TANK COMBAT IN NORTH AFRICA
THE OPENING ROUNDS

Also by Thomas L. Jentz
GERMANY'S TIGER TANKS - VK45.02 TO TIGER II
GERMANY'S TIGER TANKS - TIGER I & II: COMBAT TACTICS
GERMANY'S PANTHER TANK: THE QUEST FOR COMBAT SUPREMACY
PANZERTRUPPEN: 1933-1942
PANZERTRUPPEN: 1943-1945

TANK COMBAT IN NORTH AFRICA

THE OPENING ROUNDS

Operations Sonnenblume, Brevity, Skorpion and Battleaxe

FEBRUARY 1941 - JUNE 1941

Thomas L. Jentz

Schiffer Military History
Atglen, PA

Book Design by Robert Biondi.

Printed in the United States of America.
ISBN: 0-7643-0226-4

We are interested in hearing from authors with book ideas on related topics.

Published by Schiffer Publishing Ltd.
4880 Lower Valley Road
Atglen, PA 19310
Phone: (610) 593-1777
FAX: (610) 593-2002
E-mail: Schifferbk@aol.com.
Please write for a free catalog.
This book may be purchased from the publisher.
Please include $3.95 postage.
Try your bookstore first.

CONTENTS

Introduction

The focus of this book is the tank battles fought during the opening phase of the war in North Africa. It is aimed at explaining what really happened during tank engagements, how tanks were fought, and what caused success and losses – not in simplified generalities, but substantive, basic facts gleaned from searching for details in the surviving original records. Accounts of each battle are included, excerpted from original reports written by the participants directly after each engagement.

To understand the basis for the outcome of each battle, it is necessary to possess a basic understanding of the capabilities of each type of tank, its opponents, and how they were tactically employed. The first five chapters provide descriptions and technical attributes of the British, German, and Italian tanks and anti-tank guns along with the tactical doctrine from the period.

Chapters 6 through 11 contain the details of the tank battles fought in North Africa. Translated excerpts from the **Deutsches Afrikakorps** war diary are used as a backdrop to provide a chronological guide as events progressed. An interesting feature of this war diary was the brief daily weather report revealing how hot it was and when sandstorms occurred. Details on the actions in the tank battles are taken from after-action accounts written directly after the engagements, enhanced by excerpts from war diaries of the armored units involved to fill in the preliminary moves, buildup of strength, combat losses, and details on the actions that weren't contained in the after-action reports.

When lessons learned were reported, they have been included in the tactical analysis sections in Chapters 6 through 11 along with comments by the author. The author's comments are intended to incite the reader into thinking about tactical brilliance and blunders. The reader is encouraged to perform detailed tactical analyses by comparing each of the after-action accounts against the tactics recommended in Chapter 5. Don't accept at face value excuses for failure. Excuses given by losers are the same obstacles that are surmounted by winners. A second exercise recommended to the reader is to perform a detailed comparison of the contents of the British and German tactical manuals against each other. Tactics aren't ethnical. There are appropriate situational tactics for employing tanks regardless of the crews' country of origin.

To maintain a set of accurate data, the reader is advised to use data obtained only from primary sources to enhance the technical data contained in this book. The basis for and explanatory details behind the data in most other secondary sources simply are not present. As an example, many books provide comparative armor-penetration ability of various tank and anti-tank guns. But in most cases, the type of round fired (AP, APC, APCBC, APCBC/HE), the initial velocity, the description of the target material, the definition of what constitutes successful penetration, or the angle of impact is not provided. The claim that the British 2-Pounder tank gun could penetrate 44 mm at 1000 yards is in and of itself meaningless without data on the type of round fired, at what muzzle velocity, the target material, whether penetration is defined by the depth that the tip sank into the steel, or if the entire round cleanly penetrated as a free missile with sufficient kinetic energy remaining to damage equipment inside the tank.

The dust of battle hadn't even settled before creative minds were busy inventing stories concerning the relative performance and tactics of the tanks that had fought in North Africa. For the most part these stories weren't based on anything factual such as actual observations, battlefield investigations, or systematically conducted trials. These stories have survived, however, disguised as official reports and histories that were derived from the inaccurate gleanings recorded in military intelligence reports. Hundreds of books have been published elaborating on and embellishing these war stories, and they are readily available for those interested in entertainment. This is not one of them. Don't get me wrong; I like to be entertained by a good story and greatly appreciate the skills of a good storyteller. However, war stories are not history. The events occurred in only one way. You can't get to the truth by compiling, reading, and analyzing the contents of storybooks. This can be achieved only by digging into the original records of those who took part in the events and were responsible for the technical and tactical decisions.

The following documentary is compiled from the results of digging through original records for over 30 years in an attempt to find data that would aid in assessing and understanding the tank battles that took place in North Africa. The record is far from complete. Those recording and preserving information did not consider what data would be needed to answer the myriad of questions that would be posed by future historical analysts. Therefore, many holes in the data exist which will never be filled because experiments were not conducted in the detail needed to evaluate the effect of every type of armor-piercing shell striking every type of armor at every conceivable thickness, combination, and angle. Even in those cases in which experiments were conducted and recorded in appropriate detail, the data often are not comparable to other experimental results, because the way tests were conducted was different in Germany from that in America and Britain. However, sufficient data have survived from original reports to provide a basis for a fairly comprehensive comparison of the capabilities of opposing tanks. But the reader shouldn't try to determine which was the "superior" tank simply based on its armament, armor, and automotive characteristics. When manned by crews who recognized and exploited opponents' weaknesses and applied situational tactics, tanks with inferior characteristics frequently won tank-versus-tank engagements against "superior" tanks.

Thanks are especially due to Walter J. Spielberger, Wolfgang Wahl, Kurt Liestmann, Peter Chamberlain, and the late G. B. Jarrett for providing copies of rare and unique photos. Thanks also go to Hilary Doyle for inking the maps and Stanley Thawley for proofing the text.

This is the first of three volumes on the North African Campaign in World War II. The second volume is to cover the period from July 1941 to December 1941 and the third volume from January 1942 to May 1943. My first attempt to publish this work was in 1972. Letters from well-known publishing houses, to which I had sent a draft manuscript, informed me that they weren't interested at the time. So it has taken over 25 years to get this book published. This proves that there is still hope for other unpublished authors.

But the manuscript didn't just lie around gathering dust. Research continued right up to July 1997 in my quest to find additional details on the exact number of tanks by type shipped to North Africa and accurate technical data on the tanks. In the interim I kept busy by writing and contributing to over 20 other books on German armor in World War II. This has given me a reputation as someone solely interested in German armor. But the campaign in North Africa has always been my favorite subject because I could obtain detailed data from primary sources about the tanks and tank battles from all the participants. Surviving documents in English, German, and Italian allow the creation of a comprehensive balanced view, instead of being stuck with the biased reports from only one side (as is the case in most other campaigns in World War II). This documentary was formatted to let original report writers from the opposing factions have their say, free from being summarized into "historical" accounts by non-participants. I hope readers will appreciate these first-hand accounts as much as I did when each one was found.

Tom Jentz
Germantown, Maryland
10 July 1997

1

British Tank Forces

Between the wars British tank design had evolved into three specialized classes known as Light, Infantry, and Cruiser Tanks. Light Tanks were designed to fulfill the tactical roles of reconnaissance and scouting as mechanized cavalry. The Infantry Tank was developed from an entirely new idea in 1935 to produce an infantry support tank with sufficient armor protection to withstand an attack by enemy anti-tank weapons. Being heavily armored, the Infantry Tank was not designed to achieve more than a limited speed. The Cruiser Tank was designed to be a fast, lightly armored tank which carried a 2-pounder gun as well as one or more machineguns. It was intended for mobile warfare and to be particularly suitable for use in open country.

1.1 LIGHT TANKS

Only the Mark VI series of Light Tanks designed by Vickers was ready for production when the rearmament program was launched in mid-1936. Being cheap to manufacture, these Light Tanks were the first to be mass-produced in quantity and used to outfit entire Light Tank Battalions in both the Royal Tank Regiment (R.T.R.) and the mechanized cavalry. A total of 1218 Mark VI Series Tanks were produced from 1936 to 1940, including 91 Mark VI, 85 Mark VIA, 874 Mark VIB, and 168 Mark VIC. Most of the Mark VI series still in service in 1941 were Mark VIB. There were still a number of Mark VI and Mark VIA in service along with Mark VIC in the Infantry Tank Battalions.

1.1.1 LIGHT TANK MARK VI, VIA, AND VIB

The armament of the Mark VI, VIA, and VIB consisted of one 0.303-inch Vickers machinegun and one 0.5-inch Vickers machinegun coaxially mounted in a No.10 dual mounting in the turret. The gunner had a No.24 sighting telescope (1.9 x magnification and a 21° field of view) adjustable in 100-yard increments to a range of 1500 yards. The turret could be traversed by hand only through 360°, and machineguns could be elevated through an arc from -10 to +37°. 200 rounds of AP ammunition were carried for the 0.5-inch Vickers along with 2500 rounds of Ball ammunition for the 0.303-inch Vickers. A pair of smoke projectors were fitted externally on the turret. The turret had been enlarged at the rear to accommodate a No.9 W/T (wireless transmitting-receiving) set. A second electrical generator was incorporated for the purpose of charging the W/T battery.

All of the Mark VI series of Light Tanks had the same armor protection designed to be proof against 0.303-inch armor-piercing bullets. The armor protection was designed to be a slightly modified 14 mm basis. Vertical front plates were 14 mm basis, the engine side was 11 mm basis, and the left side 14 mm basis. Armor plates 14 mm and below 7 mm thick plates were homogeneous hard (Specification No. I.T.70); all other plates were face-hardened (Specification No. I.T.60). The 14 mm basis provided immunity against 7.92 mm A.P. rounds with striking velocity 2450 f.s. These tanks were immune to 0.303-inch class weapons firing A.P. rounds at point blank range.

FOOTNOTE:

British Official Armor Specifications		Thickness	Brinell Hardness
I.T.60	Face-hardened	7 – 12 mm	Face 550 – 650
			Back 350 – 440
I.T.70	Thin Homogeneous Hard	3 – 30 mm	440 – 475
I.T.80	Thick Homo-Machineable	15 mm & over	300 – 331
I.T.90	Cast Armor	All thicknesses	293 – 332
I.T.100	Thin Homo-Machineable	3 – 14 mm	340 – 390
I.T.110	Carbon Manganese Steel for backing plates		260 – 310

Mark VIA Light Tank (TTM)

The drive train consisted of a 6 cylinder Meadows ESTB water-cooled gasoline engine delivering 88 B.H.P. at 3000 rpm through a 5-speed transmission onto the clutch-brake steering gear and final drives, designed to provide a maximum speed of 30 miles per hour. The combat weight of 5.2 tons was distributed over two sets of rubber-tired roadwheels with coil spring suspension per side.

The principal improvements incorporated into the Mark VIA were:

• A rearrangement of the cupola, redesigned to facilitate command.

• A redesign of the driver's front flap and shutter to give increased safety and wider vision.

• An improved suspension which incorporated wider tracks and bogie wheels. The front-cross tube was repositioned in the Mark VIA 4-3/4 inches forward of its previous position. This gave a similar increase in the track base, increased riding comfort and caused no ill-effects to the steering.

• The cooling was found to be unsatisfactory, and two additional air louvers were added to render the tank suitable for use in Egypt. These additions and the provision of an efficient air cleaner were tested out in Egypt for

1,000 miles in dust clouds. The results were satisfactory, and there was no longer any danger of very abnormal wear taking place or insufficient cooling of the engine under desert conditions.

India decided to order a considerable number of tanks, and it was obviously desirable that the British and Indian patterns should be the same. Although the cooling had been improved, there was insufficient draught through the fighting compartment for use under tropical conditions. In addition, the increased cooling arrangements on Mark VIA had been carried out hurriedly in an emergency. These points and certain other details were therefore rectified, and the tank was classified as Mark VIB. It differed only in minor details from the Mark VIA, but these alterations enhanced the fighting value appreciably.

Owing to the necessity to rearm as early as possible, experimental work was not carried out for strengthening and lengthening the track and suspension to compensate for the increased weight over previous models. As a result the tracks on the Mark VI series of Light Tanks were a little too short and were heavily loaded. The consequence was a reduced life of these parts and a tendency to pitch on rough ground.

1.1.2 LIGHT TANK MARK VIC

With a change in armament from Vickers to Besa machineguns came the redesignation as Tank, Light, Mark VIC. A 15 mm Besa machinegun and a 7.92 mm Besa machinegun were mounted coaxially in the dual Besa M.G. Mounting No.14 in the turret. The gunner had a No.30 sighting telescope (1.9 x magnification and a 21° field of view) adjustable in 100-yard increments to a range of 1500 yards. The turret could be traversed by hand only through 360° and machineguns could be elevated through an arc from -10 to +34°. 175 rounds of AP ammunition were carried for the 15 mm Besa machinegun along with 2700 rounds of Ball ammunition for the 7.92 mm Besa machinegun. In addition, the commander's cupola was dropped, being replaced by a split hatch with a periscope.

1.1.3 EXPERIENCE GAINED AGAINST THE ITALIANS

After their experience in the winter campaign against the Italians in North Africa, the user's opinion of the Light Tanks was: "These are not now considered effective for other than merely light reconnaissance work, and for this purpose their cross-country ability is so low that a wheeled vehicle would be preferred."

1.2 INFANTRY TANKS

Producing an Infantry Tank armored against anti-tank weapons was an entirely new idea that originated in 1935. The Infantry Tank was a heavily armored tank not designed to achieve more than a limited speed. It was essential for this tank to be proof against the majority of anti-tank weapons so as to enable it to remain on the enemy position and cooperate closely with the infantry.

The first Infantry Tank was designed by Vickers in 1935 in accordance with General Staff specification A.11. Its only armament was an 0.5-inch Vickers machinegun in the cast turret. The second Infantry Tank (designated as the A.12) was designed by the Mechanization Board in cooperation with Messrs. Vulcan during 1937. The original intention was to mount only a machinegun and to have a crew of three men. But the design was soon changed to carry a 2-pounder gun and a machinegun with a crew of four men. In June 1940, in

Mark VIC Light Tank (TTM)

order to avoid confusion, the designations for the Infantry Tanks were all officially changed as follows:

Infantry Tank Mk.I, previously also known as A.11 or Matilda I

Infantry Tank Mk.II, previously also known as A.12 or Matilda II

Infantry Tank Mk.II.A, previously also known as A.12 or Matilda II

Infantry Tank Mk.II.A.*, previously also known as A.12 or Matilda II

The Mk.II still had a 0.303-inch Vickers machinegun. The Mk.IIA was upgraded to a 7.92 mm Besa machinegun. The addition of an asterisk signified an alteration in the type of engine. The Infantry Tank Mk.IIA* was equipped with two Leyland engines, whereas the Mk.IIA was propelled by A.E.C. engines. None of the 139 Infantry Tank Mk.I produced between June 1939 and June 1940 were shipped to the Middle East. A total of 537 Infantry Tank Mk.II, Mk.IIA, and Mk.IIA* had been produced and delivered up to the end of March 1941. Only Mk.IIA and Mk.IIA* versions were shipped to the Middle East through May 1941.

1.2.1 INFANTRY TANK MARK IIA

The armament of the Infantry Tank Mark IIA consisted of one 7.92 mm Besa machinegun and one 2-pounder coaxially mounted in the turret. The gunner had a No.30 sighting telescope (1.9 x magnification and a 21° field of view) adjustable in 100-yard increments to a range of 1800 yards. The turret could be traversed by hydraulic motor or by hand through 360° and the guns could be elevated through an arc from -15 to +20°. 93 rounds of AP ammunition were carried for the 2-pounder along with 2925 rounds of Ball ammunition for the 7.92 mm Besa machinegun. A pair of 4-inch smoke projectors were fitted externally on the right side of the turret. A No.11 W/T (wireless transmission/receiving) set was mounted in the rear of the turret.

The armor protection was designed with castings at 75 mm basis and rolled plate at 70 mm basis. Certain rear plates covering the transmission (55 mm thick) were below the basis. The 70 mm rolled plate was not at all immune to 2-pounder solid shot and the 75 mm cast turret was perforated by this attack. Immunity was obtained at approximately 1000 yds.

The drive train consisted of twin 6 cylinder A.E.C. water-cooled diesel engines delivering 94 B.H.P. at 2000 rpm

Mark IIA Infantry Tank (TTM)

through a 6-speed Wilson pre-selective, air servo operated transmission onto the cam-operated clutch steering gear and final drives, designed to provide a maximum speed of 15 miles per hour. The combat weight of 25 tons was distributed over five sets of steel roadwheels with coil spring suspension per side.

1.2.2 INFANTRY TANK MARK IIA*

In the Infantry Tank Mark IIA*, two Leyland diesel engines rated at 95 B.H.P. at 2000 rpm were mounted instead of the A.E.C. engines. Otherwise there were no significant differences from the Infantry Tank Mk.II.

1.2.3 EXPERIENCE GAINED AGAINST THE ITALIANS

Previous experience in using Infantry Tanks during the campaign against the Italians from December 1940 through early February 1941 is related in the following excerpts from reports written after the campaign:

"The Infantry Tank Mark II was considered to have put up an extremely good performance. It was largely responsible for the breakthrough at Sidi Barrani, which formed the basis for the subsequent series of victories ending in the capture of Cyrenaica. Machines of this type also were used in Bardia, Tobruk and a few survivors were on the way to Benghazi, when recalled. The armour of the tank withstood everything which was fired against it, including in some instances, field gun shell, but it should be noted that in no case was the enemy using solid shot from his heavy caliber weapons. The unit operating these machines was the one which has had most experience and must be presumed to have reached the highest state of training. In spite of this, they experienced a fair amount of mechanical trouble, although by doing their approach marches at a very low speed, they usually managed to get most of their equipment to the battle. At the same time, mechanical unreliability was such that after each phase of a battle approximately 50% of the tanks engaged were unable to go on to the next phase, due mostly to mechanical breakdowns. The tank can be considered a first class fighting machine but the standard of reliability is not high enough.

"The following are the actions fought by 7th R.T.R., each action being spread over three days:

Sidi Barrani:	1st Day	1st Phase	44 tanks reached the battle.
		2nd Phase	22
		3rd Phase	9
	2nd Day		11
	3rd Day		17
Bardia:	1st Day		23
	2nd Day		6
	3rd Day		8
Tobruk:	1st Day	1st Phase	18
		2nd Phase	8
	2nd Day		10

"Exclusive of the last run after Tobruk the average distance covered by the tanks was between 500 and 600 miles. After Tobruk ten tanks started for Benghazi and got about another 100 miles when they were recalled and returned, with four being towed by the others. The machines which were not new before the campaign, are now badly worn and all need complete overhaul. One was lost and set on fire to prevent capture and, of the remainder, probably three more are beyond local repair and will be cannibalized.

"It is the opinion of most officers of the 7th R.T.R., which opinion is supported by that of most other responsible staff officers who are in a position to know, that this Regiment and its tanks was, more than any other single factor, responsible for the surprising series of victories resulting from the demoralization of the Italian Armies at Sidi Barrani.

"The Italians did not know that this type of tank was in Egypt and when the attack was made, they concentrated the fire of every available anti-tank weapon and a good many field guns on the advancing tanks. The fire was intense and sustained up to the point when the tanks were in the line of defended localities, but when these gun crews had been silenced from the rear by machines which were apparently impervious to anything which could be hurled against them, the Italians – or those who remained – left and never again did they offer opposition nearly so tenacious. The tanks were plastered, but in no case was the full armor of the machine penetrated. Casualties were slight – just about double figures and these were all caused by unlucky shots penetrating revolver ports or to commanders with their heads out of the cupolas.

"The unit is delighted with the machines, the armor and fighting qualities are held to be first class. Even the mechanical aspect, which has come in for so much criticism, is considered satisfactory – provided approach marches are done slowly. This unit worked out its march table at five miles in the hour, which gave a day's march of forty miles and stoutly resisted all attempts to improve upon this performance and it is to this insistence that they ascribe their success.

"The 2-pounder gun behaved perfectly, and was much more efficient than the corresponding enemy weapon. Crews felt the need of a proportion of H.E. in addition to the **solid shot now the sole issue**. This is wanted for use against A.T. guns, field guns, and enemy scout vehicles. Suggest one third H.E.

"The Besa is a very good weapon and its high rate of fire is an excellent feature, but it is apt to be temperamental. Unless it is "warmed up" by firing 30 or 40 rounds before going into action, it is liable to fire only single shots. The same fault occurs when the gas regulator is coated with sand, as frequently happens.

"Observation arrangements have proved to be good. In only one or two cases were periscope prisms hit and it is considered that the scale of spares can be reduced. Vision is adequate for an Infantry tank though, naturally, any improvements would be welcomed.

"The emergency look-out of double slit type covered with a flap is not liked and its abolition is suggested. It is probable, however, that this is due to the unsatisfactory design of the flap which is easily carried away. The flap must be wholly or partially recessed into the main casting and its edges should be bevelled off on the outside. It is useless to rely on hinge pin, however stout, to take the shock of a shell hit.

"Besa ammunition seems to be sufficient and in no cases did it run out. The 2-pounder is a different matter and, although, in the later actions extra rounds were carried in every corner, it was frequently necessary to replenish between objectives. This unit definitely wants more and says that, although the heavy expenditure may be partly due to imperfect fire discipline, it is impossible to expect a higher standard of training than they have reached.

"The crew compartment is too cold when closed down, but the weather was not warm and it should be about right for summer conditions. There was no gassing noticed.

"Both the Lamp, Signalling, Tank and the Spotlamp are useless and can be dispensed with. This unit does not want any outside lamps at all but it will probably be necessary to retain side and tail lamps for use at home.

"The Dischargers Smoke Generator were never used and many were destroyed. They can be left off.

"Flags are not much use and, if they are to be retained, the bag to hold them should remain outside.

"It is the opinion of the unit that outside stowage of any important article of equipment is bad, because so much of this gets damaged in action. At the same time they do not want anything more inside, which inevitably means reduction of the equipment to be carried. They agree that tank sheets, camouflage nets, Bren guns etc. will have to be left off before an action and brought up by the 1st Line transport.

"The unit was only once attacked from the air and this had no effect whatever. They got into their tanks and stayed there till it was over.

"Power traverse was an essential item of equipment and was always used for laying. Gunners have got thoroughly used to it and won't willingly go into action if there is anything wrong with it. It required a good deal of maintenance but otherwise gave no trouble.

"Technical (automotive) performance was adequate and speed sufficient. Very little obstacle crossing was done so that there is no new information on this. The radius of action is not really enough in view of the role in which the tanks were employed. On one occasion some tanks did as much as 50 miles running inside the defenses on mopping up work. As a rule it was possible to refill during a long action of this sort.

"The suspension is fairly efficient though rather hard over the type of going in Northern Libya. All tanks were suffering from worn final drive races by the end of the campaign and some went out of action from this cause during it. There are no spares in M.E.

"The power traverse was generally very satisfactory and no pumps gave trouble. Sand in the turret races did not appear to affect its performance.

"The W/T was used a lot but the battery charging arrangements are adequate."

1.3 CRUISER TANKS

Development of a large Medium Tank had been suspended in 1932, mainly for financial reasons, and work was then concentrated on lighter and cheaper types of Medium Tanks. These developed into what became known as the Cruiser Tank. A demand had arisen in 1936 for a Cruiser Tank for the Tank Brigade – an intermediary between the present Light and Medium Tank. The Cruiser Tank was designed to be a fast, lightly armored tank which carried a 2-pounder gun as well as one or more machine guns. It was intended for mobile warfare and to be particularly suitable for use in open country.

It had long been realized that, when a tank was traveling across country and picking its course to avoid exposing itself

Mark I Cruiser Tank (TTM)

unnecessarily, or to avoid obstacles, the task of the gunner attempting to keep his sight on a target was so exhausting that accuracy in shooting was bound to suffer. In 1936 it was decided to apply power traverse to the turret to remedy this condition and an experimental hydraulic gear was fitted to a Light Tank Mark VI. Tests with this equipment showed that the problem of obtaining a gear sensitive enough for laying single-shot weapons and yet capable of rapid traverses was one on which much work had to be done before a final satisfactory solution was arrived at. It was nevertheless clear that, even in an imperfect state, power traverse was better than hand. Much development work was done to produce a very much improved gear which was tested in the pilot model of the Cruiser Tank Mark I, and all the larger tanks on order in 1938 were designed to take a gear of this nature.

1.3.1 CRUISER TANK MARK I

Of the lighter and cheaper Medium Tanks which had evolved between 1934 and 1938, one type, the A.9 constructed by Vickers, was selected as a Cruiser Tank. Designated as the Cruiser Tank Mk.I in June 1940, 89 were pro-

duced with a 2-pounder and 36 as a close support version with a 3.7-inch mortar between January 1939 and June 1940.

A 2-pounder gun and a 0.303-inch Vickers machinegun were mounted coaxially in the main turret and two 0.303-inch Vickers machineguns were mounted in separate subsidiary turrets. The gunners had No.24 sighting telescopes (1.9 x magnification and a 21° field of view) adjustable in 100-yard increments to a range of 1800 yards for the 2-pounder and 1500 yards for the machineguns. The main turret could be traversed by hydraulic motor or by hand through 360° and the coaxial guns could be elevated through an arc from -15 to +25°. The subsidiary turrets were traversed by hand through a limited arc of 110° with the machinegun elevation arc limited to -10° to +20°. 100 rounds of AP ammunition were carried for the 2-pounder gun along with 7000 rounds of Ball ammunition for the 0.303-inch Vickers. A pair of smoke projectors were fitted externally on the turret. A No.9 W/T (wireless transmission/receiving) set was mounted in the rear of the turret.

The armor protection was designed to meet a 14 mm basis. Armor plates 14 mm and below 7 mm thick plates were homogeneous hard; all other plates were face-hardened. The 14 mm basis provided immunity against 7.92 mm A.P. rounds with striking velocity 2450 f.s. These tanks were immune to 0.303-inch class firing A.P. rounds at point blank range.

The drive train consisted of a water-cooled 6 cylinder A.E.C. A.179, 9.64 liter gasoline engine delivering 150 B.H.P. at 2200 rpm through a 5-speed transmission onto the clutch-brake steering gear and final drives, designed to provide a maximum speed of 25 miles per hour. The combat weight of 13.9 tons was distributed over two sets of three rubber-tired roadwheels with coil spring suspension per side.

1.3.2 CRUISER TANK MARK I, CLOSE SUPPORT

The armament in the turret of the Cruiser Tank Mark I, Close Support consisted of a 3.7-inch mortar and one 0.303-inch Vickers machinegun mounted coaxially. 36 rounds of smoke, 4 rounds of high-explosive were carried for the 3.7-inch mortar along with 5000 rounds of Ball ammunition for the 0.303-inch Vickers. The armor and automotive features of the close support version were the same as the basic Cruiser Tank Mark I.

1.3.3 CRUISER TANK MARK IIA

In the meantime it was decided to produce a tank along the A.9 lines with heavier armor to withstand the attack of A.P. bullets fired by the 0.50-inch caliber class of weapons. Designed to General Staff specification A.10, it was officially designated as the Cruiser Tank Mk.II in June 1940. Twenty-three Cruiser Tank Mk.II with coaxially mounted Vickers machineguns and 141 Cruiser Tank Mk.IIA with coaxially mounted 7.92 mm Besa Machineguns were delivered up to March 1941. The addition of the letter "A" after the Mark signified the difference in armament.

The Cruiser Tank Mk.IIA turret was a modified Mark I design. In addition to increasing the armor protection, a 7.92 mm Besa machinegun was mounted coaxially with the 2-pounder gun in a new cast gun mantle design. Instead of subsidiary turrets, a second 7.92 mm Besa machinegun was mounted in the superstructure front plate using a ball mount with a limited traverse of 30° and limited elevation through an arc of -15 to +15°. 100 rounds of AP ammunition were carried for the 2-pounder gun along with 4050 rounds of Ball ammunition for the 7.92 mm Besa machineguns. A pair of smoke projectors were fitted externally on the turret. A No.9 W/T

Mark IIA Cruiser Tank (TTM)

(wireless transmission/receiving) set was mounted in the rear of the turret.

The armor protection was designed to meet a 30 mm composite plate basis. Composite armor consisted of a front plate of homogeneous-hard armor backed up by a second plate of D.1 quality, with the plates being securely held together by screwed rivets. The 30 mm composite basis was designed to be immune to 13.2 mm Hotchkiss A.P. bullet attack at a striking velocity of 2700 ft./sec. It was not immune to 20 mm class attack at point blank range.

The drive train was the same as in the Cruiser Tank Mk.I. It consisted of a water-cooled 6 cylinder A.E.C. A.179, 9.64 liter gasoline engine delivering 150 B.H.P. at 2200 rpm through a 5-speed transmission onto the clutch-brake steering gear and final drives, designed to provide a maximum speed of 25 miles per hour. The combat weight of 14 tons was distributed over two sets of three rubber-tired roadwheels with coil spring suspension per side.

1.3.4 CRUISER TANK MARK II, CLOSE SUPPORT

The armament in the turret of the Cruiser Tank Mark II, Close Support consisted of a 3.7-inch mortar and one 7.92 mm Besa machinegun mounted coaxially. 36 rounds of smoke, 4 rounds of high-explosive were carried for the 3.7-inch mortar along with 2475 rounds of Ball ammunition for the 0.303-inch Vickers. The armor and automotive features of the close support version were the same as the basic Cruiser Tank Mk.IIA.

1.3.5 CRUISER TANK MARK IVA

A Christie chassis was brought from America in November 1936 to assist in the development of a Cruiser Tank. In the form in which it was received, this chassis had practically no room for a fighting compartment at all. The turret ring was smaller than that of the smallest British Light Tank. This, as well as the fact that the American tank proved unreliable on trial, necessitated considerable redesign. This work was undertaken by Nuffield Mechanization, Ltd., which constructed two pilot models, the first being delivered two months after the work had started. This tank was designed under General Staff Specification A.13 and originally was to be known as the Cruiser Tank Mark II.

A 2-pounder gun and 0.303-inch machinegun were mounted coaxially in the main turret without any other sec-

Mark IVA Cruiser Tank (TTM)

ondary armament. It was planned to have a maximum speed of 35 to 40 miles an hour on good going. The suspension was smooth at speed on rough ground, and small obstacles could be taken without slowing down. Armor protection for the first production series was designed to be proof against 0.303-inch A.P. bullets. Armor protection was improved for the Cruiser Tank Mk.IV, and the 7.92 mm Besa machinegun replaced the Vickers machinegun in the Mk.IVA. Sixty-five Cruiser Tank Mk.III, 64 Cruiser Tank Mk.IV, and 206 Cruiser Tank Mk.IVA were produced between January 1939 and January 1941. From the A.13 series, only the Cruiser Tank Mk.IVA was shipped to the Middle East for use in combat.

The turret for the Cruiser Tank Mark IVA turret was a modified Mark I design. In addition to an increase in armor protection, a 7.92 mm Besa machinegun was mounted coaxially with the 2-pounder gun. There was no secondary armament. 87 rounds of AP ammunition were carried for the 2-pounder gun along with 3375 rounds of Ball ammunition for the 7.92 mm Besa machinegun. A pair of smoke projectors were fitted externally on the turret. A No.9 W/T (wireless transmitting/receiving) set was mounted in the rear of the turret.

Increasing the armor protection while attempting to minimize the additional weight resulted in non-uniform armor protection. Various armor bases were specified as follows: 30 mm casting for the cupola, 30 mm for the turret front, 28 mm for the turret sides with skirting plates, 25 mm for the driver's hood, 20 mm for the front of the hull, and 14 mm for the remainder. All plates were manufactured as homogeneous-hard armor. All of the armor surfaces were completely immune to 0.303-inch class attack. The 30 mm was immune to 13.2 mm class attack at point blank range.

The drive train consisted of a water-cooled 12 cylinder Nuffield-Liberty 27 liter gasoline engine delivering 340 B.H.P. at 1550 rpm through a 4-speed transmission onto the clutch-brake steering gear and final drives, designed to provide a maximum speed of 30.9 miles per hour. The combat weight of 14.75 tons was distributed over four rubber-tired roadwheels per side.

1.3.6 EXPERIENCE GAINED AGAINST THE ITALIANS

Previous experience in using Cruiser tanks during the campaign against the Italians from December 1940 through early February 1941 is related in the following excerpts from reports written after the campaign:

"Cruiser Tanks, Mark I – These performed well, although their armor standard restricted their use to very open warfare. They proved reliable.

"Cruiser Tanks, Mark II – These were considered the best Cruiser Tank in Egypt at the time of the operations. The particular type of armor used (homogeneous outer plates bolted on to a D1 welded inner skin) was found to be most effective, and its resistance to all sorts of attack was very much higher than was expected. Mechanically the tank was very reliable indeed, and great distances were covered without trouble.

"Cruiser Tanks, Mark IVA – These machines, by virtue of their high performance, were well liked, but thin armor of the hull made them vulnerable, and they suffered from a fair amount of mechanical trouble. Chief defects were suspension – much trouble with shock absorbers and engines – the life of the engine, due possibly to the unfavorable positioning of the air cleaners, did not exceed 800 miles on the average.

"The 2-pounder performed faultlessly and easily outmatched the anti-tank weapons fitted in enemy tanks. The 7.92 mm Besa machinegun was used for the first time in large numbers on A.F.V.'s and was considered a satisfactory gun on account of its high rate of fire and freedom from feed stoppages. At the same time, it is very susceptible to troubles caused by sand clogging up the gas vent, and also from friction due to thickening of the oil. No trouble was reported due to gassing from this gun.

"The 1st R.T.R. was equipped with Cruiser Tanks Mks.I and II and had seen a good deal of fighting (ten actions). They were very satisfied with their Tanks which had run an average of 1100 miles during the campaign without any outbreaks of serious trouble.

"Five tanks had been lost through enemy action. Thirteen tanks had broken down mechanically in the six weeks of the operations and had had to be evacuated to repair organizations in rear.

"This unit had had very little track trouble, though they had heard of the troubles which had occurred at home with this type of tank. Their tracks were of the original type, some with welded end links, but this modification was not popular and they preferred to replace lost silver-steel kup-pins by split pins.

"They ascribe their freedom from troubles to the following causes:

1. Going slow. They worked on ten miles in the hour.
2. The steering gear is not used as much in the desert as on roads.
3. Lack of metalled roads which cause hammering on the tracks.
4. Care when "swinging." No one ever attempts a 90° turn at rest without moving forward at intervals to clear the track from stones etc.

"Sand in turret races did not give trouble.

"Charging wireless batteries is insufficient for H.Q. tanks. Batteries from Light Tanks were carried on the roofs of A.9 Cruisers.

"There is one recorded case of two Mk.II Tanks of H.Q. 7th Armoured Division having done 800 miles without track trouble."

The 5th R.T.R. reported that:

"On the whole, there had been very little mechanical trouble in spite of the fact that the Mk.II (C.S.) and Mk.IV Cruisers were mixed in units. At the speed at which approach marches were made i.e. 10-15 miles in the hour, the Mk.II was able to keep up, but, had any forced marches been necessary this would not have been the case. On the other hand it is probable that the Mk.IV would have developed troubles if driven much faster.

"The only serious mechanical defect on the Mk.IV was with the front shock-absorber anchorage and this was cured by removing the shock-absorber, but it is a long job.

"The speed of the Cruiser Mk.IVA is quite sufficient in that no more than 10 to 15 mph has been required and therefor full throttle is never used. The Cruiser Mk.IIA is able to maintain this speed but if a forced march was necessary it could not hope to keep up with the Mk.IVA.

"The radius of action, with the auxiliary petrol tank is sufficient but it is considered that in the event of a surprise attack the petrol tank outside greatly increases the fire risk.

"The suspension of the Mk.IIA is satisfactory mechanically but is such that it pitches very badly.

"The trouble with the front shock absorber has to be stopped by removing it which has in no way impaired the gun platform or the riding, always being considered excellent.

"Sandguards are essential as they prevent most of the dirt and sand thrown up the tracks being drawn into the engine compartment by the fan.

"The tracks of the Cruiser Mk.IVA are trouble free.

"It would appear that the life of the Mk.II Nuffield-Liberty engine is still only in the region of 1000 miles or 100 hours running, attempts to run these engines at any greater milage results in excessive oil consumption by burning due to oil passing the pistons and rings. The engine begins to lose power at approx. 850-900 miles of running.

"A great deal of trouble has been experienced with batteries and starting on the electric starter mainly due to running at an engine speed which limits the dynamo output. A number of the tanks appear to have had the air starter assembly removed without having the modified batteries and starter fitted.

"Owing to the batteries on the Mk.IVA Tank serving both wireless and tank a fair amount of wear and tear takes place and frequent charging other than provided by the tank dynamo is necessary, especially when the tanks are moving as a battalion the road speed is insufficient to allow the dynamo to cut in and produce full charge. The Signals Charging Lorry when stationary is working almost continuously and it is necessary at times to have batteries charges elsewhere as well."

On 3 March 1941, the S.O.M.E. of the 7th Armoured Division related:

"All types of Cruiser Tanks behaved very well during operations and this satisfactory performance is, in his opinion almost entirely due to restriction of speed to approximately, 12 mph. On the occasion of the final operation south of Benghazi when an armored force advanced 200 miles across the desert to cut off Italian columns retreating along the coast from Benghazi, this speed was not exceeded. A.9's, A.10's and A.13's all participated."

He stated that:

"The armor of the A.9's and A.13's was frequently penetrated by 20 mm A.P. which usually passed through both sides, sometimes without harming the crew. There was little or no "flaking" with our machines, unlike the Italians in which the crews were nearly always killed by flake fragments when the tanks were hit. A certain amount of mine damage was caused and personnel acting as drivers or forward gunners were injured by concussion and the disruption of the belly plates.

"Cruiser Tanks Mark IV gave little trouble though their life is short, not exceeding 1000 miles. After this distance, tracks, engines and steering assembly are worn out. There was considerable trouble with the front suspension assembly anchorage (swivel plate) and nearly all machines suffered from fracture of the shock absorber end cap. This did not necessarily put the tanks out of action and he suggests eliminating the shock absorber on this assembly.

"Cruiser Marks I and II performed very well indeed and only gave serious trouble with the locking device on the steering shaft. Contact breaker springs also broke frequently through an unknown cause.

"Engines behaved well though there were a few cases of piston seizure. Tracks were good. Only troubles were through seizure of pin in link, possible due to failure to lubricate on assembly. There was a steady loss of silver steel keep-pins but these were satisfactorily replaced by split pins or mild steel rod. Average loss per day 6 per tank. Frequent inspection prevents track breakage from this cause."

1.3.7 CRUISER TANK MARK VI

The A.15 Cruiser Tank was designed by the Nuffield Organization in conjunction with the Mechanization Board as a heavy cruiser with increased armor protection. With the addition of a second 7.92 mm Besa machinegun in a subsidiary turret, the crew was increased to five. Maintaining the Christie suspension for high speed, a fifth roadwheel was added to support the increase to the design basis weight of 18 tons.

Deliveries of the Cruiser Tank Mk.VI (as it was officially designated in June 1940) first began in November 1940, with only two delivered by the end of the year. Production efforts in January through March of 1941 resulted in 92 deliveries. The first batch of Cruiser Tank Mk.VI arrived in Egypt with the Tiger Convoy on 12 May 1941.

As usual, the 2-pounder gun was mounted coaxially with a 7.92 mm Besa machinegun with an elevation arc limited to -15° to +20°. Secondary armament consisted of a 7.92 mm Besa machinegun mounted in a subsidiary turret on the hull glacis plate. 130 rounds of AP Shot ammunition were carried for the 2-pounder gun along with 4950 rounds of Ball ammunition for the 7.92 mm Besa machineguns. A No.9 W/T (wireless transmission/receiving) set was mounted in the rear of the turret.

Armor protection had been increased with the turret and front of the hull on a 40 mm basis and the remainder on a 30 mm basis. Composite armor consisted of a front plate of homogeneous-hard armor backed up by a second plate of D.1 quality with the plates being securely held together by screwed rivets. The 40 mm composite basis was just immune to 20 mm Madsen A.P. bullet attack at a range of 200 yards. The 30 mm basis was immune to 13.2 mm class attack at point blank range.

With the exception of the steering gear the drive train remained the same as in the Cruiser, Tank Mk.IVA. Its water-cooled 12 cylinder Nuffield-Liberty 27 liter gasoline engine delivered 340 B.H.P. at 1550 rpm through a 4-speed transmission onto the steering gear and final drives, designed to

Mark VI Cruiser Tank (TTM)

provide a maximum speed of 27.5 miles per hour. Steering was controlled by the driver operating the Wilson epicyclic steering gear in conjunction with skid brakes. The combat weight of 17 tons was distributed over five rubber-tired roadwheels with a Christie suspension per side.

1.4 STATUS OF BRITISH TANKS IN MIDDLE EAST

The British reported the following inventory of tanks on hand in the Middle East on 1 March 1941:

Light Tanks Mark				Cruiser Tanks Mark					Infantry Tanks	
VI	VIA	VIB	VIC	I	IIA	IVA	ICS	IIACS	IIA	IIA*
36	55	276	1	66	89	85	6	12	30	35

In addition 6 Mk.VIC Light Tanks, 8 Cruiser Tanks, and 38 Mk.IIA Infantry Tanks were in transit and expected to arrive by the end of April. The only war wastage so far reported had been 5 Mk.I Cruiser Tanks, 13 Light Tanks, and 1 Infantry Tank.

Out of this total, 149 Mk.VI series Light Tanks, 62 Mk.I and 5 Mk.IIA Cruiser Tanks had been allocated to the 7th Armoured Division. The 7th Armoured Division was composed of the 4th and 7th Armoured Brigade with the 1st and 6th R.T.R. and the 7th and 8th Hussars.

The 2nd Armoured Division had been shipped to the Middle East with 169 Mk.VIB Light Tanks and 6 Mk.I C.S., 12 Mk.II C.S., 74 Mk.IIA and 83 Mk.IVA Cruiser Tanks. The 2nd Armoured Division was composed of the 1st and 2nd Armoured Brigades with the 2nd, 3rd, and 5th R.T.R. and the 3rd Hussars, 4th Hussars and King's Dragoon Guards.

Mark VI Light Tanks ready to move off into the desert. (TTM)

One of the six Mk.I Close Support Cruiser Tank along with two Mk.IIA Cruiser Tanks belonging to the 2nd R.T.R. in December 1940. (TTM)

Mark IIA and Mark IVA Cruiser Tanks unloaded in the harbor at Alexandria. (TTM)

The Infantry Tanks belonged to the incomplete Infantry Tank Brigade with the 7th R.T.R. and elements of the 4th R.T.R. The 7th R.T.R. had 50 Mk.IIA and Mk.IIA* Infantry Tanks and 7 Mk.VIB Light Tanks and B Squadron 4th R.T.R. had 16 Mk.IIA* Infantry Tanks and 1 Mk.VIC Light Tank. An additional 34 Mk.IIA Infantry Tanks and 6 Mk.VIC Light Tanks belonging to the balance of the 4th R.T.R. along with 4 spare Infantry Tanks were still in transit.

The British also added 60 Italian medium tanks to their inventory from those captured at Beda Fomm. These were being refurbished, outfitted with No.11 Wireless Sets, and issued to the 6th R.T.R.

This inventory of 365 gun-armed tanks should have been more than adequate to handily defeat the German force that landed in Tripoli with only 78 gun-armed Panzers. But the number of British tanks available for action was but a small fraction of the total. After the highly successful campaign against the Italians, all of the Cruiser Tanks with the 7th Armoured Division were worn out and returned to ordnance base workshops for complete overhaul.

The 7th R.T.R., credited with much of the success in quickly breaking Italian resistance, had also turned in its full inventory of 7 Mk.VIB Light Tanks and 49 Mk.II Infantry Tanks for a much-needed overhaul. The only other unit with Infantry Tanks, B Squadron 4th R.T.R. with 1 Mk.VIC Light Tank and 16 Mk.II Infantry Tanks, had been sent to Eritrea to assist in rapidly concluding the campaign in East Africa.

Of the tanks that belonged to the 2nd Armoured Division: One of its Light Tank battalions (the King's Dragoon Guards) had been converted to armoured cars. Two of its tank battalions (the 2nd R.T.R. with 6 Mk.I C.S., 28 Mk.IIA, and 18 Mk.IVA Cruiser Tanks and the 3rd Hussars with 52 Mk.VIB Light Tanks) had been loaned to the 7th Armoured Division. Except for Light Tanks left behind with the 3rd Hussars, the rest of the tanks were completely worn out and returned to ordnance base workshops. The 1st Armoured Brigade (3 Mk.VIB Light Tanks and 7 Mk.IVA Cruiser Tanks in the HQ squadron) with the 3rd R.T.R. (6 Mk.II C.S. and 46 Mk.II Cruiser Tanks)

and the 4th Hussars (52 Mk.VIB Light Tanks) were dispatched to Greece.

This left a total of 64 Cruiser Tanks and 68 Light Tanks assigned to units under the 2nd Armored Division in the Western Desert as follows:

5 Cruiser Tanks and 3 Light Tanks in HQ 2nd Armd.Div.,
7 Mk.IVA Cruiser Tanks and 3 Light Tanks in HQ 3rd Armd.Div.,
6 Mk.II C.S. and 46 Mk.IVA Cruiser Tanks in the 5th R.T.R.,
52 Light Tanks in the 3rd Hussars,
4 Light Tanks in the 1st R.H.A., and
6 Light Tanks held for the 3rd Hussars.

As reported in the Half Yearly Report on the Progress of the Royal Armoured Corps, the following reinforcements were dispatched to the Middle East during the period from 1 January to 30 June 1941:

Month	Formation or unit	Light	Cruiser	Infantry	Total
January	4th R.T.R. (less 1 Sqn.) & reserves	6	8	38	52
February			5		5
March			5		5
April	1st Army Tank Bde. & reserves	28	99	194	321
May		1	50	50	101
June		0	20	20	40

Those sent in late April 1941 with the "Tiger" convoy (W.S.8), which cut through the Mediterranean, were the last tanks to arrive in time to participate in Operation Battleaxe. Having lost one ship with 57 tanks, the "Tiger" convoy arrived in Alexandria on 12 May 1941 with 21 Mk.VIC Light Tanks, 15 Mk.IVA and 67 Mk.VI Cruiser Tanks, and 135 Mk.II and Mk.II* Infantry Tanks. The normal convoys took over two months en route from England to Egypt as they went around South Africa into the Indian Ocean and up the Suez Canal.

2

German Tank Forces

Unlike the British, who designed three different tank types for specialized roles, the German tank design specifications concentrated on acquiring tanks suitable for operational employment in all roles. Starting without the hindrance of old equipment and ideas, the German army embarked on a phased program that resulted in acquiring a large number of light tanks quickly and cheaply while building up the technical and manufacturing base needed to produce the heavier types. As the program evolved, four different types of tanks were produced: the **Pz.Kpfw.I**, **Pz.Kpfw.II**, **Pz.Kpfw.III**, and **Pz.Kpfw.IV**. In addition, for purposes of operational control, command tanks known as **kl.Pz.Bef.Wg.** and **Pz.Bef.Wg.** were produced by utilizing chassis that had been developed for the **Pz.Kpfw.I** and **Pz.Kpfw.III**.

2.1 PANZERKAMPFWAGEN I

One thousand **Pz.Kpfw.I** were ordered into production to fill the six **Panzer-Regiments** created by the second phase of the German army expansion program in 1935. The first model of **Pz.Kpfw.I**, designated **Ausf.A**, had a 4-cylinder Krupp air-cooled engine. A 6-cylinder Maybach water-cooled engine was installed to increase power in the second model, designated the **Pz.Kpfw.I Ausf.B**. Contracts to produce the **Pz.Kpfw.I** were subsequently expanded resulting in the production of 1175 **Pz.Kpfw.I Ausf.A** and about 397 Pz.Kpfw.I

Ausf.B from 1935 through 1937. In addition, 184 **kl.Pz.Bef.Wg.** had been produced in 1936 and 1937.

2.1.1 PANZERKAMPFWAGEN I AUSF.A

The armament of the **Pz.Kpfw.I Ausf.A** consisted of two **7.92 mm M.G.13k** machineguns coaxially mounted in the turret. The commander/gunner had a **T.Z.F.2** sighting telescope (2.5 x magnification and a 28° field of view) adjustable in 100-meter increments to a range of 800 meters. The turret could be traversed by hand through 360° and machineguns could be elevated through an arc from -10 to +20°. 2250 rounds of S.m.K. (armor piercing) ammunition for the 7.92 mm machineguns were loaded in 25 round magazines. A rack with five smoke candles was fitted on the upper hull rear. One **Fu.2** receiver radio set was mounted to the right of the driver.

The **Pz.Kpfw.I** armor protection was designed to be proof against small-caliber armor-piercing bullets. Homogeneous hard (BHN 529 to 560) chrome-nickel armor plates 13 mm thick were used on all vertical surfaces. Thinner plates on well sloped or horizontal surfaces provided equivalent protection. The finished plates and their weld seams were immune to attack by **7.92 mm S.m.K.** rounds fired at a range of 30 meters.

The drive train consisted of a 4 cylinder Krupp M315 air-cooled gasoline engine delivering 60 metric horsepower at

---

FOOTNOTE: Detailed accounts of the technical development and tactical capabilities of the Panzers are available in Chapters 5 and 6 of the Panzer Truppen. Tactics employed and combat experience gained prior to engagements in North Africa are related in Chapters 10 through 13 of the Panzer Truppen (see page 224).

FOOTNOTE: Brinell Hardness Range of German Armor
529-560 for homogeneous hard (chrome nickel) up to 13 mm thick
435-465 for homogeneous hard (nickel free) up to 14.5 mm thick
353-382 for homogeneous machineable (nickel free) 16 to 30 mm thick
>555 face, 353-382 body for face hardened armor 30 mm thick
309-353 for homogeneous machineable 35-50 mm thick

Panzerkampfwagen I Ausfuehrung A (WJS)

2500 rpm through a 5-speed transmission onto the clutch-brake steering gear and final drives, designed to provide a maximum speed of 37 kilometers per hour. The combat weight of 5.4 tons was distributed over two pairs of rubber-tired roadwheels and a trailing idler wheel with a combination of coil and leaf spring suspension per side. The engine cooling system of the **Pz.Kpfw.I Ausf.A** was not modified for employment in the tropics.

2.1.2 PANZERKAMPFWAGEN I AUSF.B

The armament and armor protection of the **Pz.Kpfw.I Ausf.B** remained unchanged from the **Pz.Kpfw.I Ausf.A**. A 6 cylinder Maybach NL 38 TR water-cooled engine delivering 100 metric horsepower at 3000 rpm replaced the Krupp engine in the same length motor compartment. The gears in the transmission were also altered, resulting in an increase in the maximum road speed to 40 kilometers per hour. The hull rear was extended only for the purpose of structural support for the rear idler wheel mount. The idler wheel was raised off the ground and a fifth roadwheel was added to the suspension in an effort to reduce the chance of throwing a track while steering in heavy ground.

Prior to shipment to Libya, all **Pz.Kpfw.I Ausf.B** were modified for the tropics by improving cooling air circulation for the engine. Holes were cut in the rear deck and engine hatches and the radiator fan speed was increased. Only **Pz.Kpfw.I Ausf.B** with larger radiators were to be sent to Libya.

2.1.3 KLEINE PANZERBEFEHLSWAGEN

The **kl.Pz.Bef.Wg.** was created by using a modified **Pz.Kpfw.I** chassis. The superstructure sides were extended upward to form a larger crew compartment with room for three men along with **Fu.6** transmitting and **Fu.2** receiving radio sets. The only armament provided was an **M.G.34** machinegun in a ball mount located in the superstructure front. The **K.Z.F.1** gun sight (1.8 x magnification and 18° field of view) was graduated to a range of 800 meters. Traverse was limited to 40° degrees and elevation to an arc from -10° to +20°. 900 rounds of **S.m.K.** ammunition were carried in 150 round belts stowed in bags. Automotive and armor features were the same as in the **Pz.Kpfw.I Ausf.B**. **Kl.Pz.Bef.Wg.** were modified for tropical employment in the same way as the **Pz.Kpfw.I Ausf.B**.

Panzerkampfwagen I Ausfuehrung B (NA)

kleine Panzerbefehlswagen (NA)

2.2 PANZERKAMPFWAGEN II

By 1933, it had been determined that the **Pz.Kpfw.I** was too small to mount a 2 cm gun in a fully traversable turret. Therefore, a decision was made in February 1934 to design a series of light tanks with some armor piercing capability and not to exceed the weight restriction of the 8 ton engineer bridge. The first two production series of **Pz.Kpfw.II**, designated **Ausf.a** and **Ausf.b**, had three sets of paired roadwheels per side. This was changed to five independently sprung roadwheels per side with the **Ausf.c**. The design was stabilized with the **Ausf.A**, no further armament, armor, or automotive changes being introduced with the **Ausf.B** and **Ausf.C**. The latter two models were merely extensions to contracts to keep the assembly firms in business until the **Pz.Kpfw.III** was ready for mass production. A total of 1300 **Pz.Kpfw.II** chassis were produced between April 1936 and April 1940 (including those used for flamethrowers and bridgelayers). Only the **Pz.Kpfw.II Ausf.A**, **B**, and **C** models were modified for the tropics and shipped to Libya in early 1941. Changes in armor specification and a switch to a different assembly firm

had delayed production of the **Pz.Kpfw.II Ausf.F**, the first one being completed and accepted in March 1941.

2.2.1 PANZERKAMPFWAGEN II AUSF.A, B, UND C

The armament of the **Pz.Kpfw.II** consisted of a **2 cm Kw.K.30** and a **7.92 mm M.G.34** machinegun co-axially mounted in the turret. The commander/gunner had a **T.Z.F.4** sighting telescope (2.5 x magnification and a 25° field of view) adjustable in 100 meter increments to a range of 1200 meters. The turret could be traversed by hand through 360° and the coaxial guns could be elevated through an arc from -10 to +20°. Stowage was provided for 180 rounds of 2 cm **Pzgr.** (AP) or **Sprgr.** (HE) ammunition loaded in 10-round magazines and 1500 rounds of **S.m.K.** ammunition for the 7.92 mm machineguns loaded in 150-round belts in bags. A rack with five smoke candles was fitted on the hull rear. Platoon leaders' tanks were outfitted with a **Fu.5** transmitter-receiver and an **Fu.2** receiver radio set. The section leaders' tanks were outfitted with a **Fu.5** transmitter/receiver and the remain-

Panzerkampfwagen II Ausfuehrung C mit Zusatzpanzerung (APG)

ing two tanks in the light platoon were outfitted only with a **Fu.2** receiver.

As originally assembled, all **Pz.Kpfw.II Ausf.A**, **B**, and **C** had a rectangular hatch in the turret roof for the commander, closed by a two-piece cover. In experience reports from France, the troops had complained that vision from a buttoned-up **Pz.Kpfw.II** turret was too limited. Prior to shipment to Libya, all **Pz.Kpfw.II Ausf.A**, **B**, and **C** were modified by replacing the rectangular commander's hatch with a cupola housing eight periscopes.

As originally produced, the armor protection of all **Pz.Kpfw.II Ausf.A**, **B**, and **C** was only designed to be proof against small-caliber armor-piercing bullets. Homogeneous hard (BHN 435 to 465) nickel-free armor plates 14.5 mm thick were used on all vertical surfaces. Thinner plates on well sloped or horizontal surfaces provided equivalent protection. The finished plates and their weld seams were immune to attack by **7.92 mm S.m.K.** rounds fired at a range of 30 meters.

In early 1940, the armor protection on the front of the **Pz.Kpfw.II** was increased as a response to experience reports stating that the Polish 7.92 mm anti-tank rifle had penetrated the 14.5 mm thick armor. **Pz.Kpfw.II** were backfitted at ordnance depots by bolting on additional armor plates to the frontal surfaces. These additional plates were 20 mm thick on vertical plates and 15 mm thick on well sloped surfaces. The double plates provided protection equivalent to a single 30 mm plate.

The drive train consisted of a 6 cylinder Maybach HL 62 TR air-cooled gasoline engine delivering 140 metric horsepower at 2600 rpm through a 6-speed transmission onto the clutch-brake steering gear and final drives, designed to provide a maximum speed of 40 kilometers per hour. The combat weight of 8.9 tons was distributed over five independently sprung rubber-tired roadwheels with leaf spring suspension per side.

Prior to shipment to Libya, all **Pz.Kpfw.II** were modified for the tropics by improving cooling air circulation for the engine. Holes were cut in the rear deck, and the radiator fan speed was increased. Only **Pz.Kpfw.II Ausf.A**, **B**, or **C** with larger radiators were to be sent to Libya.

2.3 PANZERKAMPFWAGEN III

Authorization to design a gun armed tank for the specific purpose of engaging other tanks was first obtained in January 1934. The first four models, designated **Pz.Kpfw.III Ausf.A** through **D**, were experimental series produced in very limited numbers with coil or leaf spring suspensions and armor protection that was proof only against armor piercing rounds fired

by 7.92 mm rifles or machineguns. These had all been pulled out of service in regular **Panzer-Regiments** in February/ March 1940.

The **Pz.Kpfw.III Ausf.E** was designed at the leading edge of automotive technology for the period. State of the art features such as torsion bar suspension, lubricated tracks with rubber pads and a semi-automatic 10-speed transmission were incorporated into the initial design in an attempt to achieve a maximum speed of 67 kilometers per hour. Problems were encountered with all three of these features: the torsion bar suspension needed new telescoping shock absorbers, the rubber track pads flew off, and the 10-speed transmissions disintegrated internally. All of these problems resulted in setting back the production timetable for the **Pz.Kpfw.III** by over one year.

In the interim, authorization and contracts had been issued for production of 96 **Pz.Kpfw.III Ausf.E**, 435 **Pz.Kpfw.III Ausf.F**, 800 **Pz.Kpfw.III Ausf.G**, and 759 **Pz.Kpfw.III Ausf.H**. The **Ausf.F** and **Ausf.G** were merely mass production orders with very minor improvements over the **Ausf.E** base model. The **Ausf.H** was designed to be the first model outfitted with the **5 cm Kw.K. L/42** instead of the **3.7 cm Kw.K. L/46.5**.

As originally designed, the **Pz.Kpfw.III Ausf.H** was to possess the same 30 mm armor protection as its predecessor, the **Ausf.G**. However, the 30 mm frontal armor of the **Pz.Kpfw.III** and **Pz.Kpfw.IV** was proven to be vulnerable to fire from the Polish 37 mm anti-tank guns. Therefore, the decision had already been made early in 1940 to increase the armor protection of the **Pz.Kpfw.III Ausf.H** by producing them with 30 mm thick face-hardened plates bolted on in front of the 30 mm thick face-hardened plates on the superstructure and hull front. In addition, a 30 mm thick face-hardened armor plate was bolted onto the hull rear over the 30 mm thick homogeneous armor plate. This increased armor protection wasn't introduced on the **Pz.Kpfw.III Ausf.F** and **G** until January 1941 after the major problems with the 10-speed transmission had been solved.

Problems with the 10-speed transmission were solved only by a modification that controlled the transmission's internal speed and by an order issued to the troops limiting the top speed to 40 kilometers per hour. The normal six-speed transmission designed for a maximum speed of 42 kilometers per hour, proven to be successful in the **Pz.Kpfw.IV**, was slightly modified and reintroduced in the **Pz.Kpfw.III Ausf.H**.

As a direct result of feedback from the front that the **3.7 cm Kw.K. L/46.5** was incapable of penetrating the French Somua tank at ranges over 300 meters, the **Wa Pruef** rapidly converted the **Pz.Kpfw.III Ausf.F** and **Ausf.G**, then in production, to mount **5 cm Kw.K. L/42** guns. This was accomplished by cutting away the old turret front with the internal mantle and replacing it with a turret front and external mantle that had already been designed for the **Pz.Kpfw.III Ausf.H**. This shift in production could be quickly carried out starting in July 1940 because the **5 cm Kw.K. L/42** guns were already being produced in preparation for the start of **Ausf.H** production in October 1940. A total of 466 **Pz.Kpfw.III Ausf.F**, **G**, and **H** with L/42 guns had been produced between July and December 1940, with a further 188 produced by the end of March 1941. Only **Pz.Kpfw.III Ausf.F**, **G**, and **H** with **5 cm Kw.K. L/42** guns were shipped to Libya in March and April 1941.

Panzerbefehlswagen were produced utilizing the basic chassis from the **Pz.Kpfw.III Ausf.E** and **Ausf.H**. A total of 45 **Pz.Bef.Wg. Ausf.E** were produced from July 1939 to February 1940. Production of the first series of 145 **Pz.Bef.Wg.Ausf.H** started in November 1940, with 29 completed in 1940 and a further 60 by the end of March 1941.

2.3.1 PANZERKAMPFWAGEN III AUSF.F

The armament of the **Pz.Kpfw.III Ausf.F** consisted of a **5 cm Kw.K. L/42** with a **7.92 mm M.G.34** machinegun coaxially mounted in the turret. The gunner had a **T.Z.F.5d** sighting telescope (2.5 x magnification and a 25° field of view) adjustable in 100-meter increments to a range of 1500 meters for **Pzgr.** and 3000 meters for **Sprgr.** The turret could be traversed by hand through 360° and machineguns could be elevated through an arc from -10 to +20°. A second **7.92 mm M.G.34** was mounted in a ball mount in the superstructure front plate directly in front of the radio operator's position. The ball mount allowed a limited traverse of 30° and elevation through an arc from -10 to +20°. Metal bins were provided for storing 99 **Pzgr.** and **Sprgr.** rounds for the 5 cm gun and the 3750 rounds of **S.m.K.** (armor piercing) ammunition for the 7.92 mm machineguns were loaded in 150 round belts stowed in bags. A rack with five smoke candles was fitted on the upper hull rear. The two **Pz.Kpfw.III** in the company headquarters section and the platoon leaders' tanks were each outfitted with a **Fu.5** transmitter-receiver and an **Fu.2** receiver radio set. The **Pz.Kpfw.III** assigned to the signals section in regiment and battalion headquarters were outfitted with a **Fu.5** transmitter-receiver. The remaining four **Pz.Kpfw.III** in each platoon were outfitted only with a **Fu.2** receiver.

The **Pz.Kpfw.III Ausf.F** armor was designed to provide protection against small-caliber armor-piercing bullets of up

Panzerkampfwagen III Ausfuehrung F (WW)

Panzerkampfwagen III Ausfuehrung G (NP)

to 20 mm. Face-hardened (greater than 555 BHN on face, 353 to 382 BHN on back) armor plates 30 mm thick were used on all frontal vertical surfaces. The turret sides and rear along with the hull sides were fabricated from 30 mm homogeneous (BHN 353 to 382) armor plates. The hull rear was protected only by 20 mm thick homogeneous (BHN 353 to 382) armor plates. Thinner plates on well-sloped or horizontal surfaces provided equivalent protection.

The drive train consisted of a 12-cylinder Maybach HL 120 TR water-cooled gasoline engine delivering 265 metric horsepower at 2600 rpm through a 10-speed transmission onto the clutch-brake steering gear and final drives, designed to provide a maximum speed of 67 kilometers per hour. The combat weight of 20.5 tons was distributed over six rubber-tired roadwheels independently sprung with torsion bars per side.

Prior to shipment to Libya, all **Pz.Kpfw.III** were modified for the tropics by improving cooling air circulation for the engine. Holes were cut in the hatch covers on the rear deck, and the radiator fan speed was increased. The openings in the hatch covers were protected by 16 mm thick armor cowlings.

2.3.2 PANZERKAMPFWAGEN III AUSF.G

With the following exceptions, the **Pz.Kpfw.III Ausf.G** remained basically unchanged from the **Pz.Kpfw.III Ausf.F**:

• Magneto ignition was added for the 12-cylinder Maybach engine which was then designated as HL 120 TRM.
• Armor protection on the hull rear was increased from 20 mm to 30 mm thick.

2.3.3 PANZERKAMPFWAGEN III AUSF.H

The **Pz.Kpfw.III Ausf.H** remained basically unchanged from the **Pz.Kpfw.III Ausf.G** with the following exceptions:

• The 6-speed SSG 77 transmission was installed with a top speed of 42 kilometers per hour.
• Armor protection on the superstructure and hull front was increased by bolting on 30 mm thick face-hardened plates over the 30 mm thick face-hardened plates of the basic structure.

Panzerkampfwagen III Ausfuehrung H (WW)

Panzerbefehlswagen Ausf.E (NA)

• A 30 mm thick face-hardened plate was bolted to the basic 30 mm thick homogeneous armor plate on the hull rear.

• To increase flotation, wider Kgs 61/400/120 tracks were introduced and other running gear components modified to fit the wider track.

2.3.4 PANZERBEFEHLSWAGEN III AUSF.E

Basically, the **Pz.Bef.Wg.Ausf.E** had the same armor protection and automotive components as the **Pz.Kpfw.III Ausf.F.** The turret was fastened to the superstructure and could not be rotated. The only mounted armament was a ball mount for an **7.92 mm M.G.34** in the flat 30 mm thick turret front plate. 1500 rounds of **S.m.K.** loaded in 150-round belts were carried in bags for the machinegun. A dummy mantle made of aluminum was fastened to the turret front plate so that the external appearance of the **Pz.Bef.Wg.** would be the same as that of a **Pz.Kpfw.III** with a **3,7 cm Kw.K.**

Pz.Bef.Wg. assigned to the signals section for the regimental headquarters were outfitted with **Fu.8** and **Fu.6** radio sets. Those assigned to the signals section for the battalion headquarters were outfitted with **Fu.6** and **Fu.2** radio sets.

2.3.5 PANZERBEFEHLSWAGEN III AUSF.H

The **Pz.Bef.Wg.Ausf.H** had the same armor protection and automotive components as the **Pz.Kpfw.III Ausf.H** and the same armament and command features as the **Pz.Bef.Wg.Ausf.E**.

2.4 PANZERKAMPFWAGEN IV

After experimental trials with the **Neubau-Fahrzeug**, the **Wa Pruef** decided to abandon the use of high torque aircraft engines as the power plant in tanks. Drive train components needed to be built stronger to withstand the applied torque from low rpm aircraft engines. Therefore these heavier components constituted a high percentage of the vehicles' weight. The allotted weight could be better utilized for thicker armor, heavier armament, more space, additional crew members, or additional ammunition stowage. Consequently development of a medium tank was delayed until an engine could be developed which was specifically designed for tanks.

The German system of rating tanks as light, medium, and heavy was based on the caliber of the gun and not by the weight of the vehicle. Therefore the **Pz.Kpfw.III** with its 3.7 cm and 5 cm guns was classified as a light tank and the

Panzerbefehlswagen Ausf.H (NA)

Pz.Kpfw.IV with its 7.5 cm was classified as a medium tank, even though various models of both tanks weighed nearly the same.

Authorization for development of the medium tank designated as the **Begleitwagen** (escort tank) with a 7.5 cm gun was given to the **Wa Pruef** in February 1935. Competing with Rheinmetall, Krupp was selected for the detailed design of both the chassis and turret. The Maybach HL 108 TR engine was installed along with a 5-speed transmission resulting in a maximum speed of 35 kilometers per hour. The first production series, 35 **Pz.Kpfw.IV Ausf.A** produced in 1937 and 1938, had 14.5 mm thick armor plate which was proof only against small-caliber armor-piercing bullets.

A second series of 42 **Pz.Kpfw.IV Ausf.B** was produced in 1938. The engine was upgraded to a Maybach HL 120 TR engine that was coupled to a 6-speed transmission capable of maximum speeds of 42 kilometers per hour. The thickness of the frontal armor of the **Pz.Kpfw.IV Ausf.B** was increased to 30 mm, while the sides and rear remained at 14.5 mm. In 1938, Krupp refused to sign a contract with the **Wa Pruef** governing control of the detailed design of the chassis and was not awarded further contracts for development of chassis designs until mid-1939. Therefore, the automotive design of the **Pz.Kpfw.IV** remained virtually unchanged through the remainder of the production series. It was only the deterioration of the political situation which resulted in contracts for Krupp to continue the production of the **Pz.Kpfw.IV**.

Except for insignificant details, the 134 **Pz.Kpfw.IV Ausf.C** produced in 1938 and 1939 were identical to the **Pz.Kpfw.IV Ausf.B**. Changes incorporated into the **Pz.Kpfw.IV Ausf.D** produced in 1939 and 1940 included an increase in the armor protection for the sides and rear from 14.5 to 20 mm thick and an external mantle for the main gun that was 35 mm thick.

The 30 mm frontal armor of the **Pz.Kpfw.IV** was proven to be vulnerable to fire from the Polish 37 mm anti-tank guns. Therefore, a decision had already been made early in 1940 to increase the armor protection of the **Pz.Kpfw.IV Ausf.D** and **Ausf.E**. The hull front of the last 68 **Pz.Kpfw.IV Ausf.D** and all **Ausf.E** was to be increased from 30 mm to 50 mm thick. The front of the superstructure was to be protected by bolting 30 mm thick face-hardened plates onto the front of the 30 mm thick face-hardened plates. In addition, 20 mm homogeneous plates were to be bolted to the sides of the superstructure and to the sides of the hull outside the fighting compartment. Production of the 68 **Pz.Kpfw.IV Ausf.D** with the additional armor protection ran from July to October 1940, followed by the production of 200 **Pz.Kpfw.Ausf.E** from October 1940 to April 1941. The same decision authorizing an increase in the armor protection for newly produced **Pz.Kpfw.IV** also specified that all previously produced **Pz.Kpfw.IV** were to have 30 mm face-hardened armor fastened to the superstructure and hull front (and for **Pz.Kpfw.IV Ausf.D** 20 mm homogeneous armor bolted to the sides) when they were returned to the ordnance depots or assembly plants for major repairs or overhaul.

2.4.1 PANZERKAMPFWAGEN IV AUSF.D

The armament of the **Pz.Kpfw.IV Ausf.D** consisted of a **7.5 cm Kw.K. L/24** with a **7.92 mm M.G.34** machinegun coaxially mounted in the turret. The gunner had a **T.Z.F.5b** sighting telescope (2.5 x magnification and a 25° field of view) adjustable in 100-meter increments to a range of 1200 meters for **Pzgr.** and 3000 meters for **Sprgr.** The turret could be traversed by an electric motor or by hand through 360° and machineguns could be elevated through an arc from -10 to +20°. A second **7.92 mm M.G.34** was mounted in a ball mount in the superstructure front plate directly in front of the radio operator's position. The ball mount allowed a limited traverse of 30° and elevation through an arc from -10 to +20°. Metal bins were provided for storing 80 **Pzgr.** and **Sprgr.** rounds for the 7.5 cm gun. The 3000 rounds of **S.m.K.** (armor-piercing) ammunition for the 7.92 mm machineguns were loaded in 150-round belts stowed in bags. A rack with five smoke candles was fitted on the upper hull rear. The two **Pz.Kpfw.IV** in the company headquarters section and the platoon leaders tanks were each outfitted with a **Fu.5** transmitter/receiver and an **Fu.2** receiver radio set. The remaining three **Pz.Kpfw.IV** in each platoon were outfitted only with a **Fu.2** receiver.

The **Pz.Kpfw.IV Ausf.D** armor was designed to provide protection against small-caliber armor-piercing bullets of up to 20 mm. Face-hardened (greater than 627 BHN on face, 353 to 382 BHN on back) armor plates 30 mm thick were used on all frontal vertical surfaces. The turret sides and rear along with the hull sides and rear were fabricated from 20 mm homogeneous (BHN 353 to 382) armor plates. Thinner plates on well sloped or horizontal surfaces provided equivalent protection.

The last 68 **Pz.Kpfw.IV Ausf.D** were produced with additional armor protection. The hull front plate was a 50 mm thick homogeneous (BHN 309 to 353) armor plate. Additional 30 mm face-hardened plates were bolted to the front of the base 30 mm face-hardened plates on the superstructure front. All of the superstructure side and the side of the hull outside the fighting compartment were reinforced by bolting an additional 20 mm homogeneous plate to the base 20 mm homogeneous plate.

The drive train consisted of a 12-cylinder Maybach HL 120 TRM water-cooled gasoline engine delivering 265 met-

Panzerkampfwagen IV Ausfuehrung D (NA)

ric horsepower at 2600 rpm through a 6-speed transmission onto the clutch-brake steering gear and final drives, designed to provide a maximum speed of 42 kilometers per hour. The combat weight of 20 metric tons was distributed over four pairs of rubber-tired roadwheels sprung with leaf springs per side.

Prior to shipment to Libya, all **Pz.Kpfw.IV** were modified for the tropics by improving cooling air circulation for the engine. Holes were cut in the hatch covers on the rear deck, and the radiator fan speed was increased. The openings in the hatch covers were protected by overlapping 10 mm thick strips of armor.

Panzerkampfwagen IV Ausfuehrung D mit Zusatzpanzerung (GBJ)

2.4.2 PANZERKAMPFWAGEN IV AUSF.E

With the following exceptions, the **Pz.Kpfw.IV Ausf.E** remained basically unchanged from the last 68 **Pz.Kpfw.IV Ausf.D**:

• A new commander's cupola was introduced with increased armor protection and easier operation of the viewing slits.
• A swiveling driver's visor was introduced, allowing the 30 mm extra face-hardened armor plate to be fastened flush with the driver's front plate.

2.5 GERMAN TANKS SHIPPED TO LIBYA

All Panzers shipped to Libya in March through May 1941 belonged to **Panzer-Regiment 5** in the **5.leichte-Division (mot.)** or **Panzer-Regiment 8** in the **15.Panzer-Division**. The only replacements shipped to Libya prior to June 1941 were those sent to replace 10 **Pz.Kpfw.III** and three **Pz.Kpfw.IV** lost to **Panzer-Regiment 5** during a fire on board a ship.

2.5.1 PANZER-REGIMENT 5

Panzer-Regiment 5 was the first German tank unit to be transferred to North Africa, arriving in Tripoli on 10/11 March 1941. As part of the **3.Panzer-Division**, it had already been

34

Panzerkampfwagen IV Ausfuehrung E (NA)

prepared and alerted to be transported to North Africa in October 1940. These earlier plans to support the Italian attempt to take Egypt were called off but not before **Panzer-Regiment 5** was issued sufficient Panzers to fill it to the complete authorized strength. Their strength report dated 26 November 1940 showed that **Panzer-Regiment 5** had 45 **Pz.Kpfw.II**, 71 **Pz.Kpfw.III**, 20 **Pz.Kpfw.IV**, and 3 **kl.Pz.Bef.Wg.** in their possession. The time at which **Panzer-Regiment 5** was issued their Panzers would have a long term impact on their tactical capability.

All 45 of their **Pz.Kpfw.II** had been produced prior to April 1940 and had seen action in Poland and France. All 45 had been modified by bolting additional armor plates to the front of the gun mantlet, turret, superstructure and hull. In addition, before they were shipped to Libya, they were all modified by replacing the rectangular hatch on the turret roof with a commander's cupola.

All 71 of their **Pz.Kpfw.III** were produced from July through October 1940 with **5 cm Kw.K. L/42** guns. Most of them were **Pz.Kpfw.III Ausf.G** (the main model that was in production at the time) along with a few **Pz.Kpfw.III Ausf.F**, and no more than four or five **Pz.Kpfw.III Ausf.H**. Complete assembly and acceptance of **Pz.Kpfw.III Ausf.H** had just started at Daimler-Benz in October 1940. Therefore, most of the **Pz.Kpfw.III** in **Panzer-Regiment 5** had 30 mm face-hardened frontal armor and 30 mm homogeneous side armor protection. Only a

handful had frontal armor reinforced by bolting 30 mm face-hardened plates over the base 30 mm face-hardened plates on the superstructure and hull front.

Panzer-Regiment 5 had 12 **Pz.Kpfw.IV** in their possession in August before being issued an additional eight to complete their authorized strength in October 1940. These eight additional **Pz.Kpfw.IV** all had reinforced frontal armor. One of these (**Fgst.Nr.80521**) was a rebuilt **Pz.Kpfw.IV** with reinforced plates and one (Tactical Number 800) was assembled in October 1940 as mixture of components with an **Ausf.D** chassis and an **Ausf.E** superstructure and turret.

Four **Pz.Bef.Wg. Ausf.H** newly produced in December 1940 were issued to **Panzer-Regiment 5** in early 1941 to supplement the three **kl.Pz.Bef.Wg.**

In the same orders dated 5 February 1941 transferring **Panzer-Regiment 5** from the **3.Panzer-Division** to the **5.leichte-Division (mot.)**, in addition to its normal establishment, 25 **Pz.Kpfw.I Ausf.A** were issued to **Panzer-Regiment 5** and another 25 **Pz.Kpfw I Ausf.A** were to be held in Germany as a reserve. The **Pz.Kpfw.I** were used to create three additional light platoons for the regiment and battalion headquarters and were also integrated into the light platoons of the medium companies.

During loading on the ships in Naples, the "**Leverkusen**" caught fire resulting in the loss of the 10 **Pz.Kpfw.III** and 3 **Pz.Kpfw.IV** on board. Thus, **Panzer-Regiment 5** arrived in

A **Pz.Kpfw.II Ausf.B** in the **leichte Zug** of the **2.Kompanie/Panzer-Regiment 5**. As shipped to Tripoli, the Panzers of the **5.leichte Division** still had the unit symbol (inverted Y with two strikes) from the **3.Panzer-Division**. (BA)

Most of the **2.Kompanie/Panzer-Regiment 5** in Tripoli harbor. It was outfitted mainly with **Pz.Kpfw.III Ausf.G**s. Two **Pz.Kpfw.II**s from the **I.Abteilung** and **4.Kompanie** are in the background. All of the Panzers in **Panzer-Regiment 5** were still painted **RAL 7021 dunkelgrau** when they arrived in North Africa. (BA)

This double column of **Pz.Kpfw.III Ausf.H**s in the **6.Kompanie/Panzer-Regiment 8** in Italy is awaiting shipment to Tripoli. For added protection, spare lengths of track were carried across the hull front. (WW)

Tripoli with 25 **Pz.Kpfw.I**, 45 **Pz.Kpfw.II**, 61 **Pz.Kpfw.III**, 17 **Pz.Kpfw.IV**, 3 **kl.Pz.Bef.Wg.** and 4 **Pz.Bef.Wg.** Replacements for the ten **Pz.Kpfw.III** and three **Pz.Kpfw.IV** were immediately issued. The ten replacements were **Pz.Kpfw.III Ausf.F** and **G** with **5 cm Kw.K. L/42** requisitioned from those previously issued to **Panzer-Regiment 6**. The three replacement **Pz.Kpfw.IV** were new production **Ausf.E** that were issued directly from the ordnance depot. Shipped to Tripoli with the 18th or 19th convoy, the replacements did not catch up to the unit at the front until 29 April 1941.

The additional **25 Pz.Kpfw.I Ausf.A** that had been held in reserve were shipped as reinforcements for **Panzer-Regiment 5**, arriving in Tripoli by 10 May 1941. On 12 May 1941, arrangements were made for the Italian division "Ariete" to supply 26 trucks to pick up the 25 **Pz.Kpfw.I Ausf.A** in Tripoli and deliver them to the unit.

2.5.2 PANZER-REGIMENT 8

Previously part of the **10.Panzer-Division**, **Panzer-Regiment 8** was reassigned on 18 January 1941 to the **15.Panzer-Division** newly created from the **33.Infanterie-Division**. The following orders were issued to bring **Panzer-Regiment 8** up to authorized strength:

- 1 **Pz.Kpfw.IV** during the period of 11-20Dec40
- 16 **Pz.Kpfw.III (5 cm)** during the period of 1-10Jan41
- 6 **Pz.Kpfw.II (neuer Art)** during the week of 27Jan-1Feb41
- 4 **Pz.Kpfw.IV**, 2 **Pz.Bef.Wg.(Sd.Kfz.267)**, 1 **Pz.Bef.Wg. (Sd.Kfz.268)** during the week of 1-8Feb41
- 31 **Pz.Kpfw.III (5 cm)** in exchange for their 31 **Pz.Kpfw.III (3.7 cm)** during the week of 15-22Feb41.
- 20 **Pz.Kpfw.III (5 cm)** during the period 11-20Mar41.

This resulted in **Panzer-Regiment 8** receiving a very high number of their Panzers with reinforced frontal armor, including about 51 **Pz.Kpfw.III Ausf.H**, 5 **Pz.Kpfw.IV Ausf.D**, 5 **Pz.Kpfw.IV Ausf.E**, and 3 **Pz.Bef.Wg. Ausf.H**. All of their 45 **Pz.Kpfw.II** had additional 20 mm plates bolted to the turret front, superstructure front and hull front, but not on the gun mantlet. Only about 20 **Pz.Kpfw.III Ausf.F** and **G**, 10 **Pz.Kpfw.IV Ausf.D**, and the 4 **kl.Pz.Bef.Wg.** did not have any reinforced armor protection.

Panzer-Regiment 8 with its 45 **Pz.Kpfw.II**, 71 **Pz.Kpfw.III**, 20 **Pz.Kpfw.IV**, 4 **kl.Pz.Bef.Wg.**, and 6 **Pz.Bef.Wg.** was shipped across to Libya, spread out over three different convoys. They landed in Tripoli and arrived at the front as follows:

In Tripoli	At Front	Unit
25Apr41	9May41	**1.Kompanie**
2May41	12May41	**2.**, **3.**, and **5.Kompanie**
6May41	28May41	**6.** and **7.Kompanie**

A **Pz.Kpfw.III Ausf.H** of the **1.Kompanie/Panzer-Regiment 8** being unloaded in Tripoli harbor. The Panzers of **Panzer-Regiment 8** were also prepared for the desert campaign by carrying two fascines of wood supported by steel straps. (KL)

3

Italian Tank Forces

The Italians purchased a Carden-Lloyd machinegun carrier and then produced a small series under license with their own engine. This experience was then exploited to develop their own light tank design. These "light tanks", designated the **Carro L.3-33** and **L.3-35**, were nothing more than machinegun carriers, roofed over to provide an enclosed fighting compartment. Employment in Spain provided hard lessons regarding tactical limitations imposed on tanks armed only with machineguns.

A program to design gun-armed medium tanks was initiated in 1935. The first series produced was designated the **Carro Armato M.11-39**. It was armed with a 37 mm gun mounted in a sponson on the superstructure front and machineguns in the turret. This was followed by a more conventional design in 1940 with a 47 mm gun mounted in a power-traversed turret, designated the **Carro Armato M.13-40**.

3.1 LIGHT TANKS

Being cheap to manufacture, the **L.3-33** and **L.3-35** were mass produced in quantity and used to outfit entire light tank battalions. A total of about 1600 **L.3-33** and **L.3-35** were produced between 1933 and 1940. Both types were still in service in Libya with the Italian light tank battalions in 1941.

3.1.1 CARRO L.3-33 AND L.3-35

The armament consisted of twin 8 mm Breda 38 or twin 8 mm Fiat 35 machineguns mounted in a sponson in the superstructure front. The machineguns could be traversed by hand only through 24° and elevated through an arc from -12 to +15°. 2400 rounds of AP and Ball ammunition were carried

for the machineguns. Only a few special command versions were outfitted with a radio set.

All of the **L.3** series of light tanks had the same armor protection, designed to be immune to attack from 8 mm armor-piercing bullets from the front and 8 mm ball ammunition from the sides and rear. Vertical front plates were 13.5 mm thick, and the side and rear plates were 8.5 mm thick.

The drive train consisted of a 4 cylinder, water-cooled gasoline engine delivering 43 H.P. at 2400 rpm through a dual range 4-speed transmission onto the epicyclic-clutch steering gear and final drives, designed to provide a maxi-

L.3-35 (BA)

L.3-35 (BA)

mum speed of 41.3 kilometers per hour. The combat weight of 3.4 tons was distributed over two sets of three small rubber-tired roadwheels with leaf spring suspension per side.

3.1.2 CARRO L.3-35/LANCIAFIAMME

An unknown number of **L.3-33** and **L.3-35** were converted to or originally manufactured as flamethrower tanks. Their armament consisted of an 8 mm Fiat 35 machinegun mounted parallel with the nozzle of the **Lanciafiamme** flamethrower. Five hundred kilograms of combustible liquid for the flamethrower were towed behind the light tank in a trailer. The armor and automotive features of these modified **L.3-33/lf** and **L.3-35/lf** were the same as the basic **L.3-33** and **L.3-35**.

3.2 MEDIUM TANKS

About 100 **M.11-39** were produced in 1939 and 1940. Most of those sent to Libya were lost at Sidi Barrani or subsequently at Bardia. The three **M.11-39** reported as being in Tripoli in March 1941 are not mentioned in any subsequent reports.

Production of an order for 1,902 **M.13-40** commenced in mid-1940. Approximately 250 were completed in 1940, with production continuing at a pace of about 75 per month in the first half of 1941.

3.2.1 CARRO ARMATO M.13-40

The **cannone da 47-32** was mounted coaxially with an 8 mm Breda 38 machinegun in the main turret, and two 8 mm Breda 38 machineguns were mounted in a sponson on the right front superstructure. A fourth 8 mm Breda 38 was carried for anti-aircraft defense. An articulated sighting telescope (1.25 x magnification and a 30° field of view) mounted in the turret was adjustable in 100-meter increments to a range of 1200 meters for the 47 mm Mod.39 armor-piercing shells. The main turret could be traversed by hydraulic motor or by hand through 360° and the coaxial guns could be elevated through an arc from -10 to +20°. The sponson-mounted machineguns could be traversed by hand through an arc of 28° with elevation from -15° to +23°. 87 rounds of A.P.B.C./ H.E. and H.E. ammunition were carried for the 47 mm gun along with 3000 rounds of A.P. and Ball ammunition for the 8 mm machineguns. The **M.13-40** produced in 1940 were not outfitted with a radio set.

The armor protection was designed to be immune to the attack of 12.7 mm class of automatic weapons firing A.P. rounds. The homogeneous armor plates on the front were 30 mm thick plates and those on the side and rear 25 mm thick.

The drive train consisted of a water-cooled V-8 cylinder, diesel engine delivering 125 H.P. at 1800 rpm through a dual range 4-speed transmission onto the epicyclic clutch steering gear and final drives, designed to provide a maximum speed of 31.8 kilometers per hour. The combat weight of 14.0 metric tons was distributed over two sets of leaf springs, each set supporting four paired rubber-tired roadwheels per side.

3.3 STATUS OF ITALIAN TANKS IN LIBYA

All but a few of the Italian tanks shipped to Libya in 1940 had been lost to the British by 6 February 1941. This left the **32° reggimento corrazato** as the only remaining Italian armored force in Libya in March 1941. There were approximately 117 **L.3** in its **I**, **II**, and **III battaglione carri L** along with 46 **M.13-40** in the **VII battaglione carri M** in the **132° divisione corrazato "Ariete."** After parading with **Panzer-Regiment 5** in Tripoli on 12 March, the **VII battaglione carri M** was moved up to the area of the Arco dei Filini, arriving on 20 March 1941.

The tactical signs stenciled on this **L.3-35** reveal that it was the **3° carro 1° plotoni 1a compagnie** in the **III battaglione carri L** of the **32° reggimento corrazato** under the **132° divisione corrazato "Ariete."** (TTM)

The only reported reinforcements of Italian tanks were the **VIII battaglione carri M**, reported as newly arrived at the front on 3 May 1941 and placed in **Korps** reserve with the **II.Abteilung/Panzer-Regiment 5**. On 10 May 1941, **D.A.K.** reported that the **VIII battaglione carri M "Rizza"** (three companies with about 45 **carri M**) had arrived east of Tobruk.

M.13-40 (WW)

4

Guns Against Tanks

Basic knowledge of the ability of tank and anti-tank guns to penetrate and destroy their opponents' armor is an important factor for comparing capabilities of the opponents' tanks, the potential for losses in combat, and the fundamentals behind tactics. It should be kept in mind that most tanks were not lost because they were penetrated. Mechanical breakdowns, combat damage, and tactics were all much more significant in causing tank losses.

The data in this chapter were selected to provide reliable statistics on the weapons capabilities. Sufficient details are included to obtain a basic understanding of the effects of the different types of armor-piercing rounds and how results differed depending on the type of armor plate. There is no legitimate reason for comparing the penetrating ability of the various guns against each other. Comparisons should be made against a specific tank's armor plate, including consideration of the ability to destroy the tank. Also, keep in mind that the penetration figures are not absolute standards. They represent a mean result obtained by conducting a series of tests in controlled circumstances and do not include significant error bands.

Accuracy figures based on dispersion tests can be useful as a basis for comparing the ability of a gun to obtain a hit on a standard size target on the practice range. However, these figures do not reflect the ability to hit a tank in actual combat conditions. Round to round dispersion is only one of the many factors which affected accuracy in combat.

4.1 ARMOR PENETRATION

4.1.1 BRITISH GUNS

In addition to the 0.5-inch, 15 mm, and 2-pounder guns mounted in the tanks, the British employed the Boys anti-tank rifle, the 2-pounder as an anti-tank gun, and provided armor piercing shot for their 18-pounder and 25-pounder artillery pieces. The armor-penetration capabilities of these guns are listed in Table 4.1.1.

The small caliber weapons (0.5", 0.55" and 15 mm) were tested against I.T.70 specification homogeneous hard (BHN 440 to 475) armor plate. The standard for determining successful perforation was the range (or striking velocity) at which three hits out of five will cause perforation (core clean through or hole greater than the diameter of the shot or core). These values were all based on a large number of results and represented a mean standard of performance.

The 2-pounder through 25-pounder were tested against I.T.80 specification homogeneous (BHN 300 to 321) armor plate. At the time of determining the perforation figures for the 2-pounder, the standard for "perforation" was defined as 80 percent success. The phrase 80 percent success meant that in four out of five cases, when the shot hit the armor plate at the given critical velocity, 20 percent or more of the shot passed though the plate. The perforation figures for the 25-pounder were determined in terms of critical velocity, corresponding to 50 percent success.

As recorded in the minutes for the Tank Board meeting dated 27 May 1941, the bases for selecting 30 degrees as the standard angle of attack were:

FOOTNOTE: The bureaucratic British weren't satisfied with using the word penetration to describe when an armor-piercing shot had successfully "penetrated" through armor. Instead, they chose to use the word perforation for a "complete" penetration. In reality, this still doesn't completely define the effect and leaves the impression that the target resembled a swiss cheese. In this text, both words, penetration and perforation, are used synonymously. They both are used to mean that as a result of the attack on the armor, at least 20 percent of the shot or shell came out the back side of the armor as a free missile. None of the penetration figures used in this book represent partial penetration as did the U.S. Army Ballistic Limit.

TABLE 4.1.1
ARMOR-PENETRATION CAPABILITIES OF BRITISH GUNS
THICKNESS OF ARMOR (mm) PERFORATED AT 30° ANGLE

Gun	0.5"Vickers	0.55"Boys	15 mm Besa
Ammunition Weight Vo Target Range	AP W.Mk.I 580 grs 2575 fps I.T.70	AP W.Mk.II 734 grs 2980 fps I.T.70	AP W.Mk.Iz 1170 grs 2920 fps I.T.70
100 yds 500 yds	11 9	15 12.5	16 15

Gun	2-pounder		25-pounder
Ammunition Weight Vo Target Range	AP-Shot 2.375 lb 2600 fps I.T.80	AP-Shot 2.375 lb 2600 fps I.T.60	AP-Shot 20 lb 1550 fps I.T.80
100 yds 500 yds 1000 yds 1500 yds	55 47 37 27	49 40 29 19	70 62 55 49

"The 30° attack as a test of tank A.P. performance was standardized some years ago for the same reasons that led to its adoption at a much earlier date for Naval A.P. projectiles.

"There are tactical and technical reasons for this decision, as under:

1. The chances of obtaining normal hits on service are very small. They are confined to engagement of A.F.Vs. which are crossing the line of fire at right angles (i.e. neither advancing on or retiring from the firer) and to hitting one or two very small areas of vertical frontal armor, e.g. driver's front plate, in the case of a direct head-on attack on the firer.

2. Most of the hitting must thus be at oblique angles. The 30° attack was chosen because a reasonable proportion of hits on some part of the tank at this angle should be obtainable at most angles of approach. **The plate performance at 30° attack of the projectile provides a useful guide to the weapon user on the maximum tactical range at which fire for effect should be opened.**

2-pounder Mark II

3. Technically 30° is also the critical angle of attack for testing A.P. projectiles.

"Trials of projectiles have shown that normal attack is a poor test of perforation efficiency. Shell designs to give the best normal, or nearly normal, perforation may prove to be very inefficient at greater angles.

"On the other hand, the reverse does not hold good. The projectile which gives the best performance under the severe stress conditions of 30° attack, will approximate closely to the best performance at normal attack."

When attacked by the British ordinary armor-piercing shot, face-hardened armor was much superior to homogeneous armor. A 60 mm plate offered a resistance equal to 85 mm of homogeneous armor when attacked by a 2-pounder gun at normal and 100-yard range.

4.1.1.1 BRITISH GUNS AGAINST AXIS TANKS

Directly after the battle of Beda Fomm, the 2nd R.T.R. conducted tests to determine the vulnerability of the Italian M.13-40 tanks. They reported on 14 February 1941: During the morning tests were carried of the effect of the two types of 2-pounder ammunition on Italian M13 tanks. These tests proved that the yellow painted explosive armour piercing projectile penetrates the armour at 900 yards and bursts inside with very destructive effect. Sand bags placed on the crew's seats were well riddled with splinters. The black painted solid A.P. projectile also penetrates at 900 yards and causes large cracks in the armor.

During the first encounters with the German forces the British did not have a clue about the appropriate ranges in which to engage the Panzers. In these early engagements, the British couldn't even identify the types of German Panzers being engaged and mistakingly referred to them as Italian M13 tanks. It wasn't until after several Panzers, captured in

Shatter failure of **M.13-40** armor when overmatched by 2-pounder AP-Shot. This armor had been designed to withstand hits only from smaller caliber (0.5-inch - 12.7 mm) weapons. (GBJ)

Tobruk on 14 April 1941, had been examined that the British had some idea of the armor type and thicknesses on the German Panzers and could therefore speculate on the ranges at which these could be successfully engaged.

Advice to the troops on the appropriate ranges to engage the enemy armor was provided in the 7th Armoured Division Technical Intelligence Summary No.1 dated May 1941: As a general guide the following table gives the maximum ranges to be employed with 2-pounder against German tanks:

Normal impact:	Mks.I & II	Hull	1000 yds
		Turret Front	800 yds
	Mks.III & IV	Hull	800 yds
		Turret Front	600 yds
30° Impact:	30 mm armor		850 yds
	40 mm armor		700 yds
	45 mm armor		550 yds

Details on the vulnerability of the Pz.Kpfw.IV were revealed by tests carried out by Lieut.Col. H.D. Drew, commander of the 5th R.T.R. at Tobruch on 4 June 1941:

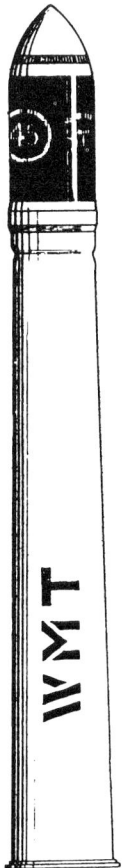

The 30 mm thick **Zusatzpanzerung** is bolted to the superstructure front of this **Pz.Kpfw.IV Ausf.D**. The 2-pounder AP-Shot failed to penetrate the 50 mm thick hull front. This **Pz.Kpfw.IV** (tactical number 401) was that of the commander of the **4.Kompanie/Panzer-Regiment 5**. (GBJ)

The combination of the 20 mm thick **Zusatzpanzerung** bolted onto the 20 mm thick base plate on superstructure side of this **Pz.Kpfw.IV Ausf.D** withstood this hit from a 2-pounder AP-Shot. It was captioned by Colonel Jarrett with the remark "2 Pdr. HIT - FUTILE." (GBJ)

2-pounder AP-Shot

TABLE 4.1.2 - RANGE IN YARDS AT WHICH 2-POUNDER AP-SHOT
(2600 fps) COULD PERFORATE THESE TARGETS AT A SIDE ANGLE OF 30°

Target Tank Model	M.13-40	PzII A-C	PzIII F-G	PzIII H	PzIV D #	PzIV E
FRONT						
Gun Mantlet	600	500	200	200	200	200
Turret	600	500	800	800	900	900
Superstructure	1300	1100	900	0	900	0
Hull	800	500	700	0	800	200
SIDES						
Turret	1400	1800	1000	1000	1600	1600
Superstructure	1600	1800	1300	1300	1800	800#
Hull	1600	1800	1300	1300	1800	800#
REAR						
Turret	1400	1800	1000	1000	1600	1600
Upper Hull	1600	1800	1500*	1000	1800	1800
Lower Hull	1400	1800	1800*	0	1800	1800

* The ranges for the 30 mm thick hull rear of the **Pz.Kpfw.III Ausf.G** were 1000 yards for the upper hull and 1300 yards for the lower hull.
\# The **Pz.Kpfw.IV Ausf.D** with additional armor could be penetrated at the same ranges as the **Pz.Kpfw.IV Ausf.E**. Those side areas without the additional 20 mm armor could be penetrated at 1800 yards.
    Additional protection was afforded by sections of spare track carried across the hull front of virtually all **Pz.Kpfw.II**, **III** and **IV** and sometimes across the superstructure front.

Penetration Tests against Pz.Kpfw.IV Tank with 2-pounder mounted in a Cruiser Mk.IVA

a. Broadside at 500-yds.

All shots on turret and whole of side armor penetrated the near side plates.

Three shots broke up inside the tank when striking some part of the gun or mounting. Three shots went completely through both sides of the tank, i.e. a total penetration of 60 mm of armor plate.

Note: This tank had one of the additional 20 mm center side plates removed, therefore the hull on that side was only 20 mm.

b. Broadside at 700-yds.

All shots penetrated the 40 mm hull plate and broke up on the far side after penetrating 10 - 15 mm.

c. Broadside at 1100-yds.

All shots penetrated the 40 mm plate on the near side of the hull but, after penetration, broke up and made little or no impression on the far side of the hull.

d. Head-On at 500-yds.

Of six rounds fired all penetrated except one. Because of the fact that one round did not penetrate and because the five that did penetrate had obviously done so with some difficulty, i.e. the hole made was only about 50% of the actual diameter of the projectile – a good deal of which had been stripped off around the edges of the hole – I stated that I considered that 500 yds is the maximum range at which penetration could be obtained against the thickest frontal armor on this type of tank.

All shots were fired at normal impact and the ranges were checked by two Barr & Stroud range finders.

These were the only test results available to the troops up to the time of Operation "Battleaxe" in June 1941. The results of these and other armor-penetration trials were used to compile ranges (shown in Table 4.1.2) at which British guns could successfully perforate the armor of their opponents' tanks. Additional protection was afforded by sections of spare track carried across the hull front of virtually all **Pz.Kpfw.II, III** and **IV** and sometimes across the superstructure front.

4.1.1.2 EFFECT AFTER PENETRATION

The destructive effect of the 2-pounder AP-Shot after penetration was based solely on whatever kinetic energy remained in the solid shot, shot fragments if it shattered, and/or fragments of armor plate broken off by the hit. Starting with the design of the **Pz.Kpfw.I**, German designers had taken extra precautions to reduce the probability of fire as a result of penetration. Fuel tanks were separated from the crew compartment by a firewall (about 5 mm thick). In the case of the **Pz.Kpfw.II**, the fuel tank, located on the right side of the crew compartment, was isolated by 8 mm thick armor plate. As a

One of the twenty-seven **4.7 cm Pak(t) Sfl. auf Pz.Kpfw.I Fahrgestell** with **Panzer-Jaeger-Abteilung 605** on parade in Tripoli. (GBJ)

further precaution, the main gun ammunition in the **Pz.Kpfw.III** and **IV** was stowed in bins whose sides were 4 to 6 mm thick. In addition, main gun ammunition in the **Pz.Kpfw.III** and **IV** was stored low in the hull. Thus, even when a 2-pounder AP-Shot managed to penetrate through the armor, it needed sufficient residual kinetic energy to penetrate the firewall or ammunition bins in order to destroy the tank by setting it on fire. Penetration of a **Pz.Kpfw.III** or **IV** by 2-pounder AP-Shot fired at 600 to 1500 yards range frequently resulted in crew members being wounded but infrequently resulted in destruction of the tank by causing irreparable damage or by setting it on fire. Of those **Pz.Kpfw.III** and **IV** knocked out in combat by AP-Shot, fewer than 20 percent were destroyed by fire or damaged so severely that they couldn't be repaired.

4.1.1.3 MACHINEGUNS VERSUS GUN SHIELDS

Only soft core (Ball) ammunition was issued to the British tanks for their 0.303-inch Vickers and 7.92 mm Besa machineguns. Therefore, these lighter machineguns could not be used to penetrate the gun shields of the enemy anti-tank guns and artillery pieces. AP rounds were issued to the light tanks for their 0.5-inch Vickers and 15 mm Besa machineguns. After the battles in France, the British reported

that the light tanks were ineffective in engaging German anti-tank guns.

In a report on the experience of anti-tank guns in Africa dated May 1941, the Germans reported that the gun shields of both the **3.7 cm Pak** and the **5 cm Pak** had not been penetrated by rifle fire or by artillery shell splinters.

4.1.2 GERMAN GUNS

In addition to the 7.92 mm, 2 cm, 5 cm and 7.5 cm guns mounted in the tanks, the Germans employed the **7.92 mm PzB** anti-tank rifle, the **3.7 cm Pak 35**, **4.7 cm Pak(t)**, and **5 cm Pak 38 L/60** anti-tank guns, and provided armor-piercing shells for their **8.8 cm Flak** anti-aircraft guns as well as the **10.5 cm le.F.H.** howitzers. The armor penetration capabilities of these guns are listed in Table 4.1.3.

German penetration statistics for armor plate were expressed in terms of the thickness in millimeters that could be cleanly perforated when the plate was laid back at an angle from the vertical of 30 degrees. The penetrating ability of armor-piercing rounds was determined by routine quality control tests of normal production lots of ammunition which proved that the results shown in Table 4.1.3 could be achieved. The target material used to test the German armor piercing shells

TABLE 4.1.3 ARMOR-PENETRATION CAPABILITIES OF GERMAN GUNS
THICKNESS OF ARMOR (mm) PERFORATED AT 30° ANGLE

Gun	7.92 mm M.G.34	7.92 mm Pz.B.38	2 cm Kw.K.30 L/50	
Ammunition Weight Vo	S.m.K. 0.0115 Kg 785 m/s	S.m.K.H. 0.0145 Kg 1175 m/s	Pzgr. 0.148 Kg 780 m/s	Pzgr.40 0.100 Kg 1050 m/s
Range				
100 m	8.0	30	20	40
500 m	3.4	25*	14	20

Gun	3.7 cm Pak 35 L/45		4.7 cm Pak(t) L/50	
Ammunition Weight Vo	Pzgr. 0.685 Kg 745 m/s	Pzgr.40 0.368 Kg 1020 m/s	Pzgr. 1.65 Kg 775 m/s	Pzgr.40 0.825 Kg 1080 m/s
Range				
100 m	35	64	52	100
500 m	29	31	47	58
1000 m	22		40	
1500 m	20		35	

Gun	5 cm Kw.K. L/42		5 cm Pak 38 L/60	
Ammunition Weight Vo	Pzgr. 2.06 Kg 685 m/s	Pzgr.40 0.925 Kg 1050 m/s	Pzgr. 2.06 Kg 835 m/s	Pzgr.40 0.925 Kg 1180 m/s
Range				
100 m	53	94	67	130
500 m	43	55	57	72
1000 m	32	21	44	38
1500 m	24		34	

Gun	7.5 cm Kw.K. L/24	8.8 cm Flak L/56	10.5 le.F.H.18 L/28	
Ammunition Weight Vo	K.Gr.rot Pz. 6.80 Kg 385 m/s	Pzgr. 9.50 Kg 810 m/s	Pzgr. 14.0 Kg 395 m/s	Pzgr. 14.0 Kg 470 m/s
Range				
100 m	41	98	56	63
500 m	38	93	52	59
1000 m	35	87	48	54
1500 m	32	80	45	50
2000 m	30	72		46

consisted of rolled homogeneous plates with the following hardness values:

Plate Thickness	Hardness (kg/mm^2)	Brinell Number
5 to 15	148 to 158	435 to 465
16 to 30	115 to 130	338 to 382
31 to 50	110 to 125	323 to 368
51 to 80	105 to 115	309 to 338
81 to 120	95 to 105	279 to 309
121 to 150	80 to 90	235 to 265

As stated in a German report on armor-penetration curves: *Basically all penetration data are valid for projectiles of good quality. The estimate of penetration for "worst" projectiles is possible only with great difficulty. The penetration can spread over a very large range below the given value. The regulations for acceptance of projectiles stipulate that a certain number of projectiles (1/2%) will be presented for inspection. Two-thirds of the projectiles which have been fired against armor plate, must satisfy the given conditions. Based on past experience, it can be stated that the largest part of the deliveries satisfy these conditions. 100% assurance is*

48

not given; it may always be expected that a small percentage do not achieve the specified penetrating ability, because of shattering prematurely. Also the explosive charge in these shattered projectiles will not detonate.

The effect of the projectile inside the tank and the probability of hitting the target are not considered in these graphical charts; thus only the **complete penetration with the total effect inside the tank is considered**. As a rule, this effect is of annihilating power when using armor-piercing shells with a high-explosive charge. When using hard core projectiles, steel or soft iron core projectiles, or hollow-charge projectiles, completely annihilating effect cannot always be expected with a single shot, because the crew, located in the

dead space of the tank, cannot be hit under certain conditions.

A limited effect, without piercing the tank by the projectile (effect produced by back-spalling of armor plate and punching holes (Stanzpfropfen) is frequently achieved with plates that are about 10% thicker than the thickness presented in the graphs.

The effect at the 30° angle of impact is set at 100% as a standard of comparison. The ability of projectiles to penetrate at other angles may be estimated from the following table:

| | Angle of Impact | | | |
Projectile Type	0°	30°	45°	60°
Pzgr. and **Pzgr.39**	120	100	60	40
Pzgr.40	120	100	60	30

Example: The penetrating ability of the **7.5 cm Pzgr.39** fired from the **Pak 40** at a range of 1000 meters is 81 mm at

7.92 mm Pz.B.39

2.8 cm s.Pz.B.41

5 cm Pak 38 L/60

8.8 cm Flak L/56

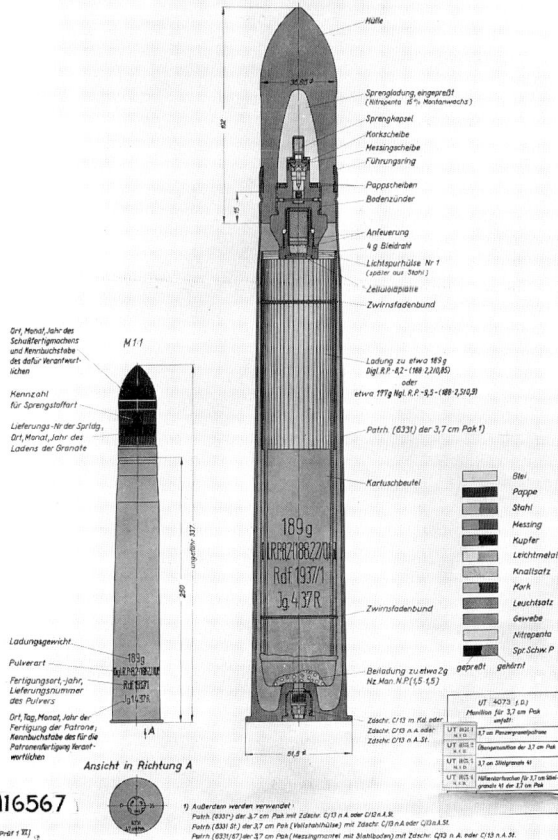

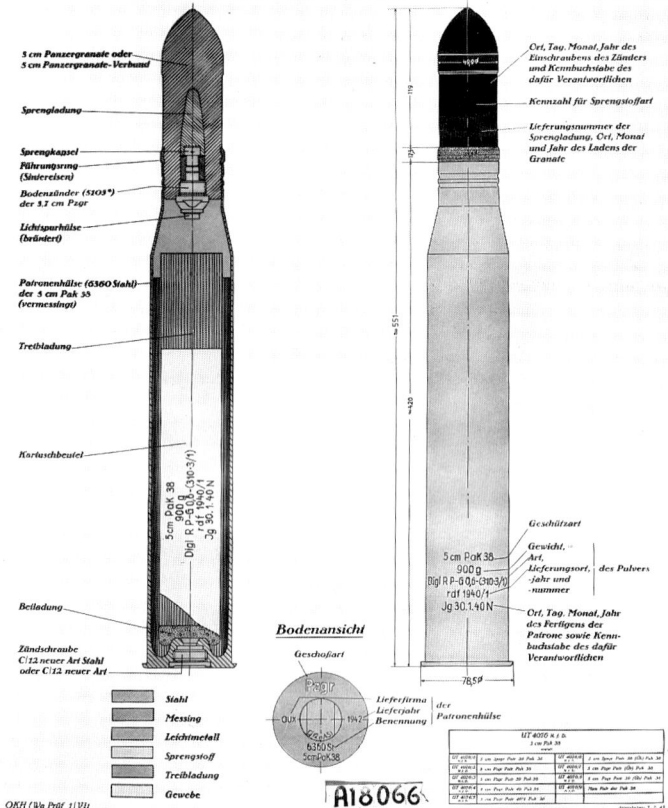

3.7 cm Panzergranatpatrone for the **3.7 cm Pak 35 L/45**. This type of shell was designated A.P./H.E. by the Allies. (APG)

5 cm Pzgr.Patr. for the **5 cm Pak 38 L/60**. It also fired the same **Pzgr.40** and **Sprgr.** as the **5 cm Kw.K. L/42**. Ammunition for the **5 cm Pak** ammunition had a longer case and more propellant than the **5 cm Kw.K. L/42** ammunition. (APG)

Ammunition for the **5 cm Kw.K. L/42**. From left to right, **Pzgr.**, **Pzgr.39**, **Pzgr.40**, and **Sprgr.** The **Pzgr.39** was not yet available for issue in early 1941. (GBJ)

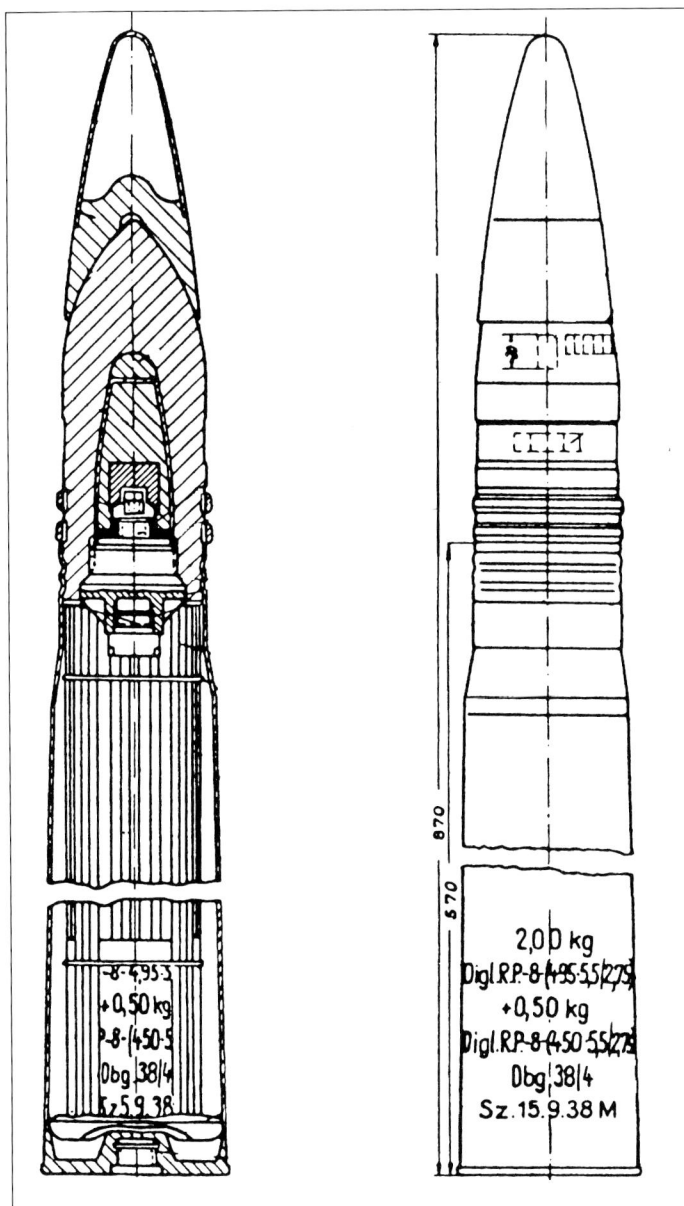

an angle of impact of 30°. Penetrating ability at this same range at 0° is 95 mm, 45° is 50 mm, and 60° is 32 mm.

The effect of penetration against cast armor parts is, under otherwise equal conditions, usually somewhat higher than against rolled plates. That is not the case if the quality of the cast armor is good. Plates hardened on the surface offer the projectile difficulties only if they cause the projectile to break. If that is not the case, the resistance might be equal to or even lower than homogeneous plates.

4.1.2.1 GERMAN GUNS AGAINST BRITISH TANKS

Having captured every type of British tank in France (except for the Cruiser Tank Mk.VI, first employed in Operation Battleaxe in June 1941), the Germans were well aware of the appropriate ranges in which to engage the British tanks. Only the infantry tanks had gained their respect and attention as being heavily armored and difficult to combat. All of the rest were thinly armored and therefore easy to penetrate within any range that the tank and anti-tank guns could manage to hit. Special bulletins were published listing the ranges and vulnerable locations of the Infantry Tank Mark II. From examining the Infantry Tank Mark IIs that had been captured in France, the Germans determined that their anti-tank guns could penetrate its armor with destructive effect at ranges up to:

200 m with the **2.8 cm Pzgr.41** fired from the **s.Pz.B.41**
200 m with the **3.7 cm Pzgr.40** fired from the **3.7 cm Pak**
100 m with the **4.7 cm Pzgr.36(t)** fired from the **4.7 cm Pak(t)**
350 m with the **4.7 cm Pzgr.40(t)** fired from the **4.7 cm Pak(t)**
200 m with the **5 cm Pzgr.39** fired from the **5 cm Pak 38**
600 m with the **5 cm Pzgr.40** fired from the **5 cm Pak 38**
1500 m with the **8.8 cm Pzgr.** fired from the **8.8 cm Flak 18/36**

Areas of the Infantry Tank Mark II vulnerable to attack by rounds fired from the **5 cm Kw.K. L/42**, **7.5 cm Kw.K. L/24**, **5 cm Pak 38 L/60**, and **8.8 cm Flak 18 L/56** are shown in the accompanying drawings. The ranges were determined based obtaining a clean penetration from armor-piercing shells striking the target at a side angle of 30 degrees.

Table 4.1.4 shows the ranges at which the three tank guns could successfully perforate the armor of British light and cruiser tanks.

LEFT: 8.8 cm Pzgr. for the **8.8 cm Flak L/56**. This type of ammunition was designated A.P.C.B.C./H.E. (armor piercing, capped, ballistic cap with high explosive filler) by the Allies.

51

5 cm 𝔎.𝔴.𝔎. 𝔏/42

𝔓𝔷gr.40 = 350 m

𝔓𝔷gr.40 = 100 m

𝔓𝔷gr.40 = 250 m

𝔓𝔷gr.40 = 100 m

𝔓𝔷gr.40 = 250 m

Possible to set on fire by hitting air loubres with Sprenggranaten

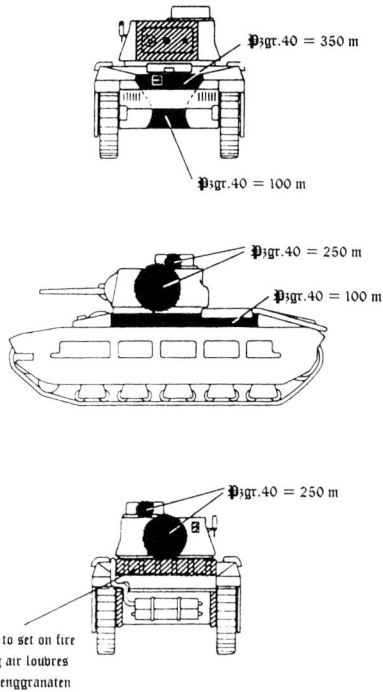

Ranges at which the **5 cm Kw.K. L/42** could penetrate the Mk.II Infantry Tank with assurance. Determined by actual firing trials at side angles of 30°.

5 cm 𝔓ak 38 𝔏/60

𝔓𝔷gr. = 200 m

𝔓𝔷gr.40 = 600 m

𝔓𝔷gr.40 = 200 m

𝔓𝔷gr. = 200 m

𝔓𝔷gr.40 = 500 m

𝔓𝔷gr.40 = 300 m

𝔓𝔷gr. = 300 m

𝔓𝔷gr. = 200 m

𝔓𝔷gr.40 = 500 m

Possible to set on fire by hitting air loubres with Sprenggranaten

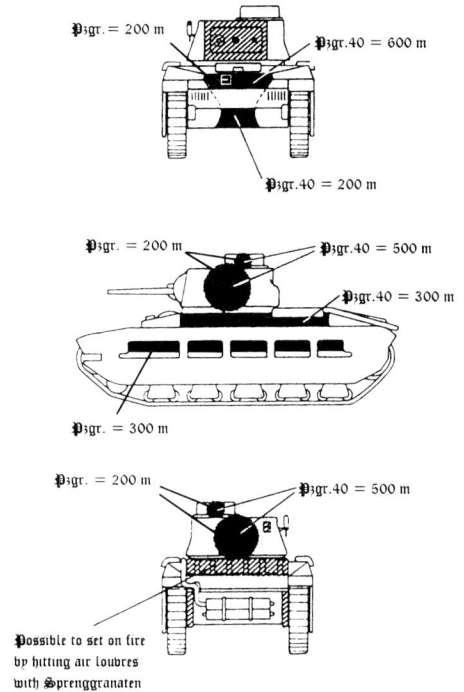

Ranges at which the **5 cm Pak 38 L/60** could penetrate the Mk.II Infantry Tank with assurance. Determined by actual firing trials at side angles of 30°.

7,5 cm 𝔎.𝔴.𝔎. 𝔏/24

Sp

Possible to set fire by hitting air loubres with Sprenggraneten

Sp

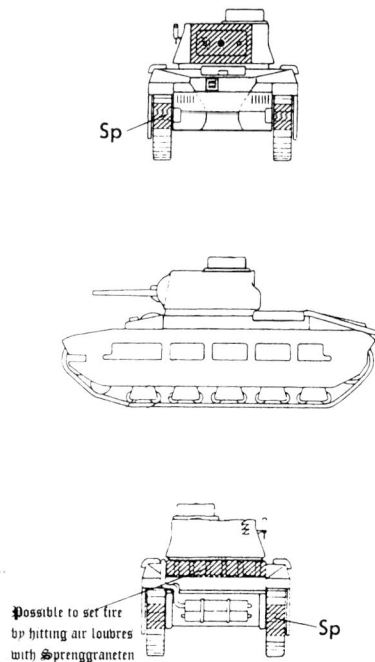

Ranges at which the **7.5 cm Kw.K. L/24** could penetrate the Mk.II Infantry Tank with assurance with the ammunition types available in early 1941. Determined by actual firing trials at side angles of 30°.

8,8 cm 𝔉lak 18 𝔏/56

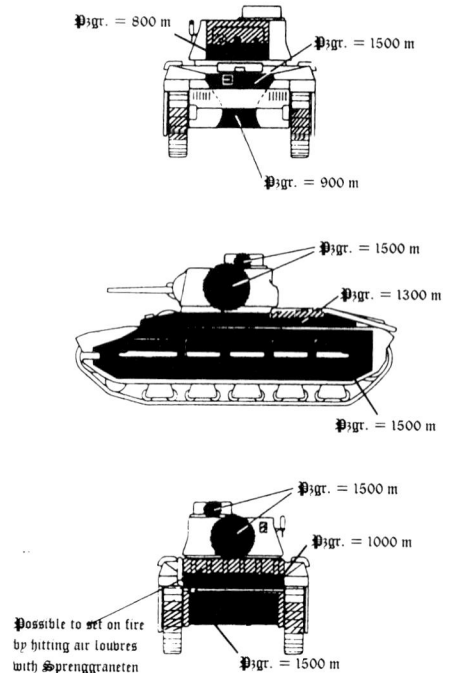

𝔓𝔷gr. = 800 m

𝔓𝔷gr. = 1500 m

𝔓𝔷gr. = 900 m

𝔓𝔷gr. = 1500 m

𝔓𝔷gr. = 1300 m

𝔓𝔷gr. = 1500 m

𝔓𝔷gr. = 1500 m

𝔓𝔷gr. = 1000 m

Possible to set on fire by hitting air loubres with Sprenggranaten

𝔓𝔷gr. = 1500 m

Ranges at which the **8.8 cm Flak L/56** could penetrate the Mk.II Infantry Tank with assurance. Based on calculations (not on firing trials) by **Wa Pruef** at side angles of 30°.

TABLE 4.1.4 - RANGE IN METERS AT WHICH THE 2 CM KW.K. PZGR.
COULD PERFORATE THESE TARGETS AT A SIDE ANGLE OF 30°

Target Tank Model	Light Mk.VI	Cruiser Mk.I	Cruiser Mk.IIA	Cruiser Mk.IVA	Cruiser Mk.VI
FRONT					
Gun Mantlet	500	100	0	0	0
Turret	400	400	0	0	0
Superstructure	500	500	0	0	0
Hull	500	600	0	100	0
SIDES					
Turret	500	500	0	100	0
Superstructure	500	600	0	300	0
Hull	500	600	0	300	0
REAR					
Turret	500	500	0	100	0
Upper Hull	500	400	0	0	0
Lower Hull	0-500	500	300	500	0

TABLE 4.1.4 - RANGE IN METERS AT WHICH THE 5 CM KW.K. L/42
PZGR. COULD PERFORATE THESE TARGETS AT A SIDE ANGLE OF 30°

Target Tank Model	Light Mk.VI	Cruiser Mk.I	Cruiser Mk.IIA	Cruiser Mk.IVA	Cruiser Mk.VI
FRONT					
Gun Mantlet	1500	1500	700	700	300
Turret	1500	1500	1300	1000	900
Superstructure	1500	1500	1400	1400	900
Hull	1500	1500	1400	1500	1100
SIDES					
Turret	1500	1500	1400	1500	900
Superstructure	1500	1500	1500	1500	1500
Hull	1500	1500	1500	1500	1500
REAR					
Turret	1500	1500	1400	1500	1300
Upper Hull	1500	1500	800	1500	1200
Lower Hull	1500	1500	1500	1500	1400

TABLE 4.1.4 - RANGE IN METERS AT WHICH THE 7.5 CM KW.K. L/24
PZGR. COULD PERFORATE THESE TARGETS AT A SIDE ANGLE OF 30°

Target Tank Model	Light Mk.VI	Cruiser Mk.I	Cruiser Mk.IIA	Cruiser Mk.IVA	Cruiser Mk.VI
FRONT					
Gun Mantlet	1200	1200	200	200	0
Turret	1200	1200	1200	1200	1200
Superstructure	1200	1200	1200	1200	1200
Hull	1200	1200	1200	1200	1200
SIDES					
Turret	1200	1200	1200	1200	1200
Superstructure	1200	1200	1200	1200	1200
Hull	1200	1200	1200	1200	1200
REAR					
Turret	1200	1200	1200	1200	1200
Upper Hull	1200	1200	1200	1200	1200
Lower Hull	1200	1200	1200	1200	1200

4.1.2.2 EFFECT AFTER PENETRATION

In all calibers of 3.7 cm and above, the normal armor-piercing round designed by the Germans contained a high explosive filler with a delay fuze. Penetration of a British tank by a German armor-piercing shell frequently resulted in crew members being wounded as well as destruction of the tank by causing irreparable damage or by setting it on fire. Not until 1942 did the British investigate the cause of fires in the tanks and began to install armored bins to protect the ammunition.

As recorded by Major G.B. Jarrett in May 1942: *The German projectiles which have caused the greatest amount of damage to Allied tanks in the Western Desert campaigns have been the A.P.-H.E. type in 47 mm, 50 mm, 75 mm and 88 mm respectively. These projectiles at long ranges need only attain a partial penetration and the explosive charge can complete the destruction of at least the tank crew. At closer ranges the destructive effect is very great, where in many cases destruction of the tank is permanent.*

When the **7.5 cm K.Gr.rot Pz.** was fitted to an American casing and fired from the 75 mm M2 gun, in May 1942 Lt.Col. Gruver reported: *Each German AP-HE round fired may safely be presumed to have put the tank out of action. In this connection it was noted that the fuze functioned perfectly, that is to say it functioned only after penetration and then always in the fighting compartment where the most damage is done. Parts also frequently penetrated into the engine compartment.*

The destructive effect of the **Pzgr.40** after penetration was based solely on whatever kinetic energy remained in shot fragments when it shattered and/or fragments of armor plate broken off by the hit.

4.1.2.3 MACHINEGUNS VERSUS GUN SHIELDS

At zero degrees obliquity, the **S.m.K.** armor-piercing bullets fired from the **7.92 mm M.G.34** could penetrate 12.5 mm at 100 meters and 8 mm at 500 meters. In gunnery manual D613/10, the Germans stated that gun shields of anti-tank guns and field guns could be penetrated by these **S.m.K.** projectiles at ranges of up to 500 meters.

This was confirmed by the British reporting that the 2-pounder anti-tank gun had a 5/16 inch (7.9 mm) thick armor shield which kept out ordinary (Ball) small arms fire but did not repel the armor-piercing bullets fired from the German tanks' machineguns. When anti-tank guns held their fire until German tanks approached to within 600 yards, the crews were frequently knocked out by machinegun fire which penetrated their shields.

4.1.3 ITALIAN GUNS

In addition to the 8 mm and 47 mm guns mounted in the tanks, the Italians employed the 20 mm Solothurn anti-tank rifle, the 20 mm Breda anti-aircraft gun, the 47 mm anti-tank gun, and provided armor-piercing shells for their 75 mm field guns. The armor-penetration capabilities of these guns are listed in Table 4.1.5.

Italian penetration statistics for armor plate were expressed in terms of the thickness in millimeters that could be cleanly perforated when the plate was laid back at an angle from the vertical of 0 and 30 degrees. The target material used to test the Italian armor-piercing shells consisted of rolled machineable quality homogeneous plates with BHN values of 210 to 245.

4.1.3.1 ITALIAN GUNS AGAINST BRITISH TANKS

In his report on his fact-finding visit to the Middle East from 10 February to 4 April 1941, Major Gordon-Hall included the following statements on the effects of Italian weapons on British tanks:

FOOTNOTE: The Italian Breda 20 mm had about the same performance as the German 2 cm Flak guns. The difference in the penetration ability shown in the tables stems from the Italians testing against softer machineable quality plate and the Germans testing against homogeneous hard plate.

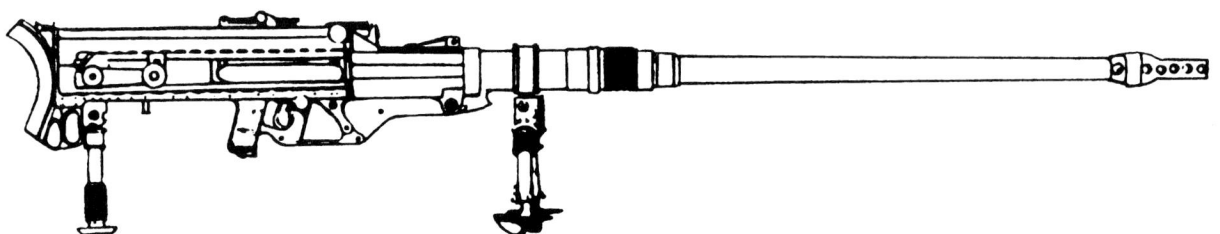

2 cm Solothurn anti-tank rifle

47-32 cannone

TABLE 4.1.5
ARMOR-PENETRATION CAPABILITIES OF ITALIAN GUNS
THICKNESS OF ARMOR (mm) PERFORATED AT 30° ANGLE

Gun	2 cm Solothurn	2 cm Breda c.a.	
Ammunition Weight Vo Target	0.138 Kg 760 m/s I.T.70	0.142 Kg 840 m/s 0 degrees	0.142 Kg 840 m/s 30 degrees
Range			
100 m	19	42	35
500 m	11	28	23
1000 m	..	20	15

Gun	cannone da 47-32		cannone da 75-18
Ammunition Weight Vo Target	c.p.mod.35 1.42 Kg 630 m/s 0 degrees	c.p.mod.39 1.44 Kg 630 m/s 30 degrees	c.p.75/13-18 476 m/s 30 degrees
Range			
100 yds	55.6	39	
500 yds	43.1	35	45
1000 yds	31.0	30	40
1500 yds	23.4	25	35

"Infantry Tanks Mk.II.A and IIA* - Both 47 mm and 20 mm penetrated skirting plates and unarmored tool boxes but did no further damage in most cases. Hits from 65 and 75 mm and heavier calibers on the turret did not penetrate but jammed the turrets. In all cases these could be freed again with lifting tackle.

"Mines certainly caused concussion but it was not serious and the crews soon recovered. The 20 mm belly plate in front seems to afford considerable protection. At the same time, the Italian mine is not a particularly effective one. Hits from shell caused practically no inconvenience to the crew and frequently they were not conscious of having been hit until examining the tank later.

"The emergency look-out of double slit type covered with a flap is not liked and its abolition is suggested. It is probable, however, that this is due to the unsatisfactory design of the flap which is easily carried away. The flap must be wholly or partially recessed into the main casting and its edges should be bevelled off on the outside. It is useless to rely on hinge pin, however stout, to take the shock of a shell hit.

"The armour of the tank withstood everything which was fired against it, including in some instances, field gun shell, but it should be noted that in no case was the enemy using solid shot from his heavy caliber weapons.

"Skirting Plates - During the recent operations in Egypt and Libya, these skirting plates have proved invaluable. They have offered adequate protection to the suspension and in no case has a tank been put completely out of action by penetration or bulging of the skirting plate.

"Only one tank was put out of action by seriously damaged suspension, and that was not due to penetration of the side plate, but by a shell of 5.9 caliber which ended its flight underneath the tank, completely wrecking the suspension.

"One case of bulging occurred when a side plate was hit but not penetrated, but the damage in no way interfered with the running efficiency of the tank. It is impossible to state with accuracy the type of shot which effected this damage, but it was thought to be fired from a medium field piece.

"At the commencement of the operations, the skirting plates were hit chiefly by Breda anti-tank shot which was equivalent to one Pounder. The effect was generally to damage or shoot away the inspection doors located in the side of the skirting plate, and break or bend a suspension lever. This did not stop the tank, and even when a bogie assembly was hit, it was not serious enough to put the tank out of action.

"One tank had its skirting plate struck by a 62 mm armor piercing shell. This penetrated and lodged in the

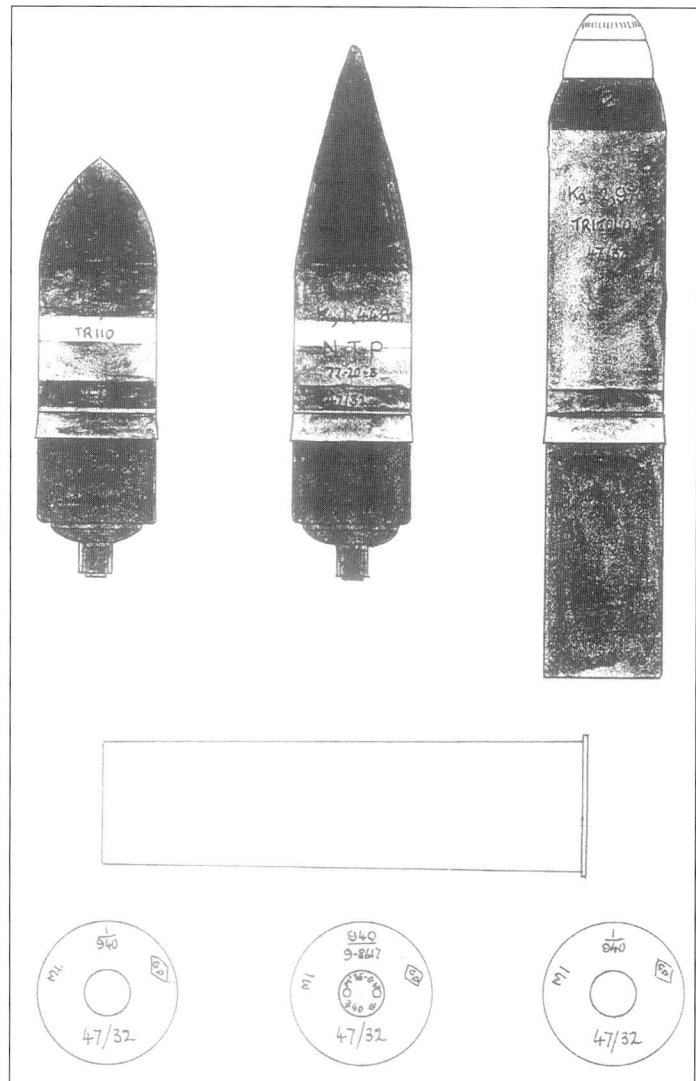

Ammunition for the **47-32 cannone**. From left to right, **perforante 35** (A.P./H.E.), **perforante 39** (A.P.B.C./H.E.), and **ordinario 35** (H.E.).

plate and stripped some teeth of the sprocket, but did not incapacitate the tank. It is interesting to note that this shell had a base charge which did not explode.

"A case occurred of a shell, equivalent to a 2-pounder anti-tank shot which struck the tank on one of the mud chutes, was deflected upwards and entered the turret. Beyond this it did no damage, either to the tank or personnel. The penetration which was approximately 2 1/2 feet long was sealed in the field by welding and inserting a double thickness of 1/2 inch mild steel.

"Generally speaking, damage done by side plates being hit has been very little, but the protection offered by such plates has been very great. From a "Battle" point of view, the fitting of skirting plates increases the fighting efficiency of the tank, and is probably one of the greatest assets possessed by the tank.

"Cruiser Tanks - A Mk.I Cruiser was penetrated by a big shell of unknown caliber in front. This exploded inside and blew a hole in the floor of a sub-turret. A 20 mm Breda penetrated the air louvres of a Mk.I Cruiser and entered the engine compartment doing very little damage. The turret of a Mk.I Cruiser was dented by large shell fragment.

"The shell hit on the Mk.I numbed the remainder of the crew for an hour or so. The tank commander was unconscious. Crew of one machine which had been mined were "dopey" and not quite coherent for some time after although there was only one casualty. It was the general opinion that heavy caliber hits do shock the crew fairly badly.

"1 R.T.R. do not think that there is any evidence that skirting plates on their Cruiser Tanks would have lessened tank casualties, as, although their suspensions were hit many times, they had no cases of tanks being put out of action from this cause. They agreed that near misses from bombs or shells might have done damage which skirting plates could save.

"The armor of the A 9's and A 13's was frequently penetrated by 20 mm A.P. which usually passed through both sides, sometimes without harming the crew. There was little or no "flaking" with our machines, unlike the Italians in which the crews were nearly always killed by flake fragments when the tanks were hit. A certain amount of mine damage was caused and personnel acting as drivers or forward gunners were injured by concussion and the disruption of the belly plates.

"The Cruiser Tanks Mark II were considered the best Cruiser Tank in Egypt at the time of the operations. The particular type of armor used (homogeneous outer plates bolted on to a D1 welded inner skin was found to be most effective, and its resistance to all sorts of attack was very much higher than was expected.

"Mk.VI Light Tanks - T.1743 Mk.VI A was hit by a 37 mm shell on side plate below air outlet louvres. Hole in plate as big as a saucer. No bulging. Subsequently on fire."

Table 4.1.6 shows the ranges at which the Italian 47 mm tank gun could successfully perforate the armor of the British tanks.

4.1.3.2 EFFECT AFTER PENETRATION

The Italian 47 mm armor-piercing round contained a high explosive filler with a delay fuze. Penetration of a British tank by a 47 mm Italian armor piercing shell frequently resulted in crew members being wounded as well as destruction of the tank by causing irreparable damage or by setting it on fire.

4.2 ACCURACY

4.2.1 FIRING AT STATIONARY TARGETS FROM STATIONARY GUNNERS

The estimated accuracy is given as the probability (in percentage) of hitting a target 2 meters high and 2.5 meters wide, representing the target presented by the front of an opposing tank. These accuracy tables are based on the assumptions that the actual range to the target has been correctly determined and that the distribution of hits is centered on the target. The first number shows the accuracy in per-

TABLE 4.1.6 - RANGE IN METERS AT WHICH THE 47 MM MOD.39 COULD PERFORATE THESE TARGETS AT A SIDE ANGLE OF 30°

Target Tank Model	Light Mk.VI	Cruiser Mk.I	Cruiser Mk.IIA	Cruiser Mk.IVA	Cruiser Mk.VI
FRONT					
Gun Mantlet	1200	1200	600	600	0
Turret	1200	1200	1200	800	700
Superstructure	1200	1200	1200	1200	700
Hull	1200	1200	1200	1200	1000
SIDES					
Turret	1200	1200	1200	1200	700
Superstructure	1200	1200	1200	1200	1200
Hull	1200	1200	1200	1200	1200
REAR					
Turret	1200	1200	1200	1200	1200
Upper Hull	1200	1200	600	1200	1200
Lower Hull	1200	1200	1200	1200	1200

Table 4.2   ACCURACY

Gun:	15 mm Besa	2-pounder	25-pounder
Ammunition:	AP Mk.Iz	AP Shot	AP Shot
Muzzle velocity:	890 m/s	792 m/s	472 m/s
Range	Percent	Percent	Percent
100 m	100 (100)	100 (100)	100 (100)
500 m	100 (82)	97 (67)	94 (66)
1000 m	82 (38)	67 (26)	81 (46)
1500 m		41 (12)	69 (28)

Gun:	2cm KwK L/50	3.7cm Pak L/45	4.7cm Pak	5cm KwK L/42
Ammunition:	Pzgr.	Pzgr.	Pzgr.36(t)	Pzgr.
Muzzle velocity:	780 m/s	758 m/s	775 m/s	685 m/s
Range	Percent	Percent	Percent	Percent
100 m	100 (100)	100 (100)	100 (100)	100 (100)
500 m	100 (87)	100 (95)	100 (100)	100 (100)
1000 m	81 (37)	90 (47)	100 (89)	100 (96)
1500 m		47 (15)	94 (59)	99 (71)

Gun:	5cm Pak L/60	7.5cm KwK L/24	8.8cm Flak L/56	10.5cm lFH L/28
Ammunition:	Pzgr	K.Gr.rot Pz	Pzgr.	Pzgr.
Muzzle velocity:	835 m/s	385 m/s	810 m/s	395 m/s
Range	Percent	Percent	Percent	Percent
100 m	100 (100)	100 (100)	100 (100)	100 (100)
500 m	100 (100)	100 (100)	100 (98)	100 (98)
1000 m	100 (95)	98 (73)	95 (64)	97 (63)
1500 m	98 (68)	74 (38)	77 (38)	76 (32)
2000 m			58 (23)	
2500 m			43 (15)	
3000 m			32 (10)	

Gun:	20mm Breda	47-32	47-32
Ammunition:		Mod.35	Mod.39
Muzzle velocity:	840 m/s	630 m/s	630 m/s
Range	Percent	Percent	Percent
100 m	100 (100)	100 (100)	100 (100)
500 m	100 (87)	100 (95)	100 (95)
1000 m	81 (37)	91 (46)	93 (52)
1500 m		53 (17)	

centage that was obtained during controlled test firing of the gun to determine the pattern of dispersion. The second number in parentheses was calculated by doubling the dispersion obtained from controlled test firing. Both the British and Germans considered that "doubled dispersion" was a close approximation of the accuracy obtained by the troops in practice and, if they remained calm, in combat. All of these accuracy values were obtained from firing tables published by the respective armies during the war. The British calculated their dispersion based on a 90% Zone and the Germans and Italians calculated the dispersion based on a 50% Zone. The 90% Zone from the British firing tables was used as the basis for calculating the percent accuracy against a 2.5 m x 2 meter target so that it could be directly compared with the other nations guns.

These accuracy tables do not reflect the actual probability of hitting a target under battlefield conditions. Due to errors in estimating the range and many other factors, the probability of a first-round hit was much lower than shown in these tables. However, the average gunner could achieve the accuracy shown by the number in parentheses after adjusting his fire onto the center of the target – if he remained calm.

4.2.2 FIRING ON THE MOVE

It was the standard British practice for their tanks to fire on the move when they couldn't take up a hull-down firing position. In a report entitled <u>Gunnery Trials</u> dated 21 March 1938, the British reported on the ability of a gunner to hit a target while firing on the move. The 2-pounder gun was controlled by the gunner's shoulder in free elevation. The following number of hits were scored while moving broadside to an 8 feet tall by 8 feet wide target at a range of 650 yards:

Speed	Rounds Fired	Hits	Percent
10 mph	19	4	21
15 mph	10	3	33
20 mph	6	2	33

The gunner managed to hit this same target 14 percent of the time while driving at the target head on at a speed of 10 mph at ranges decreasing from 900 to 600 yards.

Both the Germans and Italians instructed their crews to fire when halted, even when in the open. Panzer crews were instructed to change firing positions when they came under effective enemy fire.

5

Armored Force Tactics

Once the generals finished ordering everyone about, if it wasn't too late, small unit tactics were all that was left to save the troopers' butts. A fundamental knowledge of these tactics is required to understand and explain the outcome of all tank battles fought in North Africa. As contained in the preamble to their tactical manual, the British paid lip service to the concept of combined arms operations but didn't explain in the body of their manuals how to conduct these operations. This may be one of the key reasons that the British rarely conducted effective combined arms operations in the field. On the other hand, the Germans' fundamental tactical philosophy was based on combined arms operations. The Germans didn't stop with stating that this was an ideal; their manuals explained in detail how to conduct these operations.

The differences between the British and German tank-versus-tank tactics were of major significance in determining who won and who lost. The British believed in hull-down positions as the best firing positions. If this couldn't be achieved, the tanks were to remain and fire on the move, directing their fire to cover all of the targets. The Germans also believed in concealed, hull-down positions as the best firing positions, preferably on the enemy's flank. But the big difference was that the basic tank-versus-tank tactics in the German manual provided details on how to conduct the fight in all situations. There was to be no firing on the move or dispersed fire power. Instead, they explained how to conduct mutually supporting maneuvers with fire power concentrated as directed by the platoon leaders and company commanders. Many other significant differences are contained in the following excerpts from the original tactical manuals.

5.1 BRITISH ARMOR TACTICS

The tactics employed by the British armored units in North Africa are described in the following excerpts from the Military Training Pamphlet No.41, The Armoured Regiment, dated 1940:

Introduction

This pamphlet deals with an armoured regiment assumed to be equipped throughout with tanks armed with 2-pounder guns according to the latest war establishment.

The full power of armoured formations can only be developed by the close co-operation of tank infantry and artillery composing them, together with close and continuous co-operation by aircraft.

Armoured formations can only develop their strength when used in mass. The dissipation of these formations immediately reduces their effective strength.

The Armoured Division, Brigade and Regiment

It is essential to understand thoroughly the main characteristics of armoured formations. On these are based the principles of their employment and tactical handling.

The main characteristics are:

• <u>Armoured mobility.</u> The fighting portions are all armoured, i.e., they carry their own cover. They are also self propelled and highly mobile.

• <u>Instant readiness for action whether halted or moving.</u> Since guns are already mounted, fire can be opened at once in any direction either from the halt or on the move without exposing the personnel. On the other hand, fire from a moving tank is less accurate owing to the unstable platform.

• Capacity for crossing country. Armoured formations are not confined to roads and tracks and can cross many types of country. Their movement is, however, limited by water obstacles over a certain depth, thick woods, swampy and rocky ground, and trenches over a certain width.

• Capacity for rapid dispersion and concentration. Owing to their mobility and wireless communication, armoured formations can be moved in any direction quicker than any other arm. They can, therefore, make full use of dispersion for the purpose of concealment.

• Suitability for night operations. At night without lights drivers cannot see to negotiate obstacles, so that the cross country capacity of the tanks is very considerably reduced. Armoured units, therefore, are not suited to fighting at night. On the other hand, they can move along roads and tracks by night, e.g., carry out an approach march. They can also guard by night likely avenues of enemy approach, but, as thereby they lose one of their main assets - mobility - this duty should, if possible, be carried out by other arms, for instance by units of the support group.

• Limitations of personnel. The small number of men in a crew and the necessity for full crews for efficient working, rules out dismounted action, except of a very local nature. When closed down, the field of view is very limited and a considerable strain is imposed on the crews.

Organization of the Armoured Division

The armoured division consists of:

Divisional headquarters.

Two armoured brigades, each with a headquarters and three armoured regiments.

Support group of:

Headquarters

One Royal Horse Artillery regiment with two batteries of eight 25-pounder guns

One anti-aircraft and anti-tank regiment with two anti-aircraft batteries each of twelve light anti-aircraft guns and two anti-tank batteries each of twelve 2-pounder anti-tank guns

Two motor battalions

Royal Engineers

Headquarters, divisional engineers

One field squadron

One field part troop (carries 3016 anti-tank mines)

Armoured divisional signals

The primary role of the armoured division is to engage hostile enemy formations, but it can take on enemy troops in any other than fully fortified positions.

Organization of the Armoured Regiment

The armoured regiment consists of:

Regimental headquarters	4 tanks
Three armoured squadrons	16 tanks each
Total:	52 tanks

The armoured squadron consists of:

Squadron headquarters	2 tanks
	2 close support tanks
Four troops	3 tanks each
Total:	16 tanks

All tanks carry wireless sets capable of communicating with each other up to those distances at which a regiment is normally deployed. In addition, the four tanks on regimental headquarters carry a small wireless set with a short range of communication between themselves.

Regimental Formations

The chief regimental formations are as follows:

LINE AHEAD - Line ahead, i.e. each tank or vehicle following one behind the other, is the simplest of all formations, and is normally used for road movement. In the case of the regiment it will seldom be used on other occasions owing to the fact that it necessitates the regiment being on a minimum frontage and in the maximum depth.

LINE - Line, i.e. each vehicle facing to the front, is similarly a drill rather than a battle formation as far as the whole regiment is concerned as it presents the maximum frontage and the minimum depth.

Both "Line ahead" and "Line" may, however, be used effectively in battle by sub-units and especially by troops.

COLUMN - When a regiment is in column each squadron follows the other, regimental headquarters usually being in the lead when this formation is being used during drill, and behind the leading squadron when this formation is employed in action.

ONE UP - This formation consists in having one squadron in advance and the remaining two approximately abreast in rear of it. It is normally used in battle for the penetration of an enemy position, since its arrow-head shape is peculiarly suitable for this purpose. Its employment permits of a narrow wedge being driven into the enemy's front, of this wedge being widened by the increased frontage of the rear squadrons, of the production of great fire power in every direction, and of control by the commander of his rear squadrons, the position

REGIMENTAL FORMATIONS

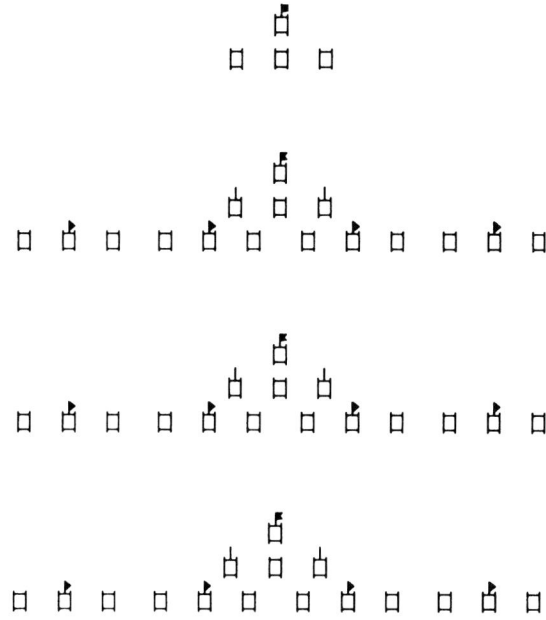

COLUMN

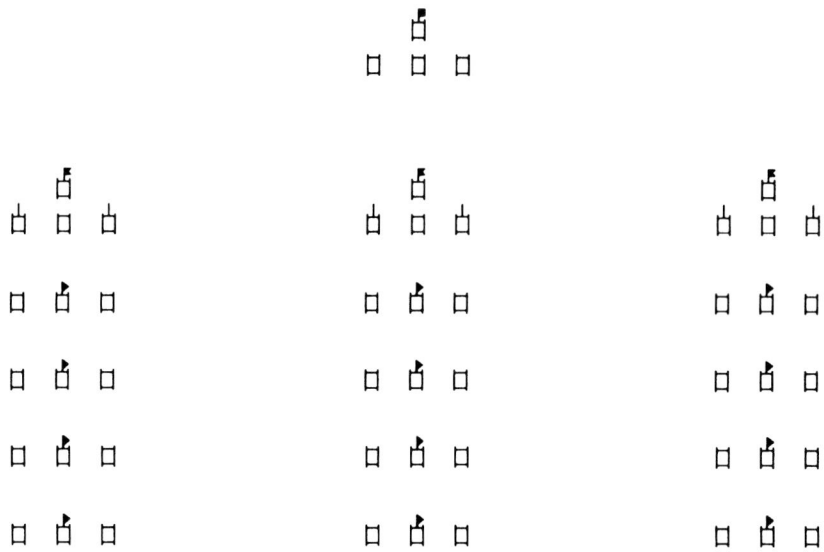

LINE OF SQUADRON COLUMNS

REGIMENTAL FORMATIONS

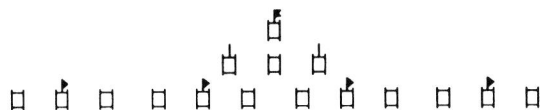

ONE UP

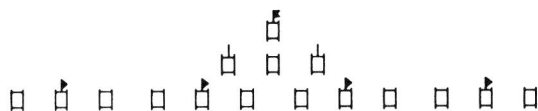

TWO UP

SQUADRON FORMATIONS

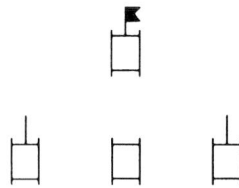

TWO UP

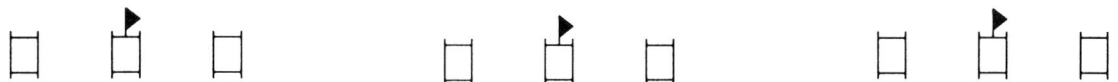

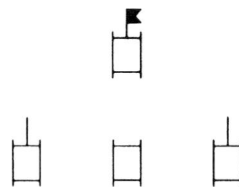

THREE UP

TROOP FORMATIONS

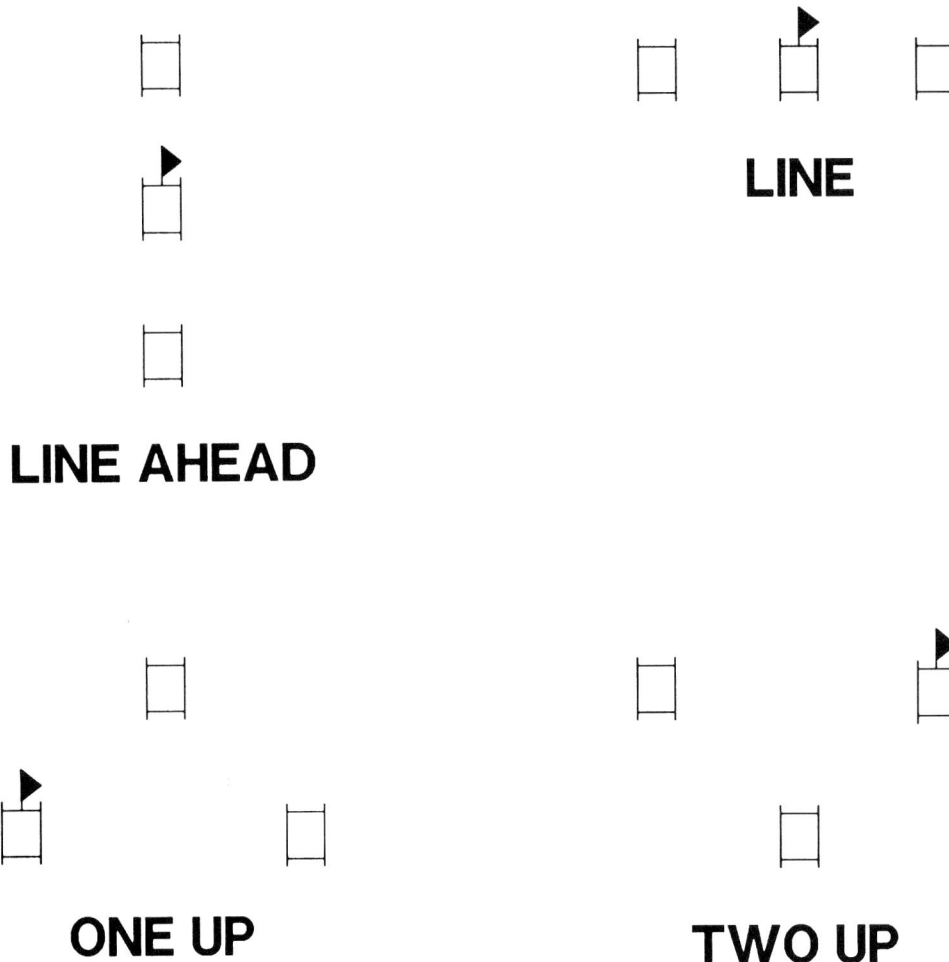

LINE

LINE AHEAD

ONE UP

TWO UP

of which he can re-adjust, if necessary, to meet any unforeseen contingency.

TWO UP - When this formation is used two squadrons lead and are followed by the third moving centrally. It is employed in battle when the frontage to be attacked is too wide for one squadron, and is in fact an inverted arrow-head.

When this formation is employed the majority of the fire will normally be directed to the front, although it permits of the enemy also being engaged by fire on both flanks. It is less handy than the "One up" formation, but can be effectively employed, especially when it is anticipated that the enemy opposition will not be very great.

During manoeuvre the normal position of regimental headquarters in both "One up" and "Two up" will be behind the leading squadron or squadrons.

The exact location of the regimental commander will depend on circumstances. It is, however, absolutely essential that he should be well forward in a position from which he can obtain the best possible view of the situation and from which he can exercise his personal influence on the battle. This principle is invariably applicable in battle, or when battle is imminent, in every type of formation.

LINE OF SQUADRON COLUMNS - This formation is usually employed when forming up for inspection or the drill purposes, the intervals between squadrons being laid down by the regimental commander.

Occasions may, however, arise when it can be effectively employed in battle, since it possesses the advantage in that either the right or the left column (or, if necessary, both), can be diverted quickly to their respective flanks and can deploy without delay while the center squadron continues on its original line of advance.

As a very rough guide it may be assumed that in battle individual tanks are usually not less than 50 or more than 100 yards from their neighbor in the same sub-unit, that troops are generally approximately double these distances from the troops next to them, and that squadrons are approximately 200 to 400 yards from each other.

Squadron Formations

Squadron formations are precisely similar in character to regimental formations. For example, squadron column consists of the squadron with each troop following behind the other.

The position of the squadron headquarters and of the squadron commander in battle are governed by the same principles as are stated for the position of the regimental headquarters and the regimental commander.

Troop Formations

A troop of three tanks is the largest sub-unit that can conveniently be directly controlled by one commander. Even in the case of a troop it is essential that the whole troop should work as a "team", and that the two subordinate tanks should, in action, operate with the minimum orders.

Owing to the small number of tanks, troop formations, though similar in principle to those of the squadron and the regiment, are simpler. The four troop formations are: Line ahead, Line, One up, and Two up.

General Tactical Principles of the Armoured Regiment

A fight is won by concentrating superior fire power at the critical time and place. This requires surprise, offensive action and full use of the characteristics of the tank, and ability to hit the target.

The mobility and speed of the tank, coupled with the correct use of ground, enables surprise to be obtained. Surprise as to the direction and time of an attack means retention of the initiative and makes easier the concentration of superior fire power.

Offensive action is obtained by the use of mobility and armor – mobility to move quickly from one fire position to another and armor to protect crews during movement. Though tanks can, if need be, operate with the utmost boldness and disregard for cover, such action may cause unnecessary casualties and is only justified under special circumstances.

The maintenance of the objective is of primary importance to armoured regiments. Soft spots must be exploited to the full, in order to achieve the ultimate object.

Offensive Battle

Armoured formations are particularly suited for offensive action on account of their armor, mobility, and fire-power. It is by offensive action that success will be achieved.

This does not mean that an attack must invariably be made, whatever the conditions. Before deciding on attack all commanders, down to the most junior, must consider the following factors:

• The general object of the operations.
• The nature of the opposition and the adequacy of the information about the enemy.
• The chance of surprise. Without it, one of the main advantages of offensive action is lost.
• The size and adequacy of the force available.

In any attack, the following principles will be observed:
1. An attack, once decided upon, must be pushed through with the greatest vigor by all ranks. There must be no half-measures.
2. The object will be to apply fire under the most favorable conditions of ground and with the greatest degree of surprise. As fire from a moving tank is less accurate than from a stationary tank, efforts should be made to find good stationary fire positions.
3. Besides attempting to surprise the enemy, a commander must guard himself against being surprised. He should, therefore, keep a reserve against any unforseen contingency. If he has to use his reserve, he must always try to create a fresh one.

Action Against Enemy Armoured Forces

Though the air may give warning of the approach of enemy armoured forces the encounter with them on the ground may be of a sudden nature. Often there will be little time for a deliberate plan or for detailed orders. Initiative and "manoeuvre sense" in subordinates is therefore essential.

The following paragraphs apply to the action of a complete regiment, which may be operating from reserve or a brigade plan, or to that of a squadron operating on a regimental plan.

In action against armoured forces, the tactical object must be to establish local superiority in a given area, even though generally outnumbered in the area of operations by forestalling the enemy in opening fire and hitting targets at decisive ranges with the main anti-tank weapons.

In the attempt to achieve this object, the following considerations arise:
1. Ground
   • The nature of the ground must largely influence the plan. The best obtainable must be used, even if this involves a

retirement by advanced troops. A headlong advance to attack on unsuitable ground would be wrong, under equal conditions of fighting power and morale.

• The ideal ground consists of a ridge, or series of ridges, running across, or diagonally to, the enemy's line of advance. This allows good hull-down positions, concealment for maneuver, and makes it difficult for the enemy to observe his fire.

• In any case commanding ground should be seized, so as to have the run of the ground in an advance or to slow down the enemy, should it be decided to await his advance.

• Ground that has many obstacles to movement and defiles should be turned to account, by manoeuvering the enemy into it. This will tend to make him bunch and to adopt lines of advance which can be foreseen and covered. His defeat in detail will then be easier.

2. Manoeuvre and opening fire

• In approaching fire positions, concealment is essential and formations must be such as to make the utmost use of the ground. Fire positions should be unobtrusively reconnoitred and tanks should be kept concealed until the last moment, though with observation forward. This requires accurate drill to ensure that all come into action simultaneously.

• The question of opening fire on advanced enemy patrols will always be difficult and must be decided on the merits of each particular case. Generally they should be ignored as long as possible and destroyed before they can give information.

• In open country, where concealment is not possible, formations must be such that all tanks can fire in most directions simultaneously and at the same time offer a difficult target to the enemy.

• A prolonged fire fight should be avoided, as this increases the risk of being out-manoeuvered.

3. Control

A regimental commander, having made his plan and allotted tasks to squadrons, cannot control the action in detail. He will influence the course of events largely by the use of his reserve.

The detail control of the action will be the task of the squadron commander, who will maneuver his troops so that they come into action under the most favorable gunnery conditions. He will, if he can, indicate targets to troops and may order the opening of fire. But actual fire control during the action must generally be the responsibility of the crew commander. Economy in the use of ammunition is essential.

Defensive Action

A defensive role will often be forced on an army for strategic reasons, and in that defensive role an armoured division must take its part. Though the word "defensive" is apt to imply something "static", an armoured division is quite unsuitable to carry out this type of defence. It is only by a combination of fire power and manoeuvre that it can achieve the best results. Tactically, therefore, it must always operate offensively.

Its most likely task will be that of a major counter-attack against an enemy armoured formation, which may have penetrated the defenses or which may have moved round a flank. Such an operation will generally be conducted on a brigade or divisional plan and will require no special methods on the part of a regiment taking part. Methods for attack as described under Offensive Battle will hold good.

There are other types of defensive action, however, which a regiment may have to conduct. These can be classified as follows: delaying action and denying an area to the enemy, denying an obstacle, and withdrawal.

General principles to be observed in these types of action are:

• Defence must be elastic. The aim should be to deny an area to the enemy, i.e., well concealed forward troops for observation and delay, reserves for counter-attack.
• Surprise is of the utmost importance. This is made easier by the ability generally to reconnoitre ground beforehand and to select routes forward and back, fire positions and lines for counter-attack.
• The use of smoke from close support tanks must be used with great discretion owing to the danger of impeding the action of our own troops. Its most likely use will be to cover a withdrawal.

Denying an Area and Delaying Action

In country, where there is no definite obstacle to be held, an armoured formation or regiment can undertake defensive action only on an elastic plan. Their action will consist in denying areas to the enemy, perhaps for a definite time, and in keeping the enemy in check by a system of delaying action. This can be achieved by attacks or by counterattacks delivered after the hostile attack has started. Liberty of manoeuvre over a wide area is required.

The principles of this type of action are:

1. A definite area will be laid down, in which delaying action is to start, and the time up to which the enemy is to be prevented from occupying that area will be stated.
2. Resistance by forward detachments will be started as far forward in the area as possible. The reserve will be suitably placed to counter-attack any penetration by the enemy.

Thus a regiment might have one or two squadrons

forward, and a squadron one, two or three troops forward, depending on the ground and the situation. Too much dispersion should be avoided, as it is by strong counterattack that this type of action must largely depend for success.

3. Personal reconnaissance and the best use of ground to achieve surprise are of the highest importance.

Additional details on the tactics to be employed by the British Light, Cruiser, and Infantry Tanks are described in the following excerpts from Military Training Pamphlet No.34 Royal Armoured Corps Weapon Training, Part 4: Fire Tactics for Tank Commanders and Troop Leaders, dated 1940:

The armoured fighting vehicle achieves its results, essentially, by fire. Its tactics will therefore always be governed by the necessity for bringing fire to bear on the most suitable targets under the most favorable conditions.

General Principles - The essential characteristics of the A.F.V. are its concentrated fire power, and its ability, by reason of its armor and cross-country mobility, to apply this fire from close effective range.

It has, however, certain limitations which fundamentally affect its tactics:

1. A moving tank is not a good gun platform and fire will always be more accurate from a stationary vehicle. Furthermore, a high standard of driving is essential if fire on the move is to be effective.

2. Although armoured, the tank is not completely proof against fire from anti-tank weapons and must therefore always make the fullest use of cover. If, to deliver its fire, it is forced to leave cover, it must remain on the move so long as anti-tank fire can be brought to bear on it.

3. Visibility for both commander and gunner is restricted under battle conditions and the tank will always be at a disadvantage when opposed by the concealed and stationary gun. It requires, therefore, the support of other tanks, or of the other arms, to cover its movement, and continual vigilance on the part of the crew.

No tank must ever be outside the support of its neighbors and equally it must be able to support them. The distance cannot be fixed as it will depend of the task in hand.

Whilst it is the duty of all members of the crew to look for targets it is the main responsibility of the tank commander; his also is the decision, when fire is suddenly opened on a tank; as to whether it should be partially or wholly closed down, and whether the fire should be replied to or ignored.

The chief duty of the driver is so to drive his tank that a good gun platform is ensured. He has also to consider the avoidance of enemy fire and choose his ground accordingly.

Constant practice is also needed to bring a vehicle into

"hull or turret down" positions. Success in taking up such positions is largely governed by the driver's ability to estimate heights.

A tank is said to be "hull down" to its target when only the turret is exposed to view from that target, i.e., when the gunner's line of sight just clears the intervening cover. It is said to be "turret down" when the tank commander from his post of observation can observe, but the tank itself is concealed from the potential target.

It will seldom be necessary for the fire of two tanks of a troop to be concentrated on the same target except when some anti-tank weapon is being assaulted under covering fire; even then too great a concentration of fire on one target may lead to the neglect of others.

"I" Tanks - "I" Tanks, which move comparatively slowly, are very heavily armoured and used primarily in support of infantry against located positions and over ground that has been previously studied, but in the face of strong opposition and in the closest and most severe conditions of battle when the tank's task is to come to close quarters with the enemy as quickly as possible.

The primary target of the tank will be weapons which may inflict casualties on our own infantry. Enemy A.F.Vs. when encountered must be immediately engaged.

Smoke projectors should be used to blind enemy anti-tank weapons. It will also be the duty of the attacking infantry to engage with fire hostile anti-tank weapons whenever and wheresoever encountered.

Halts to fire are unnecessary unless the ground has been badly cut up by shell fire, as the speed of the tank is insufficient seriously to interfere with the accuracy of aim at such short ranges.

The 2-pounder is the best weapon to use against pillboxes, houses and similar types of cover. Small arms fire will be reserved for troop targets and neutralizing fire against trenches, etc.

In the defensive battle against heavily armoured A.F.Vs., surprise fire from cover whilst the tank is still stationary will be very effective.

Cruiser Tanks - Cruiser Tanks are more lightly armoured and capable of rapid movement. They are intended for employment under the mobile conditions of more open warfare where there has been little time to organize fresh defenses. This will often involve Tank v. Tank action.

Conditions of battle will not be so severe as in Infantry Tank actions and successful action will be much more dependent on gaining by manoeuvre the most suitable ground and then by hard and accurate shooting.

Fire will often be opened at long ranges, particularly in Tank v. Tank action, when it is desired to keep the enemy at a distance until ground conditions offer a suitable opportunity to close for decisive action.

The priority of targets is:
1. Enemy A.F.Vs.
2. Enemy anti-tank weapons, including field artillery,
3. Other troops.

Should enemy cruiser tanks disclose themselves at the same time as anti-tank fire is opened, the troop or squadron leader must decide instantly how to direct his fire. The anti-tank gun may be conveniently covered by smoke from the tank's projector or, alternatively, by a close support tank and the enemy tanks then engaged.

In Tank v. Tank actions fire must be distributed to include all the enemy A.F.Vs. on a ship-for-ship basis. Every tank will engage its opposite number in the enemy formation. That is to say, flank tanks will engage the enemy flank tanks and center tanks engage those in the center of the enemy line. If in superior numbers to the enemy, spare tanks will engage the nearest enemy tanks, but flank tanks will still engage enemy flank tanks. If in inferior numbers to the enemy, flank tanks still engage enemy flank tanks, and center tanks the enemy center. This ensures that fire is distributed along the whole length of the enemy line.

Every advantage must be taken of cover and background to enable surprise fire to be carried out from a stationary position. In Tank vs. Tank action, if within decisive range in the open, tanks should keep on the move for protection and in order to retain formation, initiative and power of manoeuvre.

When crossing crests, firing from hull down positions, or engaging targets on the move individual tanks may be manoeuvred to allow of broadside fire.

The 2-pounder is best employed against enemy tanks, and anti-tank weapons or personnel in houses. When used against artillery at close range its role is to damage the equipments. Small arms fire will be used against troops in the open. When small arms fire is directed against enemy A.F.Vs. it will be concentrated as opportunity offers on the driver's visor and aiming slits.

Should Cruiser Tanks be forced to engage heavily armoured tanks their fire must be concentrated on the enemy's tracks and suspension. The Cruiser's superior speed should be used to obtain surprise by manoeuvre.

Light Tanks - Light Tanks are lightly armoured, small and handy. They are primarily concerned with the duties of reconnaissance, protection, and action against hostile light tank formations and lightly held positions.

They may expect to work over wide frontages and their successful employment will to a large extent depend on the ability of the various tanks of the troop to manoeuvre under mutual fire support.

Conditions of battle will be less severe than with either the "I" Tank or the Cruiser. Light Tanks may therefore be expected to derive advantage from bold and aggressive fire tactics combined with mobility.

On reconnaissance, fire will often be withheld, particularly when the tank commander has reason to believe he is unobserved. Enemy fire should not be considered as an invariable reason for returning fire. In the protective role, particularly when delay is necessary, fire will be opened at the longest effective range.

Enemy anti-tank weapons will be given first priority as targets.

Smoke will be used primarily for self protection. It may on occasion be used to cover the final advance of a tank against an enemy anti-tank weapon. This will only be possible when the anti-tank weapon is also being engaged by fire action from another source. It will seldom be profitable to attack an anti-tank weapon with less than three Light Tanks, and it must be borne in mind that the enemy anti-tank defence will frequently be mutually supporting and possibly defiladed from the front.

Fire will generally be from the halt from concealed positions. Exceptions to this rule will be when the tank is surprised, or when enemy anti-tank weapons are being overrun, or when the tank is caught on an exposed forward slope, or if there is a danger of being out-manoeuvred by enemy A.F.Vs.

If for any reason, fire action when on the move is necessary, the bursts of fire should be long ones, except with the 0.5-inch M.G., when short bursts give best results, and the 15 mm Besa, which is most effective as a single shot weapon.

Enemy A.F.Vs., other than light tanks, should be avoided unless they are in small numbers and can be engaged under favorable conditions. They must, however, at all times be piqueted and reported.

When crossing crests or firing from hull down positions, individual tanks may be manoeuvred to allow of broadside fire.

The heavy M.G. should be used mainly against armoured targets. Hostile M.Gs. behind brickwork can be included in this category. It is useful for "indicating fire", to observe for range, and to direct the fire of other tanks on to a target.

5.2 GERMAN PANZER TACTICS

The following excerpts from H.Dv.470/10, Guidelines for Commanding and Employing the **Panzer-Regiment** and **Panzer-Abteilung** in Combat dated 18 January 1941 provide details on the fundamental tactical approach employed by the **Panzer-Regiments** during the various battles in North Africa:

1. Because of its strong fire power, its armor and its mobility, the **Panzer-Regiment** is the main assault force of the **Panzer-Division**. Its strength lies in concentrated and audaciously conducted surprise attacks. Responsible commanders and clever employment of this strong assault force against decisive positions guarantee success. The other weapons in the **Panzer-Division** support the **Panzer-Regiment** in the accomplishment of its combat assignments.

2. The **Panzer-Regiment** is organized as follows:
   Regiments-Stab (headquarters) with
      Nachrichtenzug (signals platoon) and
      leichtem Panzerzug (light tank platoon)
   2 **Panzer-Abteilungen** (tank battalions)
   1 **Panzer-Werkstatt-Kompanie** (tank repair
   company)

3. As a rule, the **Panzer-Abteilung** is employed under the command of the **Panzer-Regiments**. Every **Panzer-Abteilung** is outfitted with the same **Panzerkampfwagen** and weapons.

4. The **Panzer-Abteilung** is organized as follows:
   Abteilungs-Stab (headquarters)
   Stabs-Kompanie (headquarters company) with
      Nachrichtenzug (signals platoon)
      Erkunderzug (scout platoon)
      leichtem Panzerzug (light tank platoon)
      Pionierzug (combat engineer platoon) and
      Fliegerabwehrzug (anti-aircraft platoon)
   2 **leichte Kompanien** (light tank company)
   1 **mittlere Kompanie** (medium tank company)
   1 **leichte Kolonne** (light supply column)

Combat Formations for the Regiment

27. The **Panzer-Regiment** can conduct an attack with one **Abteilung** behind the other (in two waves) or beside each other.

28. The **Regiment** attacking in waves strikes the enemy with a powerful blow, which is continuously fed by companies from the rear wave and makes it possible to conduct the fight in depth.

When fighting within zones of enemy resistance, the flanks of the **Regiment** are best secured by echelon in depth.

The attack in waves simplifies control of the **Regiment**. It establishes the rule.

29. The employment of both **Abteilungen** beside each other with less depth can be useful in the chase of an already decimated opponent or by breaking off combat to attack an aggressive opponent.

Combat Formations for the Abteilung

32. The **Panzer-Abteilung** takes up formation to attack in several lines. The choice of formation is based on the task, width of the available area, visibility, and room within the combat formation of the **Regiment**.

As a rule, the **leichte Kompanien** make up the front line. The **mittlere Kompanie** usually fights in the second line (in order to provide fire protection for the **leichten Kompanien**). The third **leichte Kompanie** follows in the third line behind the open flank or behind the center.

33. One should strive to employ the **mittlere Kompanie** for fire protection as a consolidated unit. The following prerequisites apply to this: Ability to view the terrain, elevated firing positions or gaps in the forward **Kompanien**, and the width of the **Panzer-Abteilung** attack formation not too wide (not greater than 1200 meters).

Close terrain can force attachment of platoons or sections from the **mittlere Kompanie** to the **leichte Kompanien**.

Attacking from a March

37. During attacks directly from a march, the key is to quickly assault the enemy with a surprise strike without scattering your own forces.

40. The combat reconnaissance by the **leichten Zug** of the **Regiment** provides the commander with information for the employment and combat formation of his **Regiment**. It is closely tied to thorough scouting of the terrain to determine the feasibility of a Panzer attack, especially scouting for tank obstacles and impediments.

If the **Regiment** has both flanks open, the **Abteilungen** are to be ordered in which flank they are to perform reconnaissance.

Timely contact with other units that should support or escort the **Regiment**'s attack is constantly to be strived for.

FORMATIONS FOR THE PANZER ABTEILUNG

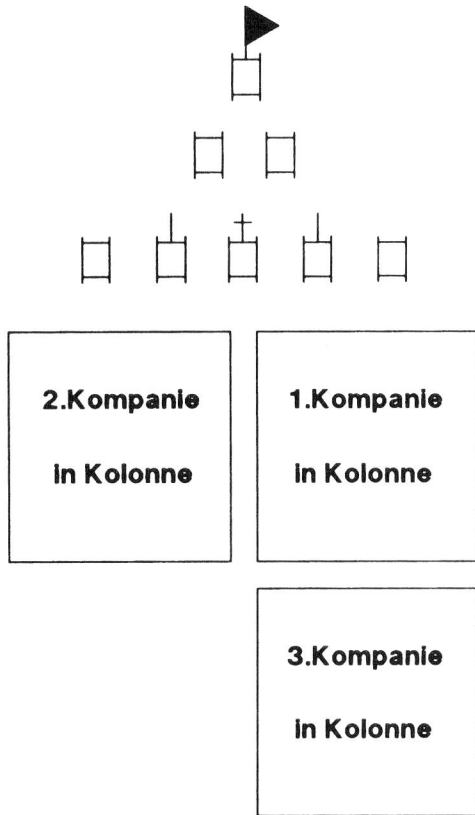

KOLONNE

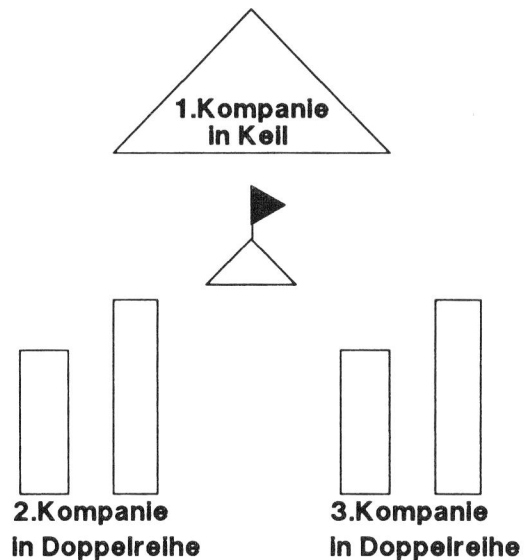

KEIL

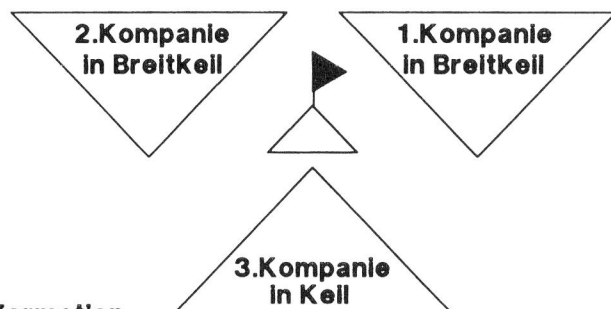

BREITKEIL

The Kolonne was used for assembly.

The Reihe was used for road marches.

The Keil was used as a narrow attack formation 500 meters wide and 1800 meters deep.

The Breitkeil was the most useful attack formation at 1000 meters wide and 1300 meters deep.

FORMATIONS FOR THE PANZER KOMPANIE

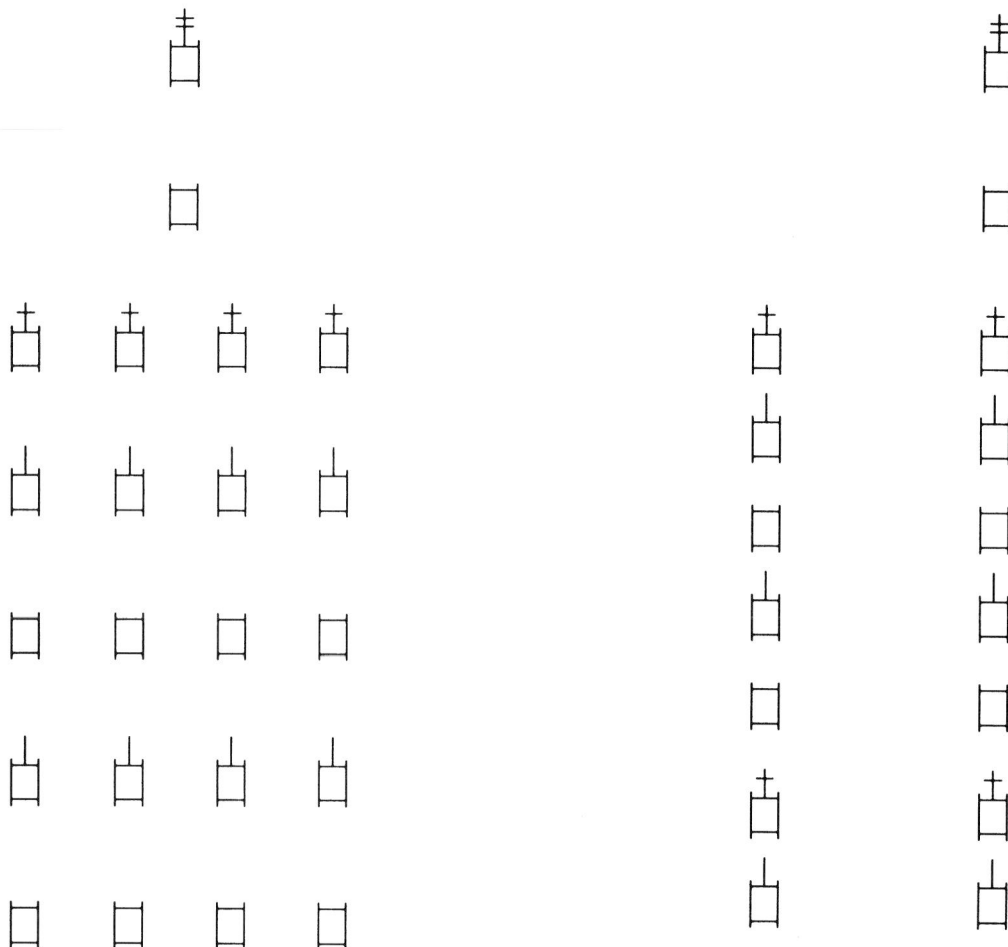

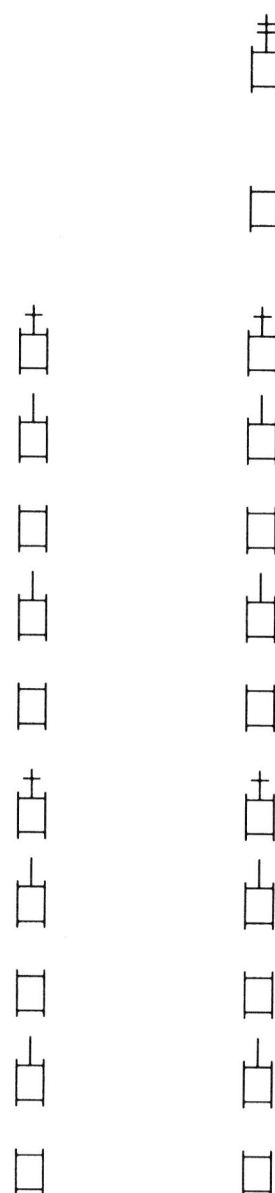

KOLONNE

DOPPELREIHE

The Kolonne was used for assembly.

The Reihe was used for road marches.

The Doppelreihe was used for approach marches.

The Keil was used as a narrow attack formation.

The Breitkeil was the most useful attack formation.

In the Breitkeil attack formation, the Kompanie occupied an area about 450 meters wide and 450 meters deep when proper intervals of 25 meters behind and 50 meters between Panzers were maintained and each Zug (platoon) spaced at 100 meter intervals.

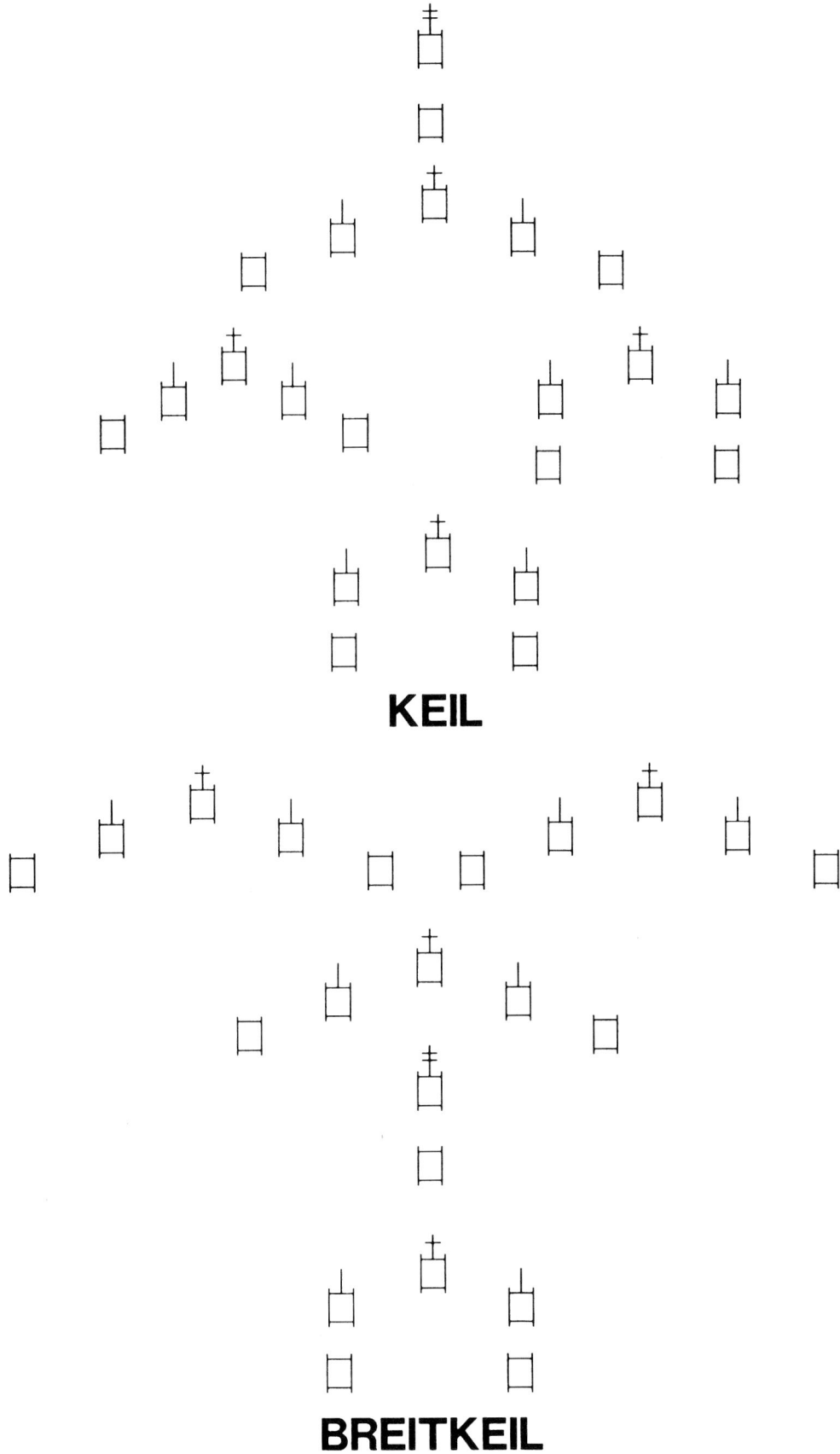

KEIL

BREITKEIL

FORMATIONS FOR THE PANZER ZUG

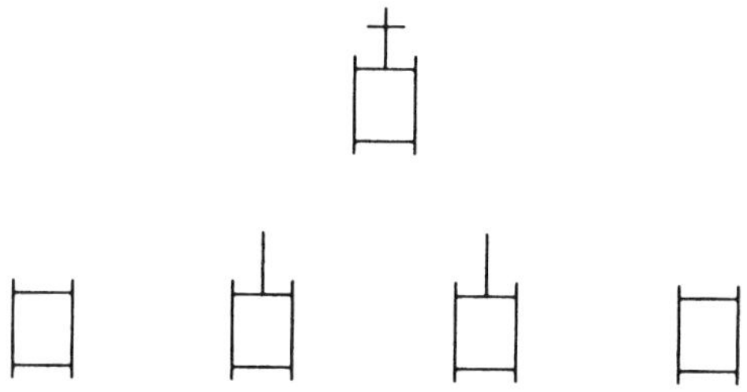

LINIE

REIHE

The Reihe was used for marches and assembly.

The Linie was used for assembly.

The Doppelreihe was used for approach marches.

The Keil was the most useful attack formation.

The intervals between Pz.Kpfw. during marches and attacks were 25 meters to the front and 50 meters to the side. Intervals could be changed depending on the terrain, weather, and enemy situation. During combat the Zugfuehrer (platoon leader) was to move to a position within the formation from where he could best direct the platoon based on the terrain and situation.

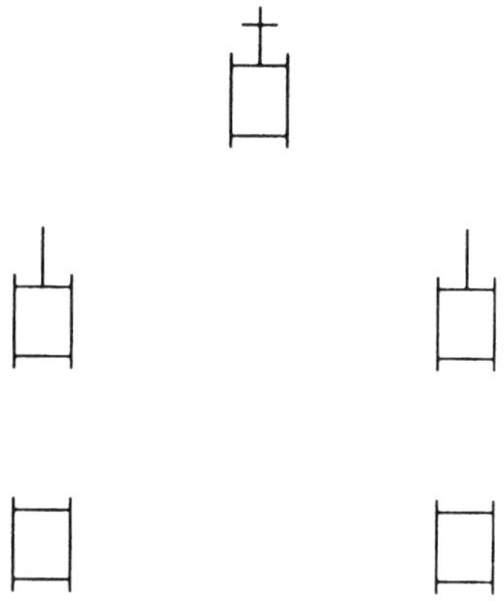

DOPPELREIHE

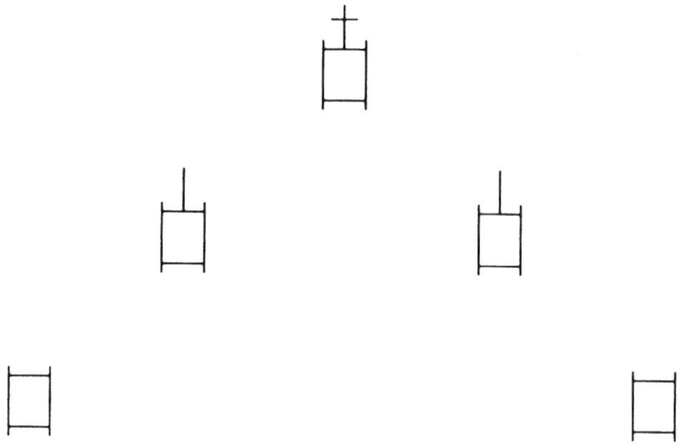

KEIL

41. When attacking from the march, the **Regiment** usually deploys the **Abteilungen** one behind the other. The first wave is to strike the known enemy and penetrate deeply into the opponents position.

The second wave is to follow along so that it can be deployed in depth. Combat assignments often will first be given as the attack is developing.

42. During the attack, close communication with the artillery commander is especially important because during an attack from a march little intelligence on the enemy is available and in most cases only a short time is available for discussion of the situation.

The artillery must be informed about the formation, width, middle line, and objective of the attack. They must be continually updated about target requests for the artillery to engage that the **Panzer-Regiment** can't engage with its own weapons.

43. Frequently the **Pionierzug** and attached elements of the **Panzer-Pionier-Bataillon** will be attached to the front wave.

45. As soon as the **Abteilung** commander receives the attack order, he deploys his **leichten Zug** to the front or to the open flank in order to expand on the information gained by the combat reconnaissance conducted by the **Regiment**. Reinforcing the **leichten Zug** with **Panzerkampfwagen** from the **leichten Kompanien** can be necessary.

46. The **Abteilung** usually attacks from the march in a "**Breitkeil**" formation.

47. During the attack, covering fire for the continuing advance of the **Kompanien** is to be continuously assured. For this, the **mittlere Kompanie** is to be advanced sector by sector. Contact between the first and second wave must not be lost.

48. The artillery commander and observer in **Panzerbeobachtungswagen** accompanying the attack in the first wave allows the **Abteilung** commander to direct the artillery fire mainly against such enemy weapons that can't be engaged by the attack of the **Panzer-Abteilung**.

Attacks from the Assembly Area

50. As much as the space and terrain allows in the assembly area, the **Panzer-Regiment** moves into formation for the attack. It completes preparations for combat.

51. All of the necessary preparations for conducting an attack are to be completed, including:

thorough scouting of the terrain to be attacked,

clearing of obstacles in front of the enemy main battle field,

obtain all of the necessary information for conducting the attack by employing combat reconnaissance,

establishing contact with the commanders of the other weapon units supporting and escorting the attack,

establishing contact with the commanders of the units and elements that already have encountered enemy activity in the terrain to be attacked, and also

establishing contact with the commanders of the infantry units that are attacking in front of the Panzers.

Exploit the intelligence gained from scouting from all units on the terrain, known enemy nests of resistance, especially anti-tank weapons and artillery.

52. Strive to show the **Kompanie** commanders and if possible many of the junior leaders the terrain for the attack, as long as thereby the intention to attack is not revealed to the enemy.

53. So that the enemy doesn't learn of the impending Panzer attack from radio intercept, radio silence is to be enforced within the **Regiment** in the assembly area.

55. If the **Regiment** attacks in several waves, as a rule the first wave has the tasks of quickly penetrating into the depth of the enemy main battlefield and destroying the enemy artillery.

Closely following, the second wave engages the enemy infantry and heavy weapons that weren't destroyed by the first wave. By quickly following with a simultaneous infantry attack, it is possible for them to exploit the success of the second wave.

56. If the **Regiment** is assigned the task of aiding the infantry to advance, the **Panzer-Regiment** commander is responsible for maintaining contact between his regiment and the infantry. The **Regiment** orders which elements - as a rule only at a strength of up to a **leichten Kompanie** - are attached to the infantry for close cooperation.

57. The **Regiment** commander can direct the second wave to employ its **mittlere Panzer-Kompanie** to reinforce the covering fire for the penetration of the first wave.

58. After succeeding in penetrating, the assault is to quickly continue into the depth of the enemy main battlefield. This is the fastest and surest way of breaking enemy resistance.

59. If elements of the **Panzer-Jaeger-Abteilung** are attached, these will be deployed in the attack in several waves directly behind the first wave of Panzers in order to support penetration into the enemy main battlefield by silencing the enemy anti-tank weapons. After the penetration, they will usually follow behind the open wing of the first wave so that they can provide support if enemy tanks are encountered and can protect the **Panzer-Regiment**'s flanks.

60. Close cooperation with the **Pioniere** that escort the attack in must be assured so that all the barriers and obstacles in the depth of the enemy main battlefield that are restricting the Panzer attack can be quickly cleared away. Protection of the **Pioniere** with **Panzerkampfwagen** while they clear barriers can come into question.

61. During attacks in waves, in so far as they aren't tied up with fighting enemy anti-tank defense, the **Abteilung** in the first wave is to silence known enemy heavy weapons and nests of resistance without allowing themselves to be diverted from the completion of their main task.

After reaching the objective, the commander immediately organizes the **Abteilung** for new deployment in the necessary combat formation. Enemy counterstrikes must always find the **Abteilung** ready to attack.

62. In the second wave, as the backstop for the first wave, the **mittlere Kompanie** is to keep up far forward. This results in the most effective covering fire in support of the **leichten Kompanien** against the enemy anti-tank weapons that weren't spotted or silenced by the first wave.

The **leichten Kompanien** must search and destroy the enemy silenced by the first wave.

A main task of the second wave is repulsion of enemy counterattacks directed against the Panzer attack and the following infantry. To achieve this, if possible, strong elements of the **mittlere Kompanie** must be quickly deployed in the decisive direction. This is to be considered when deciding the formation for the second wave after penetrating into the enemy.

63. After penetration, quickly renewing deployment of combat reconnaissance is important, especially in the open flanks.

Panzer versus Tank Combat

65. Decisive factors in tank versus Panzer combat are:
- A lighting-fast grasp of the situation and terrain as well as immediate action at all command levels.
- Timely recognition and identification of the strength and direction of the enemy tank attack.
- Knowledge of the automotive and weapons capabilities of the enemy tanks.

66. As soon as enemy tanks appear, immediately abandon the current task, attack the enemy tanks and destroy them by using all available armor-defeating weapons. The swifter the attack, the faster the enemy tanks will be destroyed and the sooner the original task can be pursued.

67. The task of combat reconnaissance is to quickly determine the enemy flanks.

68. All forces are to be concentrated to destroy the enemy tanks. This is based on quickly establishing a strong fire front that surprises the enemy with fire and forces his attack to halt. The prerequisites for deployment of the rear waves and lines should be accomplished by this. Our strength, the terrain and the weather decide if the second wave's attack is sent against the front, flank or rear of the enemy tank force. One should constantly attempt to keep the sun to the rear, the wind from the front, and tie down the enemy tanks frontally so that they will show their vulnerable wide sides to the counterattacking elements of the **Panzer-Regiment**. During attacks in waves, the **Regiment**'s commander as a rule will deploy the first wave in a frontal attack and the send the second wave – exploiting favorable terrain and at full speed – for a destructive strike against the flanks and rear of the surprised enemy.

69. Attached **Panzerjaeger auf Sfl.** accompany the Panzer attack and, in cooperation with artillery and heavy weapons, support the Panzer units' fight by delivering concentrated fire.

70. In order to quickly pull out of the aimed fire from surprise encounters with enemy tanks, win time to establish a fire front, and mask the movement of rearward waves and lines, it can be useful to lay a smoke screen between our own and the enemy tanks.

71. If a **Panzer-Abteilung** is unexpectedly attacked by enemy tanks, at first the **Kompanien** themselves check the attack, after which the commander must strive to quickly regain control of his **Abteilung**.

72. Retiring enemy tanks are to be ruthlessly pursued. Increasing to maximum speed is necessary to surround the enemy tanks and to cut them off from their path of retreat. Cooperation with reconnaissance aircraft comes into increased importance for this.

Attack Against a Fortified Position

79. The main body of the **Panzer-Regiment** will be held back – if possible under cover from the effect of the enemy weapons mounted in the fortification – until gaps through the anti-tank obstacles have been established.

Close contact is to be maintained with the **Pioniere** clearing away the tank obstacles and barriers.

80. The Panzer unit needs special fire support while driving through the lanes in the tank obstacles and the following movement to combat formation in the enemy main battlefield. It may be useful to screen the flanks with smoke.

Enemy artillery is the objective of the Panzers' attack.

The most important task for the combat reconnaissance is to prevent Panzer force from surprisingly encountering barriers, especially mines, in the depths of the main battlefield. **Panzer-Pioniere** are to be deployed far forward to spot and clear such barriers.

81. The Panzer force deployed in depth, especially the **mittlere Kompanie**, when possible in covered firing positions, provides support to the troops assigned to break into the enemy main battlefield by engaging enemy nests of resistance in no-man's land.

Defense

88. If, after gaining the attack objective, the **Panzer-Regiment** must defend the newly won territory until relieved by other units, the main body of Panzers should be held back until an enemy attack begins and be protected against the effect of enemy artillery and combat aircraft by utilizing cover and deployed formations.

89. The Panzer force prevents against surprise enemy attacks by thorough combat reconnaissance, especially in close terrain. In may be necessary to reinforce the **leichten Panzerzuege** for this task.

90. Enemy reconnaissance will be hindered by fire with long range weapons from individual Panzers that frequently change their position.

91. If the enemy attacks, he will be held back with concentrated fire that is opened early. The Panzer force that was held in reserve will be sent in to counterattack in an effective direction, into the attacker's flank if possible.

92. If enemy tanks attack, the fight will be conducted in accordance with the principles in Sections 64 to 71.

Breaking Off an Action

94. If the Panzer force is to make it possible for unarmored forces to break contact, it must repeatedly ambush the pursuing enemy by powerful short-range attacks from unexpected directions, until our own troops have managed to get well clear of the enemy. Wide attack formations are the rule.

95. Breaking off combat with superior enemy tank forces will be easier if it is possible to build up strong defensive fire in a rearward position, if possible, near a sector that is tank proof.

Active reconnaissance in the flanks and timely deployment of forces, especially attached **Panzerjaeger** and **Pioniere**, are necessary for flank protection and to prevent overtaking pursuit by the enemy tanks.

If the opponent isn't shaken off, the retreating Panzer force must exploit the terrain and favorable positions to strike with localized superior force against separate pursuing enemy elements.

96. Smoke makes it easier to break off contact with the enemy and masks the direction of the withdrawal.

Actions When Encountering Mines

105. The rapidity of the movement of Panzer forces contains the danger that the Panzers will unexpectedly drive into mines laid by the enemy.

The longer the resulting time loss as a result of encountering mines, the more time is gained by the enemy to reinforce his anti-tank defense or concentrate at decisive positions.

106. Therefore it must be taken into account that enemy mines, especially minefields, will be encountered in the attack routes. It is the most critical task of the **leichten Zuege** deployed on reconnaissance and scouting to spot and send timely reports on the position and extent of enemy-laid mines. It will be useful to attach **Pionier** scouting troops to the **leichten Panzer Zuegen** on reconnaissance in front of the **Panzer-Regiment**.

107. In order to rapidly clear mines and establish lanes through the minefields, the **Panzer-Pioniere** attached to the **Panzer-Regiment** should be deployed far forward in the first wave and attached to the lead Panzer unit.

108. In crossing terrain strewn with mines, it can be useful to advance by expanding the width and depth of the formation. Within the unit, the Panzers in the second and third lines drive in the tracks of the Panzers deployed in the first line. This also applies to the advance of units in the following wave.

109. Large minefields that are wide and deep must be by-passed. To achieve this, timely deployment of scouting and reconnaissance as well as an early decision and order to turn aside are necessary.

110. If the minefield can't be bypassed, the movement must be halted and the Panzer unit drive into cover. The combat reconnaissance is to be increased in order to obtain detailed information on the position and extent of the minefield.

111. The most important task is to scout for new opportunities, ensure covering fire for the Pionier work, and position the unit in readiness so that it can rapidly advance after establishing lanes or clearing the minefield.

112. Commanders of all ranks must continuously be self-motivated to search for gaps in the minefield or to quickly establish lanes with their attached Pionier forces working under the covering fire of the Panzers.

113. Frequently, minefields will first be recognized when the foremost Panzer has already driven into mines. Then, under the covering fire of rearward elements, the Panzers found in the minefield will be towed out and collected in a covered position.

114. When minefields are encountered, Panzers dropping smoke candles and smoke shells fired from the Panzers deployed to provide covering fire and artillery are an effective aid in screening enemy observation and fire.

Details on how to engage enemy armored formations were provided in D645, Training Directive for the **leichte** and **mittlere Panzer-Kompanie 1939** in Combat, dated 1 March 1939. These tactics had proven to be effective in the campaigns in Belgium and France. They remained unmodified and were directly referenced as the applicable tactics to use in tank-versus-tank engagements in the manuals for the **Panzer-Kompanien** written in late 1940 and early 1941.

Part C - Tank versus Tank Combat

I. General Principles

35. The decisive factors in tank versus tank combat are:
a. Knowledge of automotive and weapons capabilities.
b. Timely recognition and identification of the strength and direction of the enemy tank attack.

FOOTNOTE: Additional details on **Panzer-Kompanie** tactics are presented in Chapter 9 of Panzer Truppen.

c. A lightning-fast grasp of the situation and terrain as well as immediate action at all command levels.

The commander must travel at the point or in front of his command (commanders of rear lines or waves must travel in front of their command close behind the front units) in order to rapidly and personally observe the situation and terrain. Waiting for reports and delaying the engagement usually result in casualties to the forward line and allow the enemy to defeat our own Panzer units in sequence with superior forces.

36. The battle is to be conducted by movement and fire. The purpose of movement is to take the enemy tanks by surprise from an unexpected direction under concentrated superior firepower delivered by armor-defeating weapons and destroy them.

37. In general, the initial tasks of the forward waves and lines are to stop the enemy movement by fire and to conduct combat reconnaissance (determine the enemy flank and any accompanying enemy formations that may be following or on the flanks). This information is used to decide the engagement of rearward lines and waves. The situation, terrain, and weather are decisive in determining if they are to attack the forward elements, the flank, or the rear of the enemy tank force.

38. Target recognition and good training can make up for an inferiority in number and weapons. An attempt must be made to gain fire superiority at least at one location, even when our own forces are weaker.

39. The side which first builds superior firepower and first hits will win. In most cases, nothing more can be ordered when elements are attacked in the front or flank unexpectedly. The necessary defense has to be carried out automatically without orders. This is an essential objective of platoon and company training.

40. Concentrated fire on the enemy commander and signals tanks (knowledge of the organization and combat methods of the enemy) destroys their cohesion.

41. In difficult situations – especially during unexpected engagements – a smoke screen immediately fired in front of the enemy provides protection against aimed fire and provides time to establish a fire front.

42. Panzers with smaller caliber guns close to effective range with the enemy under the protection of the longer range, larger caliber gun armed Panzers. Firing beyond effective range is

a waste of ammunition and quickly results in ammunition shortages. The **mittlere Panzer-Kompanien** in the rear wave are to be employed as a concentrated unit.

43. Tasks for the **M.G.-Pz.Kpfw.** include securing the flanks and combat reconnaissance, especially on the enemy wing. When both opponents engage with **leichte Panzer-Kompanien**, the **M.G.-Pz.Kpfw.** are to follow the gun-armed Panzers utilizing any cover offered by the terrain.

44. Firing is most effective from stationary Panzers. Panzers that aren't being fired on, and have a good field of fire, fire when halted. Panzers without a field of fire are to use their high speed to gain a suitable position. All available cover is to be utilized when firing while halted.

If the enemy gains fire superiority, the Panzers are to leave their firing position and, utilizing available cover, drive at high speed to a new firing position. Elements that are not under enemy fire are to provide covering fire.

45. As soon as enemy tanks fire, immediately abandon the current task, attack the enemy tanks and destroy them by using all available armor-defeating weapons. The more powerful and the swifter the attack, the faster the enemy tanks will be destroyed. The enemy tanks must be quickly destroyed to win a free hand for continuing the original task.

46. The commander must attempt to maintain tight control of his unit to be able to send it against the enemy so that all weapons are utilized to full effectiveness and attack at the decisive moment.

Platoons and individual tanks are not allowed to separate from their units, in order to prevent them from being destroyed by enemy superiority. Mutual covering fire!

Ramming even smaller enemy tanks is pointless. This usually results in damaging and immobilizing the ramming Panzer.

47. Anti-tank units and artillery as well as heavy infantry weapons are to join in the battle against enemy tanks in accordance with their capabilities. Especially, mobile anti-tank weapons are to follow our own Panzers closely.

48. Fooling the enemy tanks directs their attention away from our main force and assists our own attack.

49. Constantly attempt to keep the sun to the rear and the wind from the front (prevents dust and smoke interference). During battle, cause the enemy tanks to turn so that they show their sides.

50. Rear units advancing under covering fire from the forward line utilize the terrain to attack, envelop the enemy, take them under concentrated fire, and destroy them in close combat.

51. Attacks against the enemy flanks or rear are the most effective. Use combat reconnaissance, especially when fighting in the enemy zone. Combat reconnaissance prevents unexpected encounters with enemy resistance and prevents being enveloped by enemy tanks. In addition, cooperation with our own anti-tank weapons can be very advantageous.

52. A disengaging enemy is to be recklessly pursued. Above all, high speed is necessary to envelop and cut off his retreat route. Securing against ambush, conducting combat reconnaissance, and scouting terrain may not be forgotten. Cooperation with aircraft is especially important.

II. The Battle

53. In principle, three cases are to be differentiated in tank versus tank combat:

1. Our Panzers and enemy tanks unexpectedly encounter each other.
2. Our Panzers are attacked by surprise by the enemy.
3. Our Panzers conduct a surprise attack against the enemy.

54. In each of these three cases, the tactics employed by the **Panzer-Kompanie** or **Panzer-Abteilung** are dependent upon whether the Panzers involved are in the front or in a rear line.

Our Panzers and Enemy Tanks Unexpectedly Encounter Each Other

55. In this case, the initial conditions are the same for both opponents. Swift reaction will guarantee gaining superiority.

a. Panzer units in the front line:

56. If the enemy is promptly recognized, immediately attempt to bring all available armor-defeating weapons into action at effective ranges, firing while stationary.

57. If the range is too long, the front wave is to charge at high speed, utilizing all available cover to close within effective range of the enemy tank unit. Covering fire or a smoke screen is to be attempted by the medium Panzers. Simplify all movements to hasten the start of effective fire.

58. Let the enemy advance against our favorable firing positions.

59. In a frontal engagement, all Panzers in the forward **Panzer-Kompanien** with armor-defeating weapons move to locations where they can fire at the enemy. **M.G.-Pz.Kpfw.** provide security and reconnaissance. When both opponents engage in battle, **M.G.-Pz.Kpfw.** take full cover.

60. If the enemy advances against a flank, build the "**Reihe**" formation, turned toward the threatened side or advanced toward the flank. To present a smaller target, establish a front facing the enemy as soon as possible.

61. If the enemy has the advantage and opens effective fire first, units that find themselves without cover are to pull back, zigzagging, and seek firing positions in favorable terrain. Elements that aren't receiving enemy fire provide covering fire. The battle is then conducted as related in Paragraphs 57 through 60.

62. Every Panzer that identifies enemy tanks is to give the established signal and direct the unit toward the threatened direction by corresponding actions (rapid fire or advancing toward the enemy).

The leader of the front unit immediately reports the enemy tank situation to the higher command by radio.

b. Panzer units in the rear of the first wave:

63. In general, rear units remain in the hands of the **Panzer-Kompanie** or **Panzer-Abteilung** commander. Rear units provide help by enveloping the enemy, extending the front, or compensating for reverses to the forward line.

64. Units closely following behind the front line may not hesitate to join in the battle independently. Waiting on orders costs too much time and can lead to destruction of the forward line. The **Panzer-Kompanie** commander must decide whether to reinforce or extend the front line, or to attack the enemy flank. The **Panzer-Kompanie** commander reports the selected action by radio to his commander and the commander of the forward line.

65. Rear units that identify enemy tanks on their flanks react the same as units in the front line. In addition, in this case, rear units are to react swiftly, give the established signal, and report the situation. Inform our own anti-tank unit.

c. Panzer units in the rear wave:

66. In most cases, Panzers in the rear waves will be committed in order to bring the tank battle to a decisive conclusion. Resolute command brings victory.

67. Units in the rear wave that identify enemy tanks on their flank react independently, the same as units in the front wave (refer to Paragraph 65). Timely use of our anti-tank forces and artillery aids in maintaining the Panzers' mobility.

68. If enemy tanks are observed and orders aren't received, the **Panzer-Abteilung** commander makes the decision independently. They must attack when the enemy is so strong that the front wave is endangered without committing the rear wave.

69. In most cases, the rear waves attempt to flank the enemy. Exploiting speed and terrain, the attack is carried forward on a wide front against the deep flank of the enemy tank force.

70. The decision as to where to strike cannot wait for lengthy terrain scouting. Swift action is usually more decisive than an attack that is delayed awaiting lengthy scouting or delayed due to a long detour to gain an attack direction that is presumed to be especially favorable. Our own flanks must be especially protected during every flank attack.

Our Panzers Are Attacked by Surprise by Enemy Tanks

71. This case is the least favorable because the enemy surprisingly attacks when the attention of our Panzers is directed toward the accomplishment of their combat mission.

72. Many times, at least some elements of the enemy will take up covered positions and let our Panzers advance into his fire zone. These hidden elements can only be identified with difficulty. Because they are usually hull down, only the turret is seen and is difficult to hit.

73. When units find themselves in such a situation, it is usually better to pull back from the enemy's superior firepower – if possible under smoke screen from the medium Panzers – and advance against the enemy flank from the next available cover. If this is not possible, implement the same tactics described in Paragraph 61.

a. Panzer units in the front line:

74. Every Panzer positioned in cover or not receiving fire immediately opens fire to cover the enemy tanks and thereby make it possible for other Panzers to maneuver. Covering

the enemy with smoke allows movement to the side and can be used to create a fire front in an unexpected location.

75. Continue the battle as related in Paragraphs 56 through 62.

b. <u>Panzer units at the rear of the first wave:</u>

76. Rear units that are attacked by surprise react the same way as the forward units.

77. Directly opposing, frontally attacking enemy are engaged the same as related in Paragraphs 63 through 65. Maximum speed is demanded to relieve the forward line.

78. It is especially important to swiftly identify and subdue enemy elements that are firing from hidden positions. Request artillery support from the forward observer.

c. <u>Panzer units in the rear wave:</u>

79. If they themselves are attacked, elements in the rear wave react the same as the first wave.

80. If the front wave is attacked, the commander of the rear wave decides if, which elements, and in which direction his units should attack. Employment of these elements follows the tactics described in Paragraphs 66 through 70. Commitment of the **mittlere Panzer-Kompanie** is urgent.

Our Panzers Conduct a Surprise Attack Against the Enemy

81. Surprise is an essential prerequisite for success. Surprise can be achieved only through good camouflage, good combat reconnaissance, and good contact with reconnaissance units, especially aircraft.

82. The troops must be trained to rapidly deploy into commanding positions from an advancing formation and surprise the enemy with aimed fire. The correct choice of hidden or hull-down positions is to be carefully practiced. Every Panzer commander and driver is to be taught to read the terrain during individual instruction.

83. Fire control is based on determination of the range, fire distribution or concentration, and above all, the moment for opening fire. Surprise attacks are to be carefully practiced.

84. Essential combat principles are:
   • Tie down the enemy front from hidden or hull-down positions,
   • Choose alternate positions in case of effective enemy fire,
   • Lead the reserves to attack the flanks,
   • Pursue until the opponent is destroyed.

85. Employing Panzers in a counterattack is executed from the same point of view as the principles for tank versus tank combat. The fire front can often be built or in all cases can be reinforced by anti-tank units.

Coordination with Other Arms in the Tank Battle

86. As far as possible, all other weapons have to support the battle of their own Panzers.

87. Infantry provide support by observation and reconnaissance. Motorized infantry remain under cover in the area of the tank battle. Other elements, including the heavy infantry weapons, engage identified enemy anti-tank weapons.

88. The main part of the anti-tank weapons should face toward the enemy tanks. Elements should secure the flanks of our own Panzers against tanks and anti-tank guns.

89. Artillery take enemy tanks under concentrated fire. Especially suitable are terrain features that constrict the tanks' movement, such as gaps between woods that they must pass through or obstacles on which tanks will be delayed. The artillery pins down identified enemy anti-tank guns and hinders the employment of new anti-tank units.

90. The combat engineers can achieve surprising results by swiftly laying mine barriers.

91. Aircraft scout for enemy tank forces and warn their own Panzer units. They report by radio and signal the direction of attack and strength of the identified enemy tanks.

6

Rommel Strikes Out

Only after the Italian forces had been thoroughly beaten by the British in four successive battles did the Germans come to their aid in North Africa. At first, on 11 January, they only intended to send **Sperrverband Lybien** with a single company of 30 Panzers. By 5 February the proposed force had been expanded to a division, the **5.leichte Division** with **Panzer-Regiment 5**. Overall command of the German army forces in North Africa was awarded to General Rommel, who had made a name for himself as the audacious commander of the **7.Panzer-Division**. Along with the expansion of the expeditionary force by another division, the **15.Panzer-Division** with **Panzer-Regiment 8**, on 19 February a corps headquarters was created and designated as the **Deutsches Afrikakorps**.

As the name **Sperrverband** suggested, the original plan for employment of the German units was merely as a blocking force to impede further British expansion. But the first German combat units pushed forward past Sirte without meeting any enemy resistance, and radio intercepts confirmed that the British were pulling back some forces. Therefore the Germans became bolder. On 21 March the **Oberkommando des Heeres** (army high command) approved plans for a limited reconnaissance probe against the Marsa el Brega position. But no attempt was to be made to retake Libya until the entire **15.Panzer-Division** was transferred and available at the front in May 1941. In the final preparations, the narrow defile through the salt marshes at El Agheila was occupied on 24 March as a staging area for the reconnaissance probe against Marsa el Brega to take place on 31 March 1941.

6.1 GERMAN FORCES

Panzer-Jaeger-Abteilung 39 and **Aufklaerungs-Abteilung 3** were the first German combat units to land at Tripoli, on 14 February, but without any armor-piercing ammunition. Next came the three **8.8 cm Flak Batterien** of I./ **Flak-Regiment 33** who had yet to gain their reputation as the most dreaded of tank destroyers. The very weak infantry element, consisting of the **2.M.G.Bataillon** and **8.M.G.-Bataillon** under **Regiment-Stab z.b.V.200**, arrived in Tripoli next in the period from 27 February to 6 March. Finally, the tanks in **Panzer-Regiment 5** arrived on 8 to 10 March. Additional German units are listed with their date of arrival in Appendix B.

Panzer-Regiment 5 and the Italian medium tank battalion, **VII battaglione carri M**, paraded before the Castello in Tripoli on 12 March. Directly after the parade, the **II.Abteilung/Panzer-Regiment 5** started their advance to Sirte which they conducted in four night marches. The **I.Abteilung/Panzer-Regiment 5** also advanced slowly to the front and arrived in the forward area on 23 March.

The German forces in the forward area on 31 March are listed in the order of battle for the **5.leichte Division**. The number of Panzers in each sub-unit in **Panzer-Regiment 5** is shown as it was organized based on original documents and the tactical numbers on the turrets. Due to a fire on board a ship, 10 **Pz.Kpfw.III** and 3 **Pz.Kpfw.IV** had been destroyed and replacements for these 13 didn't arrive at the front until late April 1941. The first **Pz.Kpfw.III** was lost on 24 March 1941 when El Agheila was occupied, burned out as a result of detonating an Italian anti-tank mine. No record has been found stating the exact number of Panzers that were operational (out of the available 25 **Pz.Kpfw.I**, 45 **Pz.Kpfw.II**, 60 **Pz.Kpfw.III**, 17 **Pz.Kpfw.IV**, 3 **kl.Pz.Bef.Wg.** and 4 **Pz.Bef.Wg.**) for the attack. But due to their precautions during the long road marches forward from Tripoli and the low mileage on the **Pz.Kpfw.III** and **IV**, most should have been operational when they attacked Marsa el Brega on 31 March 1941.

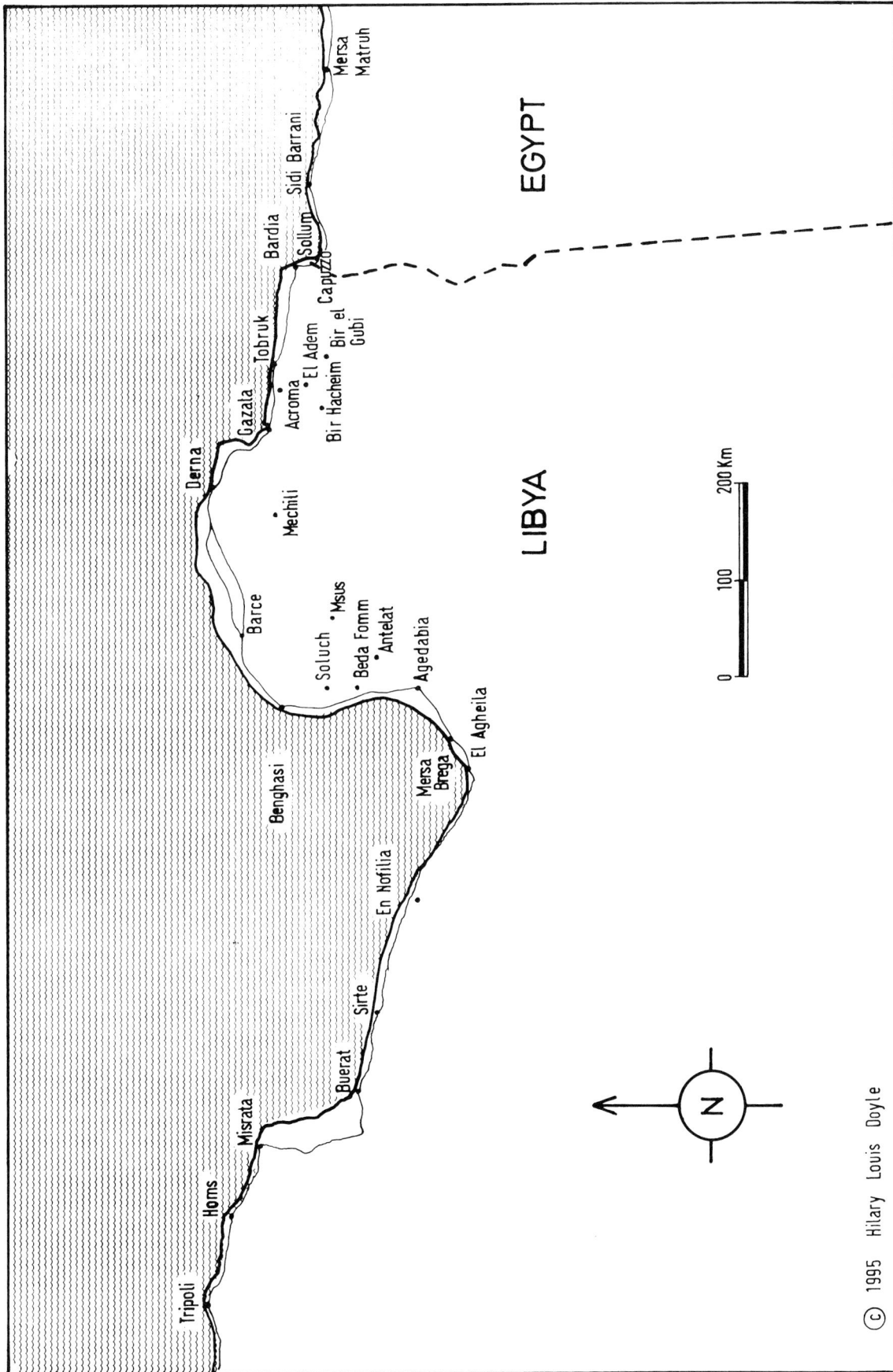

Map of Libya/Egypt

EGYPT

LIBYA

Mersa
Matruh

Sidi Barrani

Sollum
Bardia

Capuzzo

Bir el
Gubi

El Adem

Bir Hacheim

Acroma

Tobruk

Gazala

Derna

Mechili

Barce

Msus

Soluch

Beda Fomm

Antelat

Agedabia

Benghasi

El Agheila

Mersa
Brega

En Nofilia

Sirte

Buerat

Misrata

Homs

Tripoli

N

200 Km

100

0

© 1995 Hilary Louis Doyle

5.leichte Division

Panzer-Regiment 5

Stab u. Nachr.Zug	2 gr.Pz.Bef., 1 kl.Pz.Bef., 1 Pz.III, 3 Pz.II
le.Pz.Zug	3 Pz.II, 5 Pz.I
le.Pz.Zug	1 Pz.II, 4 Pz.I
I.Abteilung	
Stabs-Kompanie	1 gr.Pz.Bef., 1 kl.Pz.Bef., 2 Pz.III, 1 Pz.I
le.Pz.Zug	5 Pz.II
le.Pz.Zug	1 Pz.II, 4 Pz.I
1.le.Kompanie	17 Pz.III, 5 Pz.II
2.le.Kompanie	16 Pz.III, 5 Pz.II
4.m.Kompanie	10 Pz.IV, 3 Pz.II, 2 Pz.I
II.Abteilung	
Stabs-Kompanie	1 gr.Pz.Bef., 1 kl.Pz.Bef, 2 Pz.III
le.Pz.Zug	5 Pz.II
le.Pz.Zug	1 Pz.II, 7 Pz.I
5.le.Kompanie	16 Pz.III, 5 Pz.II
6.le.Kompanie	17 Pz.III, 5 Pz.II
8.m.Kompanie	10 Pz.IV, 3 Pz.II, 2 Pz.I

Regiments-Stab z.b.V.200

M.G.Bataillon (mot) 2	10 m.SPW (Sd.Kfz.251)
Stabs-Kompanie	8 le.M.G.
1.Kompanie	12 s.M.G., 3 Pz.B., 3 le.Gr.W.
2.Kompanie	12 s.M.G., 3 Pz.B., 3 le.Gr.W.
3.Kompani	12 s.M.G., 3 Pz.B., 3 le.Gr.W.
4.s.Kompanie	6 s.Gr.W., 6 3.7cm Pak, 2 le.M.G.
5.Pi.Kompanie	9 le.M.G.
6.Pi.Kompanie	9 le.M.G.
M.G.Bataillon (mot) 8	10 m.SPW (Sd.Kfz.251)
Stabs-Kompanie	8 le.M.G.
1.Kompanie	12 s.M.G., 3 Pz.B., 3 le.Gr.W.
2.Kompanie	12 s.M.G., 3 Pz.B., 3 le.Gr.W.
3.Kompanie	12 s.M.G., 3 Pz.B., 3 le.Gr.W.
4.Pz.Jg.Kompanie	9 3.7cm Pak, 3 le.M.G.
5.s.Kompanie	6 s.Gr.W., 6 3.7cm Pak, 2 le.M.G.
Pi.Zug	3 le.M.G.

Aufklaerung-Abteilung (mot) 3

Stab u. Nachr.Zug	3 le.M.G.
Pz.Sp.Wg. Schwadron	6 s.Pz.Sp.Wg., 18 le.Pz.Sp.Wg.
Krad-Schtz.Schwadron	18 le.M.G., 2 s.M.G., 3 le.Gr.W.
s.Schwadron	3 le.I.G., 3 3.7cm Pak, 2 le.M.G.

Panzer-Jaeger-Abteilung (mot) 39

1.Kompanie	3 5cm Pak, 8 3.7cm Pak, 6 le.M.G.
2.Kompanie	3 5cm Pak, 8 3.7cm Pak, 6 le.M.G.
3.Kompanie	3 5cm Pak, 8 3.7cm Pak, 6 le.M.G.

Panzer-Jaeger-Abteilung (Sfl.) 605

Stab u. Nachr.Zug	1 Pz.I
1.Kompanie	1 Pz.I, 9 4.7cm Pak Sfl.
2.Kompanie	1 Pz.I, 9 4.7cm Pak Sfl.
3.Kompanie	1 Pz.I, 9 4.7cm Pak Sfl.

I.Abteilung/Artillerie-Regiment (mot) 75

1.Batterie	4 10.5cm le.FH, 2 le.M.G.
2.Batterie	4 10.5cm le.FH, 2 le.M.G.
3.Batterie	4 10.5cm le.FH, 2 le.M.G.

Fla-M.G.-Bataillon (Sfl.) 606

1.Kompanie	12 2cm Fla Sfl.
3.Kompanie	12 2cm Fla Sfl.

I.Abteilung/Flak-Regiment (mot) 33

1.Batterie	4 8.8cm Flak
2.Batterie	4 8.8cm Flak
3.Batterie	4 8.8cm Flak
4.Batterie	8 2cm Fla
5.Batterie	8 2cm Fla.

6.2 ITALIAN FORCES

The Italian armored division, **132o divisione corrazato "Ariete"**, transported to Tripoli between 24 January and 26 February, was placed under Rommel's command on 7 March and ordered to move to the front. Its medium tank battalion, the **VII battaglione carri M**, paraded with Panzer-Regiment 5 in Tripoli on 12 March and didn't arrive in the forward area until 20 March. The composition of the **132° divisione corrazato "Ariete"** is shown in their order of battle. It is not known how many of the Italian tanks were forward and operational on 31 March. Most of the medium tanks in the **VII battaglione carri M** should have been operational at the start

of the attack, because they still had about 40 operational **M.13-40** early on 5 April 1941.

A second Italian division, the **27a divisione fanteria "Brescia"**, was attached to the **Deutsches Afrikakorps** on 17 March. Rommel had requested that it be moved to the front, where between 19 and 23 March it relieved the **5.leichte Division** from their defensive positions. **27a divisione fanteria "Brescia"** was composed of two infantry regiments each with two battalions (the third battalion in each regiment was still back in Tripoli), an 81 mm mortar company, and a 65/17 infantry gun company. It also had an artillery regiment with sixteen 75/27 guns and sixteen 20 mm anti-aircraft guns. Additional artillery support was provided by the attached **XV**

gruppo 16° reggimento artigliere with twelve 105/28 howitzers. Anti-tank protection was provided by four batteries each with eight 47/32 guns supplemented by an additional twelve **3.7 cm Pak**. Only one battalion in each of the infantry regiments was mobile. The division only possessed sufficient transport to move about six companies at the same time.

6.3 BRITISH FORCES

Having achieved their objective of eliminating any Italian threat to Egypt, the British left minimal forces behind on the Cyrenaica frontier and turned their primary attention to reinforcing Greece. With their worn-out tanks, the 7th Armoured Division returned to Egypt to rest and rebuild. Only the 3rd Hussars were left behind with 63 Mk. VIB Light Tanks, of which 46 passed as possible to go another 500 miles. On 26 February, the 3rd Hussars sent 18 Mk. VIB Light Tanks to repair shops for overhaul; they didn't return prior to the start of Rommel's offensive.

It wasn't until 22 February 1941 that the 6th R.T.R. arrived in Tobruk harbor without vehicles or tanks. They were

A **carri armato M.13-40** from the **VII battaglione carri M** of the **132° divisione corazzato "Ariete"** on parade in Tripoli. (APG)

then sent forward to Beda Fomm to be outfitted with the serviceable M13 tanks that had been abandoned by the Italians. On 28 February, A Squadron personnel moved forward to Beda Fomm. On 4 March, B Squadron personnel left to move forward to Beda Fomm and arrived on 6 March. A Squadron

A **Pz.Kpfw.III Ausf.G** and a **carri armato M.13-40** flanking a statue of the conquering hero in Tripoli as the rest of **Panzer-Regiment 5** passes by in a parade. (BA)

had received their M13 tanks at Beda Fomm and held a trial shoot on 7 March. On 12 March, Headquarters and C Squadron of the 6th R.T.R. also arrived at Beda Fomm to equip with the Italian tanks.

BRITISH ORDER OF BATTLE FORCES IN THE FORWARD AREA 30 MARCH 1941

Cyrenaica Command Headquarters

9th Australian Division Headquarters
20th Australian Infantry Brigade
2/13th Battalion
2/15th Battalion
2/17th Battalion
20th Aust. AT Company
24th Australian Infantry Brigade
2/28th Battalion
2/43rd Battalion
24th Aust. AT Company
26th Australian Infantry Brigade
2/23rd Battalion
2/24th Battalion
2/48th Battalion
26th Aust. AT Company
1st Royal Northumberland Fusiliers M.G. Bn.
51st Field Regiment R.A.
2/1st Australian Pioneer Bn.

2nd Armoured Division Headquarters
3rd Armoured Brigade
3rd The King's Own Hussars
5th Bn. Royal Tank Regiment
6th Bn. Royal Tank Regiment
1st Royal Horse Artillery
2nd Armoured Division Support Group
1st Bn. Tower Hamlet Rifles Motor Bn.
1st Co. Free French Motor Bn.
104th Royal Horse Artillery
16th Australian AT Company
J Battery 3rd Royal Horse Artillery
1st King's Dragoon Guards

132o divisione corazzato Ariete	
32o reggimento carrista	
I btg. carri L	
1a cp.	1 carri L, 4 carri L lf
2a cp.	13 carri L, 4 carri L lf
II btg. carri L	13 carri L, 4 carri L lf
1a cp.	1 carri L, 4 carri L lf
2a cp	13 carri L, 4 carri L lf
III btg. carri L	13 carri L, 4 carri L lf
1a cp.	1 carri L, 4 carri L lf
2a cp.	13 carri L, 4 carri L lf
VII btg. carri M	13 carri L, 4 carri L lf
1a cp.	7 carri M13/40
2a cp.	13 carri M13/40
3a cp.	13 carri M13/40
batteria	13 carri M13/40
	10 c.c.37/45
8o reggimento bersaglieri	
III btg. motociclisti	
1a cp.	9 IMG, 3 MG, 3 c.c.37/45
2a cp.	9 IMG, 3 MG, 3 c.c.37/45
3a cp.	9 IMG, 3 MG, 3 c.c.37/45
V btg. bersaglieri	
1a cp.	9 IMG, 3 MG, 3 c.c.37/45
2a cp.	9 IMG, 3 MG, 3 c.c.37/45
XII btg. bersaglieri	
1a cp.	9 IMG, 3 MG, 3 c.c.37/45
2a cp.	9 IMG, 3 MG, 3 c.c.37/45
132a cp. cannoni	8 c.c.47/32
142a cp. cannoni	8 c.c.47/32
132o reggimento artiglieria	
I gruppo	12 cannoni 75/27
II gruppo	12 cannoni 75/27
7a batteria c.a.	8 c.a. 20
8a batteria c.a.	8 c.a. 20
batteria	8 c.a. 20
ATTACHED:	
I gruppo 24o regt. art.	12 cannoni 105/28
72a cp. cannoni	8 c.c. 47/32
I btg. 39. regt. fant.	

132° divisione corazzato Ariete (Organization)

On 18 March, A Squadron of the 6th R.T.R. left Beda Fomm for the forward area and joined the 3rd Hussars after dusk. They had started forward with 15 M13 tanks and arrived with 12, of which only 9 were fit. Prior to starting out on the march, the M13 tanks had been test driven for 20 miles. During the march, M13 T2888 was evacuated to the L.R.S. when it overheated after the bottom radiator hose pulled off, M13 T2903 was left 10 miles south of Agedabia because it overheated, and M13 T2854 was left behind because the engine was overheating and power was very poor. Another three M13 tanks, T2873, T2920, and T2944, completed the trip but were overheating and had no power towards the end of the journey.

On 21 March, the 3rd Hussars had 26 operational Mk.VI Light Tanks with 6 in repair, along with 4 operational M13 tanks. These four M13 were handed over to A Squadron 6th

Order of Battle of British Forces

Two of the four or five **Pz.Kpfw.III Ausf.H** (tactical number II02 and II03), brought to Libya with **Panzer-Regiment 5**, on parade in Tripoli. (BA)

The **5.Kompanie/Panzer-Regiment 5** pulled over for a rest stop on the long drive from Tripoli to the front. These **Pz.Kpfw.III**s had all been "tropicalized." To increase air flow through the engine compartment, rectangular holes were cut into the hatch covers and then covered by armor caps. (BA)

Pz.Kpfw.III Ausf.H (tactical number II03) followed by the **leichte Zug/ II.Abteilung/Panzer-Regiment 5** pass through the Arco dei Filini on the Cyrenaica border. The Panzers still haven't been repainted for the desert. (BA)

R.T.R. on 22 March to reinforce the 15 M13 tanks (9 runners) already in their possession. B Squadron 6th R.T.R. was sent down to the 3rd Hussars on 23 March to take over 13 of their Mk.VI Light Tanks. In exchange, on 25 March, B Squadron of the 3rd Hussars arrived at Beda Fomm to take over the M13 tanks left behind by B Squadron 6th R.T.R.

The only unit outfitted with British Cruiser Tanks, the 5th R.T.R. with 46 Mk.IVA and 6 Mk.II C.S., had been moved to El Adem (south of Tobruk) on 6 February 1941. It wasn't until 13 March 1941 that part of the unit was sent forward to the frontier when

A Squadron (14 Mk.IVA and 2 Mk.II C.S.) left the battalion and came under command of 3rd Armoured Brigade. The average mileage of their Cruiser Tanks was over 1400, although it was laid down that engines require overhaul at 1000 miles. Arriving in the forward area on 19 March, A Squadron had lost seven Mk.IVA to mechanical failure and were down to 7 runners, having turned the two Mk.II C.S. Tanks over to the 6th R.T.R.

It wasn't until 21 March that the rest of the 5th R.T.R. started forward to the frontier from El Adem with 33 Mk.IVA and 3 Mk.IIA Cruiser Tanks, arriving in Bir Gefara in the Wadi Faregh on 26 March. They reported 28 Mk.IVA runners (including those in A Squadron) on 28 March. The Mk.II C.S. had been taken into the Light Repair Section to be handed

over to the 6th R.T.R., as these Mk.II C.S. were found to be unable to keep up with the Mk.IVA Cruiser Tanks. The fit tanks of A Squadron (six Mk.IVA) went forward with King's Dragoon Guards on patrol on 30 March. One Mk.IVA broke down at 1030 and one at 1900. This left the 5th R.T.R. with 25 operational Mk.IVA Cruiser Tanks when Rommel struck on the morning of 31 March 1941.

The 3rd Armoured Brigade had turned over their seven Mk.IVA Cruiser Tanks to the 5th R.T.R., retaining only their three Mk.VIB Light Tanks, and arrived in the Beda Fomm area on 22 February. The 2nd Armoured Division Headquarters arrived at El Abiar on 20 March and took command of the forward area. The number of operational Cruiser and Light Tanks with the Headquarters Squadron of the 2nd Armoured Division has not been found in the surviving records.

The status of the British operational armored forces in the forward area on the morning of 31 March 1941 was:

3rd Armd.Bde.HQ: 3 Mk.VI Light Tanks
3rd Hussars: 26 Mk.VI Light Tanks and 12 M13 tanks
5th R.T.R.: 25 Mk.IVA Cruiser Tanks
6th R.T.R.: 36 M13 tanks at Beda Fomm

Other British forces in the forward area on 31 March are listed in the order of battle for the Cyrenaica Command.

On 24 March 1941 the first Panzer was lost in the campaign. **Pz.Kpfw.III Ausf.G (Fgst.Nr.65853)** hit a mine at El Agheila. The powerful blast not only broke the track, it split the weld seam for the hull front and set the Panzer on fire, resulting in its total loss. By this time, **RAL 8000 gelbbraun** camouflage paint had been applied over the base coat of **RAL 7021 dunkelgrau**. (BA)

6.4 THE OFFENSIVE BEGINS

With the exception of a few after-action accounts, due to the loss of the **5.leichte Division** war diary the only original account of actions by and decisions affecting **Panzer-Regiment 5** are contained in the **Deutsches Afrikakorps'** war diary (DAK KTB) as follows:

<u>DAK KTB 31 March 1941</u> - *The attack of the **5.leichte Division** to take the British advanced positions by Maaten Biscer continued through 2200 hours. Partial success was made in capturing the fortified positions by Marsa el Brega. The combat elements of **Aufklaerung-Abteilung 3** captured Bir es Suera. A counterattack by enemy tanks was repulsed.*

The Panzers and vehicles were located in positions by Bleidat and Marsa el Brega.

On the evening of 31 March, General Rommel issued orders covering defensive operations by the divisions after

Bir es Suera was captured and bridgeheads established at Marsa el Brega.

Details on the action at Marsa el Brega were described in the following account of the operations of the **6.Kompanie/Panzer-Regiment 5** on March 31 and April 1, 1941:

*Reinforced by the medium platoons of the **8.Kompanie** and supported by a company from **Panzer-Jaeger Abteilung 605**, at 0600 hours the **6.Kompanie** left their assembly area (9 kilometers to the west of El Agheila) and advanced toward El Agheila. The column under the command of Major Rau was divided into two groups with the **2.Zug** and **4.Zug** on the right and the **1.Zug**, **3.Zug** and medium platoons on the left. The column advanced along the Via Balbia with a **Panzer-Aufklaerungs** section at the head, followed in order by an **8.8 cm Flak** anti-aircraft gun, a platoon of **4.7 cm Pak(t) Sfl.**, the commander, the **6.Kompanie**, and the **Panzer-Jaeger Kompanie**.*

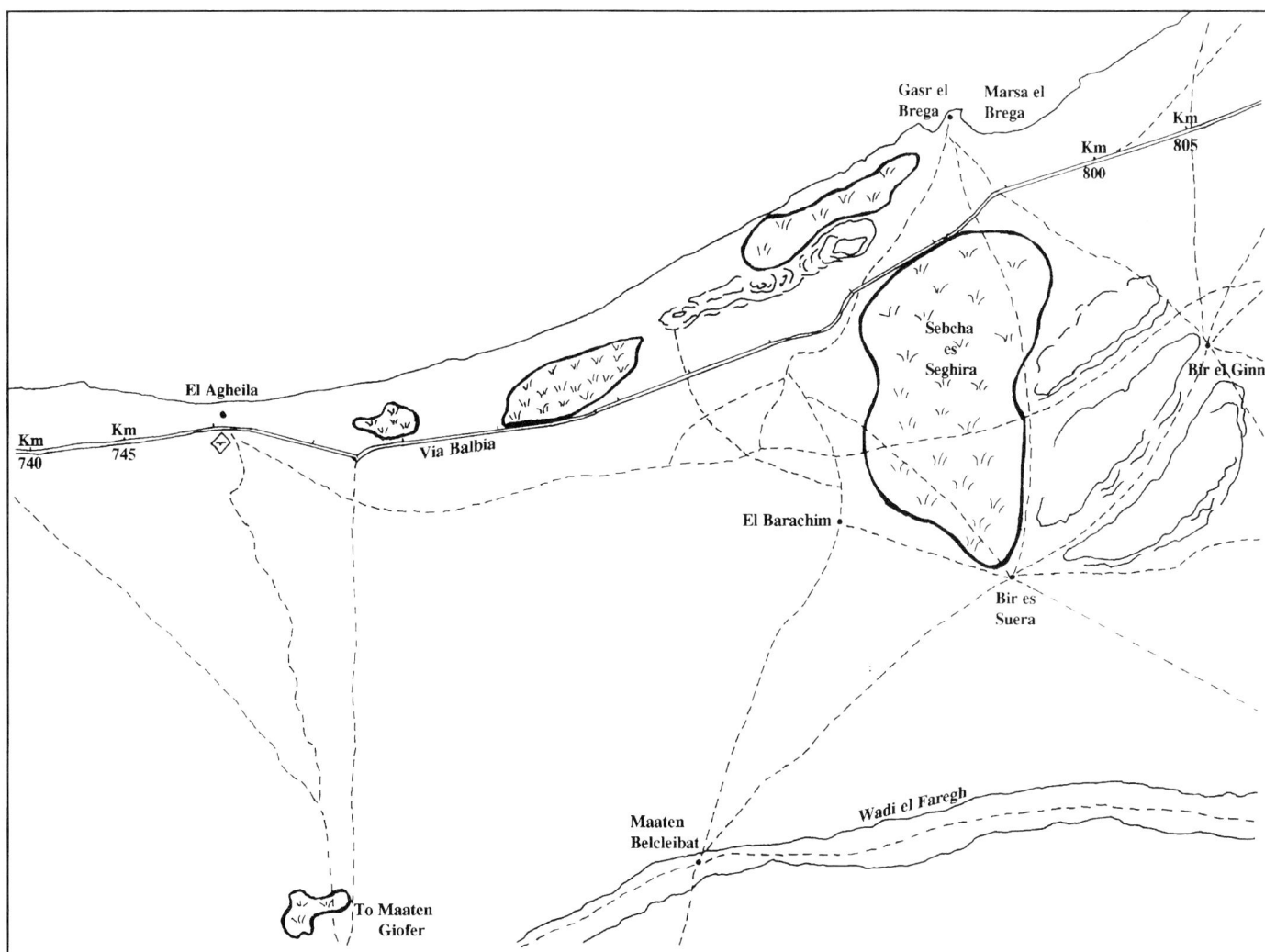

Map of Marsa el Brega

Two **Pz.Kpfw.III**s advancing along the coast road to attack Marsa el Brega on 31 March 1941. The **RAL 8000 gelbbraun** camouflage paint was sparsely applied with a spray gun in criss-crossing stripes over the original coat. (BA)

The right group had orders to reconnoiter through Sebcha el Seghira toward the southeast. It did not make contact with the enemy. Because there weren't any tracks through the salt marsh, it returned to the Via Balbia in the afternoon.

*At about 0800 hours, having opened fire near Kilometer 6, the head of the column attacked four or five enemy tanks at Kilometer 3 on the Via Balbia. The **8.8 cm Flak** went into action, dispersing the enemy with its fire without hitting any. The enemy then retired some 6 kilometers, made another attack, and was once again driven off.*

*Toward noon, the head of the column advanced to within 1 kilometer of the positions occupied by the enemy east of the junction between the Via Balbia and the track leading southwest from Marsa el Brega. The **6.Kompanie** took up positions on both sides of the road with orders to assault the enemy positions by overwhelming firepower. Covering the left flank, a **Panzer-Jaeger** platoon after a short engagement shot up an enemy tank, which burst into flames. After a long bombardment of the enemy positions by the tank guns, the enemy were observed to be retreating.*

*A **Pz.Kpfw.III** section from the **3.Zug** advanced in combat formation with the engineer platoon to clear mines off the*

*road. The British had withdrawn their outposts. The **6.Kompanie** took to the road again and came under artillery fire. The main concentration came down about 100 meters from the left-hand curve about 4 kilometers south of Marsa el Brega, preventing the engineers from continuing to clear mines off the road. About 2000 meters to the west, a strongly fortified position was observed. This was apparently the enemy main battle line. Behind this position a limbered troop of guns covered the track which ran south through a salt marsh and north over a mine-infested sand dune which was under fire from the enemy. Isolated tanks and gun tractors were observed at long range. Numerous vehicles, including tanks, were spotted behind the enemy position and taken under fire as soon as they were within range. Our successes were indicated by tall columns of black smoke. An anti-tank ditch was clearly visible due to the excavated sand. An attempt by the **1.Zug** and the engineers to advance further caused them to run into a concentration of enemy fire.*

The company commander went back to Major Rau, reported the situation, which in turn was reported to Rommel. Half an hour later, a Stuka squadron escorted by fighters not only strafed the enemy position, but in spite of the recogni-

tion markings and white Very light signals, also dive-bombed our own tanks. Two non-commissioned officers were badly wounded.

The company commander then returned to the front and moved the company back about 800 meters behind a chain of hills. He had been informed by Major Rau that a machine-gun battalion reinforced with tanks intended to attack Marsa el Brega at 1700 hours and roll up the enemy line toward the southeast. When a flag was seen to go up over Marsa el Brega, the **6.Kompanie** was to renew the attack.

At 1700 hours, our own artillery laid down a surprise barrage on Marsa el Brega. During the night our infantry pushed forward up to the town. At dusk, the **3.Zug** under **Stabsfeldwebel** Gendert received orders to feel its way forward along the road with the engineers, so that the company would know the way through the minefield when it advanced the following morning. The **3.Zug**, under the covering fire of the medium platoons, negotiated the minefield, mopped up the left-hand curve of the road and the minefield among the sand dunes, shot up an enemy ammunition trailer, and advanced to a point 1.5 kilometers short of Marsa el Brega. The **3.Zug** was then recalled so that it would not come under fire from our own troops investing Marsa el Brega.

The **II.Abteilung/Panzer-Regiment 5** was to have advanced toward Marsa el Brega during the night. At 0500 hours, April 1, the **6.Kompanie** received orders to occupy Marsa el Brega as soon as the **II.Abteilung** began an attack at dawn. The **6.Kompanie** was also to advance on the right side of the road and act as a guard on the heights 4 kilometers southeast of Marsa el Brega. However, the enemy had withdrawn during the night. The company after making contact with the **II.Abteilung** on the left, reached its objective without encountering resistance.

At dawn a patrol of the King's Dragoon Guards with A Squadron of the 5th R.T.R. (four Mk.IVA Cruiser Tanks) was hit by Panzers near the road north of Giofer. The 5th R.T.R. recorded: At 0630 hours, A Squadron encountered main force of enemy moving east. One tank hit and turret jammed, so withdrew from action. Remaining three tanks stayed in position of observation. Enemy casualties uncertain, probably about 3 M13 tanks.

The British having had no intent of holding this exposed position. At 0900 hours, the codeword "Laxative" was given for the units to prepare to withdraw. At 1730, the 5th R.T.R. moved to line "AARON" on orders from Brigade HQ and took up defensive positions after dark with their remaining 23 operational Cruiser Tanks. The rest of the 3rd Armoured Brigade had not been involved in the fighting on 31 March.

DAK KTB 1 April 1941 - At 0700 hours, the **5.leichte Division** succeeded in establishing the planned bridgeheads at Marsa el Brega. There wasn't any activity in the enemy positions, because the enemy was pulling back in headlong flight toward Agedabia. The advanced spearhead of the **5.leichte Division** (consisting of **M.G.-Bataillon 8** reinforced with elements of **Aufklaerung-Abteilung 3**, a **Pionier-Kompanie**, **Panzer-Jaeger-Abteilung 39**, and the **I.Abteilung/Flak-Regiment 33**) maintained contact with the enemy forces. At 1830 hours, they arrived 35 kilometers east of Marsa el Brega and reported that enemy forces from the Bilal area were now north of the Via Balbia and enemy forces from the Bir el Metfun area were now south of the Via Balbia.

The main body of the **5.leichte Division** was located in the area directly to the southwest of Marsa el Brega. The **132° divisione corazzato "Ariete"** relocated part of its forces, moving them from the area near Agheila to the eastern edge of the Sebcha es Seghira. The **27a divisione fanteria "Brescia"** were ordered by General Rommel to move their artillery from el Agheila into new positions by Marsa el Brega on 1 April and to bring up the rest of the division on the afternoon of 2 April.

For 2 April, General Rommel ordered the advanced elements to maintain contact with the enemy but withheld permission to take Agedabia. The **5.leichte Division** reported their intention to send the reinforced **Aufklaerung-Abteilung 3** forward on reconnaissance toward El Gtafia and Agedabia.

The Italian Comandante Superiore was against the plans and actions taken by the **Deutsches Afrikakorps**. He was hesitant and wanted to fully plan and phase each action. In a letter dated 1 April, General Garibaldi expressed his fears, stating: "Considering the strong enemy resistance, it is too early to become entangled in a large action before the necessary forces have arrived."

On 1 April 1941, the 3rd Armoured Brigade continued to withdraw in accordance with prearranged plans. At 0400 hours, on orders received from the Brigade commander, the Brigade was to move back on prearranged center line to a position about 4 miles north of El Grafia. The 3rd Hussars were to do protection rear. Withdrawal from the present position (about 8 miles southwest of El Grafia) was to commence at 0600 hours and was completed at 1000 hours. The 5th R.T.R. took up a line of observation outside the Gtafia-to-Agedabia track about 4 miles north of El Gtafia.

At 1400 hours, orders were received from the Brigade for the 5th R.T.R. to withdraw to Bir el Tombia area and take up positions of observation outside track. This move was completed by 1500 hours. The Mk.IVA Cruiser Tank "Eggesford" was abandoned due to an unserviceable engine and destroyed. The 5th R.T.R. remained at Bir el Tombia for the rest of the day and all night.

<u>DAK KTB 2 April 1941</u> - The **5.leichte Division** closed up with their advanced elements during the night of 1/2 April. The foremost elements were located on the Via Balbia south of M. Tobilba.

The enemy columns that had been located north and south of the Via Balbia by Bir Bilal and Bir el Medfun had retired toward the east during the night. On the morning of 2 April, the enemy again put up some resistance but retired to an area 20 kilometers west of Agedabia after several rounds of artillery fire.

At 1300 hours, General Rommel issued the following orders: **5.leichte Division** attack Agedabia. Then advance northwestward to the port of Zuetina and occupy both positions. The main body of the division is to advance immediately toward Agedabia and the area to the west.

At 1500 hours, the **132° divisione corazzato "Ariete"** was ordered to occupy the area 7 kilometers southeast of Cantoniera, south of Mn. Tobilba-Regh et Teneb, as soon as possible.

After a short struggle, advanced elements of the **5.leichte Division** took Agedabia at 1615 hours. **Aufklaerung-Abteilung 3** attacked to the northwest past Agedabia and took Zuetina.

At 1700 to 1745 hours, the **II.Abteilung/Panzer-Regiment 5** fought an action against 20 British Light Tanks south of Agedabia. Seven enemy tanks were destroyed and 11 men were taken prisoner. Three Panzers were lost.

The operational orders for 2 April directed the organization of the defense of the Agedabia-Zuetina area by the **5.leichte Division, "Ariete"**, and **"Brescia."**

A radio message was received from the Italian **Comandante Superiore** stating: "From reports which I have obtained, I take it that your advance continues. This directly opposes my decisions. I request that you await my arrival before you continue the advance."

In the face of enemy pressure, the 3rd Armoured Brigade continued its steady preplanned withdrawal on 1 April. At 1100 hours, the code word "Oxford" was broadcast to initiate withdrawal to a line about 8 miles northeast of and parallel to track Agedabia-El Haseiat, starting at 1130. Brigade Center Line - Bir el Tombia - El Ghinan - El Selich. The Brigade withdrew in three parallel columns: 3rd Hussars right, 1st RHA on center line, 5th R.T.R. left (southeast flank).

Between 1130 and 1700 hours, the withdrawal was carried out as ordered, moving at an extremely slow rate owing to mechanical casualties and to slowness of 1st RHA. By radio, the Brigade ordered the 5th R.T.R. to ensure the protection of the southeast flank of the Brigade. One troop of C Squadron (three Mk.IVA Cruisers) was detached to give protection to the 1st RHA.

At 1715 hours, C Squadron doing protection rear reported a large mass of tanks with crews on the outside and vehicles about 2 to 3 miles away. This report was passed on to Brigade, which warned at 1730 hours that 6th R.T.R. might be in the position of these vehicles. At 1732 hours, the approaching Panzers opened fire, with the setting sun directly behind them obscuring their position. C Squadron (with nine Mk.IVA Cruisers) returned fire. At 1745 hours, the 5th R.T.R. commander ordered the unit to withdraw behind the next ridge. C Squadron acknowledged the order and at 1750 hours, the 5th R.T.R. reformed behind the ridge approximately 1 mile north. The enemy, with an estimated strength of 40 to 60 tanks, a number of field guns, and a large quantity of vehicles, did not follow up. The 5th R.T.R. thought that the enemy tanks were mostly M13 with wireless masts on the sides, the leading tank carrying four flags on the aerial similar to our navigation flags, along with some larger tanks.

Of the four tanks left in C Squadron, all four of them are sure they had several hits each and knocked out two or three each, a number going on fire. The fact that this large enemy force did not follow up the Battalion withdrawal to the next ridge was taken as corroboration of their having suffered considerable casualties.

Five Mk.IVA Cruiser Tanks were lost and one damaged by 47mm shell entering the turret and preventing rotation. Of the five, one was set on fire - one man got out, one was set on fire - no news of the crew, one was last seen advancing - no news of the crew, one was set on fire, all got out, and there was no information on the fate of the last one.

Later the survivors had a chance to record the following after-action account of this fight, which has been edited to incorporate significant comments made by the commander of the 5th R.T.R.:

It is impossible to get an accurate or complete description of events of the 2nd April as at present none of the Tank Commanders or Gunners of the surviving tanks are here; this is a resume of what happened based on certain 1st Driver's stories.

On 2nd April the Battalion was withdrawing from an area 3 miles north of Fort Gtafia to a position on the track Aghedabia-Saunnu in accordance with a plan put into force on receipt of a code word "Oxford" which had been given us at 0800 hours that morning. By this plan, at about 1000 hours, 3rd Armoured Brigade were to withdraw to a line north of Aghedabia, with the 3rd Hussars on the right (facing the enemy) of the 5th R.T.R. The 3rd Hussars had attached to them one squadron of the 6th R.T.R. with M13 tanks.

The timing of our withdrawal was regulated by the speed of A/E Battery R.H.A. for whose protection in the withdrawal we were responsible. Their speed was about 7 mph compared to our 15 mph.

ABOVE AND TWO BELOW: A Mk.IVA Cruiser Tank from the 5th R.T.R. knocked out on 2 April is examined by Oberleutnant Liestmann of the **1.Kompanie/Panzer-Regiment 8** about a month after the battle. The Mk.IVA lost a track and was hit in the right side and caught on fire. The over-caliber sized hole in the side shows the brittle failure of homogeneous hard plate when over matched. (KL)

The strength and disposition of the Battalion during this move was as follows: C Squadron less one Troop (9 tanks) was giving protection rear to Regimental Headquarters (4 tanks) and a combined AB Squadron (6 tanks). One Troop C Squadron (3 tanks) was giving close support to A/E Battery 1 R.H.A. At the time of the action the Battalion had been still further depleted by two mechanical casualties to tanks of AB Squadron.

At about 1300 hours the Battalion halted for an hour to allow the R.H.A., part of whom we had passed, to get ahead of us. At 1245 hours, Sergeant C. of "EDGEWORTH" (No.10 Troop) and his driver saw 40 to 50 vehicles covering a 2 mile front, through his glasses. They were about 3 to 4 miles away, and were following up our centerline. At the same time a Major in the R.H.A. came up to see Sergeant R. of "EDGEHILL" (No.10 Troop) and asked him what he made of a cloud of dust behind. Sergeant R. directed this Major to the commander of 5th R.T.R. who was nearby. At about 1300 hours, the withdrawal resumed before this cloud of dust was close enough to be properly identified; in the next two hours there were two major delays - one being mechanical and the other due to an order being given by Brigade and then countermanded.

At about 1625 hours the Battalion met two of its petrol lorries; it halted just as it was and the petrol lorries went round to the tanks refuelling them. Outside fuel tanks were filled by certain drivers, though in most cases unsatisfactory running had caused their use to be discontinued.

At that time 3rd Armoured Brigade called commanders to be on the air to receive orders. Squadron Commanders assembled with the Commanding Officer by the rear link tank to receive orders. Owing to excessive talk on the air the passing of these orders took over 3/4 hour, and were to the effect that Support Group had encountered enemy tanks; that 5th R.T.R. were to send a Troop to assist them and that contact with Support Group was to be made through 3rd Hussars. At this time and while refuelling was in progress "EDGEHILL" (No.10 Troop) reported to Lieutenant. R. the Troop Leader: "30 to 40 vehicles are approaching from the southwest." Lieutenant. R. wirelessed to Major W's tank asking "Have you heard that message?" It was taken over to Major W. standing by the commander's tank; Major W. informed the commander and had a reply send, "Keep an eye on them and report anything further as regards their identification." Major W. then went over to his own tank and immediately wirelessed to Lieutenant R. "Have you anything further to report about those vehicles?" Lieutenant R. asked Sergeant R. who replied that he was still unable to distinguish them.

The vehicles concerned were then between 3 and 4 miles away.

Major W. then ordered: "10 and 11 Troops will take up a hull down position on the ridge to the rear and do protection to the Battalion. I will come up as soon as I can to see the situation myself." As our tanks started to move, the enemy tanks stopped behind a small ridge. They were some 5000 yards away. Our own tanks got into hull down positions on two shoulders of a ridge (as shown in the sketch).

By the time our tanks had reached this position the enemy had left behind some vehicles which appeared to be lorries and had pushed further forward a column of about 60 vehicles. There was further talk on the air about the identity of this column and the fact was then brought out that their crews appeared to be riding on the outside and that they carried no flags. Lieutenant R. said, "They must be enemy as they have wireless masts on the side." The presence of these vehicles was reported to Battalion Headquarters and by them to Brigade. Brigade reported "Be careful they are not the 6th Bn. R.T.R. who may be on your front" This was passed to Major W. and passed on by him to his Squadron.

It should now be pointed out again that one Squadron of 6th R.T.R. were isolated, doing protection rear to 3rd Hussars, and that previously tanks of the 6th R.T.R., some of which had no flags or masts for flags, had passed through us. Again we had no contact with, or information about, the enemy on our front that day.

The enemy force advancing where their lorries had been left, split when about 3000 yards from our tanks. 30 to 40 vehicles came straight for us in arrowhead formation and a separate column broke away to our right.

When the enemy were 2000 yards away, Major W. gave the order "Stand by to open fire at 800 yards." Information that Major W. had given a preparatory was passed to the commander who ordered a message to be sent to Major W. that they must make certain they were not the 6th Bn. R.T.R. Major W. passed this on again to his Troop Leaders but no sooner had he done so than heavy fire was opened on us by 47 mm and either mortar or light artillery. Major W. sent a message to the Battalion: "They must be enemy as they have opened fire on us."

"Within the first minute Lieutenant M's tank "ENDEAVOUR" had been hit on the auxiliary petrol tank and set on fire. Lieutenant M. and his complete crew bailed out and running to the right rear of the left hand tank of his troop took cover. They have not been seen since. The line held by 10 and 11 Troops was now reinforced by 2 regimental headquarter tanks. In spite of the fact that we were firing directly into the sun we returned their fire effectively. The ranges given by Tank Commanders in their fire orders varied from 900 to 1500 yards, and at least 8 enemy tanks are claimed to have been put out of action by our surviving gunners.

Owing to the intensity of the enemy fire, and our bad position relatively to the setting sun - and as several of our leading tanks were seen to be burning, Colonel D. decided to

withdraw. He sent a message, "SURA (C Squadron) is to withdraw to conform to my movements - IBUN (AB Squadron) will give protection until this movement is completed."

Major W. was heard to acknowledge and say "Yes it is getting rather hot." He then ordered his Troop to withdraw.

Details of the action of individual tanks most prominently engaged are as follows:

Of the Tanks of 10 Troop - "EDGEWORTH" fired 15 rounds and claims two hits of these, one hit was most definitely seen on an enemy tank the crew of which baled out. In his excitement the Gunner put another 2-pounder shell into the crew as they were getting away which caused them to disappear.

"EDGEHILL's" gun went out of action after five rounds. They twice sent a message to Lt. R. asking to withdraw to get it put right; they could not get a reply but Major W. took up and call and said "O.K. 10 A withdraw."

Earlier in this fight "EMU" (Lieutenant R.) was hit early in the action and was seen to be in flames.

There were no known survivors of the tanks of 11 Troop.

The part of the action taken by "ENTERPRISE" (Corporal Green) cannot be gauged as none of the crew are yet back in Tobruch.

The action of "ENDEAVOUR" (Lieutenant M.) has been described.

"ENCOURAGE" (Sergeant K.) received a 47 mm shell under the running board as it was withdrawing from the action; this severely wounded Trooper S., who died shortly afterwards.

Of the tanks of C Squadron - "EARN" (Major W.) was hit as it was turning to come out of action and was set on fire; one man is said to have got out, who is believed to have been Lance-Corporal B., the wireless operator, but there is no evidence as to where he went to.

"ESK" (Captain C.) was also seen on fire, while none was seen to leave his tank.

As for "EDGECUMBE" (Captain E.), he is reported to have last been seen waving the flag signal for the advance and moving up towards the enemy.

The tanks of AB Squadron holding a rear position did not properly come into action, though they appear to have fired some few rounds.

The withdrawal was successfully covered by AB Squadron and the Battalion rallied in a line 2 miles behind that on which the action had taken place. The action was reported to 3rd Armoured Brigade and the casualties evacuated from the tanks.

No attempt to follow us up was made by the enemy.

Our withdrawal according to our original plan was then continued.

In the five tanks that had been put out of action, we lost five officers and 18 other ranks. There was one additional casualty in a tank that came out of the action.

After this action, the 2nd Armoured Division was ordered to withdraw to Antelat. At 1600 hours, the 6th R.T.R. at Beda Fomm with about 36 M13 tanks was ordered to move to Antelat. During the day the 3rd Hussars lost five Mk.VI Light tanks due to mechanical failure and three M13 tanks were abandoned due to mechanical failure and lack of diesel fuel.

<u>DAK KTB 3 April 1941</u> - *On the morning of 3 April, aerial reconnaissance reported that the Via Balbia was free of enemy forces up to 60 kilometers north of Agedabia. Thirty vehicles by Sidi Abd el Aati were moving toward the north and northeast. At 1030 hours, scattered enemy tanks were reported halted 35 kilometers east of Agedabia, in all probability out of fuel. The impression given by the enemy was that the retreat continued to the north and northeast.*

General Rommel resolved to harass the enemy in their southern flank by deploying advanced elements in the Ben Gania area with their forward units near Tengeder in order to determine if the British wanted to hold Cyrenaica. If not, the units would advance further on this flank and to their rear toward Tmimi.

On the morning of 3 April, a reconnaissance platoon of **Aufklaerung-Abteilung 3** *reported 20 to 30 enemy tanks 20 kilometers north of Cantoniera Zuetina. General Rommel sent a reinforced* **Panzer-Abteilung** *against them with the objective of reaching Bir el Ageradt.*

In the midday hours, Leutnant Bernd of Korps headquarters drove alone on a motorcycle on the Via Balbia. He reported locating abandoned Italian tanks and that Magrun was free of enemy forces.

The main body of the **5.leichte Division** *remained in defensive positions in the Agedabia-Zuetina area. They were bringing water, ammunition, and supplies forward. At 1730 hours, the division reported that it had sufficient fuel to move 150 kilometers. At least four days would be required to bring forward an adequate supply if they used all of the vehicles.*

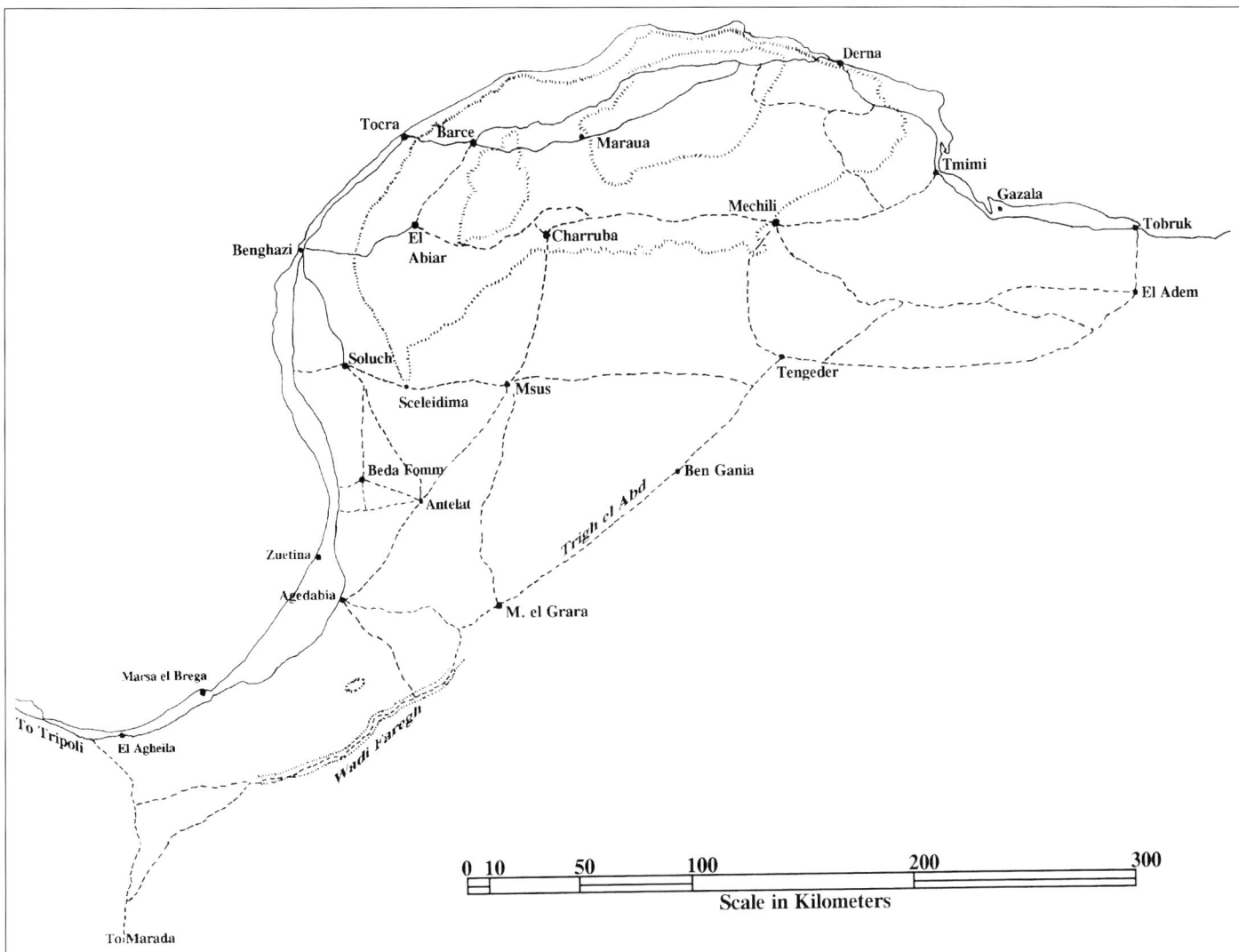

Map of Cyrenaica

General Rommel ordered that all available supply and unit vehicles were to be unloaded and to transport fuel from Arco dei Fileni in one day and night. Rommel stated: "This will spare blood and win us Cyrenaica." Officer patrols were organized to hold the road open for uninterrupted travel. All available supply columns were ordered forward out of Tripoli.

The **5.leichte Division** was immobilized for 24 hours by this undertaking. Only **Aufklaerung-Abteilung 3** and a strong advanced unit were kept ready for action.

At 2100 hours, General Garibaldi arrived at the headquarters of the Afrikakorps. In a discussion with General Rommel lasting to midnight, the **Comandante Superiore** voiced his wishes that the **Afrikakorps** always report the situation to him and then await orders before any movement was made, especially by the main body of divisions. General Rommel strongly opposed this. He must issue his orders according to the existing situation. There was no basis to the Italian's idea that the supply situation was inadequate. General Rommel stated that he must have complete freedom of command. Toward the end of the conversation, a radio message arrived from **O.K.H.** that ensured General Rommel full tactical freedom, and the discussion came to a close.

On 3 April, the 3rd Armoured Brigade continued to withdraw through the night to Antelat and then continued north to Esc Scelidina. At 0730 hours, the 5th R.T.R. reached Antelat and were ordered to continue to Esc Scelidina. At 1300 hours, the 3rd Armoured Brigade ordered the 5th R.T.R. to destroy the enemy tanks approaching Antelat. These turned out to be 6th R.T.R. as was expected. Many did not have recognition flags flying. At 1330 hours, the 5th R.T.R. moved forward to the fort at Esc Scelidina.

At 1900 hours, the 5th R.T.R. was ordered by Brigade to send one troop to assist the 3rd Hussars at eastern end of pass. The 3rd Hussars had reported enemy AFV movement. This order was canceled at 1905 hours as the suspected enemy turned out to be armoured cars from the King's Dragoon Guards.

The operational tank strength in the 3rd Armoured Brigade was:

3rd Armd.Bde.HQ	3 Mk.VI Light Tanks
3rd Hussars	15 Mk.VI Light and 4 M13 tanks
5th R.T.R.	12 Mk.VIA Cruiser (plus 3 detached)
6th R.T.R.	22 M13 tanks left in the afternoon.

DAK KTB 4 April 1941 - *During the course of the day the enemy appeared to be retiring from the south and southeast toward Barce. A rear guard covered the line of retreat 24 kilometers east of Bengazi. It was learned that the main enemy force was retreating from Barce to the east. At 1000 hours, it* was reported that a strong enemy group of 100 tanks and vehicles was moving east out of Msus, probably a flank guard that would travel to Ben Gania-Tengeder or Mechili to defend the enemy flank. At about 1800 hours, small groups of tanks and vehicles between Ben Gania and Tengeder were reported by **Abteilung Graf Schwerin**.

At midday, General Rommel traveled forward to Bengazi to **Aufklaerung-Abteilung 3** and ordered them to start immediately for Mechili after the arrival of the advanced unit from Brescia. The 30 to 35 enemy tanks reported by a reconnaissance platoon are to be immediately attacked.

At 1800 hours, advancing in the ordered direction, **Aufklaerung-Abteilung 3** struck an enemy rear guard protected by a minefield 24 kilometers east of Bengazi. Their resistance could not be broken until the morning of 5 April. The attached **Panzer-Kompanie** had taken large losses because of mines and were immobilized.

On the night of 4/5 April, **Stab 5.leichte Division** with the reinforced **M.G.-Bataillon 8** (consisting of the **I.Abteilung/Panzer-Regiment 5** minus one company, one company from **Panzer-Jaeger-Abteilung 39**, a **Pionier-Kompanie**, a platoon from **Aufklaerung-Abteilung 3**, two **10.5 cm leFH** from the **I./Artillerie-Regiment 75** and signals) were in the M. el Grara area. The **I./Flak-Regiment 33** was also advancing with this group.

Every unit reported large losses of vehicles due to the rugged nature of the terrain. It was thought that only four-wheel-drive vehicles would be able to resupply the **5.leichte Division**.

At 0530 hours, the 5th R.T.R. moved off toward Msus with a strength of 10 Mk.IVA Cruiser Tanks. Two Cruiser Tanks which had become hopelessly unserviceable had had to be destroyed the night before. On the move to Msus another Mk.IVA Cruiser Tank fell out with engine failure and was destroyed. The withdrawal was continued in the direction of Bir el Melezz at 1430 hours and the 5th R.T.R. leaguered 15 miles north of Bir el Melezz at 1600 hours. A fuel convoy with 1600 gallons of petrol destined for the 3rd Armoured Brigade had been destroyed by enemy fighters and bombers during the day. At 2030 hours, orders were issued to the 2nd Armoured Division to withdraw to Tecnis and the 3rd Armoured Brigade to Charruba.

DAK KTB 5 April 1941 - *At 1200 hours, Oberstleutnant Olbrich (with **Panzer-Regiment 5** minus one **Abteilung**, **M.G.-Bataillon 2**, one battery of **I./Artillerie-Regiment 75** and one **Panzer-Jaeger-Kompanie**) was ordered to advance from Zuetina through Antelat to Msus. He was to send **M.G.-Bataillon 2** by good roads through Solluch to Msus to cut it off from the west and await the arrival of the Panzers. From*

*Msus, **Gruppe Olbrich** was to advance further northeast. Orders as to whether this would be toward Mechili or Tmimi would be issued later. The **VII battaglione carri M** (with about 40 M.13-40 tanks) from the **132° divisione corazzato "Ariete"** was attached to **Gruppe Olbrich** and was to join them.*

*At 2230 hours, the southern group of the reinforced **Panzer-Regiment Olbrich** was located near Antelat and the northern group near Raberbet bel Gordon. He planned to join both elements together in Msus at 0800 on 6 April. Msus was reported to be free of enemy troops at midnight.*

In the afternoon, the 3rd Armoured Brigade moved north and reached the El Abiar-Charruba track. The 6th R.T.R. ordered that the nine best M13 tanks be selected (two for HQ and seven for C Squadron) to continue. The remaining tanks were drained of fuel, water and rations were transferred, and then the tanks were destroyed.

<u>DAK KTB 6 April 1941</u> - *On the morning of 6 April, the **Ia** had the impression that the British were retreating with the main body of their troops toward Tobruk and were possibly embarking in Tobruk harbor. In the absence of General Rommel, the **Ia** ordered all forces to concentrate on Mechili. Nevertheless, the hoped-for objective was Tobruk, to cut the coast road, delay the loading, and merely to hold the enemy by Mechili.*

*Oberstleutnant Olbrich received orders to accelerate the advance of every attached unit to Mechili. The **132° divisione corazzato "Ariete"** was to immediately start advancing through Agedabia to Ghemines, Solluch, and Sceleidima.*

*On 6 April, Leutnant Konrad flew to General Rommel (near Mechili) and gave the following situation report on the advancing units as of 1000 hours: A **Panzer-Abteilung Stab** and 12 Panzers are by Ben Gania. The Panzers are immobile since the oil is hot and oil pressure low. Several advancing Panzers lost their way from the track in the area southwest of Ben Gania and several of them are stationary. There are additional scattered Italian columns of guns and tanks on the Trigh el Abd toward M. el Grara.*

*Understandably, **Gruppe Olbrich** came forward slowly. The last report on their location was 20 kilometers east of Msus at 1300 hours on 6 April.*

Oberstleutnant Olbrich was at the end of the fuel supply (that had been calculated to last 500 kilometers) and demanded 50,000 liters of fuel and 10,000 liters of water be sent to Msus.

At 0600 hours, the 3rd Armoured Brigade recorded the operational strength as:

3rd Armd.Bde.HQ	2 Mk.VIB Light Tanks
3rd Hussars	12 Mk.VIB Light and 2 M13 tanks
5th R.T.R.	8 Mk.IVA Cruiser Tanks

The regimental commander's **Pz.Bef.Wg.** (tactical number R01) turning off the coast road toward Soluch. Produced in November/December 1941, this **Pz.Bef.Wg. Ausf.H** still had the **Ausf.E** style drive and idler wheels but they were modified by inserting spacers for use with the 40 cm wide track. (BA)

Cutting across the desert, this **leichte Zug** leaves the track for a rest halt. The crew member appears to be inspecting the roadwheel tires for wear for which spares were carried on the rear deck. (BA)

6th R.T.R. had abandoned all their M13 tanks due to fuel shortage and mechanical breakdown.

At 0700 hours on 6 April, a troop of B Squadron fired a few 2-pounder rounds. The troop leader reported that he had engaged what he thought were enemy armored cars at 2000 yards range. The commander reprimanded him for firing at extreme range. These vehicles subsequently turned out to be part of 6th R.T.R., who had been out of touch with the Brigade for nearly 24 hours. No damage was done.

At 1000 hours, the 5th R.T.R. received orders to remain in present position and cover withdrawal of the 6th R.T.R., who by this time had lost all their tanks through lack of diesel or for mechanical reasons. At the commencement of the day's march, the 5th R.T.R. had an operational strength of eight tanks. One Mk.IVA in hopeless mechanical condition was destroyed before they started off.

At 1400 hours, the 5th R.T.R. commander's tank hit a dump of thermos bombs and, severely damaged, had to be abandoned. Orders came in from the 2nd Armoured Division at 1600 hours that tanks becoming mechanical casualties were not to be destroyed or burned, but merely stripped. This order was not passed on to the Brigade Recovery Section, which by this time had several tanks on transporters.

At 1630 hours, the 3rd Armoured Brigade commander reported the situation that an enemy column was attacking the Indian Motor Brigade at Mechili and he had been ordered to get as many tanks together with the 1st RHA there as soon as possible. He consulted with the commander of the 3rd Hussars, who knew the area well, as to the best method of

getting there. It was decided that, owing to the shortage of petrol and the difficult nature of the terrain between the present position and Mechili, it was necessary to move back into Derna via Maraua and then to approach Mechili by the track which leaves the main road 4 miles east of Derna. The Brigade was to refuel at Maraua and Derna. The 3rd Hussars were down to five Mk.VIB Light Tanks and the 5th R.T.R. still had seven Mk.IVA Cruiser Tanks. At 2030 hours, the 5th R.T.R. arrived at Maraua, refueled, and resumed the march to Derna at 2200 hours.

DAK KTB 7 April 1941 - *The following evaluation of the enemy situation was made from radio messages between the* **Ia** *to General Rommel, Oberstleutnant Olbrich, the* **2.(H)/ 14.Pz.** *(aerial reconnaissance squadron) and* **Fliegerfuehrer Afrika**: *The troops by Tobruk do not appear to be especially strong. They have orders only to defend Acroma and to send only reconnaissance troops to the south and west. At the latest on the morning of 7 April, perhaps a large group will retreat from the area south of Derna toward Gazala and further east. It appears that the group of tanks from Msus that were already beaten by Froelich would be found again by Mechili on the morning of 7 April. If* **Panzer-Gruppe Olbrich** *would meet this group again, they can conclusively defeat them.*

An attack on Mechili didn't materialize on 7 April, because on a reconnaissance flight in the early afternoon, General Rommel discovered that **Gruppe Olbrich** *was still 50 kilometers to the southwest,* **Aufklaerung-Abteilung 3** *was 60 kilometers to the west, and the mass of* **Gruppe Streich** *with* *part of a* **Panzer-Kompanie** *first arrived near Mechili at nightfall.*

At 1400 hours, **Gruppe Olbrich** *reported that the group was resting because of the rough going 15 kilometers south of Bir el Betir and that only very slow progress could be made. Several urgent messages were sent by the* **Ia** *to* **Gruppe Olbrich,** *telling them to advance on Mechili, if only with partial strength.*

Moving through the night of 6/7 April, the 5th R.T.R. halted on the side of road near Slonta at 0300 hours for 3 hours' rest. At 0400 hours, the Brigade commander's AFV had an accident and fell down the steep bank off the road. The march was resumed toward Derna at 0600 hours. By this time all other units in the 3rd Armoured Brigade had passed through and 5th R.T.R. was doing rearguard. The 3rd Hussars abandoned their last Mk.VI Light Tank in the morning near Derna.

At 1100 hours, the 5th R.T.R. halted at the western head of Derna Pass for a short maintenance break and refueled. Continuing at 1200 hours, the remaining seven Mk.IVA Cruiser Tanks went down the pass into Derna.

Encountering German troops at 1600 hours, only four tanks succeeded in getting into action and were knocked out. The remaining three were in such bad mechanical condition that they had failed to climb the pass out of Derna.

5th R.T.R. reported the following losses during their withdrawal to Tobruk. Of the 55 Mk.IVA Cruiser Tanks:

5 never started from Tobruk.
2 recovered to Beda Fomm, then unknown.
10 never recovered on approach route.
5 sent to LRS at Beda Fomm and arrived, then unknown.
4 destroyed on receipt of code word "Laxative." They had been awaiting recovery.
8 sent toward LRS during withdrawal, never arrived.
6 stripped and destroyed during withdrawal.
1 wrecked on thermos bomb.
1 destroyed to clear road at Barce.
2 abandoned in Derna, unable to climb the pass.
9 lost in action.
2 returned to Tobruk.

Of 6 Mk.II Close Support Tanks:
1 in Tobruk before advance.
4 handed over temporarily immobilized to the 6th R.T.R.
1 destroyed during withdrawal.

DAK KTB 8 April 1941 - *At 0800 hours, the* **5.leichte Division** *with the* **I.Abteilung/Panzer-Regiment 5** *under the command of Major Bolbrinker (with eight Panzers) took Mechili. One general, 60 officers, about 200 enlisted men, an undeterminable amount of vehicles, weapons, ammunition, and food were captured. At dawn the occupants had brought a*

The regimental doctor's **Pz.Kpfw.II Ausf.B** (tactical number RA with a stylized caduceus) is pulling off to the side of the well worn track. The **RAL 8000 gelbbraun** camouflage paint was applied as a thin coat in patches instead of stripes. (BA)

A **Pz.Bef.Wg. Ausf.H** pulling into Mechili followed by the short line of Panzers that had survived the attempted dash through the desert. The dust cloud kicked up by the **Pz.Kpfw.III** and **Pz.Bef.Wg.** was drawn into the engine compartment where it was sucked into the engine intake air filters. (BA)

relief force forward from the west and had attempted to break out through the surrounding ring several times.

At 1200 hours, General Rommel ordered: The Italian troops will occupy Mechili. **5.leichte Division** secure the area to the north and northwest. **Vorausabteilung Schwerin** and all of the elements that have arrived from **Kampfgruppe Olbrich** advance on Derna.

Kampfgruppe Olbrich didn't arrive before the attack on Mechili was finished. At 1000 hours, their foremost elements were still only halfway between Bir el Beter and Mechili.

DAK KTB 9 April 1941 - At 1830 hours, General Rommel arrived at the **5.leichte Division** where they had secured Mechili toward the north and northwest and were occupied repairing the vehicles. General Rommel ordered all mobile elements to assemble, to be by Gazala on the Via Balbia at dawn standing ready to arrive at the starting positions for the attack as soon as possible.

DAK KTB 10 April 1941 - General Rommel reviewed the situation: The enemy has retired before our advance; we must pursue him with all our forces. So that every man understands, the objective is the Suez Canal. With all available forces, we need to completely envelop Tobruk to prevent the enemy forces from breaking out.

The foremost unit of the **132° divisione corazzato "Ariete"** was located around Tengeder. They received orders to proceed at once via the track through Gadd el Ahmar to El Adem. They were to immediately send a mixed combat unit ahead of the division to arrive at the latest on 11 April and remain under the direct command of General Rommel.

For the night of 10/11 April, General Rommel ordered that the **27a divisione fanteria "Brescia"** was to replace **Vorausabteilung Graf Schwerin**. The **Vorausabteilung** was to advance behind **Aufklaerung-Abteilung 3**. The main body of the **5.leichte Division** with all units was to advance on a night march behind these **Vorausabteilungen** and make contact with them.

The first phase of the campaign was completed on 11 April 1941 when the **Deutsches Afrikakorps** reported: The ring around Tobruk was closed in the east and south by the **5.leichte Division**. It was yet to be seen which of the two opponents had been trapped by this move.

A Mk.VIB Light Tank abandoned by the 3rd Armoured Brigade. (WW)

Two Mk.IVA Cruiser Tanks of the 5th R.T.R. which broke down and were abandoned during their withdrawal. (WW)

6.5 TACTICAL ANALYSIS

6.5.1 BRITISH TACTICS

The 2nd Armoured Division reported the loss of 49 Cruiser Tanks, 47 Light Tanks, and all the M13 tanks. All but ten of the Cruiser Tanks were lost due to mechanical failure and lack of fuel. But they hadn't even made their opponent pay for these losses (with the exception of three Panzers on 2 April). However, this wasn't a unique feat since the 3rd R.T.R. in Greece didn't lose a single tank in action; all 52 of their Mk.IIA Cruiser Tanks were lost to mechanical failure.

Initially, the withdrawal of the forward elements of the 2nd Armoured Division was conducted in accordance with preplanned stages. Having a plan was mentioned in their tactical manual on how to successfully conduct delaying actions. However, as recommended in their tactical manual, the plan should have been elastic – not fixed, offensive – not defensive; and conducted as surprise counterattacks – not as a rear guard screen. Due to the mechanical state of the tanks and their lack of fuel, the British didn't have anything to lose in conducting ambush counterattacks as recommended in their tactical manual. At no time was the British armored force a threat of a hindrance to the advancing German-Italian forces, mainly due to the method in which it was tactically handled.

The firefight between C Squadron of the 5th R.T.R. and the **II.Abteilung/Panzer-Regiment 5** on 2 April leaves no doubt of the British tankers' courage, as they took on a far superior force. However, lining up tanks to have a shoot at the enemy is not an example of tactical ingenuity. The worst was the revelation that individual tanks, troops, and squadrons did not have the right to maneuver without permission from the next higher command. Such inflexibility, where an individual tank wasn't allowed to move on its own

commander's decision to an alternative firing position when registered by enemy fire, is key in explaining their rapid losses in such a short firefight.

6.5.2 GERMAN TACTICS

The initial attack on Marsa el Brega by the **6.Kompanie/ Panzer-Regiment 5** is an outstanding example of combined arms tactics at its best. They worked as a well-synchronized team to systematically take on the enemy defenses without charging blindly into the fray and taking unnecessary risks. During their advance across the desert, three of the German **Kampfgruppen** had also been well organized into combined arms teams. If they had met significant enemy resistance, which they didn't, they were very well organized to meet any tactical challenge.

In their attack against the 5th R.T.R. on 2 April, the **II.Abteilung/Panzer-Regiment 5** did not demonstrate any tactical competence let alone ingenuity. The Panzers simply approached the enemy position head-on and opened fire. This was not the tank-versus-tank tactics recommended in the tactical manual. Even against a significantly weaker opponent, an attempt should have been made to pin the opponent down on the front while sending a swift enveloping strike at a flank. Their straight on advance resulted in the unnecessary loss of two **Pz.Kpfw.III** and a **Pz.Kpfw.IV** along with an unrecorded number damaged.

A major failure with longlasting consequences resulted from misjudging the opponent's intentions. The British forces were not retreating because of perceived threats from the advancing German-Italian forces. They were leaving because they never had any intention of remaining in their untenable forward positions. These positions could easily be outflanked, just as the British had succeeded in outflanking and cutting off the Italians in early February. There was no need to rush the entire German-Italian force forward through extremely difficult terrain. As a result of unnecessarily rushing through the desert, **Panzer-Regiment 5** was decimated by mechanical breakdowns, not by the enemy. Therefore, only a small fraction of their strength was available when they attempted to crack the defenses at Tobruk.

The effects of the attempted charge through the desert was reported on 5 May 1941 by the **Werkstatt-Kompanie** of **Panzer-Regiment 5**: *The average journey of 700 kilometers in the desert had a very adverse effect on the Panzers. Up to the time that the regiment moved into position before Tobruk, the following Panzers had been delivered to the two workshop companies because of severe motor and suspension damage: 12 out of 25* **Pz.Kpfw.I***, 2 out of 3* **kl.Pz.Bef.Wg.***, 19 out of 45* **Pz.Kpfw.II***, 44 out of 65* **Pz.Kpfw.III** *and* **gr.Pz.Bef.Wg.***, and 6 out of 17* **Pz.Kpfw.IV***. In all 83 Panzers out of a total of 155. The reason the stretch of desert in the Trigh el Abd caused so much damage to the Panzers was the high speed which tactical reasons demanded. Because of the necessary haste, parts of the route unsuitable for tanks could not be avoided.*

Of the 65 **Pz.Kpfw.III** *and* **gr.Pz.Bef.Wg.***, 44 fell out during the desert march because of severe damage to the engines. The fault was always the same. The engine cut out and the oil pressure fell, and after fluctuating, finally fell to nothing. The engine stopped. If an attempt was made to drive on after the oil was changed, cylinders and pistons seized. Finally, the connecting rod of the third or fourth piston broke. The cause was the same in each case. The crankshaft was clogged up by the fine dust as if with a paste, which caused a break in the oil circulation. Cylinders and pistons showed wear of as much as 6 mm. Out of the 83 broken-down Panzers, the workshop company changed engines in 58.*

The present air filters are entirely unsuitable for desert travel since it is impossible to stop the fine dust with them. Hence, clogging of the crankshaft. The use of a dry felt filter such as is fitted on British cars, trucks, and tanks was proposed.

Fifty shock absorbers had become useless and were changed on the 65 **Pz.Kpfw.III** *and* **gr.Pz.Bef.Wg.** *Twenty broken springs and 16 shackles were changed on* **Pz.Kpfw.IIs***. Spring and shock absorber failure was partially due to the bad going and partially due to mines. Lubrication of the auxiliary brakes was a common fault because of defective shims. Sixty instances with* **Pz.Kpfw.IIIs** *were due in part to bad inspection by the firms. The fan shafts had to be changed in 40 cases since the thrust bearings were defective. Difficulties arising from sand in the turret races were found in eight* **Pz.Kpfw.IIIs***. Five Variorex transmissions had to be changed.*

Lastly, General Rommel continued to charge forward, disobeying orders from both his superior Italian commander and the **O.K.H.** In hindsight, this probably cost him the campaign in North Africa. Jumping the gun in Libya had directly resulted in the British holding back forces which they had prepared to send to Greece. These same forces were then used against Rommel in North Africa. If these forces had been sent to Greece, the British did not have the capacity to pull them back out. When forced to evacuate Greece, British shipping was unable to rescue all of the forces that had been sent to Greece prior to Rommel's attack. The record doesn't state whether Rommel was informed of the impending offensive against Greece and Yugoslavia, scheduled to start on 6 April 1941. But even if he wasn't aware of the grand strategy, Rommel had purposefully disobeyed direct orders to cease and await the arrival of additional forces.

Waiting for the complete **15.Panzer-Division** would have given Rommel a tactically superior force capable of sustained offensive victories. But previous experience had taught Rommel to charge ahead as rapidly as possible, causing the opponent to panic, retreat in confusion, and remain off balance when struck by additional blows. This had worked very well in both phases of the campaign against the French. And, it was also apparently working against the British in North Africa. However, the British withdrawal wasn't the same as the French debacle. Abandoning an untenable position had been mistaken by Rommel as a panicked retreat. Therefore, as will be seen in the next chapter, the German forces were confused and shaken when the British forces steadfastly stood their ground at Tobruk.

7

Repulsed at Tobruk

Having surrounded Tobruk, the German-Italian forces attempted to quickly take the port with a few hastily organized strikes. Possessing scant knowledge of the terrain, the German forces unexpectedly ran into the anti-tank ditch which had been blasted out of the rock by the Italians. Several unsuccessful attempts were made before they realized that the defenses consisted of a continuous belt of prepared positions without an apparent weak point.

Finally, after obtaining maps of the defenses from the Italians, a combined arms team assault was assembled for an attack from the south down the main road leading to the port. It came as a complete surprise to the Germans that their assault force consisting of two companies of Panzers, two companies of infantry, and two batteries of artillery would fail to take prepared fortifications defended by four infantry brigades, eight artillery batteries, five anti-tank batteries and three weak squadrons of tanks.

7.1 GERMAN FORCES

Most of the units of the **5.leichte Division** had managed to get forward to Tobruk by 11 April. However, these units were at greatly reduced strength. Due to their attempt to dash across the desert, many of their motor vehicles and equipment were broken down, some in workshops, the rest still scattered over a stretch of 700 kilometers all the way back to the west coast of Cyrenaica.

On 11 April 1941, **Panzer-Regiment 5** could only scrape together 25 operational Panzers. This is the equivalent of one company with a few spares, not a regiment. Additional repairs brought them up to 38 operational Panzers for the assault on the morning of 14 April.

Additional reinforcements and the first elements of the **15.Panzer-Division** were arriving in the forward area.

At 0800 hours on 10 April, the **I./Flak-Regiment 18** and the **2.Kompanie/Panzer-Jaeger-Abteilung 33** stood at the crossroads by Mteifel el Chebir and requested urgently needed supplies of food and fuel. The units had been without water for 24 hours. On 11 April, the **Stab, 1., 2.,** and **3.Kompanie/Kradschuetzen-Bataillon 15** and **Panzer-Jaeger-Abteilung 33** arrived in the forward area by Tobruk.

During the evening of 11 April, **Aufklaerung-Abteilung 3** was to start immediately on the Via Balbia with the objective of reaching Bardia during the night. **Vorausabteilung Knabe** was assembled from **Kradschuetzen-Bataillon 15, Panzer-Jaeger-Abteilung 33**, one **8.8 cm Batterie** and one **2 cm Batterie** from **I./Flak-Regiment 18**. They were ordered to start at dawn on 12 April and advance through El Adem with Sollum as their initial objective. The rest of the **I./Flak-Regiment 18** was ordered to El Adem.

7.2 ITALIAN FORCES

The foremost unit of "**Ariete**" was located by Tengeder on 10 April. They were ordered to proceed at once to El Adem. On 11 April, Colonne Montemurro (**XII battaglione bersagliere autoportato**) and Fabris (**III battaglione bersagliere**) of "**Ariete**" were to be brought forward through Derna and placed under the command of the **5.leichte Division**. The "**Ariete**" could only muster 6 **M.13-40** and 12 **L.3** operational tanks to support an attack on Tobruk on 16 April.

On 8 April, the **D.A.K.** sent a request to the **Comandante Superiore** to expedite the advance of the **102a divisione fanteria motorizzato "Trento"** and the rest of "**Brescia.**" On 11 April, "**Brescia**" held positions on the Wadi el Sehel on both sides of the Via Balbia. The first elements from "**Trento**" arrived in the vicinity of Kilometer 42 on the Via Balbia west of Tobruk in the late afternoon of 13 April. These

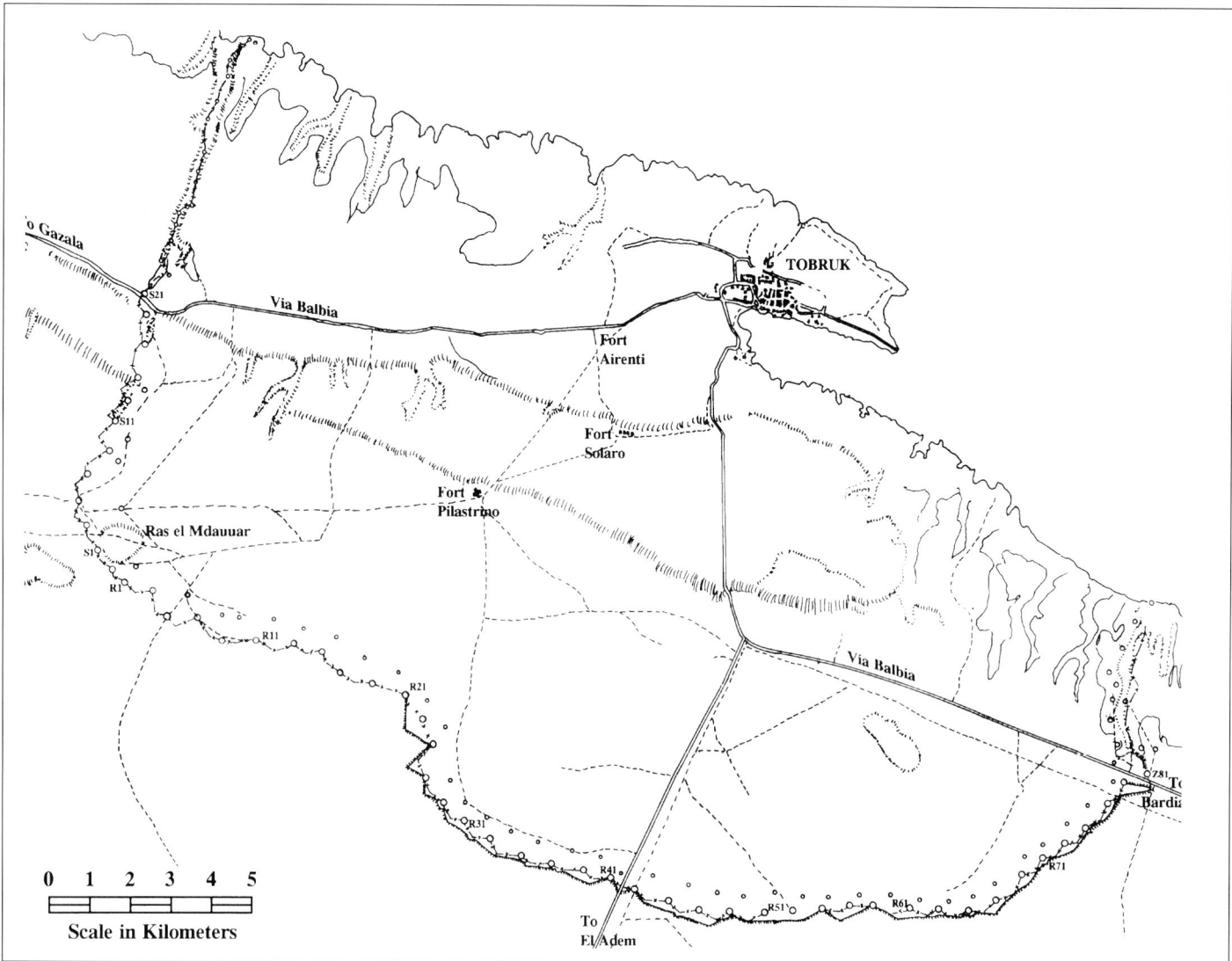

Map of Tobruk

units included the **61° reggimento fanteria motorizzato**, the **I gruppo 46° reggimento artiglieria**, the **104a** and **106a compagnia cannoni 47/32** and the **160° battaglione carabinieri**. On 14 April, most of the remainder of **"Trento"** arrived at positions near Tobruk, including the **62° reggimento fanteria motorizzato** (without the **II battaglione** left at Barce), **DLI battaglione mitraglieri divisionale, 161° battaglione carabinieri** and the **7a** and **8a batteria c.a. 20 mm. Gruppo artiglieria Frongia** arrived in the area of Bir Scerif and was attached to **"Ariete."**

7.3 BRITISH FORCES

The British forces inside the defensive perimeter at Tobruk on 11 April included the 9th Australian Division with the 18th, 20th, 24th, and 26th Australian Infantry Brigades; 18th King

Edward VIII's Own Cavalry Motor Battalion,; 1st Northumberland Fusiliers M.G. Battalion; 1st, 104th, and 107th RHA each with 16 25-pounder guns, 51st Field Regiment R.A. with 12 18-pounder guns and 12 4.5-inch howitzers; five anti-tank batteries; the 2/1st Australian Pioneer Battalion; four engineer field companies; and the 4th Anti-Aircraft Brigade.

The tank forces in Tobruk consisted of remnants of the 3rd Armoured Brigade and the newly arrived 1st R.T.R. with a detachment from the 4th R.T.R. A composite squadron from the 3rd Hussars and the 5th R.T.R. had been formed on 8 April. It was issued 15 Mk.VIB Light Tanks in the morning of 10 April, three Mk.IVA Cruiser Tanks on 10 April, one Mk.IVA on 11 April, two Mk.IVA on 12 April and another Mk.IVA on 13 April.

The 1st R.T.R. drew 1 Mk.IIA Cruiser Tank, 10 Mk.I Cruiser Tanks and 16 Mk.VIB Light Tanks during the night of 3/4 April which they used to outfit two mixed squadrons. The 1st R.T.R.

and the detachment from the 4th R.T.R. with four Mk.IIA Infantry Tanks left Egypt by sea at 0630 hours on 6 April and were unloaded by lighters in Tobruk harbor on 8 April.

British forces on the Egyptian-Libyan border consisted of the 1st King's Royal Rifle Corps, a composite company of the 1st Tower Hamlet Rifles, a company of the 1st Durham Light Infantry, the 11th Hussars, 4th RHA, and two batteries of anti-tank guns. A squadron of the 7th Hussars had been outfitted with 17 Mk.VI Light Tanks and sent forward to the border. It arrived at Halfaya at noon on 10 April and took up a position on the frontier wire near Capuzzo.

The following British units were located between the border and the Suez Canal:

7th Australian Infantry Division (with two infantry brigades), 16th British Infantry Brigade, and part of the 22nd Guards Brigade were at Mersa Matruh.

The 5th Indian Infantry Brigade had just arrived near Mersa Matruh.

The Polish Infantry Brigade was holding the approaches to Alexandria.

The remainder of the 7th Armoured Division was by the Nile Delta awaiting the repair and reconditioning of its tanks.

At midnight on 13 April, the "Cyrenaica Command" was replaced by the "Western Desert Force Headquarters" and the forces in Tobruk were designated as the "Tobruk Fortress."

7.4 THE ATTACKS BEGIN

<u>DAK KTB 11 April 1941</u> - *After the first reconnaissance advance by* **Panzer-Regiment 5** *west of the El Adem-Tobruk road in the direction of Fort Pilastrino, the commander reported that there is an anti-tank ditch with many anti-tank guns and mines south of Tobruk in Sghifet el Cherr.*

This entry in the **Deutsches Afrikakorps** war diary is misleading. The attempt by **Panzer-Regiment 5** wasn't merely a reconnaissance foray. This was a serious attempt to assault Tobruk, as related on 15 April 1941 by Oberst Olbrich in his after-action report:

<u>11 April 1941</u> - *At 0730 hours, the* **Regiment** *received orders to attack. It was to move to Acroma from Kilometer 32 on the Via Balbia and sweep around to attack Tobruk from the south.*

At 0830 hours, the **Regiment** *(with* **M.G.-Battalion 8**) *moved off and was met in Acroma by an officer from the* **D.A.K.** *under whose direction it turned off to the east about 10 kilometers south of Acroma and reached a position 12 kilometers southwest of Tobruk at about 1500 hours. The element of surprise was lost, since the assembly area immediately came under enemy fire. Rommel personally pointed out the layout of the enemy position to the regimental commander.*

At 1600 hours, the **Regiment**, *which had shrunk to 25 Panzers (***Regiment-Stab** *and* **II.Abteilung** *with all the operational Panzers) began the attack. It met with heavy artil-*

The assembly area of **Panzer-Regiment 5** prior to their initial attack on Tobruk on 11 April. The crew of **Pz.Kpfw.II** (tactical number I21), platoon leader for the **2.leichte Zug** of the **I.Abteilung**, prepare for combat. (BA)

During the afternoon of 12 April a sandstorm rolled, in further hampering the attempts by **Panzer-Regiment 5** to penetrate the defensive perimeter at Tobruk. **Pz.Kpfw.II** (tactical number 241) is in the foreground with **Pz.Kpfw.III**s silhouetted against the approaching storm on the horizon. (BA)

lery fire as it advanced across heights within direct view of the enemy.

The regiment's advance was unexpectedly held up by an impassable anti-tank ditch which surrounds Tobruk. The **Regiment** *then turned right to try and find a place to cross further to the east. It advanced for 4 kilometers along the trench under heavy anti-tank fire and extremely well directed artillery fire.*

At 1715 hours, the van of the **Regiment** *reached the Tobruk-El Adem road where it encountered a thick mine field. The order was given to withdraw to the south. The light platoon of the* **II.Abteilung** *was sent out to reconnoiter further to the east. This reconnaissance continued until late in the night and advanced about 20 kilometers south of Tobruk. The* **Regiment** *returned to its previous assembly area and drew up facing Tobruk.*

Reports provided to the **Regiment** *had led it to believe that the enemy would retire immediately on the approach of German Panzers. Nothing had been reported about the old Italian anti-tank ditch or about the large number of British anti-tank guns and artillery pieces.*

The British description of the actions of the 1st R.T.R. on 11 April are contained in the following extracts from their war diary:

The 1st R.T.R. was ordered to head for area 406423 where enemy tanks were reported to have broken through. It moved south from Pilastrino area and kept west of the El Adem road. Upon reaching the perimeter there was no sign of enemy tanks. The 1st R.T.R. then turned east along the perimeter toward the El Adem road. Before reaching the road,

at 1830 hours, they sighted two heavy tanks larger than our own Cruisers, eight M13 tanks and twenty light tanks.

The enemy tanks were engaged by B Squadron and it was believed that one and possibly three were disabled. The enemy tanks than moved east to 40804210 where they were engaged by our artillery.

1st R.T.R. continued east toward the El Adem road. On reaching the area of the El Adem road, ten enemy tanks (consisting of two heavy tanks and eight M13 tanks) were observed facing north astride the El Adem road about one mile outside the perimeter.

These advanced at 1900 hours and were engaged by both Squadrons (at 410421) and taken under heavy artillery fire. This action lasted for 30 minutes. The enemy withdrew south and left the following tanks disabled within 300 yards of the perimeter: one heavy tank believed to have been knocked out by artillery and two M13 tanks (plus one light tank which had joined the enemy force). Two Cruiser Tanks were destroyed by burning after being hit by shellfire. One of these tanks was knocked out after receiving five direct shell hits. The Mk.I Cruiser Tank of the commanding officer of B Squadron was disabled.

The composite squadron of the 3rd Hussars/5th R.T.R. were positioned two miles east-southeast of Fort Pilastrino and did not take part in the fighting.

DAK KTB 12 April 1941 - *The encirclement of Tobruk was completed on the east side by* **Abteilung Graf Schwerin** *on both sides of Sidi Duad. An attack by* **Panzer-Regiment 5** *on Tobruk from the southeast had to turn back because of the anti-tank ditch.*

Orders were issued to the **5.leichte Division** and **divisione fanteria "Trento"** concerning the capture of Tobruk.

The exact layout and construction of the permanent fortifications of Tobruk were still not known by the **D.A.K.** on 12 April. Decisions and orders were based on a 1 to 400,000 scale map. A full report on the defenses still had not arrived from the **Comandante Superiore**.

The tanker "Persiana" with 2,200,000 liters of fuel was torpedoed and sunk.

From Oberst Olbrich's after-action account:

12 April 1941 - An officer from the engineers reported that there probably was no anti-tank ditch 4 kilometers west of the point where the **Regiment** was to have broken through on the 11th. Acting on this information, at 1515 hours, the **Regiment** with 24 Panzers was led up to the point to renew the attack.

Upon its approach, British artillery began to fire into it with superb accuracy. At the same time, bombers attacked dropping large-caliber bombs. Under covering fire from the **Regiment**, the attached engineer platoon was detailed to create a passage through any anti-tank ditches there might be. As the **Regiment** advanced, the enemy fire grew so intense that in spite of their great dash and daring, the engineers could not follow.

At 1600 hours, the enemy position could be clearly distinguished. At 1645 hours, the leading elements of the **Regiment** reached the anti-tank ditch, which proved to be completely impassable at this point also.

Artillery and anti-tank guns were firing at point blank range on the **Regiment**, which first halted while waiting for the engineers and returned the fire. When, after 15 minutes, the engineers failed to appear, the order to withdraw was given and was carried out in good order, accompanied by British artillery fire.

DAK KTB 13 April 1941 - Sandstorm.

At about 1500 hours, the advance guard of the "**Ariete**" arrived at El Adem. Elements of "**Ariete**", including one **battaglione bersaglieri** (Colonna Fabris), one **battaglione carri L**, one **gruppo artiglieri**, and several small anti-tank and anti-aircraft units, were to move north of El Adem and intervene in the battle, if necessary.

At 1800 hours, the **5.leichte Division** with **M.G.-Bataillon 8** and several Panzers supported by the **2º reggimento artiglieri** under Colonnello Grati and the **I./Flak-Regiment 18**, conducted an attack to secure an assembly area for the attack on Tobruk and to establish artillery positions at the important crossroads south of Tobruk. On the right flank, **M.G.-**

This **Pz.Kpfw.I Ausf.B** of **Panzer-Jaeger-Abteilung 605** was knocked out on the road heading south out of Tobruk toward El Adem. The road block at the anti-tank ditch can be seen in the background. (AWM)

Bataillon 8 had failed to reach their objective because of the anti-tank ditch and wire.

DAK KTB 14 April 1941 - At 0430 hours, the various attacks of the **5.leichte Division** began against Tobruk. **M.G.-Bataillon 8** broke through the defensive belt directly west of the El Adem-Tobruk road. However, they could not extend the flanks of their position. The attack by **Panzer-Regiment 5** had to turn back about 5 kilometers south of Tobruk in the face of combined artillery and anti-tank fire after **M.G.-Bataillon 8** was not able to follow their attack. A large part of **M.G.-Bataillon 8** was cut off and captured or killed. The attack had been supported by elements of **I./Flak-Regiment 18** and the **3.Batterie/Artillerie-Regiment 75** from open positions in the front file. A Stuka attack was made at 0600 to 0630 hours on the center of Tobruk and up to 5 kilometers to the west.

At midday the **Korps** ordered the troops investing Tobruk to switch over to the defensive.

Details on the unsuccessful attack were recorded in Oberst Olbrich's after-action account as follows:

In order to mislead the enemy, on the night of 12/13 April, engineers made a sham demolition of the anti-tank ditch on the western sector of the British positions around Tobruk. On the night of the 13th, **M.G.-Battalion 8** and engineers made a bridge-head at the road fork 7 kilometers south of Tobruk. Here, crossing points were to be created over the ditch for the subsequent attack by the Regiment.

A platoon from **Panzer-Jaeger-Abteilung 605** and a battery from **I./Flak 33** were attached to cooperate with the

Regiment. The force was to assemble by 0230 hours on 14 April to the south of the bridgehead. The initial attack was to be directed toward the north against Point 99. As the attack developed, the **I.Abteilung** with the platoon from **Panzer-Jaeger-Abteilung 605** was to advance to the Via Balbia and pursue the retreating enemy to the west. The **II.Abteilung** would turn off to the east and advance against Tobruk. While the Regiment was preparing, enemy artillery opened barrage fire on it, but no losses were inflicted.

At 0430 hours on 14 April, **Panzer-Regiment 5** with 38 Panzers (**II.Abteilung** leading, followed by the **I.Abteilung**), then three 4.7 cm self-propelled anti-tank guns from **Panzer-Jaeger Abteilung 605** crossed the bridgehead 4 kilometers west of the point it had originally been ordered to penetrate. On first contact with the enemy, a few elements of **M.G.-Battalion 8** came forward (2 1/2 platoons instead of 300 men).

The situation seemed to be developing favorably, since we had the advantage of surprise. At 0530 hours, liaison between the Panzers and machine gunners continued. But with the approach of dawn, anti-tank fire concentrated on the **Regiment** from all sides, and the machine gunners were pinned down.

At 0600 hours, the **Regiment** crossed Point 99 and prepared to advance on the Via Balbia. Completely alone, 6 kilometers deep in enemy territory, the **Regiment** came under direct artillery fire from near Fort Solara east of Point 99 and from Fort Ariente. The enemy advanced his anti-tank units on both flanks and to our rear succeeded in closing the gap where we had broken in. The **Regiment** was forced to defend itself in all directions. At the same instant, six enemy fighters came roaring down in a low-level attack and enemy bombers dropped heavy-caliber bombs as well.

THIS PAGE AND OPPOSITE: **Pz.Kpfw.IV Ausf.D** (tactical number 811) being examined by the British after its capture on 14 April. The 20 mm **Zusatzpanzerung** on the superstructure side was knocked off by an artillery round which also blew out a section of the fender. The slots cut into the rear deck hatches were part of the tropicalization modification to improve engine compartment ventilation. (TTM)

*While in this unpleasant situation, an attack was launched from the right rear by 14 enemy tanks. Among them two Mk.II Infantry Tanks were definitely identified. Orders were given to the **I.Abteilung** to engage their front and the **II.Abteilung** was to attack from the right flank. During the battle, enemy anti-tank fire grew more and more intense. Visibility was considerably reduced by bursting shells, burning Panzers, and the smoke from shells, adding greatly to our difficulties. When the Panzer casualties had far exceeded unbearable proportions, the **Regiment** began to retire in good order, firing in every direction and recovering the dead and wounded from the knocked-out Panzers.*

At 0800 hours, the gap in the anti-tank ditch, now held by the enemy, was reached. Upon our approach, they opened fire with their anti-tank guns and from well-camouflaged machine gun posts, concentrating their fire on the Panzers as they were passing through the narrow gap. The 200 prisoners we had taken threw themselves on the ground to avoid the fire of their comrades, jumped into the ditch, and escaped.

Several of our own men riding on the outside of the Panzers were killed or wounded.

*The **I.Abteilung** was detailed to cover the retreat by opposing the fire of the enemy anti-tank and machine guns. Heavy, well-directed enemy artillery fire pursued the **Regiment** to a point about 2 kilometers southwest of the gap. Here the **Regiment** assembled, drew up its units in battle order, and prepared to repulse an enemy counterattack; however, this did not materialize. The enemy merely advanced a few tanks to the position where we had broken through.*

Thirty-eight Panzers entered the battle, 17 of which were destroyed by the enemy. Two officers were missing and 7 wounded; 21 men missing and 10 wounded. This amounted to a loss of 50 percent.

A personal account of the events was recorded in the following extract from a diary written by Leutnant Schorm of the **6.Kompanie/Panzer-Regiment 5**:

This **Pz.Kpfw.IV** had its turret blown off during the dual with the 25-pounders. The loss of five **Pz.Kpfw.IV**s in the battle on 14 April, several of them like this one with **Zusatzpanzerung**, was a severe setback to **Panzer-Regiment 5**. (TTM)

<u>14 April 1941</u> - At 0100 I am called and ordered to report with the company commander at 0100 hours. Situation: Engineers have worked a gap through the anti-tank defenses. **Panzer-Regiment 5, M.G.-Battalion 8**, anti-tank guns, and **8.8 cm Flak** will cross the gap under cover of darkness and will overwhelm the positions. Stuka attack at 0645 hours.

Storming of Tobruk. With least possible noise the **II.Abteilung, Regiment-Stab**, and **I.Abteilung** move off with vehicles completely blacked out. Bitterly cold. Of course, the opponent recognizes us by the noise, and as ill luck would have it, a defective spotlight on one of the vehicles in front goes on and off.

Soon artillery fire starts up on us, getting the range. The shells explode like fireworks. We travel 10 kilometers, every nerve on edge. From time to time isolated groups of soldiers appear – the men of **M.G.-Battalion 8** - and then suddenly we are in the gap. Already the Panzer is nose first in the first ditch. The motor whines; I catch a glimpse of the stars through the vision port, when for the second time the Panzer goes down, extricating itself backward with a dull thud with gears grinding.

We are through and immediately take up file in battle order. In front of us the **8.Kompanie**, then the **II.Abteilung-Stab**, then the **5.Kompanie**. With my troops I travel left of the company commander. With the **II.Abteilung**, 60 men of **M.G.-Battalion 8** are marching in sparse groups with their commander Oberstleutnant Ponath. Panzers advancing at the pace of infantry? This is against all rules! Behind us follows the **Regiment-Stab** and the **I.Abteilung**, likewise the other arms. Slowly, much too slowly, the column moves forward. We must, of course, regulate our speed by the marching troops. In this way the enemy has time to prepare resistance. In proportion, as the darkness lifts, the enemy strikes harder. Destructive fire starts up in front of us now - 1 - 2 - 3 - 10 - 12 - 16 and more. Five batteries rain their hail upon us. The company from **M.G.-Battalion 8** presses forward to get at them. Our heavy Panzers, fire for all they are worth, just as we do, but the enemy with his superior force and all the tactical advantages of his own territory makes heavy gaps in our ranks.

Radio message: 9 o:clock anti-tank gun - 17 o:clock tank!

We are right in the middle of it with no prospect of getting out. From both flanks, armor-piercing shells whiz by at 1000 meters per second.

Radio message: Turn Right, Left Turn, Retire!

Now we come slap into **I.Abteilung** which is following us. Some of our Panzers are already on fire. The crews call for doctors who alight to help in this Witches' Cauldron. British anti-tank units fall upon us with their machine guns firing into our midst; but we have no time. In the thick of it, my driver says, "The motor is no longer running properly, brakes not acting, transmission working only with great difficulty."

We bear off to the right. 600 meters off on the reverse slope a tank, anti-tank guns 900 meters distant in the hollow behind. Behind that in the next dip, 1200 meters away another tank. How many? Judging from their width and thickness, there must be at least 12 guns. Above us Italian fighter planes come into the fray. Two of them crash in our midst. The optical instruments are spoiled by the dust. Nevertheless, I register several unmistakable hits. A few anti-tank guns are silenced; some enemy tanks are burning. Just then we are hit and the radio set is smashed to bits. Now our communications are cut off. What is more, our ammunition is giving out. I follow the **Abteilung** commander. Our attack is fading out. From every side, the superior forces of the enemy shoot at us.

"Retire." There is a crash just behind us. The motor and the fuel tank are in the rear. The Panzer must be on fire. I turn around and look through the vision slit. It is not burning. Our luck is holding. Poor 8th machine gunners! We take a wounded and two others aboard, and the other Panzers do the same. Most of the men have bullet wounds. With its last strength my Panzer follows the others, which we lose from time to time in the dust clouds. But we have to press on toward the south, as it is the only way through. Good God! Supposing we don't find it? And the motor won't do any more!

Close on our right and left flanks, the British tanks shoot into our midst. We are struck in the tracks of the Panzer, which creak and groan. The lane is in sight. Everything hastens toward it. British anti-tank guns shoot into the mass. Our own anti-tank and the **8.8 cm Flak** anti-aircraft guns are almost deserted, but the crews are lying silent beside them. Italian artillery which was to have protected our left flank equally lies deserted. British troops run out of their positions, some shooting at us with sub-machine guns, some with hands raised. At pistol point they are compelled to enter our Panzers. Then British machine guns start up and the prisoners fling themselves to the ground. Oberleutnant von Huelsen and my machine gunner lie on that side of my Panzer which faces toward the machinegun battalion. We go on; now comes the gap – now the ditch! The driver cannot see a thing for the dust, nor I either. We drive by instinct.

The Panzer almost gets stuck in the two ditches, blocking the path, but manages to extricate itself with great difficulty. With their last reserves of power, the crew gets out of range and returns to camp. We examine damage to the Panzer. My men extricate an armor-piercing high-explosive shell from the right wall by the fuel tank. The fuel tank, 30 mm of armor plate, and the bracket for the roadwheel suspension arm were all cut clean through. The fuel had run out to this level without igniting. Had it not been for the roadwheel, we should not have got out alive.

At 1200 hours, we retire into the wadi to the south of us. Impedimenta follows. We cover up. Heavy cumulus clouds cover the sky. At intervals of 10 to 30 minutes, two or three British bombers swoop out of them among the Panzers. Every bomber drops four to eight bombs. Explosions all round. It goes on like this until 1900 hours without a pause. The Lion has wings; we have one, in fact several "Egons." These hateful birds immediately direct artillery fire over our post. Likewise smoke bombs, which sail down on parachutes, producing a streaming veil.

At 1900 hours, I am invited to accompany Leutnant Franke-Lindheim to the regimental commander, Oberst Olbrich. The Iron Cross 2nd class is awarded for the tank battle near Agedabia on 2 April 1941. A division officer proposes a short toast. Major Hohmann (commander of the **II.Abteilung**) says: Let's drink first to today. How fortunate that the Regiment got out again. How splendidly the men fought – indeed.

Casualties in the **II.Abteilung/Panzer-Regiment 5** are 10 Panzers, apart from the five 7.5 cm tank guns of the **8.Kompanie**. A few dead, several wounded, more missing. It went badly with the anti-tank units, the light and heavy Flak, but especially with **M.G.-Battalion 8**. The **Regiment** has lost all its doctors, presumably captured. The **Regiment** is practically wiped out.

Panzer-Regiment 5 advanced at dawn on A/E Battery of the 1st RHA. The Cruiser Tanks of the 1st R.T.R. began

THIS PAGE AND OPPOSITE: On 14 April, the British also captured one of the rare **Pz.Kpfw.III Ausf.H**s (tactical number II02) belonging to **Panzer-Regiment 5**. But even though they disassembled it for thorough examination, they didn't recognize the significance of the 30 mm face-hardened **Zusatzpanzerung** bolted onto the 30 mm face hardened armor base plates on the hull and superstructure front. Instead of reporting that there were **Pz.Kpfw.III**s with frontal hull armor that couldn't be penetrated by the 2-pounder at any range, British Intelligence reported that a few Panzers had odd bits of armor bolted or welded to the front. After test firing against a **Pz.Kpfw.IV**, the troops were informed in the Training Memorandum No.2 of October 1941 that "numbers of each type (**Pz.Kpfw.III** and **IV**) have been knocked out in Libya and Greece in a variety of methods and penetration performances of British weapons against these tanks are very good indeed..." and "The myth of German invincibility of material, when submitted to the cold light of engineering fact, makes a very sorry exhibition." (TTM)

advancing across the El Adem road onto their right flank. A troop of five 2-pounder anti-tank guns on portee of M Battery of the 3rd RHA also hit their right flank. The **II.Abteilung/ Panzer-Regiment 5** was stopped after coming to within 600 yards of A/E Battery. The Panzers turned east and were engaged by B/O Battery of the 1st RHA and a section of anti-tank guns from the 2/3rd Australian Anti-Tank Regiment. The 1st R.T.R. then attacked their right rear. After turning to fight the tanks and sustaining more losses, **Panzer-Regiment 5** turned and headed back for the gap in the outer defenses through which they had entered the fortress. On the way back they were engaged by the 425th Artillery Battery, a troop of anti-tank guns of J Battery of the 3rd RHA and some anti-tank guns from the 9th Battery of the 2/3rd Australian Anti-Tank Regiment.

As related in extracts from the war diary of the 1st R.T.R.:

At 0600 hours on 14 April, the 1st R.T.R. was ordered to position east of El Adem road at Bir el Menteghsa to take advantage of the high ground. The Regiment was proceeding from assembly area at 412427 towards 415423, when enemy tanks were sighted west of the El Adem road. 1st R.T.R. turned south and C Squadron engaged at about 1500 yards range on a line west of Bir Iasin where RHQ halted.

Long after this **Pz.Kpfw.II** was lost by **Panzer-Regiment 5** on 14 April, fuel was poured on to stage a fire for this photograph. (AWM)

B Squadron had advanced to the perimeter to about Post R40 without engaging the enemy and were ordered to turn west and harass the withdrawal of the remaining enemy AFVs as they made for the gap at Post R33. B Squadron was delayed by the anti-tank trench before reaching the El Adem road and only fired a few rounds at 2000 yards. One Light Tank which closed with the enemy was hit and damaged.

Unlike Leutnant Schorm in his **Pz.Kpfw.III**, who managed to relocate the crossing point in the anti-tank ditch that had been prepared by the **Pioniere**, this **Pz.Kpfw.III Ausf.G** did not make it back out of the Tobruk Fortress. The rubble it rests on was the stone blasted out by the Italians to create the anti-tank ditch. (AWM)

C Squadron rallied in the area of Bir Iasin less the squadron commanding officer's tank and one other Cruiser left burning near the road. The B Squadron Light Tanks assisted the infantry in clearing the enemy out of the anti-tank ditch.

The 1st R.T.R. had lost two Cruiser Tanks and one Light Tank destroyed and claimed to have knocked out 12 of the 35 enemy tanks.

The composite squadron of the 3rd Hussars/5th R.T.R. had received a warning order on 13 April that a tank attack was expected. The squadron was at 5 minutes' notice to move, throughout the night. On the morning of 14 April, information was received that enemy tanks had broken through the outer defenses. The composite squadron moved to the area of grid 404428 but there was no sign of the enemy. It appeared that the enemy had turned east. Their 7 Mk.IVA Cruiser Tanks and 18 Mk.VI Light Tanks did not get into action.

7.5 TACTICAL ANALYSIS

BRITISH TACTICS

With their lightly armoured Cruiser Tanks, the British tankers were very swift and bold in counterattacking any of their opponents' tanks even when outnumbered. They demonstrated tactical flexibility in attacking the flanks and rear instead of merely charging straight in. On 14 April, they were expending a lot of ammunition by opening fire at such long ranges as 1500 and 2000 yards. There is no mention of them closing range. It is very probable that their claims of 12 kills were way too high, and most Panzer losses were due to the anti-tank guns and artillery.

Each squadron was independently committed into action, instead of as a concentrated force utilizing mutually supporting tactics. They were somewhat hesitant in committing their weak armored force as a whole. Were they so concerned about being drawn into reacting to a diversionary attack that nothing would be left to counter when the main attack came

114

in? Also puzzling is the fact that they still couldn't identify the difference between a German **Pz.Kpfw.III** and an Italian **M.13-40** tank.

GERMAN TACTICS

It is difficult to list all of the tactical blunders committed by **Panzer-Regiment 5** during these initial attacks on Tobruk: Charging in without scouting, moving parallel to a defensive front, ignoring any combined arms tactics, and deserting escorted infantry. It was solely the tankers' responsibility to ensure that they did not get separated from the accompanying infantry. A straight comparison of these after-action accounts with the tactics recommended in the manuals reveals that these reports should be used as examples in lessons on how not to utilize tanks. They had become so confident that no enemy would dare stand in their way that they were disregarding any and all tactics recommended for engaging an enemy force in prepared positions.

As dawn broke on 14 April, the Panzers were at the artillery line, the ultimate objective when breaking through the enemy's defensive lines. Then why didn't the Panzers easily take out the eight 25-pounders as should have occurred? It was simply because the **Panzer-Regiment 5** took on the guns in a head-on attack and closed range. They made no attempt

As reported by Leutnant Schorm, **Panzer-Regiment 5** lost its doctors on 14 April, as is evident from the new owners who have dug **Pz.Kpfw.II** (tactical number RA) into a defensive position. Like all the original 45 **Pz.Kpfw.II**s sent down to Libya with **Panzer-Regiment 5**, two formed sections of 15 mm thick **Zusatzpanzerung** were bolted onto the flaps in the gun mantlet. (TTM)

to seek better firing position from which to pin down the guns and then send a quick enveloping strike around the flank to overrun the artillery position. Without AP-Shot, firing only high explosive shells, the 25-pounders won the gun duel. The Panzers were forced to turn aside and then were hit in the flank by the original battery as they encountered the second artillery battery. Their major mistake had already been committed during the night when they charged alone, deep into enemy territory, where there was no hope for supporting artillery fire.

Then they were struck in the right rear by the Cruiser Tanks of the 1st R.T.R. Their tactical training had adequately prepared them for such actions. **Panzer-Regiment 5** turned toward the tanks and correctly attempted to pin them down and outflank them. Even though the Panzers weren't outnum-bered, they were getting hit from several directions by small groups of tanks and anti-tank guns. Steadily taking casualties, **Panzer-Regiment 5** gave up and fought their way back out. Only a few of the 17 Panzers that they lost were burned out or damaged beyond repair. But losses due to mechanical failure or disabling/immobilizing hits become permanent losses for the side that is chased off the battlefield.

Oberst Olbrich reports that they were definitely engaged by two Mk.II Infantry Tanks. The mention of just two demonstrates their anxiety in having to deal with these heavily armored tanks. The presence of any Mk.IIA Infantry Tanks in this attack is not confirmed by the records of the 1st R.T.R. or 3rd Armoured Brigade. This may have been the first time that **Panzer-Regiment 5** was mistaken in their belief that they had spotted Mk.II Infantry Tanks, but it wouldn't be their last.

8

Assault on Tobruk

The **Oberkommando des Heeres General Chef des Stabes**, General Halder, concerned about the conduct of the operations in Libya, sent General Pallas to investigate. General Pallas reported:

*When I arrived at the **Deutsches-Afrikakorps** on the evening of 27 April, the commanding general briefed me on his intention to attack Tobruk on 1 May by consolidating all German-Italian forces. Further on the evening of 30 April, after Stuka and artillery preparations, strong assault troops were to break into the foremost defensive positions. He based his decision to attack on the current situation of the **D.A.K.** that wasn't tactically sustainable for the long term. His chief of staff added, that based on the climate, the present positions would not be bearable for the duration.*

*The operations previously conducted against Tobruk were all isolated hand slaps with the objective of breaking through at one position in order to win a quick victory. These operations were unsuccessful. Losses were low with the exception of the attack on 14 April, when after managing to break through, a large part of the **M.G.-Bataillon 8** was surrounded and captured; in the same event 16 out of the 38 Panzers sent in were lost. The commanding general promises a decisive success from this current attack, which for the first time is intended to be conducted according to a fixed plan in which all available German and Italian forces shall be concentrated on a narrow front.*

General Rommel's orders, dated 27 April, for the attack on Tobruk stated as its objectives: *During the night of 30 April and on 1 May, the **Afrikakorps** will conduct a decisive battle for Tobruk by attacking from the west. The first objective for 30 April is to break through the fortification line on both sides of Mdauuar. Then early on 1 May the attack on Tobruk will be continued by concentrating on Giaida-Pilastrino.*

8.1 GERMAN FORCES

Those elements of the **15.Panzer-Division** that had already arrived along with **Gruppe Kirchheim** (one-half of the **5.leichte Division**) were positioned in the center for the attack. The other half of the **5.leichte Division** was positioned on the south side of the Tobruk perimeter with orders to stage diversionary attacks and be in a position to repulse any attempts by the enemy to break out to the south. The reinforced **Aufklaerung-Abteilung 3** was the only German unit left behind near the Egyptian border.

The recent arrivals, seven companies of **Schuetzen-Regiment 115**, two companies from **Schuetzen-Regiment 104** (flown in), two companies of **Pionier-Bataillon 33** (flown in), and the **II.Abteilung/Artillerie-Regiment 33**, made up the main body of the assault force for the **15.Panzer-Division**. **Aufklaerung-Abteilung 33** and four additional companies of **Schuetzen-Regiment 104** arrived at the front on 30 April, followed by three additional companies from **Schuetzen-Regiment 115** on 1 May. These additional infantry units were committed to consolidate the position after the attack, but **Aufklaerung-Abteilung 33** was held in reserve.

Major elements of the **15.Panzer-Division** hadn't arrived yet, including **Panzer-Regiment 8**, one **Bataillon** of **Schuetzen-Regiment 104**, and two **Abteilungen** of **Artillerie-Regiment 33**. The **Stab I.Abteilung** and **1.Kompanie/Panzer-Regiment 8**, which had landed in Tripoli on 24 April, didn't arrive at the front until 9 May.

All of the operational Panzers (minus two sent to the Sollum front on 28 April) were concentrated under **Panzer-Abteilung Hohmann** under **Gruppe Kirchheim**.

Additional details on the organization and strength of the German forces are presented in the order of battle for the attack on 30 April/1 May.

ORGANIZATION FOR THE ATTACK ON TOBRUK
30 APRIL 1941

27o divisione fanteria "Brescia"
- 19o regt. fanteria "Brescia"
- 20o regt. fanteria "Brescia"
- 1o regt. artiglieria celere (9-75/27)
- 16o regt. artiglieria (24-105/28)
- 5a, 71a & 287a btr. c.c. (17-47/32)
- 502o gruppo c.a. (8-20mm)

15. Panzer-Division
- Kradschutzen-Batl.15 (without 2.Kp.)
- I./Schutzen-Regt.115 (without 2.Kp.)
- II./Schutzen-Regt.115 (without two Kp.)
- I./Schutzen-Regt.104 (without two Kp.)
- 1.Kp./Panzer-Regiment 8
- Panzer-Jaeger-Abt.33
- II./Artillerie-Regt.33
- Pionier-Batl.33 (without 3.Kp.)
- One Kp. Pionier-Batl.200
- I.Abt./Flak-Regt.18 (without one s.Battr.)
- Aufklarungs-Abt.33
- XV gruppo 16o regt.art. (12-105/28)

Gruppe Kirchheim
- Regt.Stab 200
- M.G.-Batl.2
- Panzer-Abt. Hohmann
- Panzer-Jaeger-Abt.39
- Panzer-Jaeger-Abt.605
- I./Artillerie-Regt.75 (without1-1/2 Battr.)
- Fla-M.G.Batl.606 (without 2.Kp.)
- I.Abt./Flak-Regt.33 (without one s.Battr.)
- 2o regt. artiglieria (12-100/17, 16-75/27)
- I gruppo 46o regt. artiglieria (12 100-17)

132o divisione corazzato "Ariete"
- VII btg. carri M
- btg. carri L
- XII btg. bersaglieri autoportato
- 132o regt. artiglieria (16-75/27)
- I gruppo 24o regt. artiglieria (12-105)
- Colonna mista Santamaria

5. leichte Division
- remainder of M.G.-Batl.8
- Panzer-Abt. Bollbrinker
- one Battr. Artillerie-Regt.75
- rest of Panzer-Jaeger-Abt.605
- one Zug Fla-M.G.Batl.606
- one le.Battr. I./Flak-Regt.33

102o div. fant. motorizzata "Trento"
- I btg. 61o regt. fant. mot. "Sicilia"
- II btg. 61o regt. fant. mot. "Sicilia"
- 7o regt. bersaglieri
- DLI btg. mitragliere divisionale
- 46o regt. artiglieria "Trento" (16-75/27)
- 102a, 104a & 106a batteria c.c. (24-47/32)
- 7a batteria c.a. (8-20 mm)

Gruppe Herff (Bardia - Sollum)
- Aufklarungs-Abt.3
  - one s.Battr. & one le.Zug Flak-Regt.33
  - 1/2 Battr. Artillerie-Regt.75
  - two Pz.Kpfw. & one 4.7 cm Pak Sfl.
- II btg. 62o regt. fant. mot. "Sicilia"
  - batteria c.c. & batteria c.a.
- V btg. bers. autoportato Montemurro
  - batteria art., batteria c.c. & sezione c.a.
- II gruppo 24o regt. artiglieria (12-105/28)

8.2 ITALIAN FORCES

The Italian forces available for the assault consisted of "**Brescia**" on the left wing and "**Ariete**" on the right wing along with five artillery battalions providing fire support for the German units. "**Trento**", minus one battalion in Bardia, was positioned on the east side of Tobruk. The reinforced **V battaglione bersaglieri** with three batteries of artillery were also positioned near the Egyptian border.

In the interim the Italians had lost several battalions of infantry during failed attacks and as a result of forays by the Australians. Italian reinforcements for the attack consisted of the **III battaglione** of the **20° reggimento fanteria** for "**Brescia**" and the **7o reggimento bersaglieri** for "**Trento**" on 25 April; the **II** and **III gruppo** of the **46° reggimento artiglieria** on 26 April; one **gruppo** of **16° reggimento artiglieria Dalmonte** on 28 April; the **II battaglione** of the **19° reggimento fanteria** for "**Brescia**" on 29 April, and two additional **gruppi** of **16° reggimento artiglieria Dalmonte** on 30 April to support "**Brescia.**" In addition, companies of infantry guns, mortars, and anti-tank guns that belonged to "**Brescia**" and "**Trento**" had been brought forward during the month.

No record has been found on the operational tank strength in "**Ariete**" during this period. Additional details on the organization and strength of the Italian forces are presented in the order of battle for the attack on 30 April/1 May.

8.3 BRITISH FORCES

On 19 April, D Squadron of the 7th R.T.R. arrived at Tobruk with eight Mk.IIA Infantry Tanks. During the period between 18 and 22 April, the tanks in Tobruk were redistributed. D Squadron of the 7th R.T.R. was outfitted with all 12 Mk.IIA Infantry Tanks. The 1st R.T.R. gave up all of their Mk.VI Light Tanks to the 3rd Hussars. They in turn received 9 Mk.IVA Cruiser Tanks that were used to outfit C Squadron of the 1st R.T.R.

During the night of 29/30 April, an additional six Mk.IIA Infantry Tanks were landed at Tobruk and given to D Squadron of the 7th R.T.R.

Additional details on the organization and strength of the British forces are presented in the order of battle for the Tobruk Fortress on 30 April 1941.

8.4 THE ATTACK BEGINS

The last attempt in 1941 to take Tobruk was organized as a combined arms assault by elements of four divisions on

---

TOBRUK FORTRESS
30 APRIL 1941

9th Australian Division
  20th Australian Infantry Brigade
    2/13th Battalion
    2/15th Battalion
    2/17th Battalion
    20th Austr. AT Co.
  24th Australian Infantry Brigade
    2/28th Battalion
    2/43rd Battalion
    One Company 2/23rd Battalion
    26th Austr. AT Co.
  26th Australian Infantry Brigade
    2/23rd Battalion
    2/24th Battalion
    2/48th Battalion
    26th Austr. AT Co.
  18th Australian Infantry Brigade
    2/9th Battalion
    2/10th Battalion
    2/12th Battalion
    18th Austr. AT Co.
  3rd Armoured Brigade
    1st Bn. Royal Tank Regiment
    B Squadron 3rd Hussars
    D Squadron 7th Bn. Royal Tank Regiment
  C Squadron 1st King's Dragoon Guards
  18th King Edward VII's Own Cavalry
  1st Royal Northumberland Fusiliers MG Bn.
  1st Royal Horse Artillery
  104th Royal Horse Artillery
  107th Royal Horse Artillery
  51st Field Regiment R.A.
  2/3rd Australian Anti-Tank Regiment
  3rd Royal Horse Artillery (two AT Btrys)
  4th Anti-Aircraft Brigade
  2/1st Australian Pioneer Bn.
  2/3rd, 2/4th, 2/7th & 2/13th Field Co. R.E.

Order of Battle of Tobruk Fortress

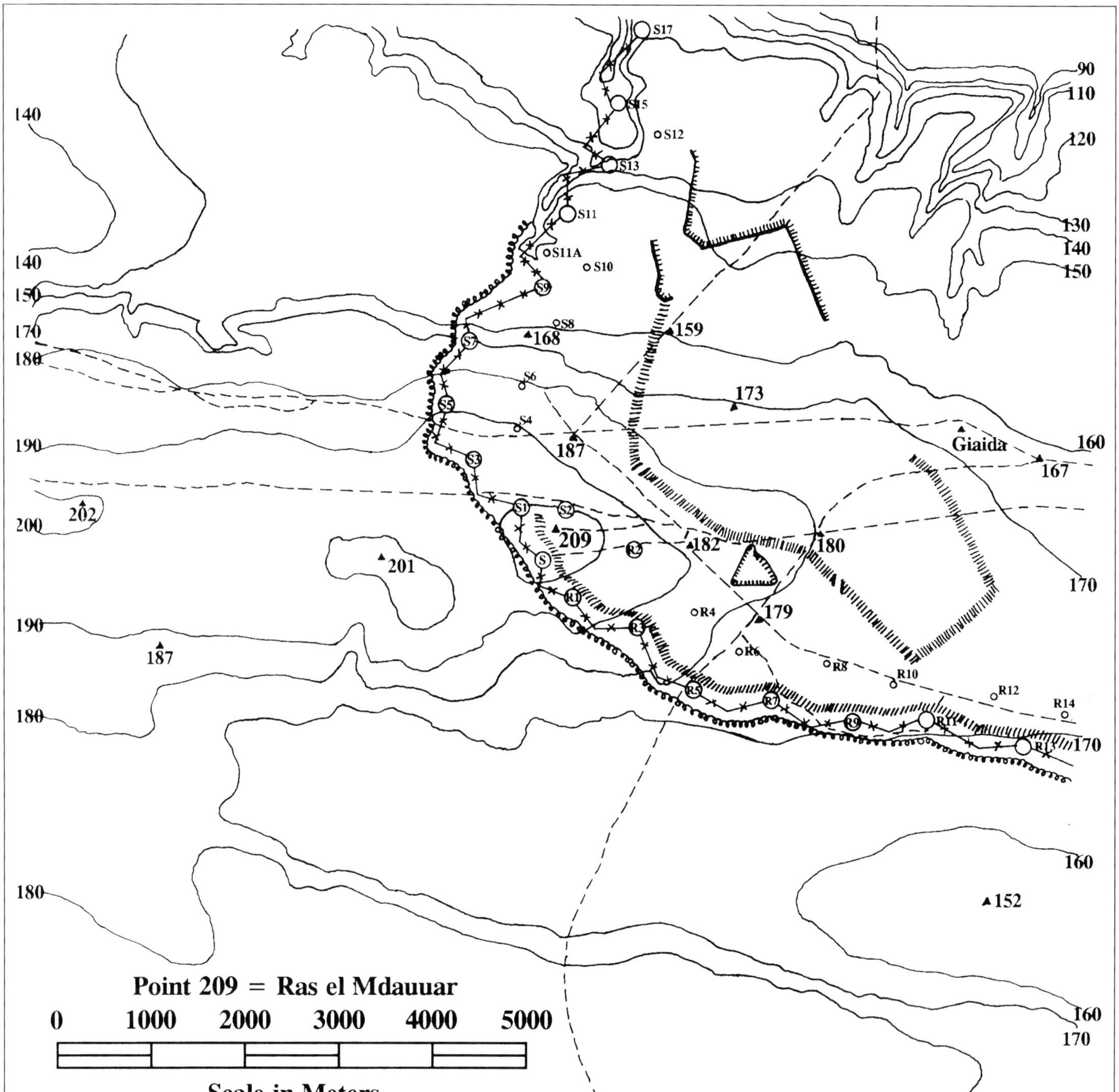

Map of Ras el Mdauuar

the southwest sector by Ras el Mdauuar. Starting on the evening of 30 April and continuing through the night, the German assault troops broke through the perimeter defenses and captured a series of concrete posts. However, exploitation of the breakthrough was halted when the lead Panzers were immobilized in a minefield.

The role played by the Panzers was recorded in the following combat report written by the commander, Major Hohmann, directly after the attack on 2 May 1941:

*Between 1900 and 1915 hours on 30 April 1941, the units from the rest of **Panzer-Regiment 5** attached to the **II.Abteilung** moved to the ordered assembly area southwest and west of Point 187 (8 kilometers east by southeast of Acroma). At 0345 hours, orders were received from the division directing the **Abteilung** to support elements of **Pionier Bataillon z.b.V. 200** and a company from **M.G.-Bataillon 2**.*

*On the way forward, the **Abteilung** passed the division command post and received orders to support the attack of*

120

advanced units of **M.G.-Bataillon 2** and a company from **Pionier-Bataillon z.b.V. 200** on the enemy-occupied Point 209.

Around 0545 hours, the leading platoons of the **Abteilung** passed through the defensive belt at Post R1. Immediately behind this position a post manned by 24 Australians was cleared out by the Panzers. In the course of this operation Obergefreiter Schaefer displayed conspicuous courage by leaping into the fortified position with hand grenades and taking several prisoners.

The **Abteilung** advanced into combat with 81 Panzers, of which 9 were **Pz.Kpfw.I**, 24 **Pz.Kpfw.II**, 36 **Pz.Kpfw.III**, 8 **Pz.Kpfw.IV** and 2 **gr.Pz.Bef.Wg.** The **5.Kompanie** (minus one platoon) commanded by Oberleutnant Sandrock went in with the **Pionier-Bataillon**, advancing along the wire toward the southeast. After the right wing of the company reached Post R5, it advanced against enemy anti-tank positions which were silenced but had succeeded in registering several hits. The detached platoon of the **5.Kompanie** (commanded by Leutnant Marschalk von Bachenbrock) detailed to clear Point 209, advanced in support of the elements of **M.G.-Bataillon 2**, engaged the enemy and took several prisoners. Later this platoon advanced along the left flank of the **Abteilung**.

Meanwhile, the left wing of the **Abteilung** had reached the triangular defense work west of Point 184. Panzers of the **6.Kompanie** which were moving in advance, ran into a minefield. However, there were hardly any losses since the mines were not powerful. Nevertheless, those Panzers which had struck mines were rendered immobile. The **Abteilung** immediately opened fire on enemy troops which were to the front. Some men, anti-tank guns, and vehicles were successfully engaged.

At 0730 hours, advance elements of **M.G.-Bataillon 2** made contact with the **Abteilung** and moved east. At 0830 hours, the **Abteilung** received orders via Oberleutnant von Huelsen to move to the right wing and there come to the aid of **Pionier-Bataillon z.b.V. 200**. The **7.Kompanie** moved between the **Pioniere** working on the wire and the **5.Kompanie** which was engaged with anti-tank guns. As it advanced with the **Pioniere**, it struck an enemy defensive position and succeeded in taking 50 prisoners. At 0945 hours, the advance was halted since the firepower of the **Pioniere** as an infantry unit was insufficient to push on. At the same time, strong, well-directed artillery fire came from the east and made the co-operation between the **Pioniere** and Panzers infinitely more difficult.

Spare track sections were added for extra protection to the superstructure front as well as the hull front of this **Pz.Kpfw.III Ausf.F** (tactical number 625) in the **6.Kompanie/Panzer-Regiment 5**. (BA)

At 1045 hours, **5.Kompanie** was informed of the presence of 10 enemy tanks to their front and immediately advanced to engage them. The distance was too great for the rest of the **Abteilung** to join this skirmish and the **5.Kompanie** turned back after setting an enemy tank on fire.

A reconnaissance was made toward **M.G.-Bataillon 2** in the east and toward the north. A second platoon attached to **M.G.-Bataillon 2** brought news at 1300 hours that the battalion was being engaged by heavy artillery fire. Concentrated fire from the tank guns was ordered. The **Abteilung** drew together and ammunition trucks were brought forward under cover of the sandstorm. At 1510 hours, ammunition replenishment was completed.

At 1545 hours, **5.Kompanie** advanced against enemy tanks. On reaching the position of **M.G.-Bataillon 2**, a message was sent back that 22 enemy tanks had been observed and that these tanks were approaching the position occupied by the battalion on a line running north of Posts R7 and R5. The **Abteilung** commander at once ordered the **7.** and **8.Kompanien** to face east and create a fire front. Soon afterward several enemy tanks were observed moving through the sandstorm toward the right flank of the **Abteilung**. These were fired upon. They swung northward and disappeared, firing as they moved toward the left wing. **8.Kompanie** reported hitting one.

Meanwhile, **5.Kompanie** had perceived that the main body of the enemy tanks was moving off toward the east and that only about 7 to 10 were approaching toward the rest of the **Abteilung**. With the rest of his company, Oberleutnant Sandrock attempted to cut off these enemy tanks' retreat to the east. He succeeded in knocking out four enemy tanks, including three Mk.II Infantry Tanks. Four of his own Panzers were hit. To make sure that he could not be outflanked from the north, three Panzers were sent on reconnaissance, came across more enemy tanks on the **Abteilung**'s left flank, and destroyed two of them.

About 1730 hours, elements from division **Ariete** arrived. The **Abteilung** was to advance with them along the wire and smash the enemy positions from the southeast. At 1800 hours, the **Abteilung** attacked in support of the Italian infantry, which advanced in good time. At Post R8, strong enemy artillery fire was received and it began to get dark at the same time. Enemy tanks again attacked from the left wing. They came under fire from the **7.Kompanie** and retired after one had been hit.

At 1900 hours, **5.Kompanie** reported that two companies of enemy infantry were advancing toward the bridgehead. At 1915 hours, the **Abteilung** accompanied by elements of Italian infantry advanced toward this sector to await the enemy attack. Upon arrival, a report was received from a pla-

Another **Pz.Kpfw.III Ausf.F** or **G** (tactical number 612) of the **6.Kompanie/Panzer-Regiment 5** out on patrol. It also has spare track sections mounted across both the superstructure and hull front. Practically the entire **6.Kompanie** were immobilized in a minefield when they charged out of the Ras el Mdauuar salient. (TTM)

toon that had been sent on reconnaissance, that the enemy was retiring.

*At nightfall, the **Abteilung** leaguered in the area of Posts R5, R6, and R3. Further supplies of ammunition and food were called up by radio. At 2045 hours and 2215 hours, the **Abteilung** received orders from the division to occupy a position southwest of Point 201 and there to stand guard over the division command post. At 0200 hours on 2 May 1941, this position was reached. At 0230 hours, maintenance vehicles arrived at the **Abteilung**.*

*After the battle 35 Panzers were still ready for action, among them 3 **Pz.Kpfw.I**, 12 **Pz.Kpfw.II**, 12 **Pz.Kpfw.III**, 6 **Pz.Kpfw.IV** and 2 **gr.Pz.Bef.Wg.** Twelve of the damaged Panzers had fallen victim to shells and mines. Losses consisted of 1 man missing and 2 officers and 12 other ranks wounded.*

As the Germans had learned to do in Spain, the nozzle of a backpack flamethrower was clamped into the mount for the right-hand machinegun in this **Pz.Kpfw.I Ausf.A** (tactical number R15). These were employed to help clear stubborn occupants out of the bunkers at Tobruk. (TTM)

Addition details on the employment of the **6.Kompanie/Panzer-Regiment 5** were recorded in the following excerpts from the diary of Leutnant Joachim Schorm:

*1 May 1941 - We intend to take Tobruk. My fourth attack on the town. Up at 0330 hours, leave at 0430 hours. We lose touch in the darkness and dust - and join up again. We file through the gap where many of our comrades have already fallen. Then we deploy at once - **6.Kompanie** on the left, **5.Kompanie** on the right. Behind **Stab**, **8.Kompanie** and **7.Kompanie**. The **Regiment** is now Hohmann's and consists of the **5.Kompanie** (previous **1.** and **2.**), **6.Kompanie** (**5.** and **6.**), **7.Kompanie** (the remainder), **8.Kompanie** (**4.** and **8.**), altogether about 80 Panzers.*

*The British artillery fires on us at once. We attack. No German patrol goes out in front to reconnoiter. Tier upon tier of guns boom out from the triangular fortification before us. The two light platoons of the company and my left section are to make a flanking movement. I attack. Radio message: "Commander of **6.Kompanie** hit on track." Then things happen suddenly. A frightful crash in front and to the right. Artillery shell hit? No? It must be a mine. Immediately send radio message: "Commander Schorm on a mine, try to turn round in your own tracks." Five meters back. New explosion - mine underneath to the left. Now it's all up with driving. Radio message: "On getting back, went on mine again. Now mounting Panzer 623." Back through the artillery fire for 100 meters. Got in. Radio order: "Panzers to pull back behind ridge." The men of the mined tank are all right. The enemy is attacking with tanks but will be put to flight.*

*Back carefully. Then with the last tank of the company and Leutnant Roskoll, I provide cover to the north. Nine **Pz.Kpfw.III** and three **Pz.Kpfw.II** in the **6.Kompanie** have had to abandon the fight owing to mines. In my platoon, the*

commander's and both of the section leaders' Panzers. Of course, the enemy went on shooting at us for some time.

*A slight change of position; forward - right - backward - left! With the commander's approval, I am to go with Leutnant Dim up in front to salvage Panzers. While we are on the way, we are fired at by machine guns and anti-tank guns at 550-meter range. I silence them with high explosive shells and drive on the tracks of Panzer 624. I bring up the rear. Then the laborious work of salvaging begins. The anti-tank fire starts up again and has to be kept in check by Leutnant Dim by constant machine gun fire. Leutnant Dim runs onto a mine and damages a track. At last, I move off slowly with Panzer 624 in tow, through the gap, and a further 800 meters. 250,000 Marks are saved! The crew is really delighted to have its tank back. Further back to the **Abteilung**. It is now late afternoon.*

Dive-bombers and twin-engine fighters have been attacking the enemy constantly. In spite of this, the British repeatedly counterthrust with tanks. As soon as the planes are gone, the artillery starts up furiously. It is beginning to grow dark. Which is friend, which is foe? Shots are being fired all over the place, often on one's own troops and on Panzers in front which are on their way back.

Suddenly – a radio message! The British are attacking the gap with infantry. It is actually true. Two companies get off their motor lorries and form a skirmishing line. All sorts of light signals go up - green, red, white. The flares hiss down near our machine guns. It is already too dark to take aim. Well, the opponent's attack is a failure.

The little Fiat-Ansaldo tanks with flamethrowers go up in front in order to clean out the triangle. Long streaks of flame from Masul oil, thick smoke, filthy stink! We cover until 2345 hours - then retire through the gap. It is a mad drive through the dust. At 0300 hours, had a snack beside the Panzer.

Twenty-four hours shut up in the tank – with frightful cramps as a result and a thirst!

The operational Cruiser and Infantry Tanks in the 3rd Armoured Brigade were organized and assigned the following code names:

STAN - HQ 1st R.T.R. 3 Mk.I and Mk.IIA Cruiser Tanks
PUDO - B Sqdn 1st R.T.R. 5 Mk.I and Mk.IIA Cruiser Tanks
DOAN - C Sqdn 1st R.T.R. 9 Mk.IVA Cruiser Tanks
DYNE 1 - 1/2 D Sqdn 7th R.T.R. 9 Mk.IIA Infantry Tanks
DYNE 2 - 1/2 D Sqdn 7th R.T.R. 9 Mk.IIA Infantry Tanks

Details on the success of their counterattacks were recorded in the following after-action report for 1 May 1941:

"At 0745 hours, DYNE 1 with two Troops from 3rd Hussars in area 403429. PUDO in area 404428. Rest in normal location.

"DYNE 1 was ordered to move two miles west and be prepared to engage enemy tanks reported at 399430. But the enemy halted when engaged by artillery and were later reported at 398430. DYNE 1 was therefore ordered to return to its original position at 403429 while the Troops from 3rd Hussars attached to DYNE 1 were pushed out, one to the west and one southwest to Post R13.

"At 0820 hours, four enemy tanks were reported at 402425 (south of Post R13), and later at 0826 hours, the number increased to 20 at 402427, that is to say in the immediate vicinity of Posts R13 and R15. Reports probably false and they weren't reported by the Light Tank patrol in this area. Possible explanation is that a party of enemy tanks about 20 in number moved east past Post R13, made a small demonstration in area of El Adem road, withdrawing at 0900. However PUDO was ordered to engage and DYNE 1 ordered to prepare to support him.

"At 0847 hours, information received that 60 enemy tanks in Ras el Medauer preparing to advance, and that there were more enemy tanks in rear. DOAN was ordered to engage

Nickname "Amy" reveals this Mk.IVA Cruiser Tank as one belonging to the 1st R.T.R. in Tobruk. It has the desert rat emblem associated with the 7th Armoured Division stenciled on the hull front, even though while at Tobruk the 1st R.T.R. was not under the command of that division. (AWM)

them. This report, however, was found to be incorrect and DOAN halted 2000 yards south of Pilastrino.

"At about 0930 hours, about 25 (mainly light, 4 or 5 medium) tanks were observed southeast within the perimeter at Post R14. These were observed by PUDO who saw Very lights being sent up from their commander's vehicle. At 0947 hours, PUDO was moved to area 403428. These enemy tanks continued to maneuver in the area for a considerable time. They were continuously shelled by artillery which appeared to confuse them. At 1014 hours, they were reported at attacking Posts R13 and R14, but according to PUDO, were north of this area. However, PUDO was ordered to engage them and, moving a little northwest, he was able to shoot at them from a hull-down position at a range of 800 to 1000 yards. Having carried out a satisfactory shoot without loss, PUDO withdrew behind the ridge to a position of observation. It is not known what damage was inflicted on the enemy, for they covered themselves with smoke. But the enemy tanks remained in their positions which our artillery continued to harass, rendering observation of their movement extremely difficult.

"At 1058 hours, DOAN was ordered to intervene in the action and the Squadron was told to advance, fire 10 rounds rapid and withdraw again, while PUDO would re-engage in support. Arrangements were made for the artillery fire to cease while our tanks engaged.

"This engagement took place at 1135 hours. DOAN engaging from the east and PUDO from the north and northwest at ranges of 700 to 800 yards. Our tanks were met with heavy fire from the enemy tanks and enemy artillery. Again it was difficult to observe results for the enemy again covered his tanks with smoke, and visibility was bad owing to dust. However, two enemy light tanks and one medium were observed to be on fire. When our tanks were on the point of disengaging, the Cruiser Tank of the commanding officer of PUDO was hit by a thermite shell and took fire, later burning out completely. One other Cruiser Tank of Pudo was damaged but was able to withdraw. The enemy tanks withdrew to the west. DOAN returned to its position south of Pilastrino while PUDO withdrew to replenish fuel and ammunition.

"At about 1300 hours, the commanding officer of DYNE 1 was summoned to HQ 3rd Armoured Brigade where verbal arrangements were made as to the action during the afternoon.

"This action involved two operations:

1. One Troop of three Infantry Tanks was ordered to cruise around the tactical minefield to the western sector, where the enemy infantry were reported to be disarming and removing our mines. This operation was known as the "small chukkar."

2. Two Troops were to cooperate with an infantry counterattack round the north of the tactical minefield in an effort to pinch out the enemy salient. This operation was known as "large chukkar."

"In fact neither of these two operations took place. The first was ordered but two of the three detailed to carry out the task became mechanical casualties. The second was never ordered owing to a threat of enemy tanks in the southwest where the Infantry Tanks were eventually employed. This threat commenced at 1325 hours when information was received that enemy tanks were massing for an attack on Posts R8 and R9. At 1340 hours, these enemy tanks were reported to be advancing, while at 1457 hours they were reported to be attacking R11 and R12. At this time DYNE 1 had lost 4 Matildas, 3 mechanical and one by dive bombing. Also the Light Tank carrying his forward and rear link radio sets had broken down. A composite force was therefore arranged which included STAN, PUDO (now 3) and DYNE 1 (now 5). STAN was in communication by R/T with HQ 3rd Armoured Brigade and with PUDO but had no R/T communication with the Matildas of DYNE. The intention was that DYNE should advance up the line of perimeter posts, supported by PUDO.

"At 1530 hours, PUDO moved towards the perimeter followed by STAN and DYNE while at 1550 hours DOAN was moved to area 407429 to guard against any enemy advance or outflanking through the minefield.

"At 1614 hours, STAN reported that R11 and R12 had been visited. Both were occupied by our own troops and neither had been attacked.

"Orders were then given to continue the advance up to the line R5 and R6. Each post was to be visited in turn and reestablished if necessary.

"At 1707 hours, STAN reported that R8 and R9 were in our hands. At this time the tanks were disposed as follows:

PUDO had been left at R14, DYNE was leading advance, STAN was following DYNE.

"STAN decided to leave two Matildas in reserve at R8 and advance to R6 with 3 Matildas leading and his HQ following. Post R6 was reached and found to be in our hands. Four German light tanks were visible in the perimeter wire at R5 while one German medium tank was visible at R4. The occupants of R6 said that these tanks had been in this position for a long time and had been knocked out. This was in fact far from being the case. A staff car was seen to drive up to the enemy tanks at R5 and personnel, evidently the tank commanders who had been to a conference, dismounted. They entered the tanks, which immediately started up and drove away northwest.

"The Adjutant (rear link for STAN) at the same time advanced towards the German medium tank in the area of Post R4. He had proceeded a short way when he saw about 14 enemy medium tanks in rear of the tank he had intended to visit. These enemy tanks advanced towards him and opened

The morale of the crew of this Mk.IIA Infantry Tank in the 7th R.T.R. at Tobruk apparently wasn't suffering from the siege, as they are all grinning and one is giving the "thumbs up" sign. The camouflage paint is worn off the glacis, revealing that the crew mounted the tank directly in front of the turret machinegun. (AWM)

At least five Mk.IIA Infantry Tanks of the 7th R.T.R. in Tobruk parked in line. From left to right, the discernible names were GALLANT, GOLIATH, and GOTOIT. (AWM)

fire at about 1000 yards range, as also did the reported "knocked-out" medium tank. The Adjutant withdrew to R6 and advanced to engage the enemy tanks. The Cruiser Tank of the commanding officer of STAN was hit at R6 by one of the first enemy shells and took fire. The crew evacuated and climbed onto the outside of the Adjutant's tank. The remaining two Cruisers of STAN now withdrew to R8 where orders were given to the two Matildas to advance to the assistance of the 3 Matildas engaging the enemy. Before they could advance however, these 3 Matildas returned to R8, one of them badly damaged with all the crew dead except the driver. There was still considerable shelling from enemy tanks advancing from R4.

"The commanding officer of STAN now entered a Matilda.

"A new threat now appeared from the northeast where a further body of enemy tanks estimated at about 14 advanced and engaged our tanks from the flank at a range of 1000 yards. They had not previously been seen owing to bad visibility. A tank from STAN which had halted southeast of R8 was hit by two shells in the engine and had to be evacuated. The Adjutant's tank, the only remaining HQ tank, now withdrew under heavy fire, southeast down the track to R14. It reached R14 safely and joined PUDO. The Adjutant immediately obtained contact with our artillery B.O.O. and asked for fire to be brought down upon the enemy tanks northeast of R8. This fire came down accurately and at once.

"In the meantime, the five Matildas were fighting a rearguard action against heavy odds. They succeeded in stopping the advance of the enemy tanks moving from R4 and attempted to withdraw towards R14 engaged by the enemy tanks on their northern flank. One Matilda was hit south of R8 and took fire. Further south another Matilda was badly damaged in the suspension and became a casualty. A third, evidently intending to move round the southern flank of the enemy tanks, was disabled in the area of R12. The remaining two Matildas reached R14 but on arrival the guns of both were out of action.

"The action now ended.

"It is not known what damage was inflicted upon the enemy; at least one enemy medium tank was observed to be burning, probably much greater damage was caused but the light was now becoming very bad and casualties could not be assessed. Further the commanding officers of three of the Matildas who could have given information were killed. The enemy didn't pursue.

Our casualties were:

2 Matildas destroyed and irrecoverable
1 Matilda damaged, later recovered
1 Cruiser Tank destroyed by fire, irrecoverable
1 Cruiser Tank damaged (recovered on 22 May 1941)."

8.5 TACTICAL ANALYSIS

BRITISH TACTICS

The Cruiser Tank squadrons demonstrated a fair grasp of offensive tactics. They first engaged the Panzers from a hull-down position from an effective range of 800 to 1000 yards. Even some coordination was shown when two Cruiser Tank squadrons were sent in for a simultaneous strike from different directions. But it was a mistake to push only a few Mk.IIA Infantry Tanks forward up the line of perimeter posts. The Cruiser squadron positioned to guard their flank was too far off to intervene when they got into trouble.

Again, the British split their small armored force into many small elements and sent them off on diverse tasks. Where was DYNE 2 all day? The British had still demonstrated that they had absolutely no concept of combined arms tactics. Sending a few troops to escort an infantry attack and calling in an artillery strike after getting into serious trouble can hardly be considered close cooperation by all arms in tackling an objective.

GERMAN TACTICS

The fact that 12 Panzers were simultaneously disabled by mines shows that after breaking into the clear the **6.Kompanie** was blindly charging forward practically on line. Fortunately for them, British mines were too weak to inflict any damage other than to break tracks and distort suspensions. Once the minefield was spotted, there was no attempt to find or clear gaps in order to continue the attack. Under intense artillery fire, the **Infanterie** and **Pioniere** were tied up with their own problems of dealing with the stubbornly defending Australians.

For the first time mention is made of tactical use of smoke in screening against both anti-tank guns and tank attacks.

All of the rest of the **Panzer-Abteilung** were employed in repulsing the British tank counterattack late in the afternoon. A very good maneuver was demonstrated when two **Panzer-Kompanien** set up a fire front while a third **Panzer-Kompanie** maneuvered onto the flank, where it succeeded in closing in on and knocking out three of the "invincible" Mk.II Infantry Tanks.

9

Operation Brevity

After the attack failed to take Tobruk, in his report on the analysis of the situation to **O.K.H.**, General Pallas concluded:

*The current tactical situation of the **Deutsches Afrikakorps** is difficult. If the opponent on the Sollum-Bardia-Front doesn't attack with strong forces before the last elements of the **15.Panzer-Division** and the reinforcements have arrived, it appears that another attack by these fresh troops with the objectives of Giaida and Pilastrino promises to be successful and will result in the fall of the Tobruk Fortress. . .*

Should the opponent on the Bardia-Sollum-Front attack with strong forces before a decisive battle for Tobruk has occurred, additional forces from the reinforcements would have to be sent to the Bardia-Sollum-Front. If these aren't sufficient, the siege of Tobruk would have to be abandoned and retirement to the Ain el Gazala position would be unavoidable. . . .

Still another difficulty, and at the present time judged to be very serious, is the supply situation both for the German as well as the Italian forces. Swift effectual measures are necessary, if a serious crisis in the African Theater is to be avoided.

Priority for further transports should be given to:

a. Supplies of all types (ammunition, fuel, and rations),

b. Vehicles to transport the supplies,

c. Only after sufficient stockpiles are available, transport further troops with priority on heavy artillery and replacement of anti-tank weapons.

As stated by Oberstleutnant von dem Borne, **Chef des Generalstabes des Deutschen Afrikakorps**, in his appreciation of the situation on 5 May:

At the present time, a continuation of the offensive into Egypt can't be considered, simply because the hottest season of the year will soon begin. Besides, the necessary forces are not available and there is a total lack of supplies.

Through their stubborn defense at Tobruk, the British had gained the initiative. Urged into action by political pressure, the British struck back on the border. Scratching together whatever mobile forces were available, they launched an attack code named "Operation Brevity" on 15 May 1941. Their first objective was to regain control of the border area, the second to relieve the Tobruk Fortress.

9.1 GERMAN-ITALIAN FORCES ON THE BORDER

When Rommel concentrated his forces for the attack on Tobruk he left the following German units behind at the border as **Gruppe Herff**: **Aufklaerung-Abteilung 3** with the **2.Kompanie/Kradschuetzen-Bataillon 15** supported by an **8.8 cm Flak Batterie**, a **2 cm Flak Zug**, two **10.5 cm leFH** howitzers, a **Pz.Kpfw.II**, a **Pz.Kpfw.III**, and a **4.7 cm Pak Sfl.**

The Italian units that Rommel had left to guard the border were the **V battaglione bersagliere autoportato** (Montemurro) with two companies, a **batteria cannoni 75/27**, **batteria c.c. 47/32**, and a **sezione c.a. 2 cm** along with the **II gruppo 24° reggimento artiglieria** (Frongia) with 12 **105/28 cannoni**. The **II battaglione 62° reggimento fanterie** (minus one company) with a **batteria c.c. 47/32** and a **batteria c.a. 2 cm**, was the only unit manning the defenses around Bardia.

On 7 May, the **Korps** ordered **Aufklaerung-Abteilung 33** to be assigned to **Gruppe Herff**. They had until 8 May to move to Bardia. In reaction to the increased activity of enemy harassing patrols on 8 and 9 May, **Gruppe Herff** was reinforced by another battalion from **"Trento"** during the night of 8/9 May. In addition, on 9 May, **Panzer-Abteilung Hohmann** and **Kradschuetzen-Bataillon 15** were assigned to **Gruppe Herff** and ordered to the border. They joined up with **Gruppe Herff** during the night of 10/11 May accompanied by a **2 cm Flak Zug**.

Additional reinforcements for the **D.A.K.** had been shipped over. **Regiment Stab, 2., 3.,** and **5.Kompanie/Panzer-Regiment 8** arrived in Tripoli on 2 May followed by the **Stab II.Abteilung, 6.** and **7.Kompanie/Panzer-Regiment 8** on 6 May. The last of **Schuetzen-Regiment 104** arrived in Tripoli on 4 May along with the **6.** and **10.Oasen-Kompanien** on 4 May, and the **2.Oasen-Kompanie** on 6 May. Under cover of a sandstorm the **I./Flak-Regiment 18** successfully recovered three **8.8 cm Flak** and a **schwere Zugmaschine** from directly in front of enemy positions. These had been abandoned during the attack on Tobruk on 14 April.

The **Stab I.Abteilung** and **1.Kompanie/Panzer-Regiment 8** along with the **10.Oasen-Kompanie** arrived in the forward area by Tobruk on 9 May followed by the **2., 3.,** and **5.Kompanie/Panzer-Regiment 8** with the **III.Abteilung/Artillerie-Regiment 33** on 12 May. But, the **Stab II.Abteilung, 6.** and **7.Kompanie/Panzer-Regiment 8** didn't arrive in the forward area until 28 May.

9.2 BRITISH FORCES FOR THE OFFENSIVE

The British could only scrape together two squadrons of Cruiser Tanks and two squadrons of Infantry Tanks to take part in the planned offensive. In addition, there were about 15 Mk.VIB Light Tanks with the 7th Hussars, turned over to D Squadron 3rd Hussars on 10 May, and up to 28 Mk.VIB Light Tanks with the 6th Australian Cavalry Regiment. The tanks that had been shipped in the "Tiger" convoy through the Mediterranean arrived too late to take part.

After the 1st R.T.R. was shipped to Tobruk, the next unit to be issued refurbished Cruiser Tanks was C Squadron 2nd R.T.R. Outfitted with three Mk.I, nine Mk.IIA, and four Mk.IVA Cruiser Tanks, it was loaded on a train on 16 April for the move up to Mersa Matruh and departed on 17 April. Between

---

BRITISH ORDER OF BATTLE ON THE BORDER 14 MAY 1941

22nd Guards Brigade
    4th Bn. Royal Tank Regiment
    2nd Scots Guards
    1st Durham Light Infantry
    3rd Coldstream Guards
    31st Field Regiment R.A.
        HQ Anti-Tank Battery
        6th Australian Anti-Tank Battery
        260th Anti-Tank Battery
        One Section 12th Field Company R.E.

7th Armoured Brigade Group
    2nd Bn. Royal Tank Regiment
    6th Australian Division Cavalry
    Prince Albert Victors Own Cavalry
        One Squadron 2nd Royal Lancers
        259th Anti-Tank Battery

7th Support Group
    D Squadron 3rd Hussars
    11th Hussars
        A Squadron Royals
    1st Kings Royal Rifle Corps
    2nd Bn. Rifle Brigade
    8th Field Regiment R.A.
        5th Battery 2nd Australian AT Regt.
        12th Battery 3rd Australian AT Regt.
        D Battery 3rd Royal Horse Artillery
        37th Light AA Battery R.A.
        38th Light AA Battery R.A.

FOOTNOTE: The British used the following "XYZ" system for reporting vehicle casualties as follows:

"X": A casualty which is due to a temporary stoppage only, and which can be repaired by the crew of the vehicle with its equipment without outside assistance; for example, a vehicle out of action due to a puncture or a tank with a broken track pin.

"Y": A casualty which requires assistance from technical personnel but is likely to be repairable in first echelon (by unit or L.A.D.), or in second echelon (by R.E.M.E. units), provided the general situation does not alter between the time of reporting and the time of recovery of the casualty.

"Z": A casualty which is beyond the capacity of first or second echelons because it requires more repair than can be carried out in those echelons or because the necessary repair cannot be carried out on account of difficulty in reaching the casualty, lack or time or other causes.

27 April and 3 May, three Mk.I and ten Mk.IIA Cruiser Tanks were issued to A Squadron and four Mk.IVA Cruiser Tanks HQ 2nd R.T.R. Loaded on a train, they left Sidi Bishr early on 4 May and rejoined C Squadron early in the afternoon on 6 May. Having been issued another Mk.I and two Mk.IIA Cruiser Tanks for A Squadron on 5 May, their total strength was reported as 30 fit, 1 X, 4 Y, and 1 Z (Mk.IIA) on 6 May.

The transport ships carrying the 4th R.T.R. with 34 Mk.IIA Infantry Tanks and 6 Mk.VIC Light Tanks were unloaded at Suez on 23 to 25 April. B Squadron 4th R.T.R., which had been fighting in East Africa, departed Massawa for Egypt on 25 April. They had taken 16 Infantry Tanks Mk.IIA* and 1 Light Tank with them to Eritrea. On 4 May 1941, their tanks arrived back at Alexandria and were taken into the RAOC Workshops in Wardian for a complete overhaul.

The 4th R.T.R. with 33 Infantry Tanks and 6 Light Tanks was loaded on tank trains which left at 1800 hours on 28 April. The tanks arrived at Maaten Bagush on 1 May, less two from a train accident. They had moved forward to Bir Scheferzen by 7 May. On the afternoon of 8 May, the 4th R.T.R. started the 100 mile march from Sheik's Tomb to Sofafi with only those tanks they thought would make it. Tank state on 8 May:

Bn HQ	2 Matilda	2 Light Tanks
A Squadron	13 Matilda	1 Light Tank
C Squadron	13 Matilda	1 Light Tank

The 4th R.T.R. arrived at Sofafi at 1600 hours on 11 May 1941. During the march two Matildas were dropped from A Squadron and one more Light Tank joined Battalion Headquarters.

Additional details on the organization and strength of the British forces are presented in the order of battle for Operation Brevity dated 14 May 1941.

9.3 PRELIMINARY MOVES

<u>DAK KTB 9 May 1941</u> - *Weather, maximum temperature 31° (88°F)*

An enemy radio message was intercepted which was directing a weather report to all their units. In the past, such reports had always been issued prior to the important enemy offensives to capture Sidi Barrani, Bardia, Tobruk, and the Gebel.

A **leichte Zug** with two **Pz.Kpfw.II**s and three **Pz.Kpfw.I**s from **Panzer-Regiment 5** on the move on 5 May 1941. A stiff breeze from the side is helping clear away the clouds of dust stirred up by each Panzer as they move cross country. On 9 May, the **II.Abteilung/Panzer-Regiment 5** was transferred to the Egyptian border. (BA)

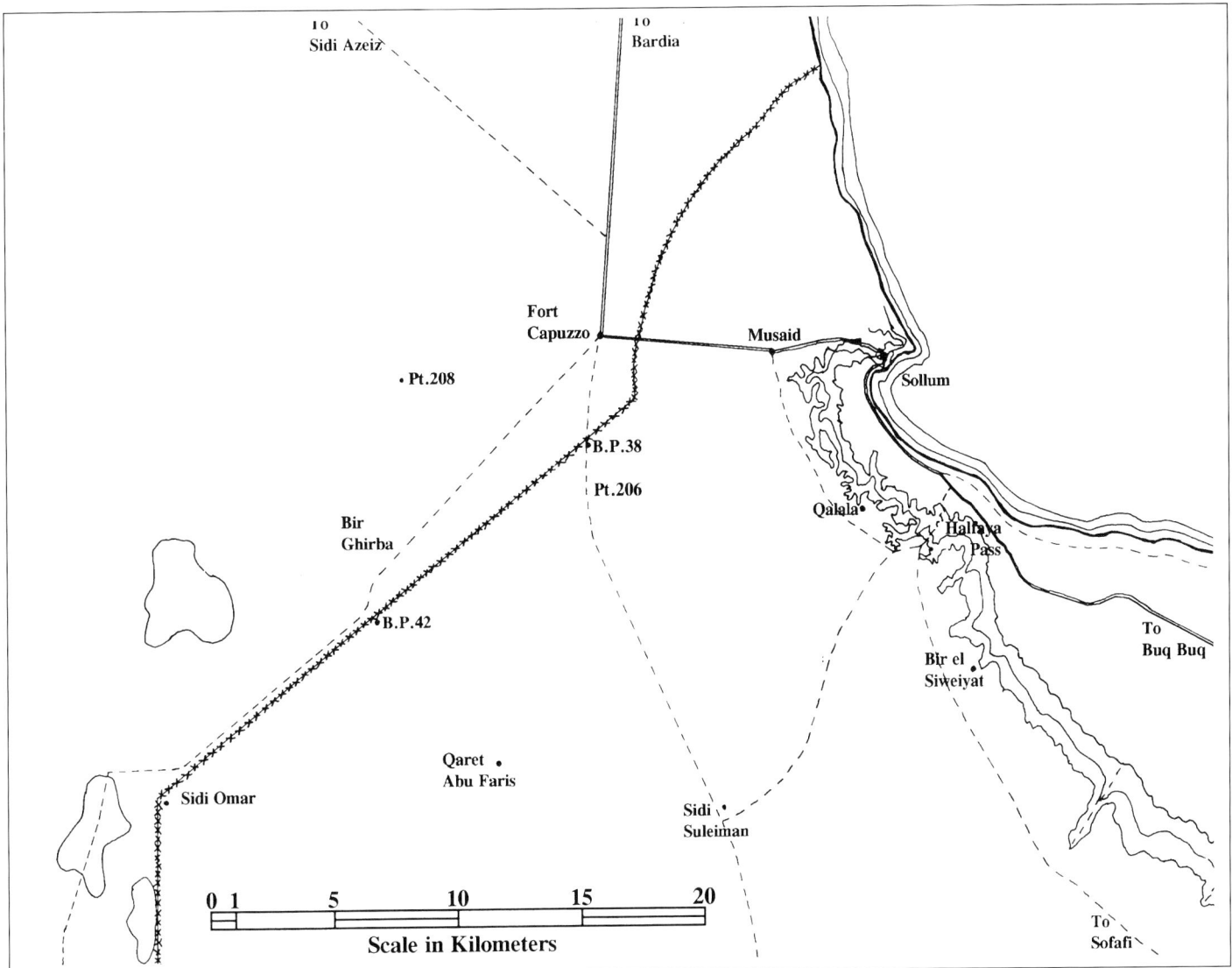

Map of Border Area

DAK KTB 10 May 1941 - *Weather, maximum temperature 27° (81°F)*

The operations order for 10 May reconfirmed the instructions to **Gruppe Herff**: *Offensively repulse the enemy to defend the area encompassed by Sidi Omar, Sollum and Bardia and aggressively reconnoitre the line Maddalena to Sidi Barrani until contact is made with the enemy.*

On 10 May, D Squadron 3rd Hussars took over the Mk.VIB Light Tanks from the 7th Hussars, who returned to Egypt. The 2nd R.T.R. moved forward to Gott el Rimeil (675323) and sent a Mk.IIA to Brigade HQ.

DAK KTB 11 May 1941 - *Weather, maximum temperature 23° (73°F)*

On the Sollum front, lively reconnaissance activity by both sides during the day. The area 50 kilometers south of Sidi Omar was reported to be free of enemy forces at 1500 hours.

Gruppe Herff *planned to start a strike against El Hamra with a southern envelopment at 2300 hours. Luftwaffe support for this attempt was not possible to the extent requested because of fuel shortages and the* **Fliegerfuehrer**'s *main objectives were targets at sea.*

The 4th R.T.R. arrived at Sofafi at 1600 hours on 11 May 1941 with 26 Mk.IIA Infantry Tanks and 5 Mk.VIC Light Tanks. The 2nd R.T.R. moved to Alam Melba (630324) arriving at 1130 hours. The Mk.IIA sent to Brigade was unfit, evacuated and replaced by another Mk.IIA from the 2nd R.T.R. An additional Mk.IIA arrived from Mersa Matruh for the 2nd R.T.R., which reported their tank status as 28 fit, 0 X, 2 Y, and 4 Z (1 Mk.I, 2 Mk.IIA, 1 Mk.IVA).

DAK KTB 12 May 1941 - *Weather, maximum temperature 24° (75°F)*

Gruppe Herff's advance started off from Capuzzo in three groups:

Panzer-Spaehgruppe Wechmar (Aufklaerung-Abteilung 3) through Sidi Omar and T.N.63 (25 kilometers north of Maddalena) to Point 213 south of Der el Hamra = 120 kilometers.

Kradschuetzen-Gruppe Knabe (Kradschuetzen-Bataillon 15) through Gasr el Abid to Point 210 south of Der el Hamra (80 kilometers).

Panzer-Gruppe Hohmann (II.Abteilung-Panzer-Regiment 5) through Suleiman toward Point 214 (10 kilometers northeast of Der el Hamra) = 60 kilometers.

The area was thoroughly combed and cleared of the enemy from south to north. Because of their great mobility and speed, the British succeeded in pulling back the mass of their troops, (probably in the direction of Sidi Barrani) before a crisis developed.

An intercepted message revealed the full surprise and confusion of the opponent. The enemy had first spotted **Gruppe Knabe** past Gasr el Abid and **Gruppe Wechmar** shortly before Der el Hamra.

A special strike was conducted by **Verband Van Nees** on the coastal plain. With their right flank on the escarpment at Minguar el Araquid, they advanced and eliminated all enemy elements northwest of Bir Baltuma-El Seyada. After a determined fight, the enemy also retired from here.

Gruppe Herff reported the following results of the fight: One officer and three men, two 25-pounders with caissons and ammunition, one Light Tank with crew and weapons were captured. One armored car, two 25-pounders with ammunition caissons, two self-propelled anti-tank guns, and several vehicles were destroyed and two Hurricanes were downed by ground fire.

At 1100 hours on 12 May, the commander of Jock Force arrived and the 4th Bn. R.T.R. came under their command as a German column was reported to be approaching rapidly. A Squadron moved to Rabia to cover the dump. Bn.H.Q. and C Squadron remained at Safafi with a Troop standing by for counterattack, remaining standing to. B Echelon moved to Bir el l'inaba. Enemy withdrew toward evening and H.Q. and C Squadron moved to Safafi East at 2000 hours. A Squadron remained at Rabia. All tanks were maintained on 13 May.

DAK KTB 13 May 1941 - Weather, maximum temperature 22° (72°F)

Gruppe Herff expects an enemy attack supported by their navy at dawn on 14 May.

Armed reconnaissance aircraft bombed a concentration of 40 to 50 tanks in the area north of El Hamra.

DAK KTB 14 May 1941 - Weather, maximum temperature 20° (68°F)

The entire day was quiet on the Sollum front. Aerial reconnaissance could not confirm the suspected changes in the enemy positions. Further enemy intentions to attack were not known.

A **Panzer-Spaehtrupp** from **Gruppe Herff** captured two mobile trucks and an anti-tank rifle near Gasr el Abid.

9.4 THE ATTACK BEGINS

DAK KTB 15 May 1941 - At 0550 hours, the enemy attacked with strong tank forces, surprising the positions of **Gruppe Herff** near Halfaya Pass. Facing 50 enemy tanks, the advanced security posts by Sidi Suleiman retired to Point 206.

At 0630 hours, enemy tanks, including heavy Mk.II Tanks against which our Pak and Flak were ineffective, followed by light tanks and one or two battalions of mounted infantry and artillery penetrated into the defensive position near Halfaya. The Italian company on the coastal plain held against reported enemy strikes with tanks.

At 0845 hours, **Gruppe Herff** reported to the **D.A.K.**: There are at least 100 enemy tanks between Capuzzo and Sollum, of which 10 are definitely Mk.II. **Panzer-Abteilung Hohmann** has been sent to counterattack.

At 0900 hours, a new report that Point 206, Sollum and Point 208 were lost. The probable enemy intention is to destroy our forces at Sollum and advance further to relieve Tobruk.

The following messages were recorded by the **Afrikakorps**:

1. Orders to the **15.Panzer-Division**: As the **Korps-Reserve, I.Abteilung/Panzer-Regiment 8** is to advance to Ed Duda, 15 kilometers east of El Adem. Take up positions there facing north and northeast. **Flak** will be sent.

2. Orders to **Flakgruppe Heckt**: Set one **8.8 cm Batterie** and one **2 cm Batterie** on the march to Ed Duda. Purpose: To hinder a breakout attempt from Tobruk and shield the besieging front toward the east against possible enemy tank attacks.

3. Orders to **VIII battaglione carri M "Rizzi"**: Immediately move off to El Adem and set up security to the south and southeast.

4. Request to **Fliegerfuehrer Afrika**: Send in the entire fighting force. Target area Sollum-Capuzzo road and Sollum itself.

5. Order to **"Trento"**: Pull in the battalion out of Gambut so that the division area can also be defended toward the east.

6. Radio message sent to **X.Fliegerkorps**, **Luftwaffe 4** and **O.K.H.**: Very strong attack with infantry and tanks made against Sollum-Capuzzo since 0800 hours. Request strongest support possible from the Luftwaffe against the enemy east to Sollum to Mersa Matruh and sea targets in the area by Sollum.

At 1050 hours, **Gruppe Herff** reported: Our forward line is directly north of Capuzzo and on both sides of the road 2 kilometers to the northeast. Montemurro is hemmed in on the border fence. Our strong flank security, **Abteilung Hohmann**, is 5 kilometers northwest of Capuzzo. Other units in old positions. **Gruppe Herff** plans to hold the line from Sidi Azeiz to Point 164 (7 kilometers southwest of Bardia) with the left flank on the coast.

At 1130 hours, message radioed to **O.K.H.**, **X. Fliegerkorps**, and **Luftflotte 4**: The situation by Sollum-Capuzzo is very critical. At this time, fighting hard, our advance units have retired to Sidi Azeiz to Bardia. **Fliegerfuehrer Afrika** can only provide limited support. Again request strong employment of all available air forces to prevent a serious setback. Because of the supply situation, it is not possible to send strong reserve forces or to counterattack.

The Italian high command was asked to employ all of the Italian air force to support the fight on the Sollum Front.

At 1200 hours, combat aerial reconnaissance and **Fliegerfuehrer Afrika** provided the following picture: Strong enemy groups each with about 50 vehicles are near TN41 and Gabr es Seghir. An artillery dual around Capuzzo. Ten enemy tanks are advancing to the north by Bir Gherbi. In general, our forces are retiring to Azeiz. At 1200 hours, about 100 vehicles were 5 kilometers southeast of Azeiz.

At 1210 hours, from intercepted radio message it was learned that a German unit with machineguns and anti-tank guns still held Halfaya Pass.

At 1235 hours, **Gruppe Herff** was able to extract Montemurro from the border area. They joined **Gruppe Herff** north of Capuzzo.

At 1330 hours, from an intercepted radio message: The German occupants of Halfaya Pass are still holding out. The British reported that mortar support was not functioning. He wanted to attempt to link up with "Upik." Upik reported that the area around Sollum was free of enemy, 500 prisoners had been taken, and they were advancing toward the airfield north of there. Near Capuzzo a British company was overrun by German tanks. The British viewed the situation there as being serious.

At 1445 hours, **Gruppe Herff** reported that Capuzzo was retaken in a counterattack and 70 prisoners were captured. Very many British were killed. They handled themselves like a new battalion that had only arrived recently.

The **Korps** orders for **I.Abteilung/Panzer-Regiment 8** were: With the attached **Flak-Batterie**, advance by the fastest route to Sidi Azeiz and establish strong flank security to the south as necessary. The **Abteilung** is to be attached to **Gruppe Herff**, on their right flank at Sidi Azeiz, for the purpose of attacking.

At 1535 hours, a radio message sent to **O.K.H.**: At 1400 hours, Capuzzo was retaken by a counterattack and 70 British captured. The British took strong losses, also in tanks. At the present, the British renewed their attack on Capuzzo from the southwest. Another **Panzer-Abteilung** with Flak is marching to Capuzzo. Halfaya Pass is still being held by a reinforced German company. The plan for 16 May is to counterattack to restore the situation. Tobruk is quiet, up to now. Request that an Italian fortress division be sent as soon as possible to free the mobile German forces and thereby similar crises at Bardia would be eliminated early.

At 1735 hours, **Gruppe Herff** reported that in the face of strong enemy attack they were pulling back on the line from Sidi Azeiz to Via Balbia to 5 kilometers southwest of the Bardia coast. The units in Capuzzo have enemy forces only to the west.

At 1740 hours, from an intercepted radio message: One British battalion should dismount and occupy Halfaya Pass.

At 1800 hours, **I.Abteilung/Panzer-Regiment 8** was rolling through El Adem.

Combat aerial reconnaissance reported: Three groups, a total of 400 vehicles, are halted near Der el Hamra. Soldiers are digging in. Sollum is strongly occupied by the enemy, about 40 tanks known. Four British armored cars at Bir Gabr Hameida, 20 kilometers west of Bardia. Our troops have established two leaguers at Bir Gabr dei Fares. About 150 British vehicles are to their south.

At 1830 hours, **Gruppe Herff** reported:

1. The impression stands that the enemy is concentrating his entire tank strength near Sidi Azeiz in order to advance in the morning to relieve Tobruk. The **Aufklaerung-Abteilung** has fought hard around Sidi Azeiz. The rest of **Abteilung Hohmann** (12 Panzers) is located there also.

2. The situation is judged as very serious. After Halfaya Pass fell, long enemy columns (150 vehicles) are freed from the coastal plain.

3. It is at least dubious if we can hold tomorrow with the reinforcements that are being sent.

At 1930 hours, **I.Abteilung/Panzer-Regiment 8** was ordered: At 1800 hours, our troops were in combat with enemy reconnaissance forces with tanks; attack there as soon as possible.

At 2000 hours, radio message sent to **Luftflotte 4**, **X. Fliegerkorps** and **O.K.H.**: Bardia-Capuzzo-Sidi Azeiz are in our hands. Several of our groups are south and southeast of

*Sollum. Strong enemy forces in Sollum. Enemy groups in Der el Hamra-escarpment, 60 kilometers southeast of Sollum. Request attacks on 16 May be made on sea targets and against traffic east of Sollum to Sidi Barrani, and on concentrations south of there, especially in Der el Hamra. Our intention is to counterattack in the direction of Sollum on 16 May. **Fliegerfuehrer** is attacking Sollum at night. During the day, they will be utilized for supporting the counterattack against ground targets.*

*At 2200 hours, **Gruppe Herff** reported that the enemy now has strong groups of 40 to 50 tanks and at least two batteries of artillery near Azeiz. Our attack with **Panzerspaeh-Kompanie** and **Abteilung Hohmann** was repulsed.*

*With a strong western flank, the enemy will again attack, at dawn at the latest. **Gruppe Herff** bound together in small groups would probably be penetrated and the mass of the enemy would strike through in the direction of Tobruk.*

Enemy strength is two divisions.

*To hinder a penetration and to conduct a forceful attack after uniting with the new reinforcements, at 2300 hours **Gruppe Herff** will began retiring to the north to Point 211 about 10 kilometers west of Azeiz.*

The line 5 kilometers south of Bardia to the coast would still be held.

Personnel losses are estimated to be one company. Material losses are heavy.

Italian troops are positioned 9 kilometers west of Bardia in the Carmuset Scegheila area.

*The plan of attack hangs on the state of **Gruppe Herff** and the arrival of reinforcements.*

*At 2230 hours, orders were sent to **Gruppe Herff**: From available reports, the enemy forces have been greatly overestimated. In general, agree with the proposed actions. In all cases, attack early through Sidi Azeiz to the south. The entire situation at Tobruk hangs on this attack.*

*From radio intercepts by the **D.A.K.**, the enemy attack was made by about five battalions, two light and one heavy artillery battalions, one armored car battalion, and one tank battalion with very many Mk.II Tanks.*

*At 2245 hours, orders to **I.Abteilung/Panzer-Regiment 8**: Beginning at 2300 hours, **Gruppe Herff** will relocate to an area 10 kilometers west of Azeiz in order to attack through Azeiz early tomorrow. Request that the advance be accelerated in order to be at the position by dawn at the latest.*

*At 2325 hours, **Gruppe Herff** reported: The reinforcements were informed to advance only to Point 221 Hariga (15 kilometers west of Azeiz). There were enemy Mk.II Tanks in Sidi Azeiz. **Gruppe Herff** advances over the Via Balbia from the north.*

The unit responsible for creating such a stir was the 4th R.T.R. with their 26 operational Mk.IIA Infantry Tanks. The record of their actions on 15 May, extracted from their war diary, is fairly sketchy as follows:

4th Bn. R.T.R. moved off at 1800 on 14 May for a night march of 32 miles to reach its lying up area for the attack next morning.

They reached Alam Batuma, the lying up area, at 0345 on 15 May. Wireless silence had to be observed until 0530 hours when netting was carried out; this had partially to be completed on the move, and as the control sets had been netted by wave meter was not very successful.

The 4th Bn. R.T.R. moved off at 0545 with C Squadron on the right and A Squadron on the left, Bn.H.Q. in the center. C Squadron advanced on the first objective Halfaya Pass. Quite heavy opposition was encountered; after a brisk action the area was made good by 0730 and the Infantry came on. Signal given to the Scots Guards who took over the area with tank support. About 500 prisoners were taken, a quantity of M.T. and a battery of six pounder guns. C Squadron had 7 tanks immobilized by enemy action but no personnel casualties.

The remainder, after a pause for the Infantry to consolidate, moved on to the second objective Musaid which was taken over without opposition.

A Squadron formed a defensive flank while the action took place at Halfaya. As soon as the area had been taken over, the Squadron (nine tanks) followed by H.Q. moved forward to attack Fort Capuzzo. On approaching the wire they were heavily engaged by anti-tank guns and batteries and by about 20 to 30 enemy tanks who were waiting in a "hull down" position behind a ridge. A Squadron suffered five tank casualties almost immediately from accurate fire on the turret and suspension; the remainder continued the advance, whereupon the German tanks retired.

Two of our tanks got through the wire into the Fort; very heavy opposition was encountered, and one became a casualty and had to be abandoned, the other retiring in the face of greatly superior opposition.

The C.O. then collected four tanks and made an attempt to get through the wire from the northeast. The tanks were engaged heavily by batteries from the Fort and were not successful in penetrating the wire. The 4th Bn. R.T.R. rallied forward in the Musaid area and re-filled with ammunition and fuel brought forward by B Echelon. Several calls for counterattacks were received and tanks sent out to deal with them. A troop was sent to assist the Durham Light Infantry in trying to take the aerodrome 6 miles up the Bardia road.

The 4th Bn. R.T.R. rallied in the Musaid area about 1900 hours. Verbal orders from the Brigadier regarding the tank role for the night were "to assist the infantry as much as pos-

Five Mk.II Infantry Tanks with their recognition pennants flying advance in line. Even though moving relatively slowly, they still raised a lot of dust. Some of the dirt picked up by the rear drive is pouring back down the rear "mud chute." (GBJ)

These Mk.IIA Cruiser Tanks belong to C Squadron of the 2nd R.T.R. This was the first Squadron outfitted with Cruiser Tanks that was sent to take on the German forces near the Egyptian border. Mk.IIA Cruiser Tank T9224 managed to survive both Operations Brevity and Battleaxe. This photo was taken in late April 1941 before Operation Brevity. (TTM)

sible" with this end in view and with so few tanks available one troop each was allotted under command to Scots Guards and Durham Light Infantry respectively for the night.

Tank state: 5 disabled.
             14 not fit for fighting, owing to enemy action.
              6 fit for action.

The 2nd R.T.R. had been assigned to screen the open left flank. At 2300 hours on 14 May, the 2nd R.T.R. at Dar el Brug reported their tank status as 29 fit, 0 X, 1 Y, and 0 Z (6 Mk.I, 17 Mk.IIA, and 7 Mk.IVA Cruiser Tanks). The following record of the actions on 15 May was extracted from their war diary:

At 0001 hours, 2nd R.T.R. moved from Dar el Burg to Bir Kireigat. Zero hour for the attack was set at 0530 hours. When they were just moving off at 0630 hours, enemy AFVs were reported 4 miles west of Bir Kireigat moving south. At 0635 hours, the AFVs were reported to have halted.

Sounds of shelling to their front were heard at 0638 hours. It was reported that 6th Australian Division Cavalry were held up on the left and had been driven back a bit by shelling. They were still, however, pushing on on the right. This was in the area of Sidi Suleiman.

At 0710 hours, two guns were reported withdrawing to southwest and the 6th Australian Division Cavalry were reported to be pushing on again and the 2nd R.T.R. was ordered to push on in support. If any minor trouble was met with, the 6th Australian Cavalry were to push round the flank, and if big trouble was met with, the 2nd R.T.R. would deal with it also from the flank.

At 0755 hours, Brigade was ordered to push on as fast as possible, as the column operating on our right had captured their first objective. Twelve enemy AFVs were reported at Cross Tracks 516361. Thirty enemy tanks or armored cars and 20 lighter vehicles were reported at 516366 at 0816 hours.

A Squadron, 2nd R.T.R. sent into action against the enemy tanks and reported on the action that took place from 0815 to 1000 hours as follows:

"On 15 May 1941, A Squadron was advancing from BP40 from cross tracks 518355. 6th Australian Division Cavalry (EPIO) was leading BEAM column when they came under fire from 75 mm guns of enemy tanks. A Squadron was ordered by O.C. 2nd R.T.R. to support BEAM.

"On reaching Sidi Suleiman, the Squadron could see a number of German tanks in their line of advance. Most of these retired on the approach of the Squadron, but three be-

THIS PAGE AND OPPOSITE: T15229 was one of the four Mk.IVA Cruiser Tanks issued to C Squadron of the 2nd R.T.R. In demonstrating its speed near Mersa Matruh in late April, it shows the dust cloud that was raised. The commander is communicating with his crew through the large hand-held Tannoy microphone. T15229 made it through Operation Brevity but didn't survive Operation Battleaxe. (TTM)

came detached and were engaged with the result that one German Mark IV was put out of action. The crew escaped with the other two tanks across the wire. Five or six 2-pounder shells hit the German tank, one of which penetrated the thick turret armor. The speed of the enemy AFVs was considerably greater than the Mk.I or Mk.IIA Cruiser Tanks of A Squadron.

"As the two enemy tanks crossed the wire about 15 more enemy tanks were seen approaching from the northwest. These were out of range of the Squadron who had worked south in the previous action to get round the enemy right flank. One tank of No.2 Troop had however broken down; the other two tanks of the Troop engaged these tanks. The result was that one Mk.III German tank was set on fire and destroyed. Hits were seen to be registered on two other tanks but they continued and with the remaining 12 retreated quickly across the wire.

"The accuracy of the enemy tank gunnery throughout this action was only fair.

"At some time during this action, one tank of A Squadron was put out of action by enemy 75 mm gun fire. Damage was caused to the turret and suspension. The turret was not penetrated. The strength of A Squadron at this time was 12 tanks. No casualties to men suffered."

Following this action, the 2nd R.T.R. maintained a watch on the enemy activity at Capuzzo and later in the day sent out a patrol to Sidi Azeiz, as follows:

At 1050 hours, enemy tanks were reported one mile north of 38 Gap. A Squadron were sent to investigate and if possible to engage, but the enemy withdrew too fast.

At 1145 hours, information was received that our forces had captured Capuzzo. Orders were received for one Squadron to watch the Capuzzo area, while HQ and one Squadron were to be in reserve at fork track 508370. C Squadron were sent off in the Capuzzo direction while A Squadron remained in reserve. Although Capuzzo was reported to be in our hands C Squadron kept querying this and reporting suspicious movement in that area at 1235 hours.

At 1415 hours, the Brigade was informed by us that we only had sufficient petrol for another 30 miles. A message from Brigade came in at 1430 hours ordering an escort to be sent to Gap 40 to meet the petrol lorries.

At 1500 hours, a report was received from the Brigade that it was possible that Capuzzo had been recaptured by the enemy. The information was immediately passed on to C Squadron.

At 1530 hours, A Squadron had 9 fit tanks, C Squadron 11 and HQ 4. C Squadron were now in the area 512377 and

were reporting enemy movement to their left rear. Aggressive movement on the part of their Mk.VIA Troop forced the enemy vehicles to withdraw.

At 1630 hours, A Squadron was ordered to carry out a loop patrol across the Trigh Capuzzo near Sidi Azeiz, northwest of Fort Capuzzo and back to the Battalion area.

At 1800 hours a heavy though brief bombing and machine gunning attack occurred. No casualties were caused to the battalion.

At 1900 hours, the following written orders were received from the Brigade: Brigade will withdraw into night dispositions. Withdrawal will be concealed as much as possible by thinning out from forward positions. In any case leaguer areas will NOT be occupied before dark.

The enemy tanks encountered by the 2nd and 4th R.T.R. belonged to the **II.Abteilung/Panzer-Regiment 5**. Details of their counterattack on 15 May with 27 operational Panzers was reported by their commander, Major Hohmann as follows:

The **Panzer-Abteilung** was alerted at 0600 hours. At 0710, the **Panzer-Abteilung** met up with a reconnaissance element several kilometers south of Point 206, then turned east and attacked a group of enemy tanks advancing toward Capuzzo. I sent the message: "British Mark II Tanks are attacking. Request **8.8 cm Flak** to Capuzzo." The engagement with about 16 Mark II Infantry Tanks was obstinately fought. In this action two Mark II Infantry Tanks were observed to be immobilized. (They were later found and blown up on 16 May by Oberleutnant Gruen of **II./Panzer-Regiment 5**). We didn't manage to stop the enemy or to force him to turn away from his objective because of the negligible effect of our weapons. I couldn't implement the tactics that had the best chance of success against the Mark II Tanks, concentrated fire at close range from several 5 cm tank guns, because of the small number of Panzers available. I only saw the risk of being forced to the west and cut off from the main battlefield. By radio message I then ordered: "Turn left, follow commander Meissel." The heavy tank combat made it difficult to break contact. Because of their high speed, the **Stab**, **5.Kompanie** and three Panzers from the **6.Kompanie** reached the border fence south of Capuzzo. The order was not received due to failure of a radio set, resulting in about 14 Panzers of the **6.Kompanie** and **8.Kompanie** turning west. Having lost radio contact with the **Abteilung**, under the command of Hauptmann Mueller, they later moved back to Sidi Azeiz.

At 0825 hours, in the area of the border fence south of Capuzzo, a firefight again occurred between Mark II Infantry Tanks and the 12 Panzers remaining with **Panzer-Abteilung Hohmann**. The Mark II Infantry Tanks pulled back. One Mark II remained stationary behind the border fence. **Panzer-Abteilung Hohmann** slowly moved back toward Capuzzo and encountered truck-borne British infantry, which were forced to take cover by machine gun fire.

At 0840 hours, I reported that Capuzzo had been occupied by the enemy and that the Panzers were out of ammunition. At 0915 hours, left with 10 operational Panzers, I pulled back to resupply with ammunition about 5 to 6 kilometers north of Capuzzo.

At 1030 hours, the reconnaissance post at Sidi Azeiz reported that 12 Panzers had arrived and at 1110 hours reported that the Panzers had left to return to Bardia. This was the **6.** and **8.Kompanie** under Hauptmann Mueller, which didn't return to Bardia but was resupplied with ammunition about 10 to 11 kilometers north of Capuzzo.

At 1130 hours, **Panzer-Abteilung Hohmann** with the operational Panzers was ordered to move to the command post of Montemurro to enable the Italian **Bersagliere Regiment** to break contact with the enemy. The **Panzer-Abteilung** advanced to Montemurro. I drove to the command post and determined the situation. The opponent lay in front of Montemurro at about 300 to 400 meters. The Italian motorcycle infantry and artillery crew were pinned down by heavy fire. The artillery battery was out of ammunition.

I decided to move around to the southeast and to attack east of Capuzzo with an assault group. Under this protection, about 1330 hours, all elements of Montemurro managed to make a clean break away from the enemy. The attack eastward past Capuzzo eliminated numerous British. A major and 16 soldiers were captured by Oberleutnant von Huelsen, leader of the **leichte Zug** of II./Panzer-Regiment 5, who turned over their prisoners at 1432 hours. I reported that the assignment had been completed and retired to the north behind the border fence.

Panzer-Abteilung Hohmann was then attached to **Gruppe Knabe** and met up with them and **8.8 cm Flak** guns at 1440 hours. At 1515 hours, I reported by radio: "Enemy tanks with the Trigh Capuzzo as their apparent objective were moving around to the north, about 6 kilometers to the west of **Gruppe Knabe** and Hohmann. Four additional heavy tanks were spotted advancing from the southeast toward Capuzzo. These can only be engaged with the **8.8 cm Flak**. Panzers with 7.5 cm guns are not available."

Since the opponent near and to the east of Capuzzo didn't advance any further, at 1600 hours I requested and received permission from the division to move to the area south of **Aufklaerung-Abteilung 3**. The Panzers needed to be urgently refueled and it was necessary to repair combat damage (tracks and road wheels had been hit by fire from enemy tanks and anti-tank rifles). At 1645, the **Panzer-Abteilung** moved back to the north toward Bardia to **Aufklaerung-Abteilung 3**.

The fort at Capuzzo with significant gaps in its walls after Operation Brevity. Mk.IIA Infantry tanks attempted to overrun anti-tank guns defending the area. (WW)

My adjutant and I reported in person to the division command post. After receiving orders to advance to Point 206 and build a leaguer there, I left the division command post at 1715 hours. Returning to the **Abteilung** I briefed my company commanders and started to advance at 1830 hours. At 1845 hours, I received the radio message that the **Panzer-Aufklaerung-Abteilung 33** had been ordered to attack Sidi Azeiz. At 1907 hours, I received an order by radio to attack Sidi Azeiz and continued the advance. Directly in front of Point 206 I spotted motorcycle infantry taking up defensive positions. I drove forward and asked Oberleutnant von Huelsen, leader of the **leichte Zug** that was leading the **Abteilung** as point guard, to determine who the motorcycle infantry belonged to. He reported that they were the **Kradschuetzen-Kompanie/Aufklaerung-Abteilung 33**. It was now about 1920 hours. Rittm. von Meyer, their company commander, came to me and reported that the **Aufklaerung-Abteilung** wasn't advancing because of the strength of the opponent. He had received orders to advance from here, but had been fired at and taken up a defensive position. Immediately following, I spoke with Leutnant von Gienenth, who came from **Aufklaerung-Abteilung 33**. He told me that the **Abteilung** wasn't getting forward. They had observed numerous enemy tanks, about 30.

Shortly before, using binoculars I had identified 7 enemy tanks as Mark II north of the track. Under the impression of the enemy situation that I had obtained from my own observations and reports from **Aufklaerung-Abteilung 33** and due to the failing light, I reported by radio to the division at 1930

hours: "**Gruppe Hohmann** is located on the track behind **Aufklaerung-Abteilung 33. Aufklaerung-Abteilung 33** not attacking. Clearly identified 7 Mark II north of Sidi Azeiz. Attack with available forces is not possible." I couldn't understand the repeated order to attack with reference to **8.8 cm Flak** because I didn't know about any **8.8 cm Flak** support. (At 1715 hours, **Aufklaerung-Abteilung 33** had reported that heavy enemy tanks had arrived near Sidi Azeiz, whereupon two **8.8 cm Flak** were sent to the **Aufklaerung-Abteilung 33** from Oberstleutnant Knabe).

At 2045 hours, unsummoned I reported in person to the division command post and repeated that Mark II Tanks had been spotted and that a breakthrough against these tanks couldn't be achieved. My concern was the total enemy situation reported by **Aufklaerung-Abteilung 33** and the pitch-dark night (no moon, visibility at 5 to 6 meters). From previous encounters at Tobruk and today's fight, the appearance of Mark II Tanks was known to me only too well. Maybe the repeated questions from the division commander were based on the fact that he had never seen a Mark II. In addition, **Aufklaerung-Abteilung 33** had reported at 1715 hours that they had also seen "heavy" enemy tanks at Sidi Azeiz. These could only have been Mark II Tanks because all of the other types fall under the classification of light and medium tanks. The heavy cruiser is a medium tank.

Operation Brevity ceased as a viable offensive operation when the British failed to take Capuzzo. However, because of the reconnaissance patrol up to Sidi Azeiz by the 2nd R.T.R, the

D.A.K. was still concerned about the British breaking through. They were still attempting to counter this move as activity continued through the night of 16 May as follows:

DAK KTB 16 May 1941 - Weather, maximum temperature 21° (70°F)

At 0000 hours, **Gruppe Herff** broke off contact with the enemy, and traveled over the Via Balbia on the Trigh Capuzzo to join **Panzer-Regiment 8**, 16 kilometers west of Azeiz. The movement was delayed due to the difficulty in finding directions at night. The most difficult task was locating an escarpment pass by Bir Junes.

At 0300 hours, the commander of **Panzer-Regiment 8** (Oberst Kramer) arrived at Sidi Azeiz with the reinforced **I.Abteilung** of the **Regiment**. He hadn't made contact with **Gruppe Herff**. The enemy had probably relocated during the night and was retiring to the south.

At 0630 hours, Capuzzo was occupied by a platoon of light Panzers. Rommel decided to send a **Kampfgruppe** under the command of General v. Esebeck as further reinforcements to the Sollum Front through Gasr el Abid-Gabr Saleh. The **Kampfgruppe** was organized with a **Schuetzen-Bataillon**, a **mittlere Panzer-Kompanie** (minus one **Zug**), the **I.Abteilung/Panzer-Regiment 5**, a **Panzer-Jaeger-Kompanie**, and an **Artillerie-Abteilung** (minus one **Batterie**). At 0855 hours, it was reported that General v. Esebeck had been wounded by a strafing enemy plane and the **Ia**, Major Kriebel, was ordered to send these reinforcements forward as fast as possible and to join **Gruppe Herff** as a general staff officer.

At 0725 hours, report to **O.K.H.**: The situation is still not totally clear. Azeiz and Capuzzo were again taken in the early morning hours by the newly sent **Panzer-Abteilung**. The intention is to fully restore the situation by sending additional forces. Tobruk front is still quiet.

At 0825 hours, **Gruppe Herff** reported that contact was made with Kramer at 0800 hours. Kramer was sent against Point 208, 8 kilometers west of Capuzzo.

At 0850 hours, aerial reconnaissance reported that our Panzers from El Adem had reached Sidi Azeiz and the German troops near Gabr bu Faris were still surrounded.

At 0900 hours, no enemy were located in the area south of Sidi Omar west of the Egyptian border. There were about 200 enemy vehicles and tanks in the area of B. Deghnasc.

At 1045 hours, There were about 300 to 400 vehicles near Der el Hamra, 150 vehicles by Sidi Suleiman, and several groups of about 50 vehicles in between.

At 1122 hours, **Gruppe Herff** reported that their position at 1030 hours was at Point 208. They intended to attack Halfaya through Suleiman. The fuel supply is exhausted. Resupply underway.

It wouldn't be possible to begin the attack until 1700 hours because of the shortage of fuel for **I.Abteilung/Panzer-Regiment 8**. Refueling with the available 3000 liters would limit the **Abteilung** to a range of 70 kilometers.

At 1205 hours, radioed report to **O.K.H.**: The attack to restore the situation has reached the area south of Capuzzo. The enemy holds Sollum. Suleiman is still on our hands and we hope to make contact there soon. Aerial reconnaissance reported that there weren't any enemy west of the Egyptian border. From intercepted messages, the enemy is retreating to the positions they held on the morning of 15 May.

At 1515 hours, **Gruppe Herff** reported that Omar is enemy free. Capuzzo was reoccupied by Knabe. Strong artillery fire on Capuzzo from Point 206. The situation at Sollum would still be tested. Reconnaissance activity along the border. Our attack delayed because of the previously reported lack of fuel for the Panzers. After refueling, in about 60 minutes we will initiate the attack on Suleiman through Point 206 to free our forces.

At 1628 hours, **Gruppe Herff** reported that there were 200 enemy vehicles with two Mk.II Tanks on the coastal plain 5 kilometers southeast of Sollum. Support was request from the Luftwaffe.

At 1650 hours, radioed report to **O.K.H.**: Sollum was retaken. The enemy forces are probably retreating. Further reinforcements are on the way. Tobruk is quiet.

At 1745 hours, Major Kriebel reported that the reinforcements intended to reach Bir el Gasr by nightfall and halt there for a supply stop. Rommel ordered them to march through the night in order to be standing in the Capuzzo-Azeiz area at dawn.

At 1805 hours, **Gruppe Herff's** attack reached Point 206.

At 1857 hours, strong enemy artillery fire in the area 6 kilometers north of Sidi Suleiman.

At 1900 hours, radio reconnaissance located enemy units south of Bir Usar to Sollum. An enemy group that had occupied Point 206 retired to the south maintaining contact with **Gruppe Herff**.

At 1920 hours, the attack by **Gruppe Herff** reached Sidi Suleiman but our troops were not found there. After repulsing a strong enemy tank attack from the south, the fight was broken off because of approaching nightfall. Strong enemy artillery fire.

At 2245 hours, **Gruppe Herff** reported that our front line is Sidi Omar to Point 206 to Sidi Suleiman to Upper Sollum. Lower Sollum is held by the enemy. **Gruppe Herff** is not qualified to conduct larger attacks because of the vehicle situation and overall condition. Further attacks are planned to first occur on 18 May. At this time there are no signs of an enemy attack. Rommel replied to **Gruppe Herff**: Agree with intentions. Go over to the defense, organize forces and assemble. Exercise greatest care.

The 4th R.T.R. didn't see any action on 16 May 1941. They merely withdrew into positions near Halfaya Pass as follows: Operation orders were received from 22nd Guards Brigade at 0200 hours and a message from the Commander of the Scots Guards at 0400 hours to say that infantry were retiring. The 4th Bn. R.T.R. withdrew to top of Halfaya Pass by 1000 hours. The Coldstream Guards took up a defensive line on the crest, the troop from the Scots Guards reverting to them on arrival at the Pass. Orders were received from the Brigadier in the evening to evacuate all unfit tanks along the coast road. This was started about 2000 hours and tanks and B Echelon were ordered to concentrate at Sidi Barrani on the following day. Nine tanks with composite crews were left at Halfaya and sufficient wheels to maintain them were concentrated at Buq Buq. Six tanks were stationed on top of the pass and three at the bottom. On 17 May 1941, the unfit tanks and remainder of wheels were ordered to concentrate at Matruh. The Commander of the 4th Bn R.T.R. visited Desert Force H.Q. 7th Armored Division and H.Q.M.E. to report on action and to arrange about tank replacements.

The 2nd R.T.R. were still in the border area in the morning. After 1000 hours, C Squadron was sent north on a patrol and didn't pull back until forced to by **Gruppe Herff**'s advance late in the afternoon, as follows:

At 0500 hours on 16 May, in accordance with orders, C Squadron moved to the area of Pt.206 and A Squadron to Pt.196 in accordance with orders. C Squadron was then split to escort various "Columns" and ordered to send one Troop to Gap 40 to meet a guide, one Troop to remain at Pt.206, and C Squadron HQ and one Troop to go to Gap 40.

At 0845 hours, A Squadron returned to Bn. HQ, which was now in area 50773697. At 0900 hours, HQ and A Squadron moved to 512365 and then moved to 516361 at 1000 hours. Most of A Squadron's tanks at this time were in a poor state due to lack of spares and maintenance and several had to be towed. During the morning and early afternoon as much work as possible was done on them and those which could not be made fit were towed back down the center line by Scammel.

The action by the 2nd R.T.R. on 16 May 1941 was then recorded as follows:

"C Squadron was dispersed in the area 508373 - 609370 under the command of Paul Column (IMAB) when orders were received at about 1000 hours to concentrate in the area 506373. At this time HQ 2nd R.T.R. with A Squadron was in the area cross tracks 516361 having returned from the west side of the wire.

"Orders were given to C Squadron to advance north along the 507 grid line to approx. track Sidi Azeiz - Capuzzo than swing northeast to approx. 506 grid line and return to concentration area.

"They were to search the area and engage any enemy they found, particularly in the area 507385.

"On the way north a broken down German tank was seen with the crew standing by it. No action was taken at this time as it was some distance away and the Squadron commander had only just sufficient time to carry out his main task before dark. He gave orders that the matter should be dealt with on the return.

"A number of enemy vehicles were seen but all retired mainly north and northeast and none could positively be identified though what looked like tanks and armored cars were among them.

"About 1830 hours information was received from HQ 7th Armored Brigade (VERO) that 80 enemy tanks were advancing south from Capuzzo. Commander of 2nd R.T.R. ordered C Squadron to return as quickly as possible. A Squadron to stand by ready to move. Crocks to be sent down track to Bir Khireigat as soon as and by any means possible. C Squadron to keep west before crossing the wire to avoid the enemy AFVs.

"2nd R.T.R. was then ordered to move south. On reaching Sidi Suleiman 518361, orders were received that Bn. was to come under orders of DUAN, then about 2 kilometers west of that point. At the same time enemy tanks could be seen advancing in force from the north. Commander of 2nd R.T.R. gave orders by wireless for A Squadron, now only 5 tanks strong and HQ tanks to take up a position to stop the advance of the enemy AFVs, which he went in his tanks to receive orders from Commander DUAN. On the way he gave orders to C Squadron, who had by this time crossed the wire, to turn north and try to relieve the pressure on A Squadron. This action was confirmed by Commander DUAN. C Squadron hit and set on fire one enemy AFV and put another out of action. A Squadron's fire was successful in stopping the enemy advance but owing to the long range and poor light its effect could not be seen. About 50 enemy tanks were engaged. C Squadron had 12 tanks in this action.

"The 2nd R.T.R. remained in position after DUAN had retired until dark when orders were given to rally in the area 514353. Owing to the dark and the uncertainty of position after the action this took a considerable time and it was about 0100 before C Squadron rejoined. The 2nd R.T.R. leaguered about one mile north of Bir Khireigat about 0230 hours. On the way in to the Bn. two enemy tanks joined the tail of C Squadron column, one was put out of action and burst into flames but the other fell back and as far as could be seen was not hit. Enemy tanks followed the Bn. to approximately the area 516361 firing many white Verey lights. As far as could be seen or heard they did not proceed beyond this point at any time.

"Enemy tanks fired at ranges beyond that of our 2-pounders. Their gunnery in this action was better than previously.

"No casualties to tanks or men were suffered from enemy action but two tanks had to be abandoned owing to
mechanical breakdown. Crews tried to effect repair but could
not carry it out owing to lack of spare parts. These tanks have
since been recovered by the Unit."

As reported in the DAK KTB on 18 May 1941:

*The total losses from the battle in the Sollum-Capuzzo-
Bardia area during the period from 13 to 16 May were:*
Personnel: 12 killed, 61 wounded, 2 officers and 183 men
missing.
*Equipment: 2 **Pz.Kpfw.III**, 1 **Pz.Kpfw.II**, 1 radio, 2 special*
*trailers, 3 cars, 1 truck, 2 **3.7 cm Pak**,*
*2 **2 cm Flak**, 3 light mortars, 4 anti-*
tank rifles, 27 M.P., 22 pistols, and
124 carbines.
*In addition to the 100 prisoners and heavy losses, the enemy
lost as booty: 3 machineguns, 3 anti-tank rifles, 3 trucks, 2
armored cars, 4 Mk.II Infantry Tanks. From intercepted radio
messages a much larger number of guns, tanks, trucks and
other equipment was damaged and out of service.*

9.5 TACTICAL ANALYSIS

BRITISH TACTICS

The British were still charging one squadron at a time without
regard to coordinating their action with any other units. They
paid the price for this, with most of their "invincible" Infantry
Tanks damaged and out of action by 0900 hours. Thus, after
their initial actions they were left with too few operational tanks
(about eight left in the morning) to sustain the offensive. It
was little compensation that the **gruppo artiglieria Frongia**
had lost all 12 of their guns.

The 2nd R.T.R. was amazingly gutsy in taking on numerically superior forces of Panzers. They were very fortunate that when they sent isolated squadrons to patrol deep

into enemy territory, they did not get entrapped or ambushed.
Yet these small patrols had proven to be very effective in
keeping the Germans off balance.

It is simply amazing how drastically the Germans had
overreacted to the scouting patrol conducted by A Squadron,
2nd R.T.R. with its nine Cruiser Tanks up to Sidi Azeiz in the
evening of 15 May. They were certain that they had lost the
battle on the border and shifted forces surrounding Tobruk to
meet an attack from the south or east. Even a limited demonstration out of Tobruk by the 1st R.T.R. (23 Cruiser Tanks)
and D Squadron 7th R.T.R. (15 Infantry Tanks) may have
caused the Germans to realign forces and possibly give up
the border.

GERMAN TACTICS

In his report, Major Hohmann reveals that they had already
developed the tactics needed to knock out Matildas with the
Pz.Kpfw.III, but he was very reluctant to use them. Mistakingly
identifying the Cruiser Tanks from the 2nd R.T.R. on patrol
near Sidi Azeiz as Mk.II Infantry Tanks, Major Hohmann refused to attack.

Although control of half of the Panzer force had been lost
in the morning, there wasn't any apparent attempt to reunite
the **Panzer-Abteilung**. This left the Germans without sufficient strength to counter a consolidated move by the entire
2nd R.T.R., had they made one.

The Germans were picking up an amazing amount of
tactically useful information by radio intercept. And it was
quickly distributed and rapidly exploited in changing tactical
decisions within hours. However, they didn't realize that the
information radioed to **O.K.H.** was also being intercepted by
the British, who then knew their anxieties and the state of
their supplies. This intercepted information was in code which
took days for the British to decipher. Therefore, the information wasn't immediately useful that same day on the battlefield, but it proved to be very useful for planning and conducting future operations.

10

Operation Skorpion

Following the failure of Operation Brevity to achieve most of its objectives, the British forces didn't bugger off with their tails between their legs. They consolidated their hold on Halfaya Pass and continued to pester the German defenders with mobile columns operating to their south.

After holding against the British attack, the German's next move was to try to restore stability on the Sollum Front and to regain control of Halfaya Pass. The code name for the operation to retake Halfaya Pass was **Unternehmen Skorpion**.

10.1 PRELIMINARY MOVES

<u>DAK KTB 17 May 1941</u> - *On the morning of 17 May, aerial reconnaissance reported that the main body of the enemy forces had relocated to the area south of Sidi Barrani. About 600 vehicles were observed, some halted, some moving, between Sidi Barrani and Bir el Aneba. There were about 100 vehicles south of Buq and smaller groups of 10 to 50 vehicles on the coastal plain in the direction of Sollum. The area in a wide circle around El Hamra was reported to be free of enemy forces other than a small group of 30 vehicles on the Habata to Bir el Aneba track. Advance enemy security forces stood in stronger groups near Bir el Chreigat and east of Halfaya Pass.*

Intercepted radio messages revealed that two of the opponent's forward elements were following our forces which were returning north from Sidi Suleiman. An enemy armored car patrol issued continuous observation reports from the area of Bir Uaar and Hagfet Uaar. An enemy group with tanks, anti-aircraft, and anti-tank units stood on the coastal plain. The enemy south of Suleiman had instructions to retire to the east and, if further attacked, cover the British supply depot near Alem er Rabia.

In contact with the enemy, reconnaissance patrols of **Gruppe Herff** *stand on line from Sidi Omar to Sidi Suleiman to Point 191. Strong enemy forces held Point 206. At 0900 hours, Lower Sollum was occupied by a German reconnaissance patrol.*

Reinforcements under Major Kriebel arrived at 1000 hours and took up positions on the border. Supplies were requested to get the troops combat ready.

At 0915 hours, Rommel provided **Gruppe Herff** *with a directive for the future conduct of the battle on the Sollum Front: Conduct a strong defense utilizing all available means. Position the* **Aufklaerung-Abteilung** *30 kilometers southwest of the right flank. The line of positions is to be Point 206 to Capuzzo to the escarpment by Sollum. The main body of Panzers are to be positioned directly behind the front, ready to counterattack immediately.*

Gruppe Herff *reported their plans for 18 May: Reinforced reconnaissance is to be conducted across the line Sceferzen Omar to Suleiman to Halfaya Pass. Enemy forces that advance over this line will be attacked and destroyed. Point 206 will be constructed as a* **Stuetzpunkt**. *Refueling and vehicle repairs will still be in progress tomorrow.*

The **Korps** *replied: From available reports, the enemy has relocated the main body of his forces clear of the battle zone. Only reconnaissance units, possibly supported by tanks, are still on the heights east of the border. Cut off the base of Halfaya Pass as soon as possible. This action is urgent and the area is navigable.*

<u>2nd R.T.R. 17 May 1941</u> - At 0835 hours, on 17 May 1941 the 2nd R.T.R. moved to Abu Shalif and took up positions on the ridge. At 2000 hours, the 2nd R.T.R. moved back into close leaguer one mile north of Bir Kireigat. The tank state was reported at 2100 hours as A Squadron 7 Fit, C 11 Fit 2 Y, HQ 4 Fit.

<u>DAK KTB 18 May 1941:</u> *Weather, maximum temperature 31°* *(88°F)*

At 0040 hours, **Gruppe Herff** *presented the plan to re-take Halfaya Pass on 19 May.*

At 0730 hours, Rommel declared his agreement and ordered that the pass be closed by artillery fire.

From intercepted radio messages, the British battery at Halfaya Pass reported at 0606 hours that the situation was critical. Their guns were probably immobile and they were possibly short of ammunition.

Combat reconnaissance located the enemy positions around Halfaya Pass.

At 1130 hours, Oberst von Herff reported his intentions to reconnoiter with reconnaissance patrols reinforced by Panzers in order to complete the preparations to retake Halfaya Pass on 19 May and to send a **Panzer-Abteilung** *through Sidi Suleiman to Bir el Chreigat to clarify the situation, and if opportunity was presented to attack the enemy tanks forces with the entire* **Panzer-Regiment**.

Rommel declared that he did not agree with the plans to advance Panzers toward Sidi Suleiman. Herff should hold his forces together and conserve fuel in order with adequate forces to be able to eventually catch the enemy.

With several calls, Rommel informed **Gruppe Herff** *of his consent after the actions were prepared by Sollum. Our forces were to return to their starting positions after dark to ensure that the enemy thought that they were still being pursued.*

At 1420 hours, the reconnaissance group sent against Halfaya Pass couldn't push through to their objective because of heavy artillery fire.

The **Panzer-Regiment** *advanced on both sides of Sidi Suleiman. The enemy retired to the south, strong security forces maintaining contact. After dark, the Panzers returned to Point 206.*

Gruppe Herff *were informed on 18 May that there would be a Ghibli (sand storm) to contend with on 19 May. They were to direct their attention to defense. Sollum and Capuzzo were not to be lost again under any circumstances.*

<u>2nd R.T.R. 18 May 1941</u> - At 0530 hours on 18 May, the 2nd R.T.R. moved back to yesterday's position. Thick mist rendered visibility very poor. Crock report sent to Brigade:

Z Casualties (all Mk.IIA Cruiser Tanks):
A Squadron   T5970 Gap 40 (already reported)

A **Pz.Kpfw.IV Ausf.D** of the **3.Kompanie/Panzer-Regiment 8** in bivouac. The crew positioned rocks alongside the roadwheels and dug under the parked Panzer to prepare a shelter safe from shell fragments and strafing aircraft. (KL)

A Squadron	T5931	526333 (previously a Y but nothing has been heard of it)
C Squadron	T9221	Bir Khireigat (turret seized, runner)
C Squadron	T5932	Bir Khireigat (2 Pdr. smashed, turret trouble, runner)
C Squadron	T5968	513363 (dropped out in re treat on 16 May, track broken, recovered on 19 May)

At 1500 hours, an enemy column of tanks, armoured cars and Met was reported on the track about the 364 E & W grid line. The leading Squadron (C) was ordered to be prepared to advance for reconnaissance purposes. Shortly afterwards the enemy column was reported halted on the 358 grid line.

At 1600 hours, an enemy column was reported moving again slowly. 2nd R.T.R. was ordered to attack head of column and then withdraw. C Squadron was sent forward and became in action with 12 enemy tanks (thought to be eight Mark III and four Mark IV). Enemy armoured cars attempted to work round right flank.

At 1740 hours, the main body of enemy withdrew to line 514360 - 518360. Code message received from Brigade not at first understood by us, but which turned out to mean that another arm would be operating in the area north of us, and we were not to advance.

At 1830 hours, a "Column" moved up his guns in van of our positions and shelled the enemy column. Main body of enemy withdrew to Pt.207 518364. 12 tanks remained in Sidi Suleiman area. C Squadron supported by A Squadron were just about to attack them when a bombing attack was delivered on them by the R.A.F. and they made off to the N.E. with a patrol of 11th Hussars watching them.

At 2030 hours, the 2nd R.T.R. rallied and moved to leaguer area.

DAK KTB 19 May 1941 - *Weather, maximum temperature 35° (95°F) Sandstorm from 1500 to 1600 hours.*

A scouting advance made on the evening of 19 May, reported Points 205 and 207 north of Sidi Suleiman were occupied by strong enemy security forces with tanks, armored cars, anti-tank guns, and artillery.

DAK KTB 20 May 1941 - *The enemy had established a screening force especially strong in armored cars and tanks, so that our **Panzerspaehtrupps** could no longer penetrate. Enemy artillery fire harassed the work on the **Stuetzpunkte** so that most of the work could be performed only at night.*

DAK KTB 21 May 1941 - *In the morning, south of Capuzzo, an attack with tanks (including several MK.II) was made against Point 206 and was repulsed by **Gruppe Herff**'s Panzers.*

In the late afternoon, during our own advance with Panzers against Point 207 (6 kilometers south of Point 206), an enemy observation tower and several anti-tank guns were destroyed.

On 21 May the units under the 7th Armoured Brigade positioned southwest of Halfaya were Prince Albert Victor's Own Cavalry, one Squadron 2nd Royal Lancers, 6th Australian Division Cavalry, 2nd Bn. Royal Tank Regiment, 259th Anti-Tank Battery RA, and 38th Light AA Battery (less one Troop).

Action by A Squadron, 2nd R.T.R. on 21 May 1941 - At 0600 hours on 21 May 1941 A Squadron (NETA) 8 tanks strong was in position about Pt.207 518364 to cover the action of DUAN whose OP was at 207 camp protected by one troop of the Squadron. Soon after first light, movement of enemy tanks and MET was observed in the area between Gap 38 and a point 4000 yards east of it. Two tanks advanced on Pt.207 apparently to reconnoitre. There were engaged by No.4 Troop and one put out of action. The crew got out but mounted again quickly on being machine gunned. A recovery vehicle came out to the damaged tank but being fired upon withdrew.

In the meantime five enemy tanks advanced from the Gap 38 area and began to work around the right flank of NETA. They were engaged by No.1 Troop only one tank strong and one enemy tank put out of action. The remaining four withdrew and shelled No.1 Troop from a position out of range. Later these four tanks began to work further round the flank and the Squadron Commander had to move his tank and that of his 2nd-in-Command to the assistance of No.1 Troop.

While this was taking place approximately 20 enemy tanks advanced slowly from the north. They were halted by fire from DUAN but later advanced again.

The tanks of the Squadron had been forced to move about a good deal to watch the movements of the enemy and to avoid shelling, and mechanical troubles began to develop. These were due to the age and poor mechanical condition of the tanks and lack of spare parts. Chiefly tracks were concerned. Efforts were made to carry out repairs on the spot, in one case pieces being taken from several tanks to try and make fit another.

The combined enemy movement from the north and east now made a withdrawal necessary and orders were given to the Squadron to carry this out. By now three tanks were out of action with mechanical trouble and one had part of its suspension shot away by enemy fire. It could still, however, move slowly under its own power. Three therefore had to be towed by others leaving only one freely in action though it was found possible to continue fire from the tanks being towed.

C Squadron (DEEP) was ordered to stand by ready to go to NETA's assistance but the Squadron Commander reported that he could manage alright. Orders were also given that should it be necessary, towed tanks must be abandoned and the crews brought out. All tanks however were got back to a rearward position about 519353 held by C Squadron.

As the Squadron was withdrawing an enemy tank appeared on the skyline at Pt.207. It was engaged by No.4 Troop and put out of action.

Throughout the action the enemy covered his movements by smoke shells fired from tanks. These are reported to have been effective and disconcerting to the defence and to have taken 4 to 5 minutes to disperse. The wind was from the northwest.

Casualties to officers and other ranks. Nil.

DAK KTB 22 May 1941 - *Weather, maximum temperature 24° (75°F)*

On the Sollum Front, two Mk.II tanks were destroyed during the repulsion of an enemy tank attack against one of **Gruppe Herff***'s forward security post.*

DAK KTB 23 May 1941 - **Gruppe Herff** *received orders to prepare for an attempt to take Halfaya Pass.*

As listed in the Operations Order #16 dated 23 May 1941 the troops under the command of the 22nd Guards Brigade were:

3rd Coldstream Guards at Halfaya with one Battery 31st Field Regiment, two Troops 260th Anti-Tank Battery, one Section 257th Anti-Tank Battery, five Bofors AA guns 4th Light AA Battery, and one Squadron 4th R.T.R.

2nd Scots Guards at Sidi Barrani with 8th Field Regiment (less one Battery), one Troop 260th Anti-Tank Battery, one Troop 257th Anti-Tank Battery, and one Section 3rd Light AA Battery.

2nd Rifle Brigade (less one company) with one Battery 31st Field Regiment, 12th Australian Anti-Tank Battery (less one Troop), and one Troop 4th Light AA Battery

B Echelon with three Detachments 4th Light AA Battery and one gun 257th Anti-Tank Battery

Brigade HQ with one gun 257th Anti-Tank Battery and HQ 4th R.T.R.

DAK KTB 24 May 1941 - *Weather, maximum temperature 26° (79°F) Sandstorm from 1000 to 1500 hours.*

DAK KTB 25 May 1941 - *Weather, maximum temperature 22° (72°F)*

Aerial reconnaissance from 1820 hours reported: 20 to 40 vehicles dug in by Der el Hamra, 62 vehicles gathered by Habata, small groups each with 6 to 12 vehicles on Hagiag el

Back from patrol, a **Pz.Kpfw.III Ausf.H** followed by a **Pz.Kpfw.III Ausf.F** of the **1.Kompanie/Panzer-Regiment 8** pull into the bivouac area. (GBJ)

Agaba, no enemy traffic or enemy on the Buq Buq to Sollum road. This gives the total impression that the enemy had pulled back the main body of his troops from above the escarpment.

The situation provided by radio intercepts: Occupants on Halfaya Pass consist of an anti-tank/anti-aircraft battalion with heavy artillery, until now weakened by the loss of a reconnaissance squadron. The stationary group that was by Sidi Suleiman is no longer there. An armored battalion with two or three artillery battalions, a motorized battalion, and an armored car battalion are located north of Der el Hamra. There are two reinforced motorized regiments on the coastal plain between Alem el Barraq and Sidi Barrani. The location of one infantry battalion and two tank battalions remains unknown.

Ground reconnaissance confirmed that the forces near Der el Hamra are still only weak. The enemy forward security line is still occupied by the previous forces.

The forces assembled for Operation Skorpion to retake Halfaya Pass were organized as:

- **Panzergruppe Cramer**: with the **I. und II.Abteilung/ Panzer-Regiment 5** and **I.Abteilung/Panzer-Regiment 8**
- **Gruppe Bach**: **I.Bataillon/Schuetzen-Regiment 104**
- **Stossgruppe Knabe**: **Kradschuetzen-Bataillon 15** and **I./Artillerie-Regiment 33**
- **Gruppe Wechmar**: **Aufklaerung-Abteilung 3** without heavy weapons.

10.2 THE ATTACK BEGINS

DAK KTB 26 May 1941 - *Weather, maximum temperature 24° (75°F)*

Fog in the morning on the Sollum Front.

Operation Skorpion 26 May 1941 - *The attack began early in the morning and encountered two enemy patrols supported by Mk.II Infantry Tanks. These had probably been sent to destroy our Panzer security forces stationed near Point 206 and Qalala. The enemy attack at Point 206 was repulsed but they forced our Panzer security force to retire with losses from Point 196. A* **Pz.Kpfw.III** *was lost. The enemy attack then failed against the consolidated stand of* **Gruppe Bach**, *which had advanced to the area of Wadi Agrab during the night.* **Gruppe Bach**, *strengthened by a reinforced* **Schuetzen-Kompanie** *and half of a* **Panzer-Jaeger-Kompanie**, *renewed their advance across tank-proof country.*

The movement of the forces went according to plan. Shortly after 1500 hours, **Panzergruppe Cramer** *and* **Divi-**

On the left, Oberstleutnant Cramer, commander of **Panzer-Regiment 8**, was praised for his tactical handling of the combined **Panzergruppe** during Operation Skorpion. Later, Cramer was assigned to command the **D.A.K.** (KL)

sion-Stab *crossed the border and deployed into a broad front with two* **Panzer-Abteilungen** *abreast and the third echeloned back to the right rear toward the southeast. Enemy armored car patrols swiftly pulled back. At 1540 hours, from the area north of Sidi Suleiman an enemy battery fired into the western flank of the attack. On orders from the division, the commander of* **Panzer-Regiment 8** *then turned toward the east with the* **II./Panzer-Regiment 5** *on the left to take the enemy battery from the rear. At this time the* **I.Abteilung/Panzer-Regiment 5** *was sent after a weak enemy tank patrol that swiftly retired to the southeast.*

At 1700 hours, the first objectives were reached (Point 203 - Qaret Abu Szid and Point 204 - 4 kilometers southeast of Sidi Suleiman). At 1715 hours, **Gruppe Knabe** *received orders to start moving southeast to Abar Abu Talaq.* **Panzergruppe Cramer** *received orders to turn northeast to the edge of the escarpment southeast of Mingar el Shaba and hit the rear of* **Gruppe Bach**'s *opponent. They were also ordered to cooperate with* **Gruppe Bach** *and* **Gruppe Knabe**.

Panzer-Gruppe Cramer *pulled the* **I. und II.Abteilung/ Panzer-Regiment 5** *back in and turned the* **Regiment** *toward the northeast with one* **Panzer-Abteilung** *in the front wave and one* **Panzer-Abteilung** *on each flank echeloned to the rear. The* **Regiment** *began the move in the new formation at 1845 hours. After a short time, strong fire was heard*

An **le.F.H.18** (with two kill rings on its barrel) from the **I.Abteilung/Artillerie-Regiment 33** was assigned to support **Kradschuetzen-Bataillon 15** during Operation Skorpion. The Germans remarked that their escorting artillery wasn't nearly as mobile as the British 25-pounders. (KL)

from the north, probably from **Gruppe Bach**. **Gruppe Bach** reported that strong enemy Mk.II Infantry Tank attacks had been renewed against his right flank. Despite the failing light, **Panzergruppe Cramer** was ordered to charge at high speed to Halfaya Pass to eliminate the enemy in front of **Gruppe Bach**. **Gruppe Knabe** was still halted north of Abar el Silgiya to sit out enemy tank attacks without tank and artillery support. Difficult sandy terrain northeast of Sidi Suleiman slowed down **Panzergruppe Cramer**'s advance. There was no moon; orientation became still more difficult. Shortly after 2020 hours, the division commander halted the **Panzergruppe** in the area 7 kilometers south of Halfaya Pass. The **Panzergruppe** was ordered to set up an all-round defense and to be prepared to continue the attack at dawn. The fuel column for **Panzergruppe Cramer** did not arrive during the night of 26/27 May, greatly limiting the **Panzergruppe**'s range.

At 1930 hours, **Abteilung Wechmar** had moved west of the border through TN68 and reached El Hamra. Their objective was to gain contact with the enemy and reconnoiter the Der el Hamra area and the edge of the escarpment by Bu Sfafi.

Gruppe Bach, **Knabe** and **Cramer** were to attack the opponent in front of **Gruppe Bach** at dawn. To achieve this, at 0430 hours **Panzergruppe Cramer** was to attack to swiftly arrive at the edge of the escarpment on both sides of Mingar el Shaba and from there fire at the artillery and enemy columns on the coastal plain. One **Panzer-Abteilung** was to be held behind the right flank, prepared to repulse any enemy advance from the southeast against the division's flank.

Gruppe Knabe was ordered to reach an assembly area 2 kilometers north of Abar Abu Talaq and start from there at 0430 hours. If possible, they were to bring the **I./Artillerie-Regiment 33** forward to arrive at Point 206 in the morning. **Gruppe Bach** was to attack along the edge of the escarpment against the base of Halfaya Pass. **Gruppe Wechmar** should disengage before dawn, move to the area east of Sidi Suleiman, and then provide security against any threat of an attack on the main body of the division from the south.

4th R.T.R. at Halfaya 26 May 1941 - Counter offensive by 10 gun tanks at Halfaya to clear the area. Enemy tanks were encountered and one destroyed. On return anti-tank gun fire was encountered and dealt with. One gun tank was evacuated with a damaged turret and suspension.

Enemy attacked in force at 1630 hours with tanks, guns and infantry. Seven gun tanks counter attacked and relieved the pressure on the Coldstream Guards. Four Bren gunners were wounded and two tanks were no longer fit for action.

A Troop counter attacked again later with a platoon of Coldstream Guards against a strong point. It was unsuccessful. Two tanks returned damaged and the third had to be destroyed.

Operation Skorpion 27 May 1941 - *At 0430 hours, **Gruppe Knabe** advanced and shortly thereafter **Panzergruppe Cramer** also started their ordered movement. The **Panzergruppe** was organized the same as on the previous day: one **Panzer-Abteilung** in the front wave and one **Panzer-Abteilung** echeloned to the rear on each flank.*

*At 0500 hours, heavy artillery fire of every caliber struck the advancing **Panzergruppe**. The artillery fire of our heavy batteries was rapidly directed onto the coastal plain by radioed orders. In spite of the artillery fire, the **Panzergruppe** arrived at the edge of the escarpment at 0530 hours and with all of their weapons laid down concentrated fire on enemy movements, artillery positions, and tanks on the coastal plain. Great confusion ensued. After a short time, the left flank was struck by very encumbering direct fire from artillery and anti-tank guns at Halfaya Pass. Then the **Panzergruppe** commander immediately ordered his left-hand **Panzer-Abteilung** to turn toward the west. The main body of a second **Panzer-Abteilung**, with only advance elements on the escarpment edge, secured the area to the southeast.*

*At the same time, around 0540 hours, **Gruppe Knabe**'s attack on Halfaya Pass had already made itself felt. Unshaken by the enemy artillery fire and direct machinegun and anti-tank gun fire, some even mounted on vehicles, the **Gruppe** advanced against Halfaya Pass. Together with elements of the **II.Abteilung/Panzer-Regiment 5**, they broke through the enemy positions. An enemy battery was stormed and those opponents that were not taken prisoner fled to the coastal plain. Halfaya Pass was firmly in our hands by 0615 hours.*

*The attack of **Gruppe Bach** at the same time also made an impression. Around 0630 hours, fighting against enemy tanks, they arrived at the foot of Halfaya Pass, took numerous prisoners, and captured considerable booty.*

*Under the pressure of the constricting attacks of the three **Gruppen** and heavy fire from all artillery, the opponents on the coastal plain fled south, suffering heavy losses and leaving their vehicles and weapons behind.*

*The pursuit was immediately taken up by **Gruppe Knabe** and **Gruppe Bach**. Because **Panzergruppe Cramer** had used up the last of their fuel to get to the edge of the escarpment, the pursuit could only be conducted with unarmored vehicles. It was strongly hampered by the enemy armored cars covering the enemy rearguard.*

*At 0630 hours, **Gruppe Knabe** and **Bach** were ordered to continue the pursuit to Alam el Kidad and from there to follow only with reconnaissance units. **Gruppe Knabe** was to be relieved as soon as possible by **Gruppe Bach** and were to regroup with their vehicles south of the pass. The*

A view from Upper Sollum looking down on Lower Sollum. In the background, the high ridge of the escarpment curves off to the east toward Halfaya Pass. The only points where vehicles could climb this escarpment near the Egyptian border were at Sollum and Halfaya Pass. The side in possession of these two locations held a distinct advantage. (KL)

Up in the defensive positions hewn into the rock on top of Halfaya Pass. The steepness of the escarpment in the background shows why it was difficult to attack this position from the east. (KL)

Panzergruppe was to refuel 3 kilometers northwest of the pass and, providing security toward the southeast, stand ready at the division's disposal.

Finally at 0800 hours, ***Gruppe Bach*** received the order to man the defenses at Halfaya Pass. The other ***Gruppen*** were to return to their previous locations with ***I.Abteilung/ Panzer-Regiment 8*** left on the Sollum Front.

4th R.T.R. at Halfaya 27 May 1941 - A heavy enemy attack developed about 0700, we only having two tanks left. The Coldstream Guards were ordered to withdraw at 0730 and the remaining two tanks covered this withdrawal. Finally these two withdrew down the pass, badly damaged under heavy fire, one tank having to be abandoned half way down.

In total 5 tanks were lost with 6 casualties at Halfaya and from the action at Capuzzo with 3 casualties. Remainder withdrew to Buq Buq.

DAK KTB 27 May 1941 - ***Gruppe Herff*** renewed their attack at 0430 hours and reported "Halfaya Pass is in our hands" at 0730 hours.

Oberst von Herff reported in several messages: Three columns succeeded in overrunning Halfaya Pass during the morning of 27 May. The enemy is in full retreat on the coastal plain. They sustained a heavy loss of equipment following a short but heavy fight. The pursuit is to halt at Alam el Kidad because of the fuel shortage. Halfaya Pass will be prepared for defense. Reconnaissance patrols are in contact with the enemy. Until now, the booty has been nine guns (of which four are operational), seven Mk.II Infantry Tanks (of which three are usable), two other tanks, many anti-tank guns and numerous other weapons along with 40 prisoners. Their combat losses are much higher from pursuing fire from the edge of the escarpment. Our own losses are few, up to now one ***Pz.Kpfw.III***. *On the coastal plain 10 to 15 kilometers east of Halfaya Pass, the enemy is burning fuel and ammunition*

A knocked-out Mk.IIA Infantry Tank with numerous scars but only one complete penetration of a **5 cm Pzgr.** below the gun mantlet at its junction with the turret. Another hit deflected off the cupola as well as three more on the turret, one of which skidded into the turret ring and may have jammed it. The strike on the upper hull below the gun appears to be from a **Pzgr.40** which may have also penetrated. The three **5 cm Pzgr.** penetrations on the skirting most likely detonated in the gap and didn't penetrate through the inner plate. (KL)

Another Mk.IIA Infantry Tank from the 4th R.T.R. being examined by officers from **Panzer-Regiment 8**. "Dorchester" was knocked out very close to the edge of the coastal escarpment, apparently from a **5 cm Pzgr.** striking the back of the turret. (KL)

With combat damage from a **5 cm Pzgr.** striking beside the driver's visor and a hit on the upper lip of the gun mantlet that may have jammed it, this Mk.IIA Infantry Tank from the 4th R.T.R. was captured in reasonable condition. "Dreadnought" was towed back **Panzer-Regiment 8**'s leaguer, repaired, and put back into service under new management. This photograph was taken prior to Operation Battleaxe. (KL)

dumps. Aerial reconnaissance reported that the enemy was no longer occupying the known positions by Bir Habata and had pulled back further to the east. Radio intercept revealed that in the region north of Sidi Barrani, most of the headquarters had changed their positions in great haste. The heavy loss of Mk.II Tanks and artillery may not be taken lightly by the opponent. Without sending new forces, an enemy attack is considered improbable. The number of prisoners taken today is 58.

Because of his excellent command and independent resolution during the conquest of Halfaya Pass, Oberstleutnant Cramer, commander of **Panzer-Regiment 8**, *is to be named in the* **Wehrmachtbericht** *and proposed for award of the* **Ritterkreuz**.

Under heavy enemy fire, Leutnant Jurg, commander of **8.Batterie/Artillerie-Regiment 33** *especially distinguished himself by advancing his battery to the edge of the escarpment and in a short time silencing two enemy batteries.*

Rommel radioed: Fullest appreciation for you and all of the associated troops for this prudent and so successfully accomplished attack performance. . . . Utilizing all available means, our defensive front is now to be prepared on the line from Point 208 to Point 206 to Halfaya Pass to the coastal plain.

10.3 TACTICAL ANALYSIS

BRITISH TACTICS

With a vastly inferior force, the British were very successful at harassing their opponents, causing the Germans to expend a large amount of fuel when they had a severe shortage. They also very aggressively held onto Halfaya Pass, which would have proven invaluable for a future offensive, saving them hundreds of miles of detours through the desert. Counterstrikes with the Mk.II Infantry Tanks were successful in keeping their opponents off balance and tying up a much larger enemy force to deal with them. Forced by circumstances, the small contingent at Halfaya Pass even resorted to combined arms tactics.

A bivouac on the coast gave the **6.Kompanie/Panzer-Regiment 8** crews a chance for a dip in the sea. Steel straps were fastened across the hull front to support the spare track sections on this **Pz.Kpfw.III Ausf.H**. White stripes were painted on the Jerry cans to distinguish those to be only used for water. The Jerry cans of fuel in the turret rack were only for marches and not carried into combat. (WW)

GERMAN TACTICS

The maneuvers to drive the British off to the south and retake Halfaya Pass are exceptionally good examples of the employment of combined arms mobile forces in a well-coordinated operation. However, it clearly demonstrates the great awe in which the Germans held the Mk.II Infantry Tanks at this time. They committed a force of three **Panzer-Abteilungen** just to wipe out less than one Squadron. Sending in such an overwhelming force rapidly expended their scant fuel supply. High-speed attacks also caused Panzers to break down from mechanical problems and combat damage, so that the **I./Panzer-Regiment 8** had only 26 of their 45 **Pz.Kpfw.III** and **IV** available in operational condition to repulse Operation Battleaxe.

To try to cut down on mechanical losses, the **6.Kompanie/Panzer-Regiment 8** was allowed sufficient time to drive from Tripoli to the front. Fuel and water were carried in "Jerry" cans in the racks on the turret roof and on the right fender. (WW)

11

Operation Battleaxe

Following their recapture of Halfaya Pass, German forces on the border set about reorganizing and constructing defensive positions, stretching about 25 kilometers inland from Halfaya. The German doctrine which formed the basis for this defensive system may be summarized as follows:

1. Effective fire is more important than cover.
2. The object of the defense is to wear down an attack before launching a counterattack, generally with armored troops.
3. Reconnaissance must be conducted to discover the enemy's intentions and to screen one's own positions, which are organized in depth.
4. A linked artillery fire plan must cover the entire front.
5. Most of the fire should be concentrated to cover the **Stuetzpunkt**, which is the key to the position and the objective toward which the enemy is likely to put forth his main effort.
6. A series of mutually supporting centers, each capable of all-round defense, must be organized in depth.

A **Stuetzpunkt** was defined as: A strongly constructed and armed point in a defensive position which is capable of being defended when the enemy has forced his way into the defensive position and is capable of attacking the flanks of the enemy when they break through.

Implementing this defensive system doctrine, the German-Italian forces set to work to reinforce and create a series of four main **Stuetzpunkte** and three secondary **Stuetzpunkte** as a series of defensive posts. The Germans, whose theory was that the defensive positions should effect a temporary check pending a powerful armored counterattack, had stocked the **Stuetzpunkte** with food and water for only 2 days.

It was against this well-prepared belt of defensive positions that the British threw the 7th Armoured Division and the 4th Indian Division in "Operation Battleaxe." Again under political pressure to obtain a victory in the only game left to them, the British rapidly planned this offensive with the really optimistic objectives of first defeating the enemy forces on the border, secondly defeating the enemy forces around Tobruk, and thirdly exploiting their success to Derna and Mechili.

11.1 GERMAN-ITALIAN FORCES ON THE BORDER

After Halfaya Pass was recaptured on 27 May 1941, it became the center of the defense. The German-Italian forces were redistributed and orders given for the defense as follows:

1. A Sollum-Halfaya Pass Gruppe was formed, consisting of the **1., 3.,** and **4.Kompanie/I.Bataillon/Schuetzen-Regiment 104**, one **leichte Flak-Batterie** with eight **2 cm Flak** and one **schwere Flak-Batterie** with four **8.8 cm Flak** from **I./Flak-Regiment 33**, and the **I gruppo (Pardi) 2° reggimento artiglieria celere** with eight 100/17 howitzers at **Stuetzpunkt Halfaya**. Both routes up the escarpment to the plateau were to be held. The bulk of the anti-tank weapons were to be put on the right wing above the escarpment. An Italian company from the **II battaglione 62° reggimento fanteria** was to be located in the center. The left wing on the coast was to be weakly held but well mined. An outpost was to be put at Bir el Siweiyat. **Stuetzpunkt Qalala** was to be held by the reinforced **6.Oasen-Kompanie** with one battery of four 100/17 howitzers from **gruppo Pardi**, and one or two Italian platoons were to be the backstop.

2. The defenses of <u>Stuetzpunkt 208</u> (at Point 208, 8 kilometers west of Capuzzo) were to be started on May 27. They were manned by the **4.M.G.Kompanie/ Kradschuetzen-Bataillon 15**, a **schwere Flak-Batterie** with two **2 cm Flak** and four **8.8 cm Flak** from the **I./ Flak-Regiment 33**, plus one **5 cm Pak** and three **3.7 cm Pak** from **Panzer-Jaeger-Abteilung 33**. <u>Stuetzpunkt 206</u> (at Point 206, 8 kilometers south of Capuzzo) was to be held by a reinforced company from **Kradschuetzen-Bataillon 15** with two batteries of the **I./Artillerie-Regiment 33** with eight **10.5 cm leFH**, three **3.7 cm Pak** and three **5 cm Pak** from **Panzer-Jaeger-Abteilung 33**, and four **2 cm Flak** from the **I./Flak-Regiment 33**.

For defense in depth, three **Rueckhalt** (backstop) positions were manned as:

<u>Stuetzpunkt Capuzzo</u> with an Italian infantry company from the **I battaglione 61° reggimento fanteria** supported by two 37/45 anti-tank guns and one 2 cm anti-aircraft gun.

<u>Stuetzpunkt Musaid</u> with an infantry and a mortar company from the **II battaglione 62° reggimento fanteria** supported by a platoon of 47/32 anti-tank guns.

<u>Stuetzpunkt Ober Sollum</u> with an infantry and a mortar company from the **II battaglione 62° reggimento fanteria** supported by a platoon of 47/32 anti-tank guns.

In addition, the **I battaglione 61° reggimento fanteria** was occupying positions in the old defense system surrounding Bardia. An observation post was established at Sidi Suleiman by **Aufklaerung-Abteilung 33**, which was also responsible for screening the defense line and conducting reconnaissance patrols.

The second element in the defensive system was a mobile infantry reserve consisting of the remainder of **Kradschuetzen-Bataillon 15**, the **3.Batterie/I./Artillerie-Regiment 33** with four **10.5 cm leFH**, and nine **2 cm Flak** from the **I./Flak-Regiment 33**.

The third element was a Panzer striking force consisting of **Panzer-Regiment 8**, the **2.Kompanie/Schuetzen-Bataillon 104**, one company from **Kradschuetzen-Bataillon 15**, one company from **Panzer-Jaeger-Abteilung 33**, and a **schwere Flak-Batterie** with four **8.8 cm Flak** and a **leichte Flak-Batterie** with eight **2 cm Flak** from the **I./Flak-Regiment 33**. This Panzer striking force was held in reserve north of Capuzzo. The **I.Abteilung/Panzer-Regiment 8** had 13 **Pz.Kpfw.II**, 18 **Pz.Kpfw.III**, and 8 **Pz.Kpfw.IV** operational on the morning of 15 June. No report has been found on the exact strength of the **II.Abteilung/Panzer-Regiment 8**, which

The **6.Kompanie/Panzer-Regiment 8** with mostly **Pz.Kpfw.III Ausf.H**s on the final stretch of their march to the front. Using a single-digit tactical number for the **Kompanie** (usually stenciled in red) on the sides and rear of the turret, each **Zug** was identified by the color of the stripe around the top of the stowage bin, red and white striped for the **Kompanie-Trupp**, white for the **1.Zug**, red for the **2.Zug**, yellow for the **3.Zug**, and light blue for the **4.Zug**. (WW)

should have been higher than the **I.Abteilung**. Two companies in the **II.Abteilung** had not been in action and shouldn't have had very many mechanical breakdowns in their new Panzers during their slow trek to the front. The 62 medium and 36 light German tanks at the border (recorded by the commander of Tobruk in his diary; may have come from a radio intercept of a coded message) appear reasonably close to what the actual figures should have been.

Most of the remaining elements of **15.Panzer-Division** were manning positions in the Ras el Mdauuar salient on the southwest side of Tobruk. **Panzer-Regiment 5** with the **5.leichte Division** were back by Tobruk. **Panzer-Regiment 5** reported 39 **Pz.Kpfw.II**, 38 **Pz.Kpfw.III**, and 19 **Pz.Kpfw.IV** as operational on 15 June 1941; some of these belonged to **Panzer-Regiment 8**.

This Mk.IIA Infantry Tank has been fitted with a hood, and the side skirts are painted in an attempt to disguise it as a truck. These hoods were fitted on 5/6 June for the approach march and were dropped prior to going into action. (TTM)

11.2 BRITISH FORCES FOR THE OFFENSIVE

The "Tiger" convoy arriving in Alexandria harbor on 12 May supplied a large portion of the tanks utilized in Operation Battleaxe. With it came a total of 238 tanks, of which 21 were Mk.VIC Light Tanks (8 required a complete overhaul), 15 Mk.IVA Cruiser Tanks (with an average milage of 700 miles out of an expected engine life of 1000 miles) and 67 Mk.VI Cruiser Tanks (new and in good shape), and 135 Mk.IIA Infantry Tanks (of which 69 were ready for issue by 28 May, each requiring an average of 48 hours in the workshops). Displaying typical British efficiency, of the 135 Infantry Tanks only 25 Mk.IIA and 77 Mk.IIA* had been unloaded by 20 May.

The number of tanks available for the offensive was slightly reduced when a Troop of the 7th.R.T.R. with six Mk.IIA Infantry Tanks embarked for Crete on 16 May along with 16 Mk.VIB Light Tanks with a Squadron from the 3rd Hussars. In addition, the 7th R.T.R. sent three Mk.IIA Infantry Tanks from A Squadron to Tobruk on 24 May and a fourth Mk.IIA Infantry Tank left for Tobruk on 27 May.

The Mk.IIA Infantry Tanks were used to reequip the 4th, 5th, and 7th R.T.R. assigned to the 4th Armoured Brigade. On 21 May, 16 Mk.IIA Infantry Tanks were sent by rail to replace casualties and breakdowns in 4th R.T.R. Completely equipped, B Squadron moved forward from Sidi Bishr on 24 May to join up with the 4th R.T.R. near the border. Between 22 and 31 May, the 7th R.T.R. drew 53 Infantry Tanks and 6 Light Tanks. One Infantry Tank from A Squadron was returned to Ordnance as unfit and four more were sent to Tobruk, leaving the 7th R.T.R. with 48 Infantry Tanks and 6 Light Tanks. 7th R.T.R. spent 5 June on maintenance and fitting canopies to disguise the Infantry Tanks as trucks. The 4th Armoured Brigade HQ drew two Mk.IIA Cruiser Tanks from RAOC on 29 May.

The third unit of the 4th Armoured Brigade, the 5th R.T.R., started slowly receiving their tanks on 2 June. They had received a total of 4 Mk.VIB and 1 Mk.VIC Light Tanks, 24 Mk.IIA and 9 Mk.IIA* Infantry Tanks, and 2 Mk.I Cruiser Tanks by the end of the day on 15 June. Outfitted too late to be used in the offensive, A Squadron 5th R.T.R. entrained in Sidi Bishr on 16 June, arriving at Mersa Matruh at 0630 hours on 17 June, followed by HQ and B Squadron R.T.R. which entrained on 19 June, arriving at Mersa Matruh at 0700 hours on 20 May.

The Cruiser Tanks were used to reequip the 2nd R.T.R. and 6th.R.T.R. assigned 7th Armoured Brigade. On 29 May, the 2nd R.T.R., with A and C Squadrons still in the forward area, reported that they only had 16 Fit Cruiser Tanks out of 18, having lost four more as crocks. On 4 June, B Squadron rejoined the 2nd R.T.R. with 16 Mk.IVA Cruiser Tanks, of which two had temporarily broken down and one was a mechanical crock. The third member of the 7th Armoured Brigade, the 7th Hussars stationed back at Amiriya were ordered to send their only tanks forward to the 2nd R.T.R. These seven Mk.I Cruiser Tanks arrived from Mersa Matruh on 9 June. The 2nd R.T.R. was sent into action understrength with 10 Mk.I, 11 Mk.IIA, and 21 Mk.IVA Cruiser Tanks.

On 17 May, the 6th R.T.R. started to draw their new Mk.VI Cruiser Tanks from the RAOC and continued to do so through 30 May. They left Amiriya by train with 52 Mk.VI Cruiser Tanks on 1 June, arriving in Mersa Matruh the next day. On 6 June, they expected to fit the tanks with sham lorry bodies. These arrived after much delay but without the hinges with which to fit them and were sent back to Mersa Matruh. The HQ 7th Armoured Brigade had a minimum of four Mk.IIA Cruiser Tanks.

One of the first batch of Mk.VI Cruiser Tanks shipped to Egypt with the "Tiger" convoy. It was still painted in the three-tone (light sandy color with black - gray) camouflage pattern. It features the earlier style internal gun mantlet and the subsidiary turret for a second 7.92 mm machinegun. (TTM)

The only other British tanks at the front were in a Squadron of the 3rd Hussars with up to 16 Mk.VIB Light Tanks and an unknown number of Cruiser Tanks with HQ 7th Armoured Division.

Back in Tobruk the British tank force was made up of the 3rd Armoured Brigade HQ with 3 or 4 Mk.VIB Light Tanks; the 1st R.T.R. with 21 Mk.VIB Light Tanks and 6 Mk.I, 9 Mk.IIA, and 12 Mk.IVA Cruiser Tanks; and D Squadron 7th R.T.R. with 4 Mk.VIB Light Tanks and 15 Mk.IIA Infantry Tanks.

Additional details on the organization and strength of the British forces are presented in the order of battle for Operation Battleaxe dated 15 June 1941.

11.3 PRELIMINARY MOVES

DAK KTB 28 May 1941 - *Weather, maximum temperature 30° (86°F)*

Stab II.Abteilung, 6. and 7.Kompanie/Panzer-Regiment 8 arrived in the forward area.

The enemy sent strong armored car patrols to feel out Gruppe Herff's new positions.

4th R.T.R. 28 May 1941 - A composite force of 15 Mk.IIA Infantry Tanks was ordered forward to the Buq Buq area. C Squadron withdrew to refit.

DAK KTB 29 May 1941 - *As determined from aerial observation, the enemy had probably again strongly occupied his field positions on Hagiag el Agaba in the Habata area.*

At around 1900 hours, a scouting Panzerspaehtrupp shot an enemy armored vehicle into flames near Sidi Suleiman.

DAK KTB 31 May 1941 - *Weather, maximum temperature 38° (100°F)*

DAK KTB 1 June 1941 - *Weather, maximum temperature 40° (104°F)*

From 1 to 7 June, A Squadron 4th R.T.R. was still in Buq Buq, B Squadron in the Habata area, and the rest of the 4th R.T.R. were refitting.

DAK KTB 2 June 1941 - *Weather, maximum temperature 32° (90°F)*

As the leader of a Panzerspaehtrupp, Leutnant Engelhardt of Aufklaerung-Abteilung 33 distinguished himself by breaking through the enemy security line southeast of Sollum and bringing back useful information on the enemy dispositions.

The 17° divisione fanteria "Pavia", recently brought forward, was to relieve the 5.leichte-Division and "Ariete" in their stationary defensive positions.

BRITISH ORDER OF BATTLE ON THE BORDER 15 JUNE 1941

7th Armoured Division
HQ 7th Armoured Division
- HQ 7th Armoured Brigade
  - 2nd Bn. Royal Tank Regiment
  - 6th Bn. Royal Tank Regiment
  - 11th Hussars
    - One Troop 38th Light AA Regt.
    - Detachment 4th Field Squadron R.E.
- HQ Support Group
  - A Squadron Royals
  - 1st Kings Royal Rifle Corps
  - 2nd Bn. Rifle Brigade
  - 4th Royal Horse Artillery
    - 12th Australian Anti-Tank Battery
    - D Battery 3rd Royal Horse Artillery
    - 3rd Battery 1st Light AA Regt. R.A.
    - 4th Field Squadron R.E
- 102nd Battery 65th Anti-Tank Regiment
- 2nd Battery 1st Light AA Regt. R.A.
- 143rd Field Park Troop

4th Indian Division
- 4th Armoured Brigade Group
  - 4th Bn. Royal Tank Regiment
  - 7th Bn. Royal Tank Regiment
  - One Squadron 3rd Hussars
  - 31st Field Regiment R.A.
    - One Co. 2nd Bn. Rifle Brigade
    - Detachment 12th Field Co. R.E.
- Halfaya Group
  - 2nd Camerons
    - One Squadron 4th Bn. R.T.R.
    - One Plat. 11th Ind.Inf.Bde. AT Co.
- 22nd Guards Brigade Group
  - 3rd Coldstream Guards
  - 2nd Scots Guards
  - 1st Royal Buffs
  - 65th Anti-Tank Regiment
    - One Sq. Prince Albert Victors Own
    - 9th Australian Light AA Battery
    - One Sect. 12th Field Company R.E.
    - Detachment 11th Field Park Co. SM
- Artillery Group
  - 6th Field Regiment R.A.
    - 212th Medium Battery R.A.
    - 4th Light AA Battery R.A.
    - One Battery 65th Anti-Tank Regt.
- Coast Force:
  - 11th Indian Infantry Brigade
  - 2nd Mahrattas
  - 1st Rajputana Rifles
  - Central India Horse
  - 25th Field Regiment R.A.
    - Two Trps. 4th R.T.R.
    - 27/28th Medium Battery R.A.
    - 4th Field Company SM
    - Detachment 11th Field Park Co. SM
- Area of Halfway House:
  - Prince Albert Victors Own
    - One Trp. 65th Anti-Tank Regt.
    - One Sect. 9th Austr. Light AA Btry.

DAK KTB 3 June 1941 - *Weather, maximum temperature 26° (79°F)*

The **Korps** *ordered further movement and reorganization of the* **Kampfgruppen***.*

DAK KTB 4 June 1941 - *In the early morning, an enemy assault unit was repulsed near Capuzzo-Sollum.*

DAK KTB 5 June 1941 - *Weather, maximum temperature 26° (79°F)*

The transport of **"Pavia"** *is proceeding with the first units arriving to relieve the* **5.leichte Division** *and* **"Ariete."**

DAK KTB 6 June 1941 - *The complete reorganization of the enemy forces on the Sollum front was discovered by radio intercept during 6 June. The British division headquarters previously at Sidi Barrani was probably relocated to the Habata area. A second regimental headquarters was added to the enemy groups on the plateau. It is possible that the artillery was reinforced by one or two batteries. Several groups were probably moved forward further to the northwest during 6 June. The enemy group on the coastal plain was reorganized and the forces previously located there were concentrated. A new, unrecognized command position was inserted between the southern and northern groups. All passes and leaves were denied to the British troops for the period from 2 to 10 June.*

The British aerial reconnaissance had increased during the past few days. They flew two or three times daily over the positions by Capuzzo and the Halfaya Pass as well as the rearward areas.

D.A.K. *ordered a reorganization of the forces on both fronts.*

DAK KTB 7 June 1941 - *The enemy east of Sollum seems to be reorganizing again. Two divisions were formed from the previously known forces, which were positioned one behind the other with the forward division in the area south of Buq Buq, the rear division south of Sidi Barrani. Strong armored forces were possibly sent to the desert plateau.*

At 0700 hours on 7 June, the 7th R.T.R. marched out from leaguer with 48 Infantry Tanks, 6 Light Tanks and 2 Cruiser Tanks. The 6th R.T.R. also started their march to the front with their 52 Mk.VI Cruiser Tanks.

DAK KTB 8 June 1941 - *Reorganization of the opponent southeast of Sollum appears to be completed. Further reports were not possible because the enemy renewed radio silence.*

Relief of the **"Ariete"** *by the units from* **"Pavia"** *was completed.*

DAK KTB 9 June 1941 - *Combat aerial reconnaissance reported a large collection of about 200 vehicles with several tanks and armored cars south of Habata. Numerous tanks were recognized in an aerial photo of the old groups of 80 to 100 vehicles west of Bir el Tlata. The number of vehicles has increased in the already known enemy groups around Alem el Behasc and Bir er Rabia.*

Radio reconnaissance was more difficult because of new cover names and call sign changes by the enemy. An intention to attack was not recognizable.

On 9 June, the 7th R.T.R. arrived south of Alum Rabia with 47 Infantry Tanks, 5 Light Tanks and 2 Cruiser Tanks.

DAK KTB 10 June 1941 - *The aerial reconnaissance reported that no important changes had been made in the enemy forces on the desert plateau. The forward enemy security line from Bir es Scegga to Gasr el Abid to Sidi el Fadeil was also verified by ground reconnaissance from* **Gruppe Herff***. The enemy reinforced his positions enormously with armored cars and mounted weapons, especially in the Bir Sceferzen-Qaret Abu Sayid sector and attempted to press further to the north. The tent city at El Hamman-Jmajid increased from 950 to 1500 to 2000.*

Following the changed enemy situation, it was not possible for the **5.leichte Division** *to pull out and relocate to quiet positions on the coast west of headquarters. In accordance with the* **Korps** *order, the division remained as* **Korps** *reserve in the El Adem-Acroma area.*

The HQ tanks of the 4th R.T.R. were moving on 9 June to join B Squadron and A Squadron (less two troops) at Sofafi. The remainder of C Squadron rejoined the 4th R.T.R. on 10/11 June.

DAK KTB 11 June 1941 - *Further minor changes were noticed in the opponent's organization east of Sollum. It is possible that another new infantry or motorized battalion has arrived in the coastal area. Increased radio traffic and use of a code word was noticed.*

All was quiet on the Sollum Front during the day. A sandstorm decreased employment of the Luftwaffe.

DAK KTB 12 June 1941 - *Weather, maximum temperature 25° (77°F) Sandstorm between 1000 and 1700 hours.*

DAK KTB 13 June 1941 - *Aerial photographs revealed further reinforcement by the enemy, aircraft between Mersa Matruh and Alexandria and growth of the tent city in the region around El Hamman to 2950 tents.*

Aerial reconnaissance and radio intercepts reported the possibility of movement of tank forces out of the Bir el Tlata area to Habata. A 1-kilometer-long supply depot was located south of Alem er Rabia. From Bir el Tlata to Bir el Aneba and Sidi Cabiso to the east, convoy traffic in both directions was observed on newly traveled trails.

All was quiet on the Tobruk and Sollum Fronts during the day.

DAK KTB 14 June 1941 - *From radio reconnaissance, the enemy had moved additional strong forces forward from the Tlata area to the region of Der el Brugh-Sofafi. The relocation of a division headquarters and the headquarters of a tank brigade to the area directly east of Dir el Hamra was discovered by radio bearings. A code word for 15 June was passed through all headquarters to the lower echelons.*

From aerial reconnaissance on the evening of 13 June, new vehicle groups of 80 to 100 vehicles each were located in the Der el Brugh-Der el Hleiliba area, and additional smaller groups were located northeast and north of them. These reports were confirmed again on the evening of 14 June.

*On the evening of 14 June, the **Korps** calculated that an enemy attack would be made on 15 June. The following orders were issued after 2100 hours:*

*Orders to **5.leichte Division**: Advance one **Panzer-Abteilung** and one battery when the moon comes up for the purpose of establishing a security force to the east near Point 183 south of Gambut. **5.leichte Division** be prepared to march at 0500 hours on 15 June.*

*Orders to **Aufklaerung-Abteilung 3, III./Artillerie-Regiment 33, battaglione carri M "Rizzi" of "Ariete"**, and **Colonno Santa Maria** were to be prepared to march after 0500 hours on 15 June.*

***Division "Ariete"** was alerted in their position on both sides of Gazala.*

***Fliegerfuehrer Afrika** was requested to maintain all forces ready to attack on 15 June.*

Reconnaissance over Tobruk located a new large group of vehicles with 10 to 15 tanks 3 kilometers east of the crossroads 8 kilometers south of Tobruk.

The 2nd R.T.R. arrived 2000 yards west of Kireigat at 1900 hours. Their tank state at this time was reported as HQ 4 Fit; A Squadron 15 Fit, 1 Z; B Squadron 15 Fit, 1 Y; and C Squadron 4 Fit, 2 Y. Starting their approach march from Bir Ramadan at 1545 hours, the 6th R.T.R. arrived at Bir Khireigat at 2230 hours, still with all 52 Mk.VI Cruiser Tanks operational. The 7th Armoured Brigade HQ had at least 4 Mk.IIA Cruiser Tanks.

At 0730 hours on 14 June, the 4th R.T.R. moved to an assembly area west of Sofafi ready to cross the start line at 1645 hours. Two troops (6 Infantry Tanks) of A Squadron had been detached to support the 11th Indian Brigade working up

the coast. The balance of the 4th R.T.R. were at Sofafi with 38 Infantry Tanks, 6 Light Tanks, and 2 Cruiser Tanks.

At 0600 hours, the 7th R.T.R. began the march to an area west of Sofafi S.W., arrived in the laying up area at 1000 hours, and leaguered by squadron. B Squadron had dropped their canopies. At 1645 hours, the 7th R.T.R. began the march out to the Halfway House area with the 4th Armoured Brigade. Not having reported any change in their operational tank status since 9 June, at this time the 7th R.T.R. should have had 47 Infantry Tanks, 5 Light Tanks and 2 Cruiser Tanks.

11.4 THE ATTACK BEGINS

DAK KTB 15 June 1941 - *Weather, maximum temperature 35° (95°F)*

*At 0615 hours, **15.Panzer-Division** reported that the enemy had made probing attacks over our security line south and southeast of Sollum since 0430 hours. The enemy was in unknown strength near Point 204, 13 kilometers east of Sidi Omar; smaller groups were near Point 207 southeast of Point 206, and on the edge of the escarpment toward Halfaya Pass. On the coastal plain the tank and motorized infantry attack was brought to a halt by our fire. Security by Sidi Omar and Gasr el Abid had not observed any enemy activity at this time. The total impression from here is that the enemy intention was not known. It may be an enemy scouting advance on a wide front or an operation to take the forward **Stuetzpunkte**. A large action is still not evident. Since 0630 hours, the enemy also moved past Sidi Omar to the north with seven tanks and artillery. The enemy's intention on the western flank was still unclear.*

A report arrived at 0900 hours: At 0730 hours, strong enemy columns moving to the north were located 15 kilometers north of Sidi Omar. Their suspected intention being to strike with strong forces into the west flank of the Capuzzo-Sollum positions and, after elimination of the German forces, to relieve Tobruk. The possibility had to be considered that in coordination with the attack on Sollum, the enemy would attempt a breakout from Tobruk.

*The observers of **2.(H)14.Pz.** reported: Probable enemy tank attack from the south and southeast against Fort Capuzzo, at 0835 hours 6 kilometers south and southeast of Capuzzo.*

*Based on these reports the **Afrikakorps** issued the following orders:*

*1. **Fliegerfuehrer Afrika** was requested to attack the enemy column north of Sidi Omar with its combat forces. A request for Stukas was added.*

*2. **Aufklaerung-Abteilung 3** and one battery of **I./Flak-Regiment 18** was attached to **5.leichte Division** as their*

Vorausabteilung (advanced element) and were ordered to march.

3. Support from **X.Fliegerkorps** was requested through **Fliegerfuehrer Afrika**.

4. The Italian high command was asked by Ecc. Garibaldi to make the mobile elements of **"Ariete"** available. After a reply was received, **"Ariete"** was ordered to be ready to march at 1500 hours.

At 1000 hours, the **III./Artillerie-Regiment 33** was attached to the **5.leichte-Division** and received orders to march. One battery was detached to support the eastern front of **"Trento."**

At 1100 hours, report sent to **O.K.H.**: Since the morning of 15 June, strong enemy forces have been attacking the Sollum Front from the plateau and the coastal plain. Their main objective is probably the western flank around Sidi Omar. All positions are still held. The Tobruk Front is quiet.

The **5.leichte Division** was ordered to start advancing the main force toward Point 193 south of Gambut at 1430 hours. Their objective was to solidly hold the area, possibly having to defend the area from the south, southeast, and northwest. Maintain readiness to attack to the southeast on the morning of 16 June.

At 1150 hours, the **Vorausabteilung** of the **5.leichte Division** was ordered to advance further through Sidi Azeiz to Capuzzo to be attached to the **15.Panzer-Division** on arrival.

Orders were issued to General Rovera, artillery commander for the **D.A.K.**, to send one **gruppo** of **reggimento artigliaria "Dal Monte"** to the eastern sector to support **"Trento."**

Up to 1200 hours, the **15.Panzer-Division** presented the following picture of the situation: The occupants of Halfaya Pass had repulsed the attack of an infantry battalion reinforced by tanks at 0900 hours. From an intercepted radio message, these were elements of the 4th Indian Division (2nd Camerons) and one company of the 4th R.T.R. The enemy fell back leaving nine prisoners and 18 armored vehicles behind, of which nine Mk.II Infantry Tanks, one armored car, and one carrier were destroyed.

At 1220 hours, strong enemy tank forces had attacked Capuzzo on the line Point 208 to 206. It succeeded in partially penetrating into **Stuetzpunkt 208**. The reinforced **Panzer-Regiment** was sent past Point 208 to counterattack. **Aufklaerung-Abteilung 33** was on security 10 kilometers southwest of Sidi Azeiz. The eastern sector of the front, east of Point 208, was quiet.

Intercepted radio messages provided: The 7th Armoured Division attacked Capuzzo with the 4th and 7th Armoured Brigades. The suspected position of both enemy divisions and a brigade headquarters was in the area south of

Sceferzen-Sidi Omar. This can be confirmation that the main enemy attack lay on the western flank. The enemy knows about the **Vorausabteilung** of the **5.leichte Division**. The British reported that they had left many prisoners in enemy hands at Halfaya Pass.

The **Korps** sent the following messages to the **15.Panzer-Division** at 1240 hours: Occupy the fortifications at Bardia along the Capuzzo to Tobruk road with the battalion from **"Trento"** stationed there. The **5.leichte Division** is advancing on the Trigh Capuzzo and by late afternoon the main body can arrive south of Capuzzo. The **Vorausabteilung**, 50 kilometers in advance, has orders to move through Sidi Azeiz and attack in the direction of Capuzzo.

At 1300 hours, Points 208, 206, and the battery northwest of 206 were again in our hands. The enemy concentrated southwest of 208 and south of 206, probably to conduct further advances. Small enemy tank units out of the area southwest of Sidi Azeiz will probably turn to the west against the **Vorausabteilung** of the **5.leichte Division**. The mobile elements of **Panzer-Regiment 8** positioned themselves northeast of Point 208, ready to counterattack. An enemy radio code list was captured which provided the exact order of battle of the attacking troops, names of the commanders, and the code names for tanks, guns, and supplies.

At 1430 hours, **15.Panzer-Division** reported that the enemy penetrated and captured Capuzzo and now stands 4 kilometers north of Capuzzo with 20 Mk.II Infantry Tanks. A counterattack was ordered to retake Capuzzo. The situation is viewed as being very serious. Request Luftwaffe support for Points 206 and 208. The southern sector of the Bardia fortress has been occupied by the Italian battalion.

At 1630 hours, the main body of the **5.leichte Division** was 22 kilometers west of Point 183.

At 1700 hours, the commander of the **5.leichte Division** arrived at the command post of the **15.Panzer-Division**. The **Vorausabteilung** of the **5.leichte Division** received orders from the **15.Panzer-Division** and were sent on the north side past Point 208 to strike to the southeast. At this moment, Capuzzo was again recaptured and the enemy tank attack advanced on both sides. Results of our Panzer attack are still unknown. Points 208, 206, Halfaya Pass, and Sollum are still in our hands.

At 1730 hours, the **5.leichte Division** was ordered to continue marching to reach the area Sidi Azeiz-Point 216 today.

At 1830 hours, the Luftwaffe reported the following picture of the enemy situation: There are 100 vehicles and some tanks 10 kilometers northeast of Sidi Omar. Strong groups of vehicles with tanks are at Bir Ghirba (north of TN41). Small groups of tanks are near Gabr el Mednar and there are strong enemy forces of unknown strength south of TN41. Four weak

A **Pz.Kpfw.III Ausf.H** of the **6.Kompanie/Panzer-Regiment 8** approaches the frontier wire as artillery fire raises a cloud of dust to its right. (WW)

groups with tanks of about 50 vehicles each were reported on both sides of the north-south track to Hamra.

At 1930 hours, the **Ia** of the **15.Panzer-Division** gave the following situation report: The **Stuetzpunkte** on Halfaya Pass, Sollum, Points 208 and 206 are still in our hands. Results of our Panzer attack are still unknown. Weak forces of ours are still in Capuzzo. The enemy penetrated the defenses and surrounded them. The enemy pressed forward up the road to Bardia. The enemy has broken off his attack on Bardia from the south and southwest. **I.Abteilung/Panzer-Regiment 8** attacked to relieve Point 208 and is now west of Point 206.

The division's plans for the night are to hold the **Stuetzpunkte**, except Capuzzo. Hold the Panzers south of Bardia ready to counterattack to the south on both sides of Capuzzo in the morning. Together with the **5.leichte Division**, we intend to strike the opponent in the flank and rear out of the area 15 kilometers west of Sidi Azeiz at daybreak.

Naturally, losses have been very heavy and several batteries have been captured by the enemy. The losses in Panzers are still unknown, but were not very many altogether. Sixty of the enemies tanks were destroyed, many of them Mk.II Infantry Tanks.

The impression of the enemy is that the intended attack on Bardia from Capuzzo was broken off. Attempts will be made to take a **Stuetzpunkt** during the evening and night. The enemy is very strong in tank forces with about 150 to 200, practically all Mk.II Infantry Tanks.

At 1900 hours, the operations officer of **"Ariete"** reported to the command post and received orders from Rommel: Taking the quickest route, elements of the division under the command of Colonello Montemurro are to reach Ed Duda-Point

157, south of the Trigh Capuzzo east of El Adem during the night. Objectives: 1) To be positioned so that the enemy who try to penetrate over this line can be repulsed and opponents who want to outflank the position to the south can be attacked in the flank. 2) To act as the rear guard and reserve for the southern sector of Tobruk in case of a possible attempt by the enemy to break out.

Battaglione carri M "Rizzi" was attached and sent to **"Ariete."**

The entire Tobruk Front was quiet. A reconnaissance patrol by six tanks against **"Pavia"** raised more alarm than the situation should warrant.

From aerial and radio reconnaissance, the **Korps** had the impression that after pulling back units from Capuzzo, the main body of the enemy was concentrated around Gerrari-TN41.

At 2030 hours, ordered were issued to the **5.leichte Division** and **15.Panzer-Division**: We agree with the previous attack plan of both divisions. Coordinate and set the earliest time possible for the attack and report it. Express requests for Luftwaffe support. We fully agree with previous actions taken.

At 2345 hours, **15.Panzer-Division** reported that the reconquest of Capuzzo was not accomplished and the situation at Point 206 is not clear. The intended attacks are as previously stated: **15.Panzer-Division** on both sides of Capuzzo toward Point 206 initiated at daybreak and **5.leichte Division** in a generally southeast direction against the enemy flank so that they reach the border northeast of Sidi Omar around 0800 hours. Request early aerial reconnaissance south of the line Point 208 to Point 206 to Halfaya Pass. Re-

quest large air strikes at daybreak against the enemy positions, especially on the western flank. There has been no contact between the 15.Panzer-Division and the 5.leichte Division. The plan of attack has been determined exactly and our intentions were sent by radio and messengers. Will report when contact is made with the 5.leichte Division.

The 4th Armoured Brigade with the 4th and 7th R.T.R. were assigned the tasks of assisting in capturing the key defensive positions and protecting the infantry from the Panzer counterattacks.

4th R.T.R. - 15 June 1941 - The planned objectives were:

Objective 1 - To capture Halfaya Pass.
Objective 2 - Point 38 on the Boundary Wire and Point 206
Objective 3 - Possible exploitation of Capuzzo, Musaid and Salum.
Two troops of A Squadron were allotted under command of 11th Brigade working on the coast. C Squadron to take Halfaya Pass in conjunction with the Camerons. B Squadron under command of the Battalion. A Squadron to take Point 38 and Point 206. Two batteries of 25-pounders which were sub-allotted to the commanders of A and C Squadrons.
Squadron Strengths:
Bn. HQ.: 1 Infantry Tank, 3 Light Tanks and 2 Cruiser Tanks from Brigade Headquarters as Rear Link
A Squadron: 9 Infantry Tanks, 1 Light Tank (plus 6 Infantry Tanks with 11th Indian Brigade on the coast)
B Squadron: 16 Infantry Tanks, 1 Light Tank
C Squadron: 12 Infantry Tanks, 1 Light Tank

The 4th R.T.R. moved out on 14 June, passing the starting area at 1745 hours, matched time so that at 0600 hours on 15 June, artillery in support of C Squadron would give a concentration of artillery fire on the Halfaya Pass area. A Squadron moved northwest so as to take Point 38 and 206 not later than 1100 hours and B Squadron in reserve to take over Point 207 from one squadron of the 11th Hussars, taking over to be completed by 0715 hours. A Company of the Coldstream Guards in the vicinity of Point 207 would occupy Point 206 and Point 38 after its capture. 4th R.T.R. HQ were placed at Point 207 with B Squadron.

Action on Halfaya Pass. For some reason, yet unexplained, the artillery failed to give concentrated fire at 0600 hours as arranged. C Squadron at 0605 hours - coming under very heavy fire. Fighting continued until 0930 hours by which time only one tank was fightable and this had a jammed turret and could not direct fire, also damaged transmission

and was therefore unable to take cover. Meanwhile the Camerons had de-bussed at Bir Elsiweiyat and moved about 1000 yards, advanced and took cover during which time they came under very heavy fire. At about 1030 hours a company of this infantry battalion was counterattacked by armoured cars and no support could be given as the tank which may have provided it was unfit to do so. By evening this tank had its turret repaired and could direct its fire. Shell fire continued during that day. Casualties for 15 June amounted to 11 Infantry Tanks, 3 officers and 14 men.

A Squadron. A Squadron arrived at Point 42 where they crossed the wire at 0945 hours and commenced the attack at 1020 hours. At this time the artillery in support of this squadron were instructed to concentrate fire on Point 206 and then switch to Point 38. Firing by observation, the F.O.O. went forward behind the tanks with the Recce. Officer in an Infantry Tank. Point 206 was attacked by one troop and Point 38 by two troops, there being no reserve. By 1100 hours Point 38 was completely subdued and some 8 field guns, some anti-tank guns, and 100 to 200 prisoners were taken, with no casualties to ourselves. Fighting was still in progress at Point 206. At 1120 hours the Squadron Leader proceeded in the direction on Point 206 for personal recce, no information as to the course of battle being obtainable to him. On the way the Squadron Leader saw an Infantry Tank on the right flank some 400 yards from the objective. The Squadron Leader proceeded in this direction and saw 7 men standing beside it together with 2 enemy motorcycle combinations. As he approached the combinations drove off to Point 206 driving the men in front of them. Fire could not be opened without endangering the crew.

At this time the Squadron Leader was under heavy fire and withdrew towards Point 38 to collect the Squadron. His tank was immobilized by shots in the engine and the turret jammed. At 1200 hours, he radioed for one troop to attack Point 206 forthwith, remainder to hold Point 38. A few minutes later one tank appeared heading for Point 206 firing heavily and itself being heavily engaged. This tank ran right along Point 206 and eventually passed out of view over the sky line. Meanwhile, as only one tank appeared, the Squadron Leader radioed for all available tanks at Point 38 for assistance. The Squadron Leader when proceeding on recce had left Point 38 in possession of five Infantry Tanks and one Light Tank and the F.O.O. In consequence of this message three more tanks came out leaving one Light Tank, one immobilized Infantry Tank and F.O.O. tank to guard prisoners. Squadron Leader now radioed for immediate artillery support at Point 206. Effective fire was brought down in about 3 to 4 minutes, the Squadron Leader acting as observation post.

This troop, being unable to find the Squadron Leader or communicate, retired to Point 38 to make a plan. At this time about 20 enemy AFVs appeared from the north. They were engaged by the Infantry Tanks who moved south through the wire to obtain a hull-down position. Meanwhile, the Light Tank trained artillery fire on to the enemy AFVs. During the tank action, one enemy AFV was put on fire and a number actually seen to be hit.

Our tanks were now under fire from front and rear; namely Point 38 and Point 206. They replied to the fire in both directions which was very hot and they slowly withdrew still engaging the enemy finally rallying 2000 yards southeast of Point 38. The troop that had originally attacked Point 206 had one tank immobilized near objective and one temporarily out of action through gun and turret jamming. This troop rejoined the remainder of A Squadron at Point 38 a minute or two before the tank action.

As a result of this engagement Point 38 again came into enemy hands but as a result of our artillery, they soon withdrew.

A report was then made by the Recce Officer regarding the situation at Point 206. SUNA ordered tanks to remain in observation. At 1555 hours, LUPE ordered an attack on Point 206 in conjunction with one company of the Scots Guards who were then at Point 207 and were ordered to meet tanks at vicinity B.P.39.

At approximately 1630 hours, an Infantry Tank attack with four tanks was launched on Point 206. A good flanking movement was made to the south and the tanks came right on to the objective wholly engaging the enemy. One tank was immobilized by gun fire. The tanks remained on the objective for about 15 minutes. At least two guns which were not seen by the tanks registered numerous hits on the tanks. The Squadron Commander reported this to the Recce Officer who also saw them. Meanwhile, infantry and artillery support had arrived at Point 39. As the position appeared untenable by the tanks, the Recce Officer advised the tanks to rally at this point in order to make a fresh concerted attack.

During this attack the Squadron Commander was enabled to get his tank recovered and moved to a place of safety. The Squadron Commander then reported to the artillery and infantry to make a plan of attack with the only tank that remained fighting fit as a result of this last action. Meanwhile medium artillery engaged Point 206. Before this fresh attack was launched, SUNA informed the Squadron Commander that REVA was to launch an attack on instruction received from LUPE at 1725 hours. This attack was carried out by REVA at 1910 hours and was successful with full artillery and infantry co-operation.

B Squadron and 4th R.T.R. HQ. At 0715 hours, B Squadron arrived at Point 207 where they relieved a squadron of the 2nd R.T.R., while 4th R.T.R. HQ proceeded to Abu Faris arriving there at 0830 hours with Brigade HQ. At 0835 hours,

an air message was dropped with a sketch of the positions Point 206, Capuzzo and area. This was shown to the A Squadron Commander and forwarded to Brigade at 0905 hours. At this time 4th R.T.R. HQ was in touch by radio with A and B Squadrons. From there 4th R.T.R. HQ moved forward to Point 207. En route, C Squadron were called up in order that the number of casualties reported could be confirmed and reported to Brigade.

4th R.T.R. HQ then proceeded to join B Squadron at Point 207 via Abu Faris, arriving at Point 207 at 0800 hours. B Squadron were here in hull down positions with hoods still on.

At 0945 hours, it was still impossible to get in touch with C Squadron. Just before midday it was suggested to Brigade that B Squadron should take Point 206 from Point 207. A reply was received that B Squadron must be kept for another role. At 1245 hours, a situation report was given to Brigade as a message had been received from C Squadron confirming that the Squadron Commander had been killed, 5 other ranks wounded and 9 other ranks missing. At 1430 hours, called up Brigade but could get no reply.

At 1530 hours, Brigade ordered 4th R.T.R. HQ and B Squadron to report to Brigade forthwith. Asked for orders for Scots Guards since Point 206 and area were still in enemy hands. Reply from Brigade some time later that Scots Guards would occupy Point 206 after it had been secured by A Squadron. A and B Squadron and Scots Guards informed. Arrived Brigade HQ at 1610 hours, where orders were received for B Squadron to take Point 206. Communication between 4th R.T.R. HQ and squadrons very bad owing to batteries being very weak. At 1930 hours situation report received from B Squadron action progressing. Further information by radio unable to be received. At 1945 hours, the 4th R.T.R. Commander proceeded to Point 206, arriving there in due course.

En route, received from B Squadron situation report stating Point 206 in our hands and no casualties to personnel or vehicles. This message passed to Brigade. Casualty details received from C Squadron about 2030 hours.

The situation of 4th R.T.R. at last light on 15 June was as follows:

A Squadron 1 officer wounded and P.O.W., 2 other ranks wounded.
B Squadron Nil
C Squadron 1 officer killed, 2 missing, 5 other ranks wounded, 9 missing.
Vehicle casualties - state of Squadrons
A Squadron: 1 Infantry Tank and 1 Light Tank
B Squadron: 15 Infantry Tanks and 1 Light Tank
C Squadron: 1 Infantry Tank fit to fight, 1 damaged and 1 Light Tank

Bn HQ: 1 Infantry Tank, 2 Light Tanks (Cruisers detached for Rear Link)

The 4th R.T.R. less C Squadron rallied with Brigade at position Pt.39, B Squadron at Point 206. During the day no information had been received regarding two troops of A Squadron on the Coastal Plain. About midnight the Brigadier ordered that by 0500 hours on the 16th, B Squadron was to take up positions to repel any enemy attack from the north and northwest.

7th R.T.R. - 15 June 1941 - At 1645 on 14 June, 7th R.T.R. commenced march with 4th Armoured Brigade to Halfway House area (543346), arriving at 0200 on 15 June. Refueled and snatched a few hours sleep. At 0415 hours, march out to Batuma (532558) and arrive in area Abu Faris (515336) at 0711 hours. Refuel and have a quick meal. At 0845 hours orders are received by radio to advance to B.P.42. Conflicting messages of action at Halfaya were received. At 1000 hours, 7th R.T.R. crossed the wire through gap at B.P.42. An enemy battery opened fire from the direction of Musaid and Capuzzo. The 7th R.T.R. formed up in area Point 206 (511372) at 1100. A Squadron on the left, B on the right, C in reserve to bring the infantry up when the objective is clear. 2nd R.T.R. could be seen operating on the Hafid Ridge and appeared to be withdrawing in our direction. At 1230 hours, orders received to advance at 1300 hours. At 1245 hours, the advance was delayed until 1330 hours.

Details on the action were recorded in the 7th R.T.R. report on the capture of Capuzzo on 15 June 1941:

The attack was delayed twice and finally started at 1330 hours. Two squadrons up, B right, A left. Objectives Bir Wair - excluding Capuzzo and A Squadron Capuzzo including the cross roads north of Capuzzo. The attack went more easily on the right than on the left.

On the left there was heavy opposition from concealed anti-tank guns and five Infantry Tanks were knocked out. The area was reported clear by the 7th R.T.R. Commander after 1505 hours. B Squadron area reported clear by 1530 hours. The link tanks gained contact with Brigade at approximately 1600 hours and stated that all tasks had been finished and it was clear for the infantry to come up. This was after an enemy counterattack from the north with 20 to 25 A.F.V.s had been beaten off.

As the infantry did not arrive until about 1730 hours, a strong fusement of enemy forces were observed 4500 yards to the north and northwest of Capuzzo. The 7th R.T.R. Commander who was lying behind the two leading squadrons did not contact link tank until 1600 hours and so went back half way and fired all green Verey lights he had in the hope that the infantry would see them. He then returned to his position,

en route driving off some guns who turned up on the left flank.

The Adjutant's link tank was suffering from engine trouble and had difficulty in keeping up with the Commander, who became involved with a demonstration from the left flank.

At approximately 1630 hours, both squadrons left troops in each position until the arrival of C Squadron and the infantry. The 7th R.T.R. Commander's tank and a few tanks, numbering about eight, rallied 1.5 miles southwest of Capuzzo and then drove off an attack by enemy A.F.V.s (from the west) and proceeded after C Squadron and the infantry into Capuzzo. A counter attack by enemy tanks was driven off by C Squadron en route to their objectives.

In Fort Capuzzo the situation was discussed with the Buffs in view of the enemy counter-attacks from the north and west. It was decided that tanks would remain and prevent any mauling of our infantry by enemy tanks.

Order received from Brigade to send sub-units to Musaid. This was impossible at the time, as many of the tanks had been knocked out and many were suffering from mechanical trouble, the result of long marches before the battle, and a large concentration of MET was seen north of Capuzzo. All available tanks were sent forward to the area of the Capuzzo aerodrome.

At 1830 hours, the enemy launched a very strong attack from the west, north and northwest, supported by all arms. This continued to dark, tanks being subjected to fire from more than one direction. Ammunition was replenished round the perimeter by transport borrowed from the infantry. No impression was made by the enemy though they knocked out five or six of our tanks.

At 2100 to 2130 hours, the tanks stood down and withdrew to leaguer south of Capuzzo. It was difficult to find the way back to the rally in the dark and it was midnight before the tanks finally rallied. From the 7th R.T.R., 17 tanks withdrew to the rally area.

The 7th Armoured Brigade with the 2nd and 6th R.T.R., outfitted with Cruiser Tanks, was to advance on the left flank to the Hafid Ridge and beyond, hoping to draw the enemy armor, while the 7th Armoured Division Support Group screened the open flank.

2nd R.T.R. - 15 June 1941 - The 2nd R.T.R. (with 38 operational Cruiser Tanks) moved off at 0315 hours on 15 June. By 0420 hours, they were 1/2 mile south of the cross tracks south of Sidi Suleiman. HQ and C Squadron halted with JAXO at 0455 hours at 51823587. A and B Squadron going on. At 0550 hours, Point 207 was reported clear and handed over to a Squadron of the 6th R.T.R. at 0740 hours. At 0745 hours, 2nd R.T.R. received orders to be ready to move to Gap 42. At 0750 hours, A and B Squadrons moved to 518364. C Squadron and HQ to one mile south of there. This was to collect the Battalion which moved on from there in the order of A, B, HQ, C and then B Echelon.

At 0910 hours on 15 June, 2nd R.T.R. crossed the wire at Gap 42 with the objective of occupying first the Nizwet Ghirba (507368) - Bir Ghirba (504370) line, and then the Hafid Ridge area (506374).

At 0910 hours, A Squadron was at Gap 42. A Squadron moved to 504370 and B Squadron moved to 507368. At 0940 hours, 2nd R.T.R. was ordered to move onto Hafid Ridge 506375. B Squadron arrived there and reported it clear. Subsequently they advanced a little further and were heavily shelled by medium artillery and anti-tank guns and forced to withdraw to the southern slopes of this feature. B Squadron position then at 504372 and A Squadron at 507371. It was discovered that the position they had reported clear was merely an intermediate ridge. At 1045 hours, occasional shelling from Bir Hafid. A few passed over the 2nd R.T.R. and landed among the assembled Infantry tanks around Gap 42.

From information received from A and B Squadrons, 11th Hussars, and 6th R.T.R., it became apparent that there were at least six field guns and six anti-tank guns about the Bir Hafid position. It was unknown what was, or might be, in the dead ground further to the north.

Orders were received from 7th Armoured Brigade that this position was to be attacked with the help of the JAXO Column. The plan of attack was:

1. B Squadron was to move from present location north for 3000 yards than east for 2000 yards onto the position, sweep through it and then rally South.

2. JAXO was to support by rapid fire for 3 minutes while the final run in was being made.

3. A link between B Squadron and JAXO observation post was established through A Squadron who moved to the position vacated by B Squadron when the attack started.

The above plan was slightly modified by the 2nd R.T.R. commander, who ordered A Squadron to support but not to become too heavily involved, as it was essential to keep some reserve in hand.

The attack started at about 1145 hours. At this time Infantry Tanks were moving in a northeast direction about 2 to 3 miles east of the enemy's position. It was hoped that this movement would assist the attack.

B Squadron was to move in a "Two Up" formation with Troop 8 left front, Troop 7 right front, Troop 6 left rear, and Troop 5 right rear. At 1132 hours, the Squadron commander gave the order to move off now, route 3000 yards north, then east to the Bir. There was a slight delay in moving off, owing to the Squadron being spread out and having to change direction 90 degrees. It actually started at 1137.

At 1138 hours, B Squadron commander reported that the enemy movement was considerable on the ridge; nevertheless he would attack. At 1147 hours, B Squadron was ordered to turn right 90 degrees and gunner support was requested. When B Squadron commander crossed the crest, the first thing he noticed was a large white flag, a considerable number of vehicles including field lorries, ammunition lorries, ambulances, and two Light Tanks, one of which was a Mk.VIB and a number of guns small and large anti-tank, probably about a dozen, dotted amongst the transport. At 1156 hours, a message was intercepted from B Squadron commander telling them to make for the white flag, pay no attention to it, and fight like hell. At 1200 hours, the Squadron commander ordered the Squadron to wheel right, go through position and get out of it, pay little attention to vehicles, be more careful of guns. It can only be concluded that the five missing tanks did not get this message and precipitated themselves into even heavier opposition. Troop 7 commander's tank was hit and caught fire as soon as he crossed the crest out of the dead ground. All the crew, however, were seen to evacuate it and ran back.

B Squadron having run right through the forward enemy position eventually rallied back into their start position. At least two guns and the crew of one were run over and destroyed. At 1207 hours, B Squadron commander reported that most opposition on the ridge had been overcome, but that the areas further northwards still held enemy. It was suggested that another Squadron would probably be able to complete the job.

While B Squadron were fighting the above action, A Squadron engaged the enemy from the south at about 1000 yards range, and when B were ordered to rally, A Squadron conformed to the movement and also rallied back in their original position.

The Hafid position was held in strength far greater than at first thought. The enemy were determined to hold this position at all costs, and had prepared many alternative positions for guns. Enemy anti-tank guns were cleverly placed and bravely fought, fire being held until the range was really effective. The attack was a surprise to the enemy and the artillery support of the utmost assistance to the attack. It appeared that failure in the wireless communications may have resulted in the loss of five tanks. Only the forward enemy defenses were encountered. The position appeared to run northwards in some considerable depth.

At 1545 hours, it was discovered that 4th Armoured Brigade had sent four A10s to support the 2nd R.T.R.. B Squadron was sent back to the wire to replenish with ammunition. At 1730 hours, B Squadron returned replenished. Four ammunition lorries came up and refilled A Squadron.

At 1755 hours, a bombing attack nearby and at 1830 hours, a heavy bombing attack on the 2nd R.T.R., neither inflicting casualties or damage.

At 2023 hours, 6th R.T.R. reported 26 enemy tanks two miles north of them. At 2030 hours, 6th R.T.R. was withdrawing. 2nd R.T.R. was ordered to move southwest to protect Gap 42.

At 2040 hours, the following crock report was sent to Brigade:

A Squadron: 12 Fit, 1 Y, 2 Z (runners with turrets damaged by enemy action).
B Squadron: 7 Fit, 3 Y, 0 Z. Battle casualties: 1 hit and destroyed by fire, 5 missing.
C Squadron: 6 Fit
HQ Squadron: 3 Fit, 1 Z (Mk.IVA T15225 on tow by unit Scammell, other Scammell sent for).
Cruisers Fit: 28.

6th R.T.R. 15 June 1941 - At 0430 hours on 15 June, the 6th R.T.R. (with 52 operational Cruiser Tanks) broke leaguer and marched to Qaret Abu Faris, arriving at 0740 hours. At 0745 hours, the 6th R.T.R. was ordered to move 2 kilometers further north and from there to BP 42. At 0810 hours, they arrived at 510360. At 0930 hours, Brigade ordered the 6th R.T.R. to move to BP 43, push through and halt southwest of Bir Ghirba. They were to keep clear and be prepared to support the 2nd R.T.R. At 0950 hours, B Squadron 6th R.T.R. passed through Gap 43. At 1000 hours, the Brigade ordered the 6th R.T.R. to stay in reserve and prepare to meet any threat from the north or northeast. At 1005 hours, 2nd R.T.R. was reported to have reached Bir Ghirba. At 1020 hours, Brigade ordered 6th R.T.R. to move to 502372 continuing in the same role, quickly followed by an order to stand fast at 1030 hours. 6th R.T.R. was now at 502371. At 1105, the Brigade reported six anti-tank guns 200 yards east of Hafid and six field guns at Bir Hafid. At 1130 hours, 2nd R.T.R. reported considerable activity in the Hafid area. The Brigade ordered that if tanks appear, 6th R.T.R. will have to intervene. At 1220 hours, 2nd R.T.R. reported that the guns at Hafid have been over-run, but they require further assistance to mop up the area as their reserve has been used up.

At 1225 hours, Brigade ordered that one sub-unit of 6th R.T.R. was to move at once to assist the 2nd R.T.R. in consolidating the area. At 1226 hours, B Squadron 6th R.T.R. was detailed. At 1234 hours, the Brigade's orders that the sub-unit was to make for the left of the large black plume of smoke was passed on to B Squadron. At 1240 hours, Brigade ordered that the sub-unit be warned that the forward guns have withdrawn and joined the guns further back. B Squadron moved forward to Hafid Ridge and were heavily shelled. Two tanks were immediately knocked out. No liaison had been effected with the 2nd R.T.R.. At 1300 hours, Brigade ordered that the sub-unit be withdrawn to the west and south and that it was not to be committed until ordered. B Squadron was ordered to withdraw. At 1315 hours, B Squadron reported being shelled by our own guns, and unable to withdraw as every time they moved they were fired on. (Later these were stated to have been enemy guns.)

At 1328 hours, Brigade ordered the 6th R.T.R. to stand by to move 3 kilometers north and send one sub-unit to Meduuar Ridge. Brigade was informed that B Squadron was still unable to rally and that they are being shelled from the north and northeast by light field guns.

At 1340 hours, 40 enemy tanks appeared at Hafid Ridge and moved southwest towards the 6th R.T.R.. The 6th R.T.R. formed a line ahead and moved northwest, engaging the enemy at long range. After this engagement the 6th R.T.R. withdrew southwest coming under shell-fire from the Hafid Ridge direction, and retired out of range.

At 1420 hours, the Brigade ordered the 6th R.T.R. to concentrate southwest of Hafid and be prepared to counter attack. At 1425 hours, Brigade ordered the 6th R.T.R. to move 2 kilometers southeast (501374) and to be prepared to counter attack to the east or northeast, through or across the 2nd R.T.R. tanks or to the northwest. At 1435 hours, B Squadron rejoined the unit less two tanks.

At 1436 hours, Brigade ordered the 6th R.T.R. to send their third sub-unit wide to the west to Meduuar and to be prepared to counter-attack towards Hafid Ridge or to go straight through to protect the left flank of the 4th Armoured Brigade. 6th R.T.R. was informed that there were 10 enemy tanks on Hafid Ridge. 6th R.T.R. reported their position at 501374 at 1445 hours. At 1450 hours, Brigade ordered to 6th R.T.R. to leave a sub-unit and go to 504373 and get in touch with 2nd R.T.R. to co-operate. 6th R.T.R. commenced this move at 1500 hours. After moving 1.5 miles southeast, at 1510 hours, they were ordered by Brigade to halt where they were.

At 1555 hours, Brigade ordered the 6th R.T.R. to remain in the present location less one subunit which was to proceed to make good the Meduuar feature. C Squadron was sent to 499374 and remained there, reporting at 1600 hours that 30 enemy tanks were approaching from the northwest. Brigade ordered the 6th R.T.R. to engage and destroy, but keep one sub-unit in hand because an enemy counter-attack was developing towards Capuzzo. At 1605 hours, Brigade ordered the 6th R.T.R., less C Squadron, to move to Bir Ghirba to meet a threat coming from the north or northeast. At 1625 hours, the column reported by C Squadron was composed of lorries at 500376.

Actions of 6th Bn. Royal Tank Regiment on 15 June 1941

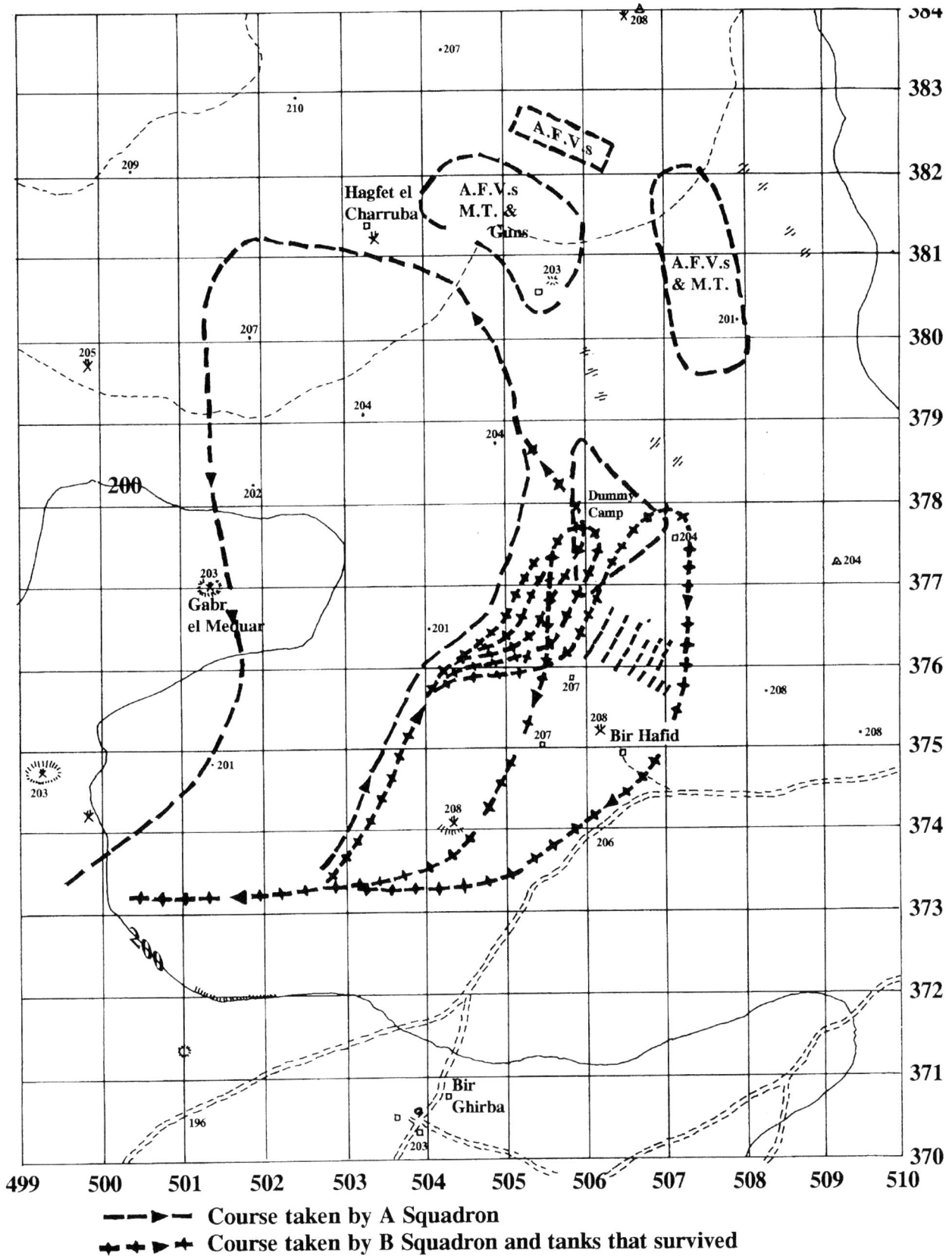

- – ►– Course taken by A Squadron
- ✚✚►✚ Course taken by B Squadron and tanks that survived

At 1645 hours, information was received from Brigade that after our shelling of Hafid Ridge the enemy have retired north. Only a few vehicles are left in the Hafid area. Brigade ordered the 6th R.T.R. to clear up the area and report when ready. Brigade suggested that the 6th R.T.R. attack from the southwest or west and to move C Squadron forward to occupy Meduuar Ridge. At 1700 hours, 6th R.T.R. were ordered to get in touch with JAXO (a mobile artillery column) to co-operate in attack if artillery support was wanted. Advantage was not taken of this offer and no liaison was effected with the 2nd R.T.R.. The liaison officer who had been dispatched for this purpose was recalled by the commander of the 6th R.T.R..

At 1715 hours, 6th R.T.R. reported to the Brigade that patrols were out and the unit was forming up for the attack. At 1720 hours, C Squadron reported the column that they were observing was moving northwest from Meduuar. At 1725 hours, Brigade informed that 30 enemy MET and some guns were at Hafid and ordered the 6th R.T.R. to get on with the attack.

At 1735 hours, A Squadron in co-operation with B Squadron were ordered to attack Hafid Ridge.

A forward patrol who had reported an enemy column consisting of lorries and a few guns and tanks was contacted by A Squadron commander. The enemy were observed 1 1/4 miles distant. The Squadron moving in line ahead closed on the column and opened fire at 800 yards. The column turned out to be a dummy camp in which were British MET and damaged A.F.V.s. No fire was returned from the camp but 3 lorries moved out north from the rear of the position. The Squadron, still in line ahead, moved northwest following the lorries and looking for new targets. To the northeast were well-dug-in anti-tank guns and behind them a large concentration of tanks and MET with field guns in support. These were engaged during the move northeast.

About 1.5 miles from the first target, which was suspected of being a dummy position, another camp consisting of MET, A.F.V.s and guns was encountered. These were engaged at 500 yards range.

Enemy tanks which moved from northeast were also engaged. The Squadron, after a good broadside shoot which was carried out at speed, withdrew westward.

The attack on the northern camps appeared to be a surprise, as artillery fire was not opened for some 10 minutes and there was much movement near the camp area. Artillery fire then became intense, and two tanks were knocked out moving west.

One tank had been previously hit and disabled by the above mentioned anti-tank guns. Crews from damaged tanks were later picked up and the Squadron withdrew southwest onto C Squadron. On the way two British Infantry Tanks were

observed on patrol to the west, and these were later suspected of being used by the enemy. The Squadron again came under shell fire from Hafid direction before rejoining C Squadron.

It was apparent that the enemy position was organized to lure an attack onto the anti-tank and field guns at short range.

The tanks to the east opened fire on the Squadron and moved out as if to counter-attack. It was suggested that these A.F.V.s were the ones which subsequently attacked C Squadron later in the evening. Some of the lorries in the camp were captured British vehicles, and one captured British ambulance was seen to supply ammunition to a gun pit.

From tank commanders' reports, the following damage was calculated to have been inflicted on the enemy:

Tanks definitely hit:	9
Tanks probably hit:	4
Lorries definitely hit:	8
Lorries probably hit:	3

Three anti-tank and one field gun knocked out. Considerable damage was done to personnel on the ground by small arms fire.

Meanwhile 14 tanks of B Squadron advanced in trident north-northeast towards the vehicles on the ridge. A Squadron as already mentioned was in line ahead on their left. B Squadron fired at the enemy vehicles and got no reply, but on crossing dead ground and mounting the rise came under heavy anti-tank fire at ranges from 500 to 300 yards, losing 6 tanks almost immediately. Two more had just previously been knocked out on the right front of the Squadron by gun fire from the northeast.

It is unlikely that any damage was done to the enemy, as the only targets were derelict vehicles covering the gun positions. The six surviving tanks picked up what crews had managed to evacuate and rallied on C Squadron. Of these six tanks, only two were fit for action the following day.

At 1820 hours, 6th R.T.R. reported to Brigade that they were withdrawing. A situation report to Brigade at 1830 hours detailed: Owing to some guns not firing until 300 to 400 yards away, we have sustained many tank casualties, and we have withdrawn 4 to 5 miles west.

At 1930 hours, while the wounded were being attended to and crock states collected, C Squadron reported a column of 70 vehicles, of which 35 were tanks moving southeast, 3 miles from the 6th R.T.R. position. At 2015 hours, 6th R.T.R. reported that they were withdrawing to the southeast and were ordered by Brigade to hold them. C Squadron was left to delay this force, while crocks, wounded, and personnel from casualty tanks were evacuated to BP 42. Three tanks were being towed.

An **8.8 cm Flak L/56** of the **I.Abteilung/Flak-Regiment 33** in a heavily sand-bagged emplacement. From these actions at Halfaya, the **8.8 cm Flak** would later gain a reputation as the greatest anti-tank gun of the war. Above the escarpments close to the coast there was only a very shallow layer of loose rock and earth covering the bedrock, making it impossible to dig in deeper than a foot or two in most places. (KL)

At 2020 hours, 6th R.T.R. reported that one sub-unit was holding them and was being shelled by enemy A.F.V.s with long range guns. Brigade informed the 6th R.T.R. that they were being shelled by 75 mm guns and ordered them to take up hull-down positions. C Squadron carried out a delaying action back to Gap 44, holding the enemy until darkness fell. In the failing light, vehicles, assumed to be enemy, were discerned moving slowly northeast. They were at close range but did not see us.

Tank Status of 7th Armoured Brigade 15 June 1941

	2nd R.T.R.	6th R.T.R.
First light effective strength	38	52
Battle casualties lost	6	13
Damaged (enemy action and mechanical)	4	18
Enemy tanks definitely destroyed	1	9
Enemy tanks damaged or possibly destroyed	0	4

The following scanty details of the defense and counter-attack by the German forces were found in <u>The Development of German Defensive Tactics in Cyrenaica - 1941</u>, Special

Series No.5 prepared by Military Intelligence Service, War Department in October 1942. The descriptions of the actions were extracted from seven after-action reports that the British had acquired when the **15.Panzer-Division** lost their war diary during Operation Crusader. Unfortunately many details in these reports were lost and distorted through being analyzed and summarized by "military intelligence." The original texts have not been found, if copies were even kept after all the valuable information was extracted through "analysis."

The Action at Halfaya on 15 June 1941

The defending forces were as follows: one company on the coastal plain behind a mine field, one Italian company facing east on the edge of the plateau, and one company facing to the south and west of the Italian company. Four **8.8 cm Flak** were sited in the front line covering the open right flank. The eight Italian 105 mm howitzers were distributed between the front line and the interval between Halfaya and Qalala, and the battalion held a company in reserve.

The main attack by the British tanks on the open right flank was stopped by the **8.8 cm Flak** after fire had been taken up by the **2 cm Flak** and all other weapons at 400 meters. When the attack had been broken, a patrol was sent out to establish the position of the British infantry, which was then pinned down by artillery. There was a counterattack by the battalion reserve in which 67 prisoners and important codes and maps were captured. A second attack by the British followed in which the defenders held fire until the infantry was within 400 meters, then opened fire with **2 cm Flak**. The British plan to attack by the coast was foreseen and one **8.8 cm Flak** was placed there.

The report of the **I.Abteilung/Flak Regiment 33** indicated that this unit played an important role in the victory. Its guns opened up on the tanks at 2000 meters at 0500, knocking out one Cruiser Tank; then they held fire until the opposing tank force approached to within 300 meters, where dust did not obscure the targets, and bagged nine Infantry Tanks. After this they fired high-explosive shell into the infantry, forcing it to take cover. The **8.8 cm Flak** on the coast knocked out three Infantry Tanks. The **Flak** thus eliminated 14 of the 20 attacking tanks, and doomed the British attack to failure.

The Action at Point 208 on 15 June 1941

When the attack alarm was given, two patrols from Point 208 were sent 2 miles to the south because of mist which blanketed the area. Fire was held for some time after tanks were first observed, because they were in the barrage area of Point 206. The **3.7 cm Pak** opened fire first to drive off armored cars which were within 150 meters. Meanwhile the barrage from Point 206 had ceased, but Paulewicz gave orders to hold all anti-tank fire until vehicles approached to within

close range in order not to give away anti-tank positions prematurely. This policy proved effective, for subsequent British artillery fire on Point 208 was inaccurate.

At 1015 on June 15, the British made a pincer attack on Point 208 with 45 tanks. The attacking force was soon reinforced to 70 tanks. Fire by all weapons was opened at close range. The left or easterly sector of the area was overrun, one **3.7 cm Pak** and one **2 cm Flak** were knocked out, and one of the **8.8 cm Flak** was silenced. The commander of Point 208 immediately ordered the three **8.8 cm Flak** on the other flank to concentrate on the eastern sector, and this saved the situation by enabling the silenced **8.8 cm Flak** to reopen fire. By 1130 hours, 11 British tanks had been smashed and the rest driven away, and in the afternoon a new 14-tank attack was thrown back, with eight tanks knocked out. After that, Point 208 was secure and was used as a base for reforming **Panzer-Regiment 8** and the mobile infantry reserve.

The **I.Abteilung/Flak Regiment 33** had knocked out 19 tanks with its **8.8 cm Flak**. The description of the battle given in the **Abteilung** report differs slightly from that of Paulewicz. The **8.8 cm Flak** opened up at 1600 meters and drove back the first tank attack without inflicting any casualties. In the pincer attack, the gun on the left flank knocked out two Cruiser Tanks before it was overrun. The three other **8.8 cm Flak** on the right opened fire upon the other arm of the pincers at 1500 meters without getting hits, but later knocked out seven Cruiser Tanks at close range. In the third attack the **8.8 cm Flak** opened at 800 meters, knocking out eight Cruiser Tanks and later two Infantry Tanks.

The Action at Point 206 on 15 June 1941

Point 206 had no **8.8 cm Flak**, but five British tanks were knocked out by its **Pak** in the first attack. The **2 cm Flak**, however, proved useless. This **Stuetzpunkt** was finally overrun after the last **5 cm Pak** had been knocked out.

The Panzer Striking Force on 15 June 1941

German defensive theory emphasizes the role of the armored striking force, stating that defense is simply a temporary expedient. **Panzer-Regiment 8** meant it to be temporary indeed, for by 1030 hours on the first day of the action they were well up from their assembly area north of Capuzzo, and by 1130 hours one company was already engaged on the frontier. Reinforced by a second company, it nevertheless had to withdraw before superior numbers. In doing this it ran out of ammunition, allowing the British to take Capuzzo.

By this time two **Pz.Kpfw.III** had been knocked out and some others had fallen out with damage to their guns and engines. A third company was now called in to prevent the British from breaking through west of Capuzzo, but it also had to retire. Later in the day the **I.** and **II.Abteilung/Panzer**

Regiment 8 attacked Capuzzo in succession, but failed to get through and withdrew before dark to a position near the Bardia road. **Panzer-Regiment 8** had violated the rules of German tank doctrine by attacking in detail.

The report of the **I.Abteilung/Flak Regiment 33** explains some of these moves. The four **8.8 cm Flak** attached to **Panzer-Regiment 8** had participated in the first frontier action. After opening up at 1900 meters, they had knocked out 12 tanks, 2 of them Infantry Tanks struck at 1200 meters. British artillery then forced the **8.8 cm Flak** to withdraw. During these engagements a **2 cm Flak** knocked out an Infantry Tank with a lucky hit on the exhaust at 250 meters.

<u>**DAK KTB 16 June 1941**</u> - *At 0100 hours, following an orientation on the situation, the **Fliegerfuehrer** was requested to attack the enemy forces south of the Point 206 to Halfaya Pass line.*

*At 0130 hours, **D.A.K.** ordered the **5.leichte Division**: Plans for the **5.leichte Division** have been discussed with the **15.Panzer-Division**. Attack early past the north of Sidi Omar, striking the enemy rear and flank. Cross the border at 0800 hours, at the latest.*

*The following message was transmitted at the same time: **5.leichte Division** intends to initiate the attack from the west of Sidi Azeiz, through Bir Chirba toward Sidi Suleiman at 0500 hours.*

*At 0455 hours, **15.Panzer-Division**'s Panzer attack on Capuzzo started. The **5.leichte Division** reported that their attack had been initiated as ordered.*

At 0745 hours, evaluation of radio interceptions provided: The 7th R.T.R. of the 4th Armoured Brigade attacked north of Capuzzo and the British reported a large tank battle. With this, the expected outflanking of the 4th Armoured Brigade failed.

*At 0800 hours, aerial reconnaissance by **2.(H)/14.Pz.** reported strong groups of tanks and trucks around Bir Hafid, Capuzzo, south of Bir Uaar by TN41, and 8 to 12 kilometers southeast of Sidi Omar.*

*At 0820 hours, the **15.Panzer-Division** reported that the outcome of the Panzer attack on Capuzzo was not known and **Stuetzpunkt Musaid** was in enemy hands.*

*At 0900 hours, **Fliegerfuehrer** completed attacks against the enemy south of Point 206 to Halfaya Pass and on the division headquarters 6 kilometers southeast of Sidi Suleiman.*

*At 1000 hours, **5.leichte Division** reported: Involved in fierce combat 8 kilometers south of Sidi Omar. Under fire from two artillery batteries. There are numerous tanks and anti-tank guns in the Chirba area.*

*From radio reconnaissance, the **5.leichte Division** was across from the 7th Armoured Brigade.*

One of the operations orders captured today provided

information that the 4th Indian Division with the 22nd Guards Brigade and the 4th Armoured Brigade was the main attack force. The 7th Armoured Brigade with the 2nd and 6th R.T.R. and 11th Hussars were placed on the left as a flank security force.

*At 1100 hours, after hard fighting, the Panzer attack on Capuzzo had to be broken off. Only 35 Panzers of the **15.Panzer-Division** were still mobile. The motorized forces of the division (**Panzer-Regiment**, one **Bataillon**, two **Batterien**, and part of the **Aufklaerung-Abteilung**) assembled in the area 5 to 10 kilometers north of Capuzzo. The **15.Panzer-Division** believed that an attack against unshaken opponents was no longer possible because of strong motives and high losses of weapons.*

Stuetzpunkt 208 *had knocked out 20 tanks and still held. Capuzzo, Musaid, and probably Point 206 were held by the enemy. Sollum was being attacked from the west. The opinion of the **15.Panzer-Division** was that prospects for continuing to hold the positions were not very high. Halfaya Pass had repulsed all enemy attacks and still held. Resupply of food, water and ammunition by air was urgently requested.*

Korps *ordered the **15.Panzer-Division**: The situation is serious. Hold back the mobile reserves until the situation of the **5.leichte Division** is clarified. Move the mobile forces further to the west and try to link up with the **5.leichte Division**.*

*At 1050 hours, **5.leichte Division** reported that after the successful conclusion of the Panzer battle north and northeast of Sidi Omar, the division began attacking with the right flank through Sidi Omar toward Sidi Suleiman.*

*At 1225 hours, **5.leichte Division** was located around and in Sidi Omar in a hard fight and the attack came to a standstill.*

*At 1235 hours, orders were sent to **15.Panzer-Division**: Behind a screen of whatever units are necessary, pull out all available forces and strike east of Point 208 toward Sidi Suleiman.*

*The **Korps** intention was, relying on the **5.leichte Division** to break the known enemy between Omar and Capuzzo, to use the mobile force of **15.Panzer-Division** to strike against the flank of the 4th Armoured Brigade and relieve Halfaya Pass.*

*At 1245 hours, the **Fliegerfuehrer** was requested to send all forces to attack the enemy in Capuzzo and Musaid.*

At 1300 hours, an intercepted radio message provided: The 11th Brigade, reinforced with tanks and artillery, received orders at 1000 hours to advance toward Sollum on the coastal plain. At 1045 hours, the brigade reported that they couldn't advance and that two tanks stood in flames.

The enemy air force attacked our columns attacking Sidi Omar.

At 1400 hours, the 2nd R.T.R. and 6th R.T.R. of the 7th Armoured Brigade were attacked while they were refueling. They were located 4 kilometers north and northeast of Sidi Omar. Small German units had already crossed the border fence. It was suspected that the enemy had a supply base at Sidi Omar.

At 1600 hours, the headquarters of the 7th Armoured Division was probably located 20 kilometers further back to the southeast.

At 1620 hours, the enemy probed to the north out of Capuzzo. He could probably no longer resolve to attack determinedly, considering the **Stuetzpunkte** still held at his rear and the strong pressure on his flank.

The **5.leichte Division** was attacked while refueling and taking on ammunition. The attack on Sidi Suleiman could be depended on starting soon. **15.Panzer-Division** had withdrawn units to cooperate with the **5.leichte Division** in an attack on Sidi Suleiman from Point 208. They received orders from the **Korps** to absolutely hold **Stuetzpunkt Halfaya-Sollum** and encourage the personnel. The situation changes favorably; hold through to the last.

At 1630 hours, message to **5.leichte Division**: Our swift strike against Sidi Suleiman is of important consequence.

Fliegerfuehrer Afrika was requested to attack Point 206 and the area to the east and southeast but not Halfaya Pass.

The **5.leichte Division** reported that they would utilize their entire force in the attack at 1700 hours to throw back the strong enemy forces at Sidi Omar and reach Sidi Suleiman.

At 1735 hours, **D.A.K.** reported to the **O.K.H.**: Heavy fighting since dawn with both divisions against a strongly superior enemy. Out of an estimated 300 to 400 tanks, up to now 80 to 100 have been destroyed. An important attack on the west flank in the area of Sidi Omar is proceeding at this time.

At 1800 hours, **Fliegerfuehrer Afrika** and **2.(H)/14.Pz.** reported: Strong elements of the **5.leichte Division** lay under heavy artillery fire on the border 7 kilometers northeast of Sidi Omar. Halfaya Pass is in German hands. There are dust clouds north of Sidi Omar from columns advancing toward the southeast. There are strong friendly forces near Sidi Azeiz.

The following order from the **Korps** was dropped on Halfaya Pass by a fighter plane: Our counterattack from the west is advancing well and the enemy is being repulsed. Success hangs upon holding Halfaya Pass and the coastal plain. Defend toward Sollum.

At 1830 hours, Sollum has probably fallen. The commander of **Panzer-Regiment 8** fell from an artillery strike. From the last report, the attack by the **5.leichte Division** and **15.Panzer-Division** failed because of artillery fire. Further to the west, the assembly area was also under fire.

At 2015 hours, the impression is that, altogether, the enemy is quiet. Twenty-five tanks are advancing to the north from Musaid.

The **15.Panzer-Division** feared that the enemy would attack Halfaya Pass from Sollum and out of the east from the coastal plain on 17 June.

The attack of the **15.Panzer-Division** was changed to the next morning, because **5.leichte Division**'s attack didn't start until 1800 hours and must be accomplished first. Radio contact between the **5.leichte Division** and **15.Panzer-Division** was poor. It is **15.Panzer-Division**'s intention to concentrate the mobile forces by Point 208 and start toward Sidi Suleiman at dawn.

At 1905 hours, north of Sidi Omar, **Panzer-Regiment 5**'s attack toward Sidi Suleiman advanced well. The attack of the main body of the division against and south of Sidi Omar suffered from artillery fire.

Detachment Montemurro arrived at Contoniere 30 kilometers west of Tobruk at 0320 hours. Although **"Ariete"** lay as a reserve by Gazala at the disposal of the Italian high command, it had so little fuel that the assembled battle groups had trouble reaching the ordered area east of El Adem. It had taken until 1900 hours on 16 June to organize as ordered. Only after considerable trouble and exertion by the **Korps** at the Italian liaison headquarters did detachment Montemurro receive sufficient fuel to be mobile for further deployment.

At 1115 hours, the mobile elements of **colonna Santa Maria**, (11 vehicles and 84 men) under the command of Major Teetz of the **Korps-Stabes**, received orders to advance through El Adem and Bir el Gubi to Gabr Saleh, raise as much dust as possible and return at night. The purpose being to simulate strong forces advancing to strike in the rear of the British forces.

At 2300 hours, detachment Montemurro received orders to advance to Sidi Azeiz on the Trigh Capuzzo at down or at the latest 0700 hours. There they were to join and be subordinate to the **15.Panzer-Division**.

2nd R.T.R. - 16 June 1941 - At 0010 hours on 16 June, orders were received to move to Point 204 507364 and to replenish there. One Troop was to be left west of the wire until replenishment was complete and all crocks had been got back east of the wire.

At 0230 hours, 2nd R.T.R. received information that enemy have moved south in two columns, one to Bir Hatid, one of 35 MET to 497369. Orders were issued to be in position at 502365 at 0530 to destroy the enemy at 497369.

2nd R.T.R. moved as ordered at 0430 hours. At 0515 hours, it was reported that the column to be attacked was moving southeast. 2nd R.T.R. arrived in position at 502365 at 0530 hours. At 0750 hours, 2nd R.T.R. was ordered to move to Bir Ghirba 504370 area to watch and be prepared to engage the enemy. Shortly after this it became apparent that the general enemy movement was southwest towards Sidi

Omar (494359) and a column of approximately 150 MET and tanks was reported moving in this direction. Orders were then received from Brigade instructing 6th R.T.R. to attack the flank of the column and force it to keep away to the west, away from the wire. 2nd R.T.R. were to operate on 6th R.T.R.'s northeast flank. A general action followed in which 6th R.T.R. attacked in a northeast direction running parallel to the enemy column. This movement was carried on as far as 2nd R.T.R.'s position, tending to mask their fire. After this attack 6th R.T.R. rallied in the area of Gap 47. Meanwhile 2nd R.T.R. continued their action on the enemy's flank and gradually moved southward conforming to their movements. Orders were then received to rally between Gap 44 and 45.

Up to this point 2nd R.T.R. lost one tank but cannot claim any definite enemy tanks put out of action although many hits were observed.

2nd R.T.R. now rallied about the 204 feature near Gap 45 and northeast to Gap 44. The time was now about 1115 hours. At 1245 hours, the enemy put in a heavy attack on the 204 feature with the obvious intention of making good the line of the wire. 2nd R.T.R. was forced to retire in a northwest direction in the face of this attack, losing one tank which burst into flames on the 204 position. Here B Squadron had a good shoot before leaving, and again scored numerous hits although none of the enemy were seen to halt or catch fire. The enemy did not attempt to follow up once the position was in their hands. Considerable activity was seen about their forward positions and it appeared evident that the enemy were replenishing and forming up for a further and stronger attack. 2nd R.T.R. then asked for more ammunition and replenishment was completed by 1730 hours.

At 1830 hours, 40 enemy tanks were reported at Gap 44. At 1915 hours, 40 to 50 medium tanks moved south along the wire to Gap 45 and there crossed the wire. As soon as these crossed the wire, a further 50 appeared out of the mirage and followed through the gap. It was then possible to see that the enemy column was moving in a southeast direction and threatening to separate 2nd R.T.R. from 6th R.T.R. Orders were received to the effect that on no account were the two battalions to become separated, so 2nd R.T.R. bent further and further to the south until both battalions were in action about the head of the enemy column, now about one mile northwest of Qaret Suweide (506356). The time was now about 2030 hours. At about this time, the 2nd R.T.R. commander was wounded and had to be evacuated. Almost at the same time the Link Tank in which the 2nd in Command was travelling had both the No.9 Set and No.14 Set put out of action, and some little time elapsed before control was gained by 2nd R.T.R. HQ. The enemy were halted on this position, and as darkness fell, the action was broken off. During the final stages one more tank was lost, making three battle casualties for that day.

The enemy used their tanks in large numbers and on very set plans. The large formations appeared to be rather unwieldy.

6th R.T.R. - 16 June 1941 - The 6th R.T.R. retired to a position 0.5 mile east of BP 44 and replenished at 0100 hours on June 16. At 0300 hours, the 6th R.T.R. reorganized as follows: 3 tanks in HQ, 7 tanks in A Squadron, and 11 tanks in C Squadron.

The liaison officer returned from Brigade with orders that the 6th R.T.R. was to be at 500365 at first light with TOGS under command. The 6th R.T.R. left BP 44 at 0430 hours, arriving at 500365 at 0530 hours.

At 0730 hours, 2nd R.T.R. were ordered to Bir Ghirba to engage and delay the enemy in the event of his moving forward. At 0755 hours, 36 enemy tanks were reported in the Bir Ghirba area. At 0830 hours, the 11th Hussars reported a large enemy column moving west southwest, estimated at 100 to 150 MET including 50 to 60 medium tanks, 20 light tanks, lorries and motorcycles. At 0900 hours, the head of this column was reported to be at 497367.

At 0910 hours, Brigade ordered the 2nd R.T.R. to move down on the right flank of the enemy column. 6th R.T.R. was to keep on the inside, delay him and keep him out, but not to get really involved unless circumstances were favorable. The 6th R.T.R. moved in line ahead and engaged the enemy on this left flank at 800 to 1000 yards. The 6th R.T.R. then swung east to clear the front of the 2nd R.T.R., enabling them to engage. Two Mk.VI Cruiser Tanks were knocked out in this action. The 6th R.T.R. re-formed at BP 44.

At 1000 hours, the Brigade ordered the 6th R.T.R. to move towards Sidi Omar to engage 20 enemy tanks advancing north from Sidi Omar. At 1015 hours, the 6th R.T.R. moved south engaging these enemy tanks from the east in line ahead on the move.

At 1030 hours, Brigade ordered the 6th R.T.R. to move to a point 2 miles west of Sidi Omar to engage a large mixed enemy force. At 1035 hours, the 6th R.T.R. moved southwest and engaged the enemy broadside, then swung south engaging another enemy tank column moving northeast with a diagonal shoot. This action continued until the majority of our tanks had swung west and taken up hull-down positions facing northeast. Then with 2-pounder and Bema M.G. fire the unit inflicted considerable damage on a large mixed force of the enemy, who withdrew in disorder in a northwest direction. At 1100 hours, the action was broken off and the unit rallied at BP 46. No tanks were lost. After evacuating the crocks to the rear, the 6th R.T.R. effective strength numbered 11.

At 1230 hours, 54 enemy medium tanks appeared from the west and heavily shelled the 6th R.T.R. The unit withdrew northeast, firing broadside and, pivoting on 2nd R.T.R., swung

Actions of 6th Bn. Royal Tank Regiment on 16 June 1941

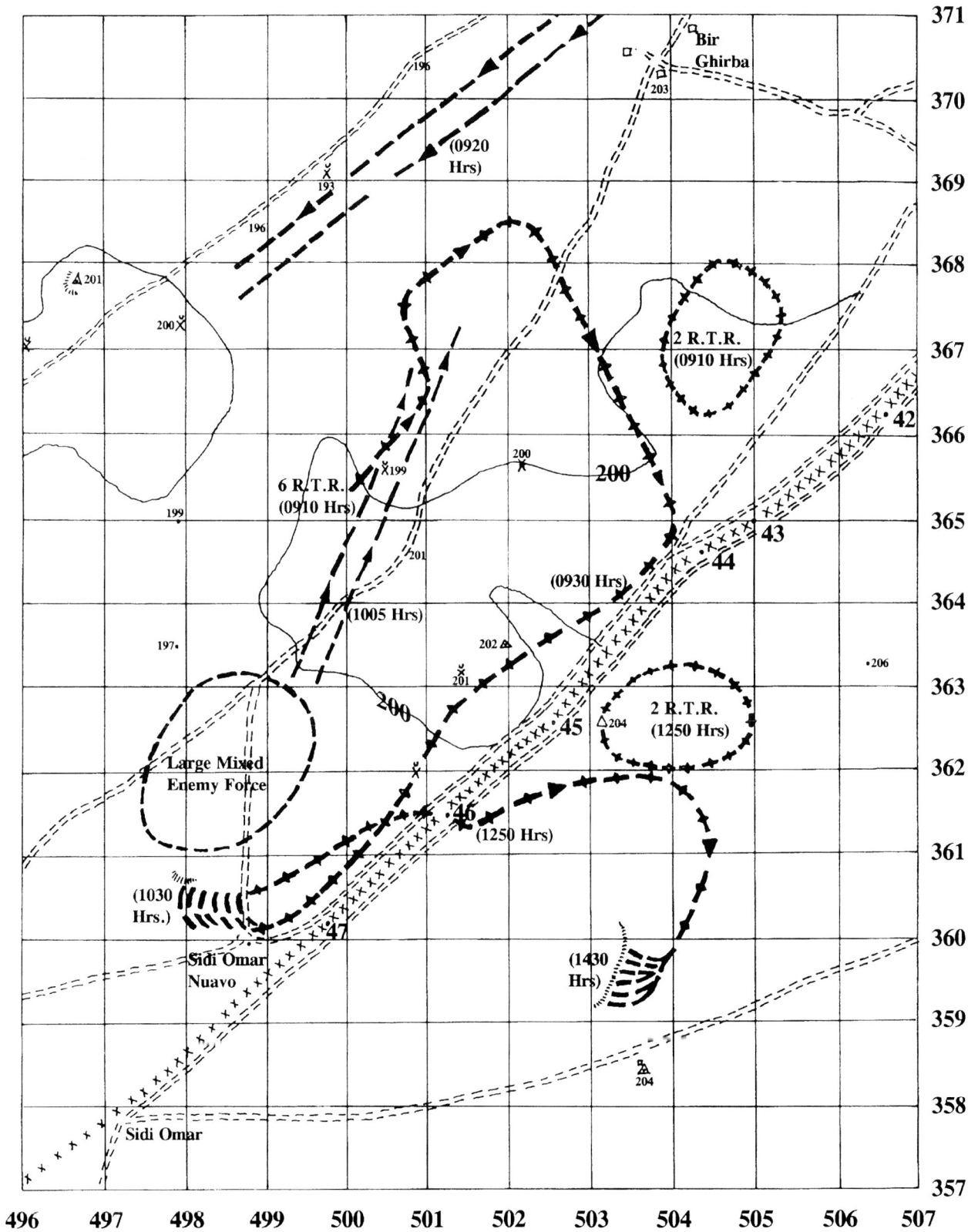

- -▶- - **Approximate enemy course**

+-+-▶-+- **Course taken by 6th Bn. Royal Tank Regiment**

east and eventually south, halting in a hull-down position facing northwest. The 6th R.T.R. position was 0.5 mile north of Qinei Qina. At 1410 hours, ammunition replenishment arrived. The 6th R.T.R. had 9 runners left.

At 1720 hours, Brigade ordered that due to indications that the enemy is about to attack, take up hull-down positions and delay him. Guns with the Brigade were to assist.

At 1900 hours, enemy tanks at BP 46 were reinforced and now numbered 80. They attacked to the east. 6th R.T.R. heavily engaged, conducted a stationary shoot and then retired southeast. The 6th R.T.R. leaguered for the night at 510351. Replenishment failed to arrive.

Tank Status of 7th Armoured Brigade

16 June 1941	2nd R.T.R.	6th R.T.R.	Bde.
First light effective strength	28	21	0
Battle casualties lost	3	3	1
Damaged (enemy action and mechanical)	10	6	0
Enemy tanks definitely destroyed	3	10	0
Enemy tanks damaged or possibly destroyed	0	3	0

4th R.T.R. - 16th June 1941

Brigade remained at Point 39 covered by B Squadron (15 Infantry Tanks). During the day enemy movement was constantly seen and reported. In the early afternoon enemy tanks were seen. There were some 25 medium tanks, 6 light tanks and a quantity of wheeled transport. A tank battle seemed imminent. B Squadron made some adjustment to meet the enemy. However, after about an hour the enemy withdrew out of sight leaving only guns in position at Hafid Ridge. Immediately after dark B Squadron tanks withdrew to a position southeast of the wire supported by a detachment of an Indian Regiment, and 31st Field Regiment R.A. to repel any enemy attack at first light.

C Squadron 4th R.T.R. at Halfaya Pass were shelled periodically during the night. At 0730 hours on 16 June, the Maharatas attacked Halfaya Pass. At 0930 hours, the attack was held up. The 2nd Camerons supported by an Infantry Tank and a Light Tank went forward in an attempt to hold the southern edge of Halfaya Wadi, but were forced to a standstill. The tanks now withdrew to the right flank to take up a position of cover.

Two tanks of C Squadron were now rallied on the right flank, namely one Infantry Tank and one Light Tank. About 1500 hours the Adjutant of the Camerons asked if anything could be done about replenishing water and ammunition. The Light Tank set out to look for B Echelon, which he found at Ali Batuma; this was the Camerons Echelon. They had of course no diesel but had petrol and ammunition, which was sent as far forward as possible, and replenishing was then carried out.

The Light Tank carried on to Halfway House where diesel and ammunition were found on a dump. This was carried forward. Had this dump not been there, any chance of saving the tank would have been out of the question.

The Commander of the remaining Infantry Tank went out during the day to ascertain if the tanks knocked out were at all recoverable. He found that they were towable but the Camerons commander was averse to risking any covering party for this recovery.

At 2330 hours, 4th R.T.R., less two squadrons, received orders to withdraw to Bir Nuh, leaving present position at 0600 hours on 17 June.

7th R.T.R. - 16 June 1941

7th R.T.R. - 16 June 1941 - At 0400 hours on 16 June, all runners of the 7th R.T.R. moved out to the north and west perimeter and took up defensive positions. The enemy attacked at dawn, shelling our positions, using artillery and 75 mm guns of the Pz.Kpfw.IV tanks. This continued throughout the day with an occasional lull. At 1700, a formation of dive bombers bombed the western sector causing several casualties.

The Action at Halfaya on 16 June 1941

Two more infantry attacks on 16 June were stopped short by an artillery barrage, accompanied by **2 cm Flak** and infantry fire. During the morning, German planes bombed their own artillery and Flak positions, and in the afternoon the ammunition situation became critical – the artillery reporting that only 600 shells remained and that **Flak** ammunition was running short. Bach was worried about food and water. A message from the **Deutsche Afrikakorps** was dropped by air at 2000 hours: "All depends on holding Halfaya." He answered: "All depends on your sending us ammunition and food." As time had not permitted him to reconnoiter positions, he did not obey Knabe's order to clear the shore and concentrate on the pass. The next day aircraft dropped ammunition for small arms and **2 cm Flak**. The British retreat began, harassed by artillery, **Flak**, and heavy machine-gun fire from Halfaya, and in the evening the position was relieved.

On the second day the **2 cm Flak** were pushed forward to eliminate machine-gun nests and an observation post at 1500 meters, while the coastal gun was used to scatter concentrations of motor transport and an infantry battalion.

In the course of the action at Halfaya 20 British tanks and 8 armored vehicles were destroyed, and 98 prisoners were taken. Losses were small – 8 killed and 32 wounded (excluding **Flak** and **Pak** personnel).

The Panzer Striking Force on 16 June 1941

Panzer-Regiment 8 was ordered to attack Capuzzo once more on 16 June, this time with both **Abteilungen** combined. The **I.Abteilung** had now only 6, 4 and 9 of the 8 **Pz.Kpfw.IV**, 18 **Pz.Kpfw.III** and 13 **Pz.Kpfw.II**, respectively, with which it started the battle. The British tanks struck out of the morning mist, and once more there were heavy casualties in the **3.Kompanie**. The commander of the **I.Abteilung** had his Panzer shot through twice by fire from Infantry Tanks at 300 meters, and the **I.Abteilung** had to withdraw with only three operational **Pz.Kpfw.III** and one **Pz.Kpfw.II**. It is clear that if the British tanks had been able to take Bardia, **Panzer-Regiment 8** would have been finished.

By the evening of the second day, two **Pz.Kpfw.II**, nine **Pz.Kpfw.III**, and two **Pz.Kpfw.IV** had been repaired (the damage had been mostly to guns), and stood ready to defend Bardia.

In the Capuzzo action of the second day **8.8 cm Flak**, firing through a mist, knocked out eight Infantry Tanks, including one hit in the turret at 500 meters. British artillery, however, forced the crews of the **8.8 cm Flak** to take cover, and British tanks meanwhile approached to within 300 meters and damaged three of the four guns. The one intact **8.8 cm Flak** and two **2 cm Flak** knocked out three more British tanks at ranges between 250 and 300 meters, but the Panzers were not in any condition to follow up this advantage.

After the battle, Oberleutnant Wahl, commander of the **6.Kompanie/Panzer-Regiment 8**, went in search of the Mk.II Infantry Tank that he remembered hitting on the gun. Missing its cupola, this Mk.IIA Infantry Tank was also penetrated at the turret ring and on the hull side by **8.8 cm Pzgr.** (WW)

DAK KTB 17 June 1941 - *Weather, maximum temperature 28° (82°F)*

At 0035 hours, orders to the **5.leichte Division** and **15.Panzer-Division**: Initiate the attack at 0430 hours on 17 June from the previously gained positions. **5.leichte Division** through Sidi Suleiman toward Halfaya Pass South with security to the south. **15.Panzer-Division** through Alam aba Dikah toward Halfaya Pass and the southern edge of Bardia, which must be held. The enemy's intention is to concentrate the tanks out of Capuzzo, probably in the area around Sidi Suleiman at 0500 hours, to attack Halfaya with an artillery barrage. Since this appears possible, an earlier attack is practical.

At 0100 hours, a radio message just arrived at **Korps** from the **5.leichte Division** reporting that at 1935 hours on 16 June, **Panzer-Regiment 5** was 13 kilometers east of Sidi Omar engaged in a hard fight with tanks, artillery, and anti-tank guns.

At 0130 hours, the **5.leichte Division** in a tough fight against enemy tanks, artillery, and anti-tank guns had reached the area 10 kilometers east of Sidi Omar. The main body of the division remained pinned down by artillery fire at the border because their attack came under artillery fire reinforced by heavy weapons. The division still intended to join the **Panzer-Regiment** during the night in order to attack in the morning and reach Sidi Suleiman.

At 0600 hours, after a fight with a strong enemy tank force, **Panzer-Regiment 5** arrived at Sidi Suleiman. Further divisional units were advancing there. The division received flanking fire from a strong enemy group south of Gasr el Abid, and **M.G.-Bataillon** advanced on them.

At 0840 hours, Sidi Suleiman was attacked from the south by tanks with attached artillery, which turned to retreat to Sidi Omar. The **5.leichte Division**, with the **Gruppe** by Sidi Omar, reverted to the defensive. **Panzer-Regiment 5** remained in Sidi Suleiman.

The **15.Panzer-Division** started the attack as ordered. At 0830 hours, **Panzer-Regiment 8** lay in combat with enemy tanks by Ghot Adhidiba. **Kradschuetzen-Bataillon 15** was behind them in the area of border marker 42. Enemy forces near Capuzzo and Musaid were engaging our weak security forces with artillery fire.

The morning aerial reconnaissance (conducted from 0600 to 0620 hours) reported two strong enemy groups with tanks near Ghot er Rereibit and a strong group with tanks two kilometers east of Sidi Omar (probably **5.leichte Division**). Directly west of TN41 there was a large concentration of ours (elements of the **15.Panzer-Division**.)

At 0823 hours, radio intercepts provided: At 0655 hours, the enemy reported that a German tank force with 75 heavy tanks are advancing on Sidi Suleiman. German infantry are advancing from the west to east and have reached the area 6 kilometers east of Sidi Omar. These columns must, by all means, be halted. At 0745 hours, the 7th Armoured Brigade reported that they were out of ammunition and the situation was very serious. The Brigade demanded immediate resupply of ammunition. The location of the Brigade is Sidi Suleiman and to the north. At 0800 hours, an enemy group south of Suleiman reported that they were advancing. It is not known whether their direction is toward Sidi Suleiman or Sidi Omar.

At 0830 hours, **Fliegerfuehrer Afrika** had dropped the requested ammunition on Halfaya Pass early in the morning. They were requested to attack Gasr el Abid-Sidi Omar as first line, the surrounded elements south of Musaid as second line, and Sollum as third line.

Orders were issued for the **15.Panzer-Division** with all forces to immediately strike through to Halfaya, leaning on the **5.leichte Division** which had arrived at Sidi Suleiman at 0645 hours. The advance of the **15.Panzer-Division** is important because the **5.leichte Division** is being strongly pushed by enemy groups south of Omar. The **5.leichte Division** holds Sidi Omar.

At 0920 hours, **Korps** orders for the **5.leichte Division** and **15.Panzer-Division**: The situation has very favorably changed. The British portray their situation as very serious. Quickly complete the penetration through to Halfaya and prevent the surrounded tank forces in the north from breaking out.

At 1000 hours, **15.Panzer-Division** reported the conclusion of the tank battle near Ghot Adhidiba. Following heavy losses, the enemy is retreating. Three enemy batteries near Sollum-Capuzzo were pinned down by our artillery.

At 1045 hours, **15.Panzer-Division** reported: From a radio intercept, the occupants of Sollum and Musaid have orders to retire. All units have been sent to disperse the rear guard.

An urgent message from **D.A.K.** to the **5.leichte Division** described the situation and ordered the division to break the rear guard.

At 1200 hours, the **15.Panzer-Division** lay near Alam Abudihak in combat with enemy tanks that were covering the rear guard from Capuzzo. Elements of the **15.Panzer-Division** were sent south in the direction of Halfaya to outflank the enemy and gain contact with the **5.leichte Division**.

At 1220 hours, **Fliegerfuehrer Afrika**'s attack, planned to relieve the flank of the **5.leichte Division** at 1430 hours, was called off and requested for Sidi Omar.

15.Panzer-Division's attack advanced to within 6 kilometers of Halfaya Pass. Sollum is probably free of enemy forces and Capuzzo is cleared. Contact has been made with Halfaya Pass. There have been no situation reports from the **5.leichte Division** for several hours.

At 1420 hours, an intercepted radio message: HQ of 4th Indian Division and HQ of 7th Armoured Brigade are located near Bir Siuyat (7 kilometers southeast of Halfaya).

This was given as an objective to the **Fliegerfuehrer Afrika**, the **15.Panzer-Division**, and the **5.leichte Division**.

At 1430 hours, the 4th Indian Division had orders to pull back in the direction of Bir Nuh.

At 1530 hours it was learned: At 1420 hours, the 7th Armoured Brigade reported to the Corps Commander that the 7th R.T.R. and B Squadron 4th R.T.R. have attacked Point 207, causing considerable damage to enemy armored cars. The 4th Armoured Brigade reported a strength of 24 Infantry Tanks and the division hoped that it was more.

At 1525 hours, from a report from the **15.Panzer-Division**, the **5.leichte Division** had struck toward Halfaya from Sidi Suleiman. Musaid and Point 206 are in our hands.

At 1540 hours, **15.Panzer-Division** reported that enemy columns were in retreat to the south 5 kilometers west of Quallala. There was an enemy battery with motorized infantry near Minguar el Shabe. The **5.leichte Division** was ordered to cut off and eliminate these.

At 1600 hours, after taking on ammunition by Gabr el Quaha, **Panzer-Regiment 8** started toward Halfaya. **Panzer-Regiment 5** arrived at Halfaya at this time. Further intentions of the **Regiment** were to fall on the enemy retreating from the north, take prisoners, and gain contact with the attacking elements of the **15.Panzer-Division**.

At 1650 hours, **Panzer-Regiment 5** had made contact with **Panzer-Regiment 8** and both attacked to the north together.

Because of the weakness of the **Gruppen** of the **5.leichte Division**, the 4th Armoured Brigade still managed to pull their main body out of Capuzzo-Sollum and to strike past **Panzer-Regiment 5** while the main body of the **5.leichte Division** was tied down at Sidi Omar. Most of the damaged tanks were towed away by the enemy.

At 1740 hours, D.A.K. ordered the **5.leichte Division** to immediately send an **Abteilung** with Panzers through Alam Battuma toward the known enemy supply bases 4 kilometers southeast of Rueibit.

At 1915 hours, **5.leichte Division** reported: Will start the pursuit with Panzers as soon as possible after refueling and taking on ammunition. The time will be reported.

At 1945 hours, message sent to the **5.leichte Division** and **15.Panzer-Division**: The three-day battle has resulted in complete success. Greatest appreciation for the extraordinary performance.

The **Korps** defense was established on the Bir Ghirba to Qubr el Qaha to Halfaya Pass line. The units reorganized and mopped up the battlefield. The troops in **Stuetzpunkt 208** remained there and were attached to the **5.leichte Division**.

At 2115 hours, orders were issued: On 18 June, an hour before sunrise, both divisions are to send a reinforced **Aufklaerung-Abteilung** across the forward line on the plateau to clear the areas up to the line of Gasr el Abid to Ghot er Rueibet to Sidi el Fadeil. Further attack and pursuit are not planned.

At 2330 hours, at the completion of the battle on the evening of 17 June, the main body of the **5.leichte Division** was located around Sidi Omar with **Panzer-Regiment 5** at Halfaya Pass. The division reported that the ordered reorganization for the defense and the start of the pursuit by an **Abteilung** from **Panzer-Regiment 5** would first be possible at dawn on 18 June.

2nd R.T.R. - 17 June 1941 - During the night, the 2nd R.T.R. was reorganized as a composite Squadron with 7 A10s, 3 A9s and 5 A13s. At 0515, June 17, 1941, B Echelon located the tanks and commenced replenishment.

At 0530, the German column was sighted in the areas Qurat Abu Faris el Gharbiya and the 2nd R.T.R. was ordered to withdraw along the center line in conjunction with the rest of the Brigade. The following crocks had to be abandoned at Kinnibish 517355: Mark IVA T15235, Mark I T3523 and Mark II T5964. At Bir Khireigat replenishment was completed. The enemy column moved to the area northwest of Sidi Suleiman and at 0900 the composite Squadron was ordered to move to the area of Abu Shalif. Patrols were sent forward with the objective of harassing outlying detachments of the column, but as nothing offered itself they were withdrawn.

At 1530, six Cruiser Tanks that had been repaired and brought up from B Echelon joined the composite Squadron. At 1600, patrols were again ordered forward by Brigade. The enemy column moved forward towards Bir Nuh. A Cruiser Tank followed on the eastern flank and destroyed one enemy medium tank. The 11th Hussars reported an apparently broken down medium tank in the area 4 miles northwest of Sidi Suleiman. A patrol was sent and destroyed that one.

At 1830, patrols concentrated with the 2nd R.T.R. Squadron at Abu Shalif. At 1900, an enemy force of 15 medium tanks advanced southeast from Qaret Abu Faris towards the Squadron's position. They were shelled by JAXO and on coming under 2-pounder fire, they withdrew northwards. At 1930, 12 Messerschmitt 110s flew over the position and bombed the area. No casualties or serious damage. At 2030, 2nd R.T.R. was ordered to withdraw to Bir Khireigat for the night.

6th R.T.R. - 17 June 1941 - At 0530, the 6th R.T.R. with 8 effective Mk.VI Cruiser Tanks moved to Qaret Abu Faris but was delayed by crocks. Arriving at 0630, they contacted JAXO, who were firing at approximately 40 enemy tanks advancing slowly towards them from the northwest. 6th R.T.R. composed

In addition to capturing 12 operational Mk.IIA Infantry Tanks, the Germans recovered several Mk.IVA and Mk.VI Cruiser Tanks which they repaired and put back into service. The flag on the turret roof of this Mk.VI Cruiser Tank was the standard method used for recognition by aircraft. (NA)

of 8 Mk.VI Cruiser Tanks, formed up hull-down to cover the withdrawal of JAXO. The enemy tanks were engaged down to 700 yards while JAXO withdrew. 6th R.T.R. then withdrew on a bearing of 110 degrees, heavily engaged and outranged by the enemy tanks.

At 0730, 6th R.T.R. arrived at Khireigat with 8 tanks fit, one tank towing and one tank being towed. At 0830, four tanks joined at Khireigat and two left for the L.R.S.

At 1145, the Brigade ordered the 6th R.T.R. to move into reserve at Alem el Arad facing north and northwest. The 6th R.T.R. arrived at 1235. At 1645, Brigade ordered the 6th R.T.R. to move 6 kilometers north of Khireigat. An enemy column was reported moving east, its head at Qaret Abu Faris. At 2005, 6th R.T.R. were ordered to move to leaguer 3 miles southeast of Khireigat.

One of the few Mk.VI light tanks that were knocked out during Operation Battleaxe. It is not known if this was one from the 7th Hussars or from the 4th Armoured Brigade.

7th Armoured Brigade

17 June 1941	2nd R.T.R.	6th R.T.R.
First light effective strength	15	12
Battle casualties lost	0	
Damaged (enemy action and mechanical)	2	6
Enemy tanks definitely destroyed	5	3
Enemy tanks damaged or possibly destroyed	0	

The total number of British Cruiser Tanks destroyed and abandoned during the three-day operation were: 12 from the 2nd R.T.R., 16 from the 6th R.T.R. and one from Brigade.

4th R.T.R. - 17 June 1941

Tank State morning 17 June 1941:

4th R.T.R. HQ	1 Mk.IIA Infantry Tank
A Squadron	1 Mk.IIA Infantry Tank in poor condition, 2 evacuated for transport
B Squadron	15 Mk.IIA Infantry Tanks
C Squadron	1 Mk.IIA Infantry Tanks and 1 Light Tank.

C Squadron. At about 2030 hours, the Light Tank went out to find and guide back the A Echelon of the Camerons to Halfway House. As it drew clear of the cover where it had been all day, it came under fire from enemy tanks at a range of about 1000 yards. No hits were made but after a little way the engine of the tank stalled. The commander dismounted to investigate, and then saw that the following enemy tanks were passing behind him and towards the wadi where the Infantry Tank was lying up. They were firing into the wadi, and probably at the Camerons who were due to evacuate the position about that time. This is the last that is known of the Infantry Tank and the crew.

The Light Tank on arriving within 500 yards of the Camerons Echelon had another engine failure, which this time was prolonged, and repeated efforts failed to clear the diffi-

culty. In view of the proximity of the enemy who appeared to be on the move, and the anxiety of the Camerons to move, the commander decided to destroy the tank. This was done. The tank commander entered a carrier of the Camerons Echelon and navigated them to Saffai.

It is now known that the remaining Infantry Tank was unable to move from the wadi owing to the proximity of the enemy. As it was now growing dark and the infantry was withdrawing, there was no alternative but to abandon the vehicle. It could not be driven down the hill.

4th R.T.R. with B Squadron. At 0600 hours the withdrawal commenced. 4th R.T.R. HQ had arrived just north of Point 207 and B Squadron covering withdrawal on the northwest slopes of Point 207. 4th R.T.R. HQ returned to Point 207 and B Squadron advanced preparing for enemy tank attack which was reported to be imminent.

The Brigadier went forward in a staff car and issued verbal orders to the B Squadron Commander at 0640 to 0710 hours. Recce of the wire showed that the enemy had broken through Gaps 40 and 41, under cover of six tanks and armored cars. Enemy guns were brought up in position west of Gap 41. At this time enemy A.F.V.s were through the wire and numbered about 20 and a large amount of enemy movement could be seen. At about 0800 to 0830 hours some enemy tanks came through Gap 41 on our right flank. Two troops from B Squadron were to repel any attack from this point. Enemy A.F.V.s halted under cover and brought up guns through Gap 41. At about 0830 hours an artillery officer reported to the 4th R.T.R. Commander and went forward with B Squadron to enable fire to be directed on the enemy position. It was suggested that he should advance with the tanks and give orders to the gunners to direct fire on enemy positions. This was done with no apparent damage.

During this time there was intermittent shelling on our tanks. At 0855 B Squadron attacked the enemy with two troops on the left and one in the center, one remaining in position of the right flank and one in reserve. Within about 10 minutes of the attack opening, B Squadron had three tanks immobilized by enemy artillery fire and the enemy commenced an outflanking movement on the left.

B Squadron now re-enforced the attack on the center. The situation on the center was now two tanks immobilized and the third tank ran out of ammunition.

At 0930 hours, the Squadron Commander was killed and a lieutenant assumed command. He reported the situation to the 4th R.T.R. Commander who passed information to Brigade asking for instructions. Report from center was now critical as our tanks were receiving continuous fire from enemy artillery and tanks. The Squadron Commander now sent in the last troop to ease the situation.

Meantime the 4th R.T.R. Commander had received orders from Brigade for B Squadron to withdraw, fighting, to Point 206. This was successfully carried out. The forward tanks were still in position. The enemy were now coming on and replenishing and bringing up more guns. At 1032 situation was, Brigade HQ had arranged for 7th R.T.R. at Capuzzo and Guards Brigade to cover the withdrawal. The position at this time was B Squadron at Point 206 with nine tanks – seven of which were fit to fight – the remainder having jammed turrets, and all tanks were short of ammunition. Casualties who were able to walk were evacuated. One officer killed, one missing, one other ranks killed and 11 missing. Enemy casualties amounted to 8 A.F.V.s burning.

Orders were now received that B Squadron Commander to hold Point 206 as long as possible and then withdraw slowly, fighting; assistance was coming. About 1050 hours the forward troop of B Squadron reported enemy advancing. In order to repel the advance the whole Squadron was put into the attack. The enemy attack was supported by intensified shell fire. The enemy center halted and left two lorries drawing up guns. These lorries were set on fire. The left flank of B Squadron was now under heavy fire with solid shot and high explosive from B.P.41. The Light Tank behind B Squadron reported enemy A.F.V.s advancing from the north and therefore threatening to cut off the withdrawal. Commander B Squadron was to withdraw, fighting, from the gap. Cover for this movement was provided by two Infantry tanks, which moved towards the enemy's right. The Squadron slowly withdrew fighting to Point 207.

Sixteen tanks then appeared from the north and supported the withdrawal. The Squadron leader's tank now suffered a broken track and repairs were commenced. The enemy advanced further, shelling and machine gunning the tank, making repairs impossible. The tank was abandoned and de-

stroyed. All tanks with one exception were out of 2-pounder ammunition. Squadron Commander returned and joined remainder of the squadron under cover of 7th R.T.R. No ammunition was discovered on the way and no ammunition could be obtained from the 7th R.T.R. as at this time the enemy were still advancing and 7th R.T.R. were preparing to make an attack.

B Squadron arrived at about 1500 hours at Bir Nuh where ammunition was collected and dispositions were taken up to cover the force which had now halted at Bir Nuh.

The situation at this time was B Squadron had six tanks which could move with difficulty and shoot. Of the remaining three, one had been destroyed short of Point 207, one had run out of ammunition earlier in the action and, being unable to return to Bir Nuh, had been destroyed, the third allotted to the 7th R.T.R.

At about 1600 hours, Brigade ordered a Light Tank patrol forward to Point 207 to get in touch with 7th R.T.R. The patrol reported a tank battle in progress between 7th R.T.R. and the enemy. Enemy were making encircling movement to the right in unknown numbers to cut off the patrol.

At 1815 hours, Brigadier ordered forces at Bir Nuh to withdraw commencing by 1915 hours. At 1600 hours the enemy staged a dive bombing attack which resulted in severe casualties to the gunners.

At 1930, Brigade HQ had a couple of their Cruiser Tanks as escort. 4th R.T.R. had 2 Cruisers (1 in poor condition) from Brigade, 7 Infantry Tanks (all poor to bad) and 3 Light Tanks (2 fair only).

At 1930 hours, the withdrawal commenced covered by 4th R.T.R. tanks. Ultimately, the vehicles of the Brigade and artillery left the tanks behind which came on in their own time, arriving in the vicinity of Sofafi at 0530 hours on the 18th June 1941.

During the march, one Infantry Tank had to be abandoned and destroyed as the gearbox collapsed. One Cruiser Tank and one Light Tank were temporarily abandoned due to mechanical trouble which could not be repaired in the dark, and were subsequently recovered.

Summary of casualties: 3 officers and 10 other ranks killed, 4 officers and 53 other ranks wounded or missing. Vehicles: 37 Infantry Tanks lost. This may be reduced if those on the coast are recovered. Lost in enemy-held territory: 32 Mk.IIA Infantry Tanks and one Mk.VIC Light Tank.

7th R.T.R. - 17 June 1941 - At 0015 on June 17th, the tanks of the 7th R.T.R. rallied back to replenish and were reorganized into four troops. The fatigue of prolonged action is apparent. At 0400 move up to positions along perimeter. By 0515 all tanks in position. Considerable movement was observed along Hafid Ridge and to the north. Capuzzo was subjected

A Mk.IIA Infantry Tank that was knocked out by an **8.8 cm Pzgr.** penetrating cleanly through the side skirts and interior side plate. Detonation of the **Pzgr.** inside the tank finished it off. A second Mk.IIA Infantry Tank in the background has been completely destroyed with explosive charges. (GBJ)

to spasmodic enemy artillery fire, to which our 25-pounders replied. The light was so extremely bad and the mirage effect was so great that it was impossible to identify anything.

At 1130, 7th R.T.R. received orders by radio that all fit tanks were to proceed to B.P.39 and 40. A squadron of the 4th R.T.R. heavily engaged by enemy superior force was withdrawing northeast. The 7th R.T.R. were to form a defensive line from B.P.40 to Point 205.

A composite squadron set off via Bir Wair to form a defensive flank to the southwest from the wire and cover the withdrawal, also to assist the 4th R.T.R. already heavily embroiled. 7th R.T.R. HQ had one Infantry, No.1 Troop three Infantry Tanks, No.2 Troop three Infantry Tanks, No.3 Troop four Infantry Tanks and No.4 Troop four Infantry Tanks. The Adjutant's Cruiser Tank broke down. As the necessary repair would take too long, and as the infantry and gunners had already begun the retirement, it was destroyed.

The column slowed down at Bir Wair – then when collected went through the wire and formed a line facing southwest and advanced on the enemy tanks. 4th R.T.R. appeared first and crossed our front from right to left. This movement drew away the majority of 7th R.T.R. in the direction of Point 207. Our tanks were thus leaving their right flank open for the enemy. The 7th R.T.R. Commander by radio ordered tanks

to return. But this proved ineffective and so he and one other tank lay back 1.5 miles from the remainder. It was later discovered that the wireless mast was hanging down the side of the tank, having been shot away. The two tanks engaged between 15 to 20 enemy tanks and did not move away to the perimeter camp in the locality of Point 207 until some time later. Two enemy tanks were hit – stopped – and did not go on firing.

Three tanks from the right-hand troop destroyed an enemy battery on the wire in the area of Gap 40. They turned southeast and passed away southwest of Point 207 and did not rejoin the composite squadron. They reported to Brigade HQ.

On arriving at Point 207, the 7th R.T.R. Commander found another 7th R.T.R. tank and one from the 4th R.T.R. As the Commander's tank was getting into position, the servo gave out. The tank could not be moved so it was destroyed by 2-pounder fire on the engine and the remaining eight rounds of ammunition fired at the enemy.

The composite squadron with about 10 Mk.IIA Infantry Tanks and two or three from the 4th R.T.R. arrived at Point 207 at about 1230 hours where former camps were located. As this position covered the entire surrounding country, it was decided that it would be held.

At 1300 hours, an enemy column seen to northwest moving on to Point 207 was engaged by light fire. They halted, spread out, and appeared to be going to use Point 207 as a base for operations against Halfaya and elsewhere.

At 1800 hours, a large enemy column was seen also making for this point and were engaged by our fire. The action was very one sided as the enemy had an overwhelming superiority in A.F.V.s and attacked from all directions. Several of the 7th R.T.R. tanks were knocked out but the enemy were held up, which allowed the Guards Brigade to be withdrawn.

At 1800 the main party rallied southeast of Point 207. An enemy covering force of six **Pz.Kpfw.IV**, thinking we had gone, moved into the camp at Point 207. They were heavily engaged and perhaps two or three put out of action. By 1830, all ammunition expended, a column of 18 enemy A.F.V.s was seen moving on our right flank in a southeast direction. At 1900 hours, the remaining 7th R.T.R. tanks of the composite squadron rallied and set off at full speed. Only four tanks escaped; the remainder were probably captured. Contact was made with a 4th R.T.R. party, the remaining 4 Infantry Tanks replenished with fuel and some ammunition and set off at dusk along the escarpment to rejoin the Brigade.

At 0300 on June 18th, B Echelon moved back to area two miles west of Sofafi-Southwest. The 7th R.T.R. composite squadron arrived at this area with four tanks by 0830 hours. Six other tanks which had crawled back also appeared in the morning, one of which was evacuated immediately.

The Panzer Striking Force on 17 June 1941

The **II.Abteilung/Panzer Regiment 8** was now ordered to cross the frontier and join with **Panzer-Regiment 5** of the **5. leichte Division**. An infantry officer who observed the resulting action attributed the regiment's success in breaking through a British tank force on the frontier to the artillery and Flak support. The **8.8 cm Flak** appear here in a new role.

The day after the battle found Oberleutnant Wahl, commander of the **6.Kompanie/Panzer-Regiment 8**, on the rear deck of his **Pz.Kpfw.III Ausf.H** drafting a message. The **Scherenfernrohr 14Z** (scissors periscopes) mounted on the cupola were not standard issue but with their 10x magnification would have been a tremendous help in estimating range and observing fire. The top edge of the stowage bin was painted in red and white stripes to designate the **Kompanie-Trupp**. (WW)

The **II.Abteilung** had picked up those which had saved Point 208, and had repaired at least two others damaged at Capuzzo. Some of these ran on the flank of the advance; others went 200 meters ahead of the leading tanks. The first group knocked out two Infantry Tanks and the second plunged straight ahead at the British formation of 20 Infantry Tanks, destroying seven of these before the German tanks had opened up. The way was clear to a rendezvous with **Panzer-Regiment 5**, as well as to Halfaya. The **I.Abteilung/Panzer Regiment 8** suffered losses from two British air attacks while en route to join the **II.Abteilung**. The first attack was by six strafing Hurricanes and the second by numerous bombers. Total losses were one **Pz.Kpfw.IV** (knocked out), one **Pz.Kpfw.III** (crew casualties), and one ammunition, one fuel, and one transport truck (rendered unserviceable). Five personnel were killed and 16 wounded. The **Abteilung** turned back from this rendezvous.

DAK KTB 18Jun41 - The number of operational Panzers in the **Deutsches Afrikakorps** was reported on the evening of 18 June as:

	Pz.Rgt.5	Pz.Rgt.8
Pz.Kpfw.I	15	
Pz.Kpfw.II	6	20
Pz.Kpfw.III	23	28
Pz.Kpfw.IV	9	12
Pz.Bef.Wg.		2

The British reported the following losses in tanks left behind on the battlefield during the period from 15 to 17 June 1941:

4th R.T.R.	30 Mk.IIA Infantry Tanks
	1 Mk.VIC Light Tank
7th R.T.R.	35 Mk.IIA Infantry Tanks
	1 Mk.I Cruiser Tank
	2 Mk.VIC Light Tanks
2nd R.T.R.	12 Mk.I, IIA, & IVA Cruiser Tanks
6th R.T.R.	16 Mk.VI Cruiser Tanks
7th Armd.Bde.	1 Mk.IIA Cruiser Tank

The Germans reported their losses as total writeoffs from the Sollum battle during the period of 15 to 17 June 1941 as:

5.lei.Div.	2 **Pz.Kpfw.II**
	2 **Pz.Kpfw.III**
15.Pz.Div.	3 **Pz.Kpfw.II**
	4 **Pz.Kpfw.III**
	1 **Pz.Kpfw.IV**

These losses were replaced by 12 Mk.II Infantry Tanks that had been captured in operational order.

The **5.leichte Division** claimed to have destroyed 57 tanks (including 13 Mk.II) and the **15.Panzer-Division** claimed 175 tanks (including 95 Mk.II). The 7th Armoured Division claimed that they had destroyed 90 enemy tanks.

11.5 TACTICAL ANALYSIS

BRITISH TACTICS

In the aftermath of the battle, the two R.T.R. battalions with the Mk.IIA Infantry Tanks recorded the following assessments of why the attacks had failed:

4th R.T.R.'s Lessons of the Action and Operations

It appears futile to attack with tanks an enemy position which has been well prepared, and which has not been reconnoitered.

The two troops of A Squadron which were working under a separate command on the coast had four tanks immobilized due to running onto an enemy mine field. This minefield was known to exist, and it would seem that the clearing of a mine field must be recognized as a minor tactical operation to be carried out before tanks can be moved in the vicinity.

The enemy tanks do not appear to have knocked out many of our tanks. The majority of tank casualties were due to enemy artillery fire.

The enemy use their tanks to cover the bringing into action rapidly and at close range, their artillery. This was noticeable at Point 39 in front of B Squadron on the 17th.

On several occasions, it was noticed that once one of our tanks had halted and appeared disabled, the enemy ceased to engage it until it showed signs of life again. This may be due to the enemy anxiety to recover our tanks in as good a state as possible.

At other times, it was noticed that after a tank had been immobilized by enemy action, usually through hits on the suspension, the enemy then deliberately directed their fire on the cupola.

The fact that Halfaya Pass was held for the period 15/17 June inclusive by the enemy, with the Camerons investing them from one side and the 11th Brigade from the other; caused some shortage to the enemy of probably rations, as efforts were repeatedly made to drop supplies from the air. This was not very successful as our aircraft intervened. It may be logically assumed from this that the garrison of the Pass was not self-supporting for any length of time and might well have been ignored with a view of its automatic capitulation after Capuzzo and Sollum had been taken.

Although Point 190 (Halfaya Pass) was known to be a strong point and contain either O.P. or guns, nothing seems to have been done to subdue this place. Guns were observed on this point, and had a large flash. These guns did considerable damage. Possibly more use could have been made of smoke.

Guides for night marches should be more plentiful. C Squadron had 6.5 miles to traverse from Batuma to the top of the Pass. This had to be covered in under an hour. Nearly all of this was done in the dark. No guides were provided for this bit of the route and the whole column followed the tanks, who moved on a compass bearing. This was inconvenient for the guns, which in many cases stuck in sand. The motor transport of the accompanying infantry suffered in a like manner.

The shortage of ammunition in B Squadron on the 17th would not have occurred had the ammunition been directly under the command of the Squadron Commander.

7th R.T.R.'s Analysis

The 7th R.T.R. claimed to have put 31 enemy tanks out of action. Attacking Capuzzo on the first night, the enemy appeared to put a second wave of tanks through, hoping perhaps that our ammunition was exhausted. Our policy should be to hold fire until 700 yards. The enemy support tank gun (75 mm on the Pz.Kpfw.IV) has quite a good moral effect, but does not shoot too well. Plenty of near misses but not hits. The Hun invariably got the sun behind him, though at Capuzzo he fired high (if he was trying to knock our perimeter tanks).

Initial impetus appeared to be lost owing to the infantry not arriving sooner. Had they done so, it is felt that we should have lost fewer tanks and sailed the infantry into position earlier with less opposition.

It is very significant that in neither case did these units specifically recognize that the **8.8 cm Flak** was one of the primary causes of their failure. However, they were slowly learning that in spite of their thick armor, they would have to improve their tactics instead of simply betting on being able to overrun any enemy opposition.

In the event that they lost the battle, the British had established a backstop of two Infantry Tank squadrons manned by crews from the 5th R.T.R. who were totally untrained in Mk.IIA Infantry Tanks.

The British were still deploying their tanks one squadron at a time. They even held complete squadrons back in reserve under Brigade control. The accounts still reflect that the individual troops and tanks did not have permission to be tactically flexible and were following their squadron commanders.

The 2nd and 6th R.T.R. both did amazingly well for a day in holding the numerically superior **Panzer-Regiment 5** off on the left flank. But the Cruiser Tanks' attempt to overrun Point 208 was a mixture of the charge of the Light Brigade and tactics borrowed from the Navy, including steaming in line ahead and turning for broadside fire. Worse yet, from their own accounts they apparently didn't realize why these tactics had failed.

The conclusions by the 2nd R.T.R. on the action at Hafid Ridge on 15 June as recorded on 20 June 1941 were:

The Hafid position was held in strength far greater than at first thought.

The enemy were determined to hold this position at all costs, and had prepared many alternative positions for guns.

Enemy anti-tank guns were cleverly placed and bravely fought, fire being held until the range was really effective.

The attack was a surprise to the enemy and the artillery support of the utmost assistance to the attack.

It appears that the failure in the wireless communications may have resulted in the loss of five tanks.

Only the forward enemy defenses were encountered. The position appears to run northwards in some considerable depth.

And, the 2nd R.T.R. conclusions from the tank-versus-tank actions on 16 June as recorded on 20 June 1941 were:

It is essential to have ammunition near the forward tanks. Preferably in Unit B.1.Echelon and under wireless control from the unit.

The enemy use their tanks in large numbers and on very set plans. The large formations appear rather unwieldy.

The need for close co-operation between units flanking each other and the possible use of Verey lights to show positions. This is done by the Germans, and it is not considered that any surprise effect would be jeopardized if used discreetly.

The most effective co-operation between guns and tanks is possible if an O.P. is with Bn.H.Q.

GERMAN TACTICS

The **8.8 cm Flak**, the **Panzer-Regiment 5** and the solid defenses of Halfaya and Point 208 won the battle. The defensive system had contributed heavily to a victory which might easily have been a defeat. It was the stubborn resistance of **Stuetzpunkte** that provided an opportunity for the employment of offensive tactics. The organization of these defensive positions in depth had allowed them to hold out until a limited counteroffensive could be put in motion.

Without the **8.8 cm Flak**, however, none of the positions could have repulsed the British drive. It opened fire either at 2000 to 1600 meters or at 800 to 500 meters, but its most effective ranges were certainly in the lower bracket. The **I./Flak-Regiment 33** chalked up 92 armored vehicles (including 82 tanks), which they claimed to have completely destroyed with 1,680 rounds of 8.8 cm shell and 13,500 rounds of 2 cm shell. As the 2 cm fire knocked out only three tanks, the **8.8 cm Flak** got a tank for every 20 shells fired in this action. In comparison, **Panzer-Regiment 8** claimed 64 kills.

With the **8.8 cm Flak** in support, the Panzers had overcome their reluctance to tangle with the Mk.II Infantry Tanks. However, **Panzer-Regiment 8** had also sent isolated companies and then separate battalions into the fray instead of the entire **Regiment** en masse to overwhelm isolated British tank squadrons. This appears to be one of their few mistakes, as they closed to short range where their **5 cm Kw.K.** ammunition could penetrate the Mk.II Infantry Tank's thick armor.

Following Operation Battleaxe, the **Panzertruppen** created a report on their "Experiences in the African Theater of War" from which the following relevant excerpts are drawn:

Combat Vehicles
- ***Pz.Kpfw.I Ausf.A und B*** - General opinion: The ***Pz.Kpfw.I Ausf.A*** continuously break down. They don't meet requirements, too weak and too slow. They are unusable in tropical conditions.
- ***Pz.Kpfw.II*** - General opinion: They have worked out well in the company HQ section or as reconnaissance vehicles. The main deficiency is their leaf-springs breaking.
- ***Pz.Kpfw.III*** - General opinion: At first there were many breakdowns. Now it is a good vehicle suitable for the tropics. The new, wider tracks have proven successful, less roadwheel wear. Due to continuously sucking in dust, the engines are usually completely done in after 1500 to 2000 kilometers, pistons with 2 to 3 mm play. The air must be drawn in from the crew compartment through larger oil bath filters. After a 40-kilometer desert journey the oil bath filters must be thoroughly cleaned. A modification has been initiated. The main deficiency is insufficient filtering of the engine intake air. High wear on the roadwheels of those with wider tires and narrow tracks. The same modification to the suspension as on the ***Ausf.H*** is already arranged. It is to be accomplished during general rebuilds back in Germany.
- ***Pz.Kpfw.IV*** - General opinion: Proved to be very good. No large deficiencies.

Directives for Training

Range estimation is to be continually practiced, especially by troops new to Africa. Because of the very good visibility in the desert on the one hand, because of air vibrations during the hottest hours of the day on the other, overestimates of the range by 2 or 3 kilometers occur at first. Along with these overestimates, ammunition tactics must also be taught.

Weapons and Ammunition

Up to now, all weapons have proven to be good. Also the **M.G.34** has shown that with correct care and belt fed, no stoppages of any significance occur. Because of the dust and dirt, the weapons are to be maintained dry and polished.

At 300 meters range, both the **5 cm Pzgr.** and **5 cm Pzgr.40** cleanly penetrate through all enemy armor. The Mark IV and VI were knocked out throughout the entire working range of the **5 cm Kw.K.**

Ammunition expenditure is high in tank battles. The cause of this is the good visibility resulting in opening fire too early or firing at retreating enemy tanks beyond the effective range of the weapons.

As a result of the British employing Mark II Infantry Tanks in large numbers (over 100 in the Sollum battle from 15 to 17 June), the weapons that come to the forefront are those that are guaranteed to penetrate its armor. Primarily the **8.8 cm Flak** and **5 cm Pak 38**, also the **s.Pz.B.41**. These build the framework for the defense, but **8.8 cm Flak** are also accompanying every attack. **T-Minen** are amply utilized.

Remarks on British Tactics

Up to now the British have employed Mark II Infantry Tanks and Mark IV and VI Cruiser Tanks. Reports stress the good cooperation between British tanks with their 85 mm and 105 mm artillery, which is very mobile as escorting artillery.

The artillery fire is very accurately placed and is often directed by employing three armored cars. Artillery fire is well placed even on moving columns, so that the troops were very irritated at first. In general, a serious effect upon the Panzers has not been achieved other than the hindrances caused from closing the hatches.

The effectiveness of their tanks' shooting was usually not high, because the British fire a lot while on the move.

British tanks can be effectively engaged by quickly establishing a firefront or closing to effective ranges. The British lack concentrated and coordinated command. All British tanks have been effectively combated within the range of our weapons (**5 cm Kw.K.**). It should be noted that the Mark II Infantry Tank catches on fire very easily and the Mark VI Cruiser Tank is very thinly armored. It is very difficult to pursue the Mark VI Cruiser Tank because it is extraordinarily fast (50 to 60 kilometers/hours with Christie-Patent suspension). Employment of a sufficient number of **8.8 cm Flak** was also necessary to effectively engage this tank at long range. The **8.8 cm Flak** can also knock out the Mark II Infantry Tanks at long ranges.

Points to aim at on British tanks are the easily jammed gun mantlets, the rear, the drive sprockets at the rear, the track, and the lower slope of the turret.

Take precautions with British trucks, because they mount anti-tank guns and cannon on them from which they surprisingly open fire over the engine or rear. British reconnaissance patrols are energetically carried out either on foot or in armored cars. They strike out of the desert deep into the rear areas, dropping off assault troops or attacking rear columns with fast armored cars.

It must be taken into account that the British will lay anti-tank mines at night in needed crossing points (passes and gaps in barbed wire).

Attacks by British aircraft are to be engaged by all the light weapons. The British have shown themselves to be especially sensitive to the 2 cm Kw.K.

In large battles, the British command is slow and ponderous. But as fighters they are tough and tenacious.

Directives for Combat

Combat reconnaissance must be deployed far ahead in the desert.

Exact target recognition is possible only in the morning and evening. Because of the heat, the air shimmers so much during the day that all contours are completely wiped out and distorted. Tanks look like bushes and bushes like tanks, etc. A lot of practice is necessary!

When advancing through areas of the desert with valleys (3 to 10 to 15 kilometers wide and up to 50 kilometers long), secure the open flank with a platoon or company on the ridgeline; when crossing them, always send out combat reconnaissance in advance to the next ridgeline. Pz.Kpfw.II are too slow and weak for this; use the Pz.Kpfw.III and IV.

In general, the principal guidelines for Panzer combat have proven completely successful and are to be used unchanged. It is ideal tank country without the restrictions of occupied areas. Combat formations of large units (regiment or brigade) and tank actions up to 100 kilometers in depth are possible at any time.

By outfitting the Pz.Kpfw.III with the 5 cm Kanone, it is not necessary to employ the mittlere Panzer-Kompanie forward in the first line. The mittlere Panzer-Kompanie is to be held absolutely concentrated in the hands of the Abteilung commander until after the direction in which the battle is developing is clarified; then it is utilized to build a Schwerpunkt.

The wide combat formation (Breitkeil) has proven successful in the desert: Two leichte Panzer-Kompanien in the front line followed by the mittlere Panzer-Kompanie in the second line. The Panzer-Regiment is deployed in two waves. Increase intervals between Panzers to 100 to 150 meters because of the dust and artillery fire. Therefore Kurskreisel (course indicator gyro-compasses) are needed in every Panzer. During attacks, constantly switch between fire and movement because the desert entices the troops to charge in.

Unlike the British, we lack mobile escorting artillery.

The Mark II Infantry tank (about 25 kilometers/hour speed, 80 mm thick armor reinforced in the front by concrete, 40 mm gun, usually employed as 10 to 12 tanks together) can be most effectively engaged by rapid fire at the gun mantlet. Without halting to fire and if possible in the flank, at their highest speed, an appropriate number of Pz.Kpfw.III charge toward the Mark II tanks down to a range under 300 meters and then open fire, switching between Pzgr. and Pzgr.40. The Mark II easily catches on fire. The 5 cm Pzgr. penetrates clean through at ranges under 300 meters.

FOOTNOTE: Like the **Panzertruppen**, in their experience report the **Panzer-Jaeger** also stated that training in range estimation was important for every single crew member. The **Panzer-Jaeger** experience was that, in general, estimates of the range were too short; Panzertruppen, on the contrary, stated that range estimates were far too long. Maybe Panzer crews were optimistic and **Pak** gunners pessimistic by nature. The **Panzer-Jaeger** stated that the causes for range estimation errors were due primarily to the lack of any reference points in the desert, being unaccustomed to the long-range visibility and the air shimmering especially during midday.

Appendices

APPENDIX A - TECHNICAL SPECIFICATIONS

Official Title:	Tank, Light, Mark VI.B
Weapons:	0.5" Vickers M.G. and a 0.303" Vickers M.G. in a dual M.G. Mounting No.10 in the turret
Elevation:	-10°, +37°, free elevation
Traverse:	360° by hand
Ammunition Types:	A.P. and Ball for machineguns
Ammunition Stowage:	200 - 0.5" rounds
	2500 rounds for the 0.303" machinegun
Gun Sight:	Telescope No.24 Mk.II (1.9 x 21°)
Range:	Graduated to 1500 yards for AP
Crew:	Gunner, Driver and Observer
Communications:	No. 9 Wireless Transmitter and Receiver

Armor (Thickness at Angle from Vertical):
14 mm armor basis. Specification I.T.70C homogeneous-hard plates for most plates including construction of the turret. Specification I.T.60B for 7 mm to 12 mm thick face-hardened plates

Commander's Cupola	18 mm I.T.70 @ 0°
Turret Roof	3.5 mm I.T.70 @ 90-83°
Turret Front	14 mm I.T.70 @ 17°
Gun Mantle	14 mm I.T.70 @ 0°
Superstructure Roof	4 mm I.T.70 @ 90°
Driver's Front Plate	14 mm I.T.70 @ 0°
Glacis	6 mm I.T.70 @ 75°
Hull Nose	11 mm I.T.60 @ 20°
Hull Front Lower	5 mm I.T.70 @ 65°
Hull Belly	3 mm I.T.70 @ 90°
Turret Side, Fore	14 mm I.T.70 @ 0°
Turret Side, Aft	11 mm I.T.70 @ 0°
Hull Nearside	13 mm I.T.70 @ 0°
Hull Offside	11 mm I.T.60 @ 0°
Turret Rear	11 mm I.T.70 @ 0°
Hull Rear Upper	6 mm I.T.70 @ 50°
Hull Rear Lower	4 mm I.T.70 @ 50-80°

Automotive Capabilities:

Average Speed	
a) Road:	40 km/hr (25 mph)
b) Cross Country:	20 km/hr (12 mph)
Maximum Speed:	48 km/hr (30 mph)
Range	
a) Road:	290 km (180 miles)
b) Cross Country:	180 km (110 miles)
Fuel Capacity:	164 liter (36 gallons)
Grade:	??°
Step:	73 cm (2.4')
Trench Crossing:	?? cm
Fording Depth:	61 cm (2.0')
Motor:	88 B.H.P. @ 3000 rpm, water cooled,
	6 cylinder Meadows ESTB, 4.43 liter gasoline
HP/Weight Ratio:	16.9 B.H.P./long ton
Transmission:	5 speed
Steering:	Clutch and brake steering
Suspension:	4 roadwheels, double wheel bogie with coil springs

Measurements:

Length Overall:	3.94 m (12' 11.25")
Width Overall:	2.05 m (6' 8.5")
Height Overall:	2.22 m (7' 3.5")
Ground Clearance:	0.33 m (13")
Combat Loaded:	5.2 tons
Ground Pressure:	0.57 kg/cm² (8.1 lb./sq.in.)

Official Title: **Tank, Light, Mark VI.C**

Weapons: 15 mm Besa M.G. and a 7.92 mm Besa M.G. in a dual Besa M.G. Mounting No.14 in the turret

Elevation: -10°, +34°, free elevation
Traverse: 360° by hand
Ammunition Types: A.P. for 15 mm and ball for 7.92 mm
Ammunition Stowage: 175 - 15 mm rounds
2700 rounds for the machinegun
Gun Sight: Telescope No.30 Mk.I (1.9x 21°)
Range: Graduated to 1800 yards for 2-pdr. AP

Height Overall: 2.13 m (7')

Other data the same as Tank, Light, Mark VI.B.

Appendices

Official Title: **Tank, Infantry, Mark II.A "Matilda II"**

Weapons: One 2-pdr. and one 7.92 Besa M.G. in coaxial mounting in the turret
                                                       plus one 2" Smoke Mortar
Elevation: -20°, +20°
Traverse: 360° by hydraulic motor (max. 24°/sec) and by hand
Ammunition Types: AP Shot for 2-pdr, ball for machineguns
Ammunition Stowage: 93 2-pdr. rounds
                                                       2925 rounds for the machinegun belted
Gun Sight: Telescope No.30 Mk.I (1.9 x 21°)
Range: Graduated to 1800 yards for AP Shot Adjustable in 100 yard increments

Crew: Commander, Gunner, Loader, and Driver

Communications: No.11 Wireless Transmitter and Receiver
                                                       Telephone AFV for intercom

Armor (Thickness at Angle from Vertical):

Specification I.T.90 armor castings at 75 mm basis and Specification I.T.80 rolled plate at 70 mm basis. Specification I.T.80 rear plates covering the transmission (55 mm thick) were below the basis.

Commander's Cupola	75 mm I.T.90 @ 0°
Turret Roof	20 mm I.T.80 @ 90°
Turret Front	75 mm I.T.90 @ 20°
Gun Mantle	75 mm I.T.90 complex
Superstructure Roof	20 mm I.T.80 @ 81-90°
Driver's Front Plate	75 mm I.T.90 @ 0°
Glacis	47 mm I.T.90 @ 68°
Hull Nose	78-21 mm I.T.90 @ 26-90°
Hull Belly, Fore	20 mm I.T.80 @ 90°
Hull Belly, Aft	13 mm I.T.100 @ 90°
Turret Side	75 mm I.T.90 @ 0-20°
Superstructure Side	70 mm I.T.80 @ 20°
Engine Deck Side	55 mm I.T.80 @ 20°
Hull Side	25 I.T.70 & 40 mm I.T.80 @ 0°
Turret Rear	75 mm I.T.90 @ 0°
Engine Deck Roof	20 mm I.T.80 @ 75°
Hull Rear	55 mm I.T.80 @ 26°

Automotive Capabilities:

Average Speed	
a) Road:	16 km/hr (10 mph)
b) Cross Country:	8 km/hr (5 mph)
Maximum Speed:	24.1 km/hr (15 mph)
Range	
a) Road:	113 km (70 miles)
b) Cross Country:	69 km (42 miles)
Fuel Capacity:	211 liter (46.5 gallons)
Grade:	35°
Step:	61 cm (2')
Trench Crossing:	244 cm (8')
Fording Depth:	91 cm (3')
Motor:	Two 94 B.H.P. @ 2200 rpm, water cooled, 6 cylinder A.E.C. 6.75 liter diesel engines
HP/Weight Ratio:	7.5 B.H.P./long ton
Transmission:	6 speed Wilson epicyclic type, air servo operated
Steering:	Two Rackman type clutches with unified operation of clutch and brake
Suspension:	5 pairs of roadwheels, bell crank coil springs

Measurements:

Length Overall:	5.72 m (18' 9")
Width Overall:	2.51 m (8' 3")
Height Overall:	2.56 m (8' 5")
Ground Clearance:	0.33 m (1' 1")
Combat Loaded:	25 long tons
Ground Pressure:	1.4 kg/cm^2 (20.0 lb./sq.in.)

Official Title:	**Tank, Infantry, Mark II.A* "Matilda III"**
Motor:	Two 95 B.H.P. @ 2000 rpm, water cooled, 6 cylinder Leyland diesel engines
Range	
a) Road:	90 km (56 miles)
b) Cross Country:	69 km (42 miles)

Other data the same as Tank, Infantry, Mark II.A "Matilda II."

Appendices

Official Title:
Tank, Cruiser, Mark I
(previously A.9, Mark I)

Weapons:
One 2-pdr., one Vickers 0.303" M.G. coaxial mounting in turret plus two Vickers 0.303" M.G., one in each subturret

Elevation: -15°, +25° (-10°, +20° subturret)
Traverse: 360° by hydraulic motor (max. 24°/sec) and by hand (110° subturret by hand)

Ammunition Types: AP Shot for 2-pdr., ball for machineguns
Ammunition Stowage: 100 2-pdr. rounds
7000 rounds for the machineguns
Gun Sight: Telescope No.24 Mk.IV (1.9x 21°)
Telescope No.24 Mk.III for Sub Turrets
Range: Graduated to 1800 yards for AP Shot Adjustable in 100 yard increments
Graduated to 1500 yards for machineguns

Crew:
Commander, Gunner, Loader, 2 Forward Gunners and Driver

Communications:
No. 9 Wireless Transmitter and Receiver
Tannoy intercom

Armor (Thickness at Angle from Vertical):
14 mm armor basis. Specification I.T.70C homogeneous-hard plates for most plates including construction of the turret.

Turret Roof	4 mm I.T.70 @ 82+90°
Turret Front	14 mm I.T.70 @ 17°
Gun Mantle	14 mm I.T.70 rounded
Sub Turrets	14 mm I.T.70 @ 0°
Superstructure Roof	5 mm I.T.70 @ 90°
Driver's Front Plate	14 mm I.T.70 @ 0°
Glacis	5 mm I.T.70 @ 62°
Hull Nose	10 mm I.T.70 @ 24°
Hull Belly	7 mm I.T.70 @ 71+90°
Turret Side	12 mm I.T.70 @ 21°
Driver's Compartment Side	14 mm I.T.70 @ 0°
Superstructure Side	5 mm I.T.70 @ 72°
Hull Side	10 mm I.T.70 @ 25°
Turret Rear	14 mm I.T.70 @ 0°
Engine Deck Roof	5 mm I.T.70 @ 61°
Hull Rear	10 mm I.T.70 rounded

Automotive Capabilities:
Average Speed
    a) Road: 31 km/hr
    b) Cross Country: 16 km/hr
Maximum Speed: 40.2 km/hr (25 mph)
Range
    a) Road: 200 km (126 miles)
    b) Cross Country: 116 km (72 miles)
Fuel Capacity: 327 liter (72 gallons)
Grade: 35°
Step: 91 cm (3')
Trench Crossing: 244 cm (8')
Fording Depth: 91 cm (3')
Motor: 150 B.H.P. @ 2200 rpm, water cooled, 6 cylinder A.E.C. A.179, 9.64 liter gasoline engine
HP/Weight Ratio: 11.8 B.H.P./ton
Transmission: 5 speed Meadows
Steering: Clutch and brake steering
Suspension: 6 roadwheels, triple wheel bogie with coil spring and double acting shock absorbers

Measurements:
Length Overall: 5.79 m (19')
Width Overall: 2.50 m (8' 2.5")
Height Overall: 2.65 m (8' 8.5")
Ground Clearance: 0.46 m (1' 6")
Combat Loaded: 13.0
Ground Pressure: 0.76 kg/cm²

Official Title: **Tank, Cruiser, Mark I Close Support**
(previously A.9, Mark I C.S.)

Weapons: One 3.7 inch Mortar and one Vickers 0.303" M.G. in coaxial mounting
in the turret plus two Vickers 0.303" M.G., one in each subturret

Elevation: -10°, +30°

Ammunition Types: Smoke and HE for 3.7 inch mortar
Ball for machineguns

Ammunition Stowage: 36 rounds smoke, 4 rounds HE
5000 rounds for the machineguns

Gun Sight: Telescope No.24 Mk.III (1.9x 21°)

Other data the same as Tank, Cruiser, Mark I.

Appendices

Official Title: **Tank, Cruiser, Mark II.A.**
(previously A.10, Mark I.A.)

Weapons: One 2-pdr. and one 7.92 Besa M.G. in coaxial mounting in the turret plus 1 7.92 Besa in hull

Elevation: -15°, +15° (±15° for the hull M.G.)
Traverse: 360° by hydraulic motor (max. 24°/sec) and by hand (±15° for the hull M.G.)
Ammunition Types: AP Shot for 2-pdr, ball for machineguns
Ammunition Stowage: 100 2-pdr. rounds
4050 rounds for the machineguns
Gun Sight: Telescope No.24 Mk.IV (1.9 x 21°)
Telescope No.24 Mk.III for Besa in Hull
Range: Graduated to 1800 yards for AP Shot Adjustable in 100 yard increments
Graduated to 1500 yards for machineguns

Crew: Commander, Gunner, Loader, Forward Gunner and Driver

Communications: No. 9 Wireless Transmitter and Receiver
Tannoy intercom

Armor (Thickness at Angle from Vertical):
Composite armor 30 mm basis. Whenever 14 mm thickness exceeded, composite construction with Specification I.T.70C homogeneous-hard front plate riveted to Specification I.T.110 backing plate.

Turret Roof 7 mm I.T.70 @ 78-90°
Turret Front 15 mm I.T.70 & 15 mm I.T.110 @ 9°
Gun Mantle 30 mm I.T.90 complex
Superstructure Roof 7 mm I.T.70 @ 77°
Driver's Front Plate 15 mm I.T.70 & 15 mm I.T.110 @ 0°
Glacis 13 mm I.T.70 @ 56°
Hull Nose 11 mm I.T.70 & 11.1 mm I.T.110 @ 24°
Hull Belly 7 mm I.T.70 @ 90°

Turret Side 13 mm I.T.70 & 13 mm I.T.110 @ 21°
Superstructure Side 14 mm I.T.70 & 14 mm I.T.110 @ 0°
Slant Superstructure 7 mm I.T.70 @ 72°
Hull Side 11 mm I.T.70 & 11.1 mm I.T.110 @ 23°

Turret Rear 15 mm I.T.70 & 15 mm I.T.110 @ 0°
Engine Deck Roof 12 mm I.T.70 @ 60°
Hull Rear 12 mm I.T.70 @ rounded

Automotive Capabilities:
Average Speed
    a) Road: 22.5 km/hr (16 mph)
    b) Cross Country: ?? km/hr
Maximum Speed: 40.2 km/hr (25 mph)
Range
    a) Road: 236 km (147 miles)
    b) Cross Country: 129 km (80 miles)
Fuel Capacity: 445 liter (97 gallons)
Grade: 35°
Step: 91 cm (3')
Trench Crossing: 229 cm (7.5')
Fording Depth: 91 cm (3')
Motor: 150 B.H.P. @ 2200 rpm, water cooled, 6 cylinder A.E.C. A.179, 9.64 liter gasoline engine
HP/Weight Ratio: 10.68 B.H.P./long ton
Transmission: 5 speed Meadows
Steering: Clutch and brake steering
Suspension: 6 roadwheels, triple wheel bogie with coil spring and double acting shock absorbers

Measurements:
Length Overall: 5.52 m (18' 1.5")
Width Overall: 2.58 m (8' 5.5")
Height Overall: 2.54 m (8' 4")
Ground Clearance: 0.44 m (17.25")
Combat Loaded: 14.0 long tons
Ground Pressure: 1.05 kg/cm^2 (15 lb./sq.in.)

Official Title: **Tank, Cruiser, Mark II Close Support**
                                       (previously A.10, Mark II C.S.)

Weapons: One 3.7 inch Mortar and one 7.92 mm Besa M.G. in coaxial mounting
                                       in the turret plus one 7.92 mm Besa M.G. in the hull
Elevation: -10°, +30°
Ammunition Types: Smoke and HE for 3.7 inch mortar
                                       Ball for machineguns
Ammunition Stowage: 36 rounds smoke, 4 rounds HE
                                       2475 rounds for the machineguns
Gun Sight: Telescope No.25 Mk.I (1.9x 21°)

Other data the same as Tank, Cruiser, Mark II.A.

Appendices

Official Title: Tank, Cruiser, Mark IV.A.
(previously A.13, Mark II.A.)

Weapons: One 2-pdr. and one 7.92 Besa M.G. in coaxial mounting in the turret
Elevation: -15°, +25°
Traverse: 360° by hydraulic motor (max. 24°/sec) and by hand
Ammunition Types: AP Shot for 2-pdr., ball for machineguns
Ammunition Stowage: 87 2-pdr. rounds
3375 rounds for the machinegun
Sight: Telescope No.24 Mk.V (1.9 x 21°)
Range: Graduated to 1800 yards for AP Shot Adjustable in 100 yard increments

Crew: Commander, Gunner, Loader, and Driver

Communications: No. 9 Wireless Transmitter and Receiver
Tannoy intercom

Armor (Thickness at Angle from Vertical):
Various armor basis were specified: 30 mm casting for the cupola, 30 mm for the turret front, 22 mm for the turret sides with skirting plates, 25 mm for the driver's hood, 20 mm for the front of the hull, and 14 mm for the remainder. All plates were manufactured as Specification I.T.70C homogeneous-hard armor.

Commander's Cupola	30 mm I.T.90 @ 0°
Turret Roof	4 mm I.T.70 @ 80-90°
Turret Front	30 mm I.T.70 @ 15°
Gun Mantle	30 mm basis I.T.90 complex
Superstructure Roof	4 mm I.T.70 @ 90°
Driver's Front Plate	25 mm I.T.70 @ 0°
Glacis	10 mm I.T.70 @ 63°
Hull Nose	20 mm I.T.70 @ 0°
Lower Hull	10 mm I.T.70 @ 64°
Belly	4 mm I.T.70 @ 90°
Turret Side	14 mm I.T.70 @ 20° plus
	4 mm I.T.70 skirts @ 30-40°
Superstructure Side	14 mm I.T.70 @ 0°
Hull Side	14 mm I.T.70 plus 3/16" M.S. @ 0°
Turret Rear	14 mm I.T.70 @ 0° plus
	4 mm I.T.70 skirts @ 25°
Engine Deck Roof	4 mm I.T.70 @ 90°
Hull Rear Upper	10 mm I.T.70 @ 60°
Hull Rear	14 mm I.T.70 @ 0°
Hull Rear Lower	8 mm I.T.70 @ 66°

Automotive Capabilities:
Average Speed
    a) Road: 40.2 km/hr (25 mph)
    b) Cross Country: ?? km/hr
Maximum Speed: 49.7 km/hr (30.9 mph)
Range
    a) Road: 161 km (100 miles)
    b) Cross Country: ?? km
Fuel Capacity: 454 liter (100 gallons)
Grade: 35°
Step: 85 cm (2.8')
Trench Crossing: 244 cm (8')
Fording Depth: 91 cm (3')
Motor: 340 B.H.P. @ 1550 rpm, water cooled, 12 cylinder M&A Ltd. VEE Mark II, 27 liter gasoline engine
HP/Weight Ratio: 23.05 B.H.P./long ton
Transmission: 4 speed M&A
Steering: Clutch and brake steering
Suspension: 4 roadwheels, coil spring, slow motion Christie

Measurements:
Length Overall: 6.02 m (19' 9")
Width Overall: 2.54 m (8' 4")
Height Overall: 2.59 m (8' 6")
Ground Clearance: 0.38 m (1' 3")
Combat Loaded: 14.75 long tons
Ground Pressure: 0.84 kg/cm² (12.0 lb./sq.in.)

199

Official Title:

Tank, Cruiser, Mark VI.A.
"Crusader I" (previously A.16)

Weapons:

One 2-pdr. and one 7.92 Besa M.G. in coaxial mounting in the turret and one 7.92 mm Besa M.G. in the subturret, plus one 2" Smoke Mortar

Elevation: -15°, +20°
Traverse: 360° by hydraulic motor (max. 24°/sec) and by hand
Ammunition Types: AP Shot for the 2-pdr.
Ball for machineguns
Ammunition Stowage: 130 2-pdr. rounds
4950 rounds for the machinegun
Gun Sight: Telescope No.30 Mk.I (1.9 x 21°)
Range: Graduated to 1800 yards for AP Shot Adjustable in 100 yard increments

Crew:

Commander, Gunner, Loader, Subturret Gunner and Driver

Communications:

No. 9 Wireless Transmitter and Receiver
Tannoy intercom

Armor (Thickness at Angle from Vertical):

40 mm basis for the turret and front of the hull, 30 mm basis for the remainder. Whenever 14 mm thickness exceeded, composite armor construction with a Specification I.T.70 front plate of homogeneous-hard armor riveted to a Specification I.T.110 backing plate of carbon manganese steel.

Turret Roof	9 mm I.T.70 @ 77°
Turret Front	20 mm I.T.70 & 19 I.T.110 @ 0°
Gun Mantle	50 mm I.T.90 complex
Superstructure Roof	7 mm I.T.70 @ 90°
Driver's Front Plate	18 mm I.T.70 & 22.2 I.T.110 @ 0°
Glacis	9 mm I.T.70 @ 85°
Upper Hull Nose	14 mm I.T.70 @ 60°
Hull Nose	14 mm I.T.70 & 12.7 mm I.T.110 @ 29°
Lower Hull Nose	14 mm I.T.70 @ 60°
Hull Belly, Fore	4 mm I.T.70 & 6.4 mm I.T.110 @ 90°
Hull Belly, Aft	6.4 mm I.T.110 @ 90°
Turret Side	10 mm I.T.70 & 9.5 mm I.T.110 @ 45°
Hull Side	14 mm I.T.70 & 14.3 mm I.T.110 @ 0°
Turret Rear Upper	12 mm I.T.70 & 12.7 mm I.T.110 @ 30°
Turret Rear Lower	14 mm I.T.70 @ 58°
Engine Deck Roof	7 mm I.T.70 @ 90°
Exhaust Louvres	14 mm I.T.70 @ 45°
Hull Rear	14 mm I.T.70 & 14.3 mm I.T.110 @ 15°
Hull Rear Lower	12 mm I.T.70 @ 60°

Automotive Capabilities:

Average Speed
    a) Road: 40.2 km/hr (25 mph)
    b) Cross Country: ?? km/hr
Maximum Speed: 44.2 km/hr (27.5 mph)
Range
    a) Road: 266 km (165 miles)
    b) Cross Country: 195 km (121 miles)
Fuel Capacity: 500 liter (110 gal. & 30 gal. aux.tank)
Grade: 35°
Step: 76 cm (2' 6")
Trench Crossing: 229 cm (7' 6")
Fording Depth: 99 cm (3' 3")
Motor: 340 B.H.P. @ 1550 rpm, water cooled, 12 cylinder Nuffield Mk.III, 27 liter gasoline engine
HP/Weight Ratio: 18 B.H.P./long ton
Transmission: 4 speed M&A
Steering: Clutch and brake steering
Suspension: 5 roadwheels, coil spring, slow motion Christie

Measurements:

Length Overall: 6.30 m (20' 8")
Width Overall: 2.77 m (9' 1")
Height Overall: 2.24 m (7' 4")
Ground Clearance: 0.41 m (1' 4")
Combat Loaded: 18.8 long tons
Ground Pressure: 1.1 kg/cm^2 (15.7 lb./sq.in.)

Official Title:

Pz.Kpfw.I (M.G.) (Sd.Kfz.101) Ausf.A

Weapons: Two M.G.13k in the turret
Elevation: -10°, +20°
Traverse: 360° by hand
Ammunition Types: S.m.K. and S.m.K.L'Spur
Ammunition Stowage: 2250 rounds in 25-round magazines
Gun Sight: T.Z.F.2 (2.5x 28°)
Range: Graduated to 800 meters

Crew: Commander/Gunner and Driver

Communications: FuG2 radio set (Receiver only)

Armor (Thickness at Angle from Vertical):
Turret Roof 8 mm @ 81 and 90°
Turret Front 14 mm @ 8°
Gun Mantle 15 mm rounded
Superstructure Roof 8 mm @ 90°
Driver's Front Plate 13 mm @ 21°
Glacis 8 mm @ 70 and 72°
Hull Nose 13 mm @ 25° and rounded
Hull Belly 5 mm @ 90°

Turret Side 13 mm @ 22°
Superstructure Side 13 mm @ 21°
Engine Deck Side 13 mm @ 6°
Hull Side 13 mm @ 0°

Turret Rear 13 mm @ 22°
Superstructure Rear 13 mm @ 22°
Engine Deck Roof 8 mm @ 81°
Engine Deck Rear 13 mm @ 22°
Hull Rear 13 mm @ 15°

Automotive Capabilities:
Average Speed
    a) Road: 20 km/hr
    b) Cross Country: 10-12 km/hr
Maximum Speed: 37 km/hr
Range
    a) Road: 140 km
    b) Cross Country: 93 km
Fuel Capacity: 140 liter
Grade: 30°
Step: 37 cm
Trench Crossing: 140 cm
Fording Depth: 60 cm
Motor: 60 metric HP, air cooled, 4 cylinder
Krupp M315, 3.5 liter gasoline
HP/Weight Ratio: 11.1 metric HP/ton
Transmission: 5 speed Zahnradfabrik F.G.35
Steering: Clutch steering
Suspension: 4 roadwheels, coil and leaf springs

Measurements:
Length Overall: 4.02 m
Width Overall: 2.06 m
Height Overall: 1.72 m
Ground Clearance: 0.295 m
Combat Loaded: 5.4 metric tons
Ground Pressure: 0.39 kg/cm^2

Official Title: **Pz.Kpfw.I (M.G.) (Sd.Kfz.101) Ausf.B**

Weapons: Two M.G.13k in the turret
Elevation: -10°, +20°
Traverse: 360° by hand
Ammunition Types: S.m.K. and S.m.K.L'Spur
Ammunition Stowage: 2250 rounds in 25-round magazines
Gun Sight: T.Z.F.2 (2.5x 28°)
Range: Graduated to 800 meters

Crew: Commander/Gunner and Driver

Communications: FuG2 radio set (Receiver only)

Armor (Thickness/Angle from Vertical):
Turret Roof   8 mm @ 81 and 90°
Turret Front   14 mm @ 8°
Gun Mantle   15 mm rounded
Superstructure Roof   8 mm @ 90°
Driver's Front Plate   13 mm @ 22°
Glacis   8 mm @ 70 and 72°
Hull Nose   13 mm @ 25° and rounded
Hull Belly   5 mm @ 90°

Turret Side   13 mm @ 22°
Superstructure Side   13 mm @ 22°
Engine Deck Side   13 mm @ 6°
Hull Side   13 mm @ 0°

Turret Rear   13 mm @ 22°
Engine Deck Roof   8 mm @ 87°
Engine Deck Rear   13 mm @ 0°
Hull Rear   13 mm @ 18 and 55°

Automotive Capabilities:
Average Speed
    a) Road: 25 km/hr
    b) Cross Country: 12-15 km/hr
Maximum Speed: 40 km/hr
Range
    a) Road: 170 km
    b) Cross Country: 115 km
Fuel Capacity: 146 liter
Grade: 30°
Step: 37 cm
Trench Crossing: 140 cm
Fording Depth: 60 cm
Motor: 100 metric HP, water cooled, 6 cylinder
                                       Maybach NL 38 TR, 3.8 liter gasoline
HP/Weight Ratio: 17.25 metric HP/ton
Transmission: 5 speed Zahnradfabrik F.G.31
Steering: Clutch steering
Suspension: 5 roadwheels, coil and leaf springs

Measurements:
Length Overall: 4.42 m
Width Overall: 2.06 m
Height Overall: 1.72 m
Ground Clearance: 0.295 m
Combat Loaded: 5.8 metric tons
Ground Pressure: 0.52 kg/cm²

Official Title: **kl.Pz.Bef.Wg. (Sd.Kfz.265)**

Weapons:	One M.G.34 in ball mount
Elevation:	-10°, +20°
Traverse:	20° left and 20° right of center
Ammunition Types:	S.m.K. and S.m.K.L'Spur
Ammunition Stowage:	900 rounds belted in 150-round sacks
Gun Sight:	K.Z.F.1 (1.8x 18°)
Range:	Graduated to 800 meters
Crew:	Commander, Radio Operator and Driver
Communications:	FuG6 and FuG2 radio sets
Armor (Thickness/Angle from Vertical):	
Commander's Cupola	14.5 mm
Superstructure Roof	8 mm @ 90°
Driver's Front Plate	13 mm @ 22°
Glacis	
Hull Nose	13 mm @ 27° and rounded
Hull Belly	5 mm @ 90°
Superstructure Side	13 mm @ 22°
Engine Deck Side	13 mm @ 0°
Hull Side	13 mm @ 0°
Superstructure Rear	13 mm @ 22°
Engine Deck Roof	5 mm @ 88°
Engine Deck Rear	13 mm @ 0°
Hull Rear	13 mm @ 19°
Automotive Capabilities:	
Average Speed	
a) Road:	25 km/hr
b) Cross Country:	12-15 km/hr
Maximum Speed:	40 km/hr
Range	
a) Road:	170 km
b) Cross Country:	115 km
Fuel Capacity:	146 liter
Grade:	30°
Step:	37 cm
Trench Crossing:	140 cm
Fording Depth:	60 cm
Motor:	100 metric HP, water cooled, 6 cylinder
	Maybach NL 38 TR, 3.8 liter gasoline
HP/Weight Ratio:	17 metric HP/ton
Transmission:	5 speed Zahnradfabrik F.G.31
Steering:	Clutch steering
Suspension:	5 roadwheels, coil and leaf springs
Measurements:	
Length Overall:	4.42 m
Width Overall:	2.06 m
Height Overall:	1.99 m
Ground Clearance:	0.295 m
Combat Loaded:	5.88 metric tons
Ground Pressure:	0.525 kg/cm^2

Official Title: **Pz.Kpfw.II (2 cm) (Sd.Kfz.121)**
Ausf. A, B und C

Weapons: One 2 cm Kw.K.30 and one M.G.34 in the turret
Elevation: -10°, +20°
Traverse: 360° by hand
Ammunition Types: 2 cm Pzgr. for 2 cm Kw.K.
S.m.K. and S.m.K.L'Spur for machinegun
Ammunition Stowage: 180 2 cm rounds in 10-round magazines
2100 rounds belted in 150-round sacks
Gun Sight: T.Z.F.4 (2.5x 25°)
Range: Graduated to 1200 meters for Pzgr. with Adjustable range scale
at 100 meter intervals

Crew: Commander/Gunner, Radio Operator and Driver

Communications: FuG5 radio set (sender and receiver)
or FuG2 radio set (receiver only)

Armor (Thickness at Angle from Vertical):
Turret Roof 10 mm @ 76 and 90°
Turret Front 20+14.5 mm rounded and 16°
Gun Mantle 15 mm rounded
Superstructure Roof 12 mm @ 90°
Driver's Front Plate 20+14.5 mm @ 9°
Glacis 14.5+14.5 @ 73°
Hull Nose 20 @ 32° + 14.5 mm rounded
Hull Belly 5 mm @ 90°

Turret Side 14.5 mm @ 22°
Superstructure Side 14.5 mm @ 0°
Engine Deck Side 14.5 mm @ 0°
Hull Side 14.5 mm @ 0°

Turret Rear 14.5 mm @ 22°
Superstructure Rear 14.5 mm @ 9°
Engine Deck Roof 10 mm @ 81 and 90°
Engine Deck Rear 14.5 mm @ 0°
Hull Rear 14.5 mm @ 6°
Hull Rear Lower 10 mm @ 63°

Automotive Capabilities:
Average Speed
    a) Road: 25 km/hr
    b) Cross Country: 12-15 km/hr
Maximum Speed: 40 km/hr
Range
    a) Road: 190 km
    b) Cross Country: 126 km
Fuel Capacity: 170 liter
Grade: 30°
Step: 42 cm
Trench Crossing: 180 cm
Fording Depth: 92 cm
Motor: 140 metric HP, water cooled, 6 cylinder
Maybach HL 62 TR, 6.2 liter gasoline
HP/Weight Ratio: 16 metric HP/ton
Transmission: 6 speed Zahnradfabrik S.S.G.46
Steering: Differential steering
Suspension: 5 roadwheels, leaf springs

Measurements:
Length Overall: 4.81 m
Width Overall: 2.22 m
Height Overall: 2.15 m
Ground Clearance: 0.345 m
Combat Loaded: 8.9 metric tons
Ground Pressure: 0.73 kg/cm^2

Official Title: **Pz.Bef.Wg. (Sd.Kfz.266, 267 und 268)**
Ausf. E (earlier **Ausf.B**)

Weapons: One M.G.34 in ball mount
Elevation: -10°, +20°
Traverse: 15° left and 15° right of center
Ammunition Types: S.m.K. and S.m.K.L'Spur
Ammunition Stowage: 1500 rounds belted in 150-round sacks
Gun Sight: K.Z.F.2 (1.8x 18°)
Range: Graduated to 800 meters

Crew: Commander, Gunner, 2 Radio Operators and Driver

Communications: FuG6 and FuG2 radio sets in Sd.Kfz.266
FuG6 and FuG8 radio sets in Sd.Kfz.267
FuG6 und FuG7 radio sets in Sd.Kfz.268

Armor (Thickness at Angle from Vertical):
Commander's Cupola — 30 mm @ 90 plus cast visors
Turret Roof — 10 mm @ 83 and 90°
Turret Front — 30 mm @ 15°
Superstructure Roof — 16 mm @ 90°
Driver's Front Plate — 30 mm @ 9°
Glacis — 25 mm @ 85°
Upper Hull Front — 30 mm @ 52°
Hull Nose — 30 mm @ 21°
Hull Belly — 15 mm @ 90°

Turret Side — 30 mm @ 25°
Superstructure Side — 30 mm @ 0°
Engine Deck Side — 30 mm @ 0°
Hull Side — 30 mm @ 0°

Turret Rear — 30 mm @ 25 and 90°, curved
Engine Deck Roof — 16 mm @ 75 and 87°
Engine Deck Rear — 21 mm @ 30°
Hull Rear — 21 mm @ 10°

Automotive Capabilities:
Average Speed
    a) Road: 25 km/hr
    b) Cross Country: 12-15 km/hr
Maximum Speed: 40 km/hr
Range
    a) Road: 165 km
    b) Cross Country: 95 km
Fuel Capacity: 320 liter
Grade: 30°
Step: 60 cm
Trench Crossing: 230 cm
Fording Depth: 80 cm
Motor: 265 metric HP, water cooled, 12 cylinder
Maybach HL 120 TR, 12 liter gasoline
HP/Weight Ratio: 13.4 metric HP/ton
Transmission: 10 speed Maybach S.R.G.32 8 145
Steering: Differential steering
Suspension: 6 roadwheels, torsion bars

Measurements:
Length Overall: 5.38 m
Width Overall: 2.91 m
Height Overall: 2.44 m
Ground Clearance: 0.385 m
Combat Loaded: 19.8 metric tons
Ground Pressure: 0.93 kg/cm^2

Official Title: **Pz.Kpfw.III (5 cm) (Sd.Kfz.141)**
Ausf. F und G

Weapons: One 5 cm Kw.K. L/42 and one M.G.34 in the turret
One M.G.34 in a ball mount

Elevation:	-10°, +20°
Traverse:	360° by hand
Ammunition Types:	5 cm Pzgr. and Sprgr. for 5 cm Kw.K.
	S.m.K. and S.m.K.L'Spur for machinegun
Ammunition Stowage:	99 5 cm rounds
	3750 rounds for the machinegun belted in 150-round sacks
Gun Sight:	T.Z.F.5d (2.5x 25°)
Range:	Graduated to 1500 meters for Pzgr. and 3000 meters for Sprgr.
	with Adjustable range scales at 100 meter intervals

Crew: Commander, Gunner, Loader, Radio Operator and Driver

Communications: FuG5 and FuG2 radio sets

Armor (Thickness at Angle from Vertical):

Commander's Cupola	30 mm @ 90 plus cast visors
Turret Roof	10 mm @ 83 and 90°
Turret Front	30 mm @ 15°
Gun Mantle	35 mm rounded
Superstructure Roof	16 mm @ 90°
Driver's Front Plate	30 mm @ 9°
Glacis	25 mm @ 85°
Upper Hull Front	30 mm @ 52°
Hull Nose	30 mm @ 21°
Hull Belly	15 mm @ 90°
Turret Side	30 mm @ 25°
Superstructure Side	30 mm @ 0°
Engine Deck Side	30 mm @ 0°
Hull Side	30 mm @ 0°
Turret Rear	30 mm @ 25 and 90°, curved
Engine Deck Roof	16 mm @ 75 and 87°
Engine Deck Rear	21 mm @ 30° (Ausf.G = 30 mm)
Hull Rear	21 mm @ 10° (Ausf.G = 30 mm)

Automotive Capabilities:

Average Speed	
a) Road:	25 km/hr
b) Cross Country:	12-15 km/hr
Maximum Speed:	40 km/hr
Range	
a) Road:	155 km
b) Cross Country:	95 km
Fuel Capacity:	320 liter
Grade:	30°
Step:	60 cm
Trench Crossing:	220 cm
Fording Depth:	80 cm
Motor:	265 metric HP, water cooled, 12 cylinder
	Maybach HL 120 TRM, 12 liter gasoline
HP/Weight Ratio:	12.9 metric HP/ton
Transmission:	10 speed Maybach S.R.G.32 8 145
Steering:	Differential steering
Suspension:	6 roadwheels, torsion bars

Measurements:

Length Overall:	5.38 m
Width Overall:	2.91 m
Height Overall:	2.44 m
Ground Clearance:	0.385 m
Combat Loaded:	20.5 metric tons
Ground Pressure:	0.97 kg/cm^2

Official Title:	**Pz.Kpfw.III (5 cm) (Sd.Kfz.141)** **Ausf. H**
Weapons:	One 5 cm Kw.K. L/42 and one M.G.34 in the turret One M.G.34 in a ball mount
Elevation:	-10°, +20°
Traverse:	360° by hand
Ammunition Types:	5 cm Pzgr. and Sprgr. for 5 cm Kw.K. S.m.K. und S.m.K.L'Spur for machinegun
Ammunition Stowage:	99 5 cm rounds 3750 rounds for the machinegun belted in 150-round sacks
Gun Sight:	T.Z.F.5d (2.5x 25°)
Range:	Graduated to 1500 meters for Pzgr. and 3000 meters for Sprgr. with adjustable range scales at 100 meter intervals
Crew:	Commander, Gunner, Loader, Radio Operator and Driver
Communications:	FuG5 and FuG2 radio sets

Armor (Thickness at Angle from Vertical):

Commander's Cupola	30 mm @ 90 plus cast visors
Turret Roof	10 mm @ 83 and 90°
Turret Front	30 mm @ 15°
Gun Mantle	35 mm rounded
Superstructure Roof	16 mm @ 90°
Driver's Front Plate	30+30 mm @ 9°
Glacis	25 mm @ 85°
Upper Hull Front	30+30 mm @ 52°
Hull Nose	30+30 mm @ 21°
Hull Belly	15 mm @ 90°
Turret Side	30 mm @ 25°
Superstructure Side	30 mm @ 0°
Engine Deck Side	30 mm @ 0°
Hull Side	30 mm @ 0°
Turret Rear	30 mm @ 12° curved
Engine Deck Roof	16 mm @ 75 and 87°
Engine Deck Rear	30 mm @ 30°
Hull Rear	30+30 mm @ 10°

Automotive Capabilities:

Average Speed	
a) Road:	25 km/hr
b) Cross Country:	12-15 km/hr
Maximum Speed:	42 km/hr
Range	
a) Road:	155 km
b) Cross Country:	95 km
Fuel Capacity:	320 liter
Grade:	30°
Step:	60 cm
Trench Crossing:	220 cm
Fording Depth:	80 cm
Motor:	265 metric HP, water cooled, 12 cylinder Maybach HL 120 TRM, 12 liter gasoline
HP/Weight Ratio:	12.3 metric HP/ton
Transmission:	6 speed Zahnradfabrik S.S.G.77
Steering:	Differential steering
Suspension:	6 roadwheels, torsion bars

Measurements:

Length Overall:	5.38 m
Width Overall:	2.95 m
Height Overall:	2.50 m
Ground Clearance:	0.385 m
Combat Loaded:	21.5 metric tons
Ground Pressure:	0.97 kg/cm^2

| **Official Title:** | **Pz.Bef.Wg. (Sd.Kfz.266, 267 und 268)** |
| | **Ausf. H** (earlier **Ausf.C**) |

Weapons:	One M.G.34 in ball mount
Elevation:	-10°, +20°
Traverse:	15° left and 15° right of center
Ammunition Types:	S.m.K. and S.m.K.L'Spur
Ammunition Stowage:	1500 rounds belted in 150-round sacks
Gun Sight:	K.Z.F.2 (1.8x 18°)
Range:	Graduated to 800 meters

| **Crew:** | Commander, Gunner, 2 Radio Operators and Driver |

Communications:	FuG6 and FuG2 radio sets in Sd.Kfz.266
	FuG6 and FuG8 radio sets in Sd.Kfz.267
	FuG6 and FuG7 radio sets in Sd.Kfz.268

Armor (Thickness at Angle from Vertical):

Commander's Cupola	30 mm @ 90 plus cast visors
Turret Roof	10 mm @ 83 and 90°
Turret Front	30 mm @ 15°
Superstructure Roof	16 mm @ 90°
Driver's Front Plate	30+30 mm @ 9°
Glacis	25 mm @ 85°
Upper Hull Front	30+30 mm @ 52°
Hull Nose	30+30 mm @ 21°
Hull Belly	15 mm @ 90°

Turret Side	30 mm @ 25°
Superstructure Side	30 mm @ 0°
Engine Deck Side	30 mm @ 0°
Hull Side	30 mm @ 0°

Turret Rear	30 mm @ 12° curved
Engine Deck Roof	16 mm @ 75 and 87°
Engine Deck Rear	30 mm @ 30°
Hull Rear	30+30 mm @ 10°

Automotive Capabilities:

Average Speed	
a) Road:	25 km/hr
b) Cross Country:	12-15 km/hr
Maximum Speed:	42 km/hr
Range	
a) Road:	155 km
b) Cross Country:	95 km
Fuel Capacity:	320 liter
Grade:	30°
Step:	60 cm
Trench Crossing:	220 cm
Fording Depth:	80 cm
Motor:	265 metric HP, water cooled, 12 cylinder
	Maybach HL 120 TRM, 12 liter gasoline
HP/Weight Ratio:	12.3 metric HP/ton
Transmission:	6 speed Zahnradfabrik S.S.G.77
Steering:	Differential steering
Suspension:	6 roadwheels, torsion bars

Measurements:

Length Overall:	5.38 m
Width Overall:	2.95 m
Height Overall:	2.50 m
Ground Clearance:	0.385 m
Combat Loaded:	21.5 metric tons
Ground Pressure:	0.97 kg/cm^2

Official Title: **Pz.Kpfw.IV (7.5 cm) (Sd.Kfz.161)**
Ausf. D

Weapons: One 7.5 cm Kw.K. L/24 and one M.G.34 in the turret
One M.G.34 in a ball mount

Elevation: -10°, +20°
Traverse: 360° by electric motor and by hand
Ammunition Types: 7.5 cm Pzgr., Sprgr. and Nebel-Gr. for 7.5 cm Kw.K.
S.m.K. and S.m.K.L'Spur for machineguns
Ammunition Stowage: 80 7.5 cm rounds
2700 rounds for the machinegun belted in 150-round sacks
Gun Sight: T.Z.F.5b (2.5x 25°)
Range: Graduated to 1200 meters for Pzgr. and 2000 meters for Sprgr. with adjustable range scales at 100 meter intervals

Crew: Commander, Gunner, Loader, Radio Operator and Driver

Communications: FuG5 and FuG2 radio sets

Armor (Thickness at Angle from Vertical):
Commander's Cupola   30 mm @ 90 plus cast visors
Turret Roof   10 mm @ 83 and 90°
Turret Front   30 mm @ 10°
Gun Mantle   35 mm rounded
Superstructure Roof   11 mm @ 85 and 90°
Driver's Front Plate   30 mm (+30 mm) @ 9°
Glacis   20 mm @ 72°
Hull Nose   30 mm (+30 mm) @ 14° (50 mm for last 68)
Hull Belly   10 mm @ 90°

Turret Side   20 mm @ 25°
Superstructure Side   20 mm (+20 mm) @ 0°
Engine Deck Side   20 mm @ 0°
Hull Side   20 mm (+20 mm) @ 0°

Turret Rear   20 mm @ 25 and 0°, curved
Engine Deck Roof   10 mm @ 88°
Engine Deck Rear   20 mm @ 10°
Hull Rear   20 mm @ 10°

Automotive Capabilities:
Average Speed
    a) Road: 25 km/hr
    b) Cross Country: 20 km/hr
Maximum Speed: 42 km/hr
Range
    a) Road: 210 km
    b) Cross Country: 130 km
Fuel Capacity: 470 liter
Grade: 30°
Step: 60 cm
Trench Crossing: 230 cm
Fording Depth: 80 cm
Motor: 265 metric HP, water cooled, 12 cylinder
Maybach HL 120 TRM, 12 liter gasoline
HP/Weight Ratio: 13.2 metric HP/ton
Transmission: 6 speed Zahnradfabrik S.S.G.76
Steering: Differential steering
Suspension: 8 roadwheels, leaf springs

Measurements:
Length Overall: 5.92 m
Width Overall: 2.84 m
Height Overall: 2.68 m
Ground Clearance: 0.40 m
Combat Loaded: 20 metric tons
Ground Pressure: 0.83 kg/cm^2

Official Title: Pz.Kpfw.IV (7.5 cm) (Sd.Kfz.161)
Ausf. E

Weapons: One 7.5 cm Kw.K. L/24 and one M.G.34 in the turret
One M.G.34 in a ball mount
Elevation: -10°, +20°
Traverse: 360° by electric motor and by hand
Ammunition Types: 7.5 cm Pzgr., Sprgr. and Nebel-Gr. for 7.5 cm Kw.K.
S.m.K. and S.m.K.L'Spur for machineguns
Ammunition Stowage: 80 7.5 cm rounds
3150 rounds for the machinegun belted in 150-round sacks
Gun Sight: T.Z.F.5b (2.5x 24°)
Range: Graduated to 1200 meters for Pzgr. and 2000 meters for Sprgr. with
adjustable range scales at 100 meter intervals

Crew: Commander, Gunner, Loader, Radio Operator and Driver

Communications: FuG5 and FuG2 radio sets

Armor (Thickness at Angle from Vertical):
Commander's Cupola   30 mm @ 90 plus cast visors
Turret Roof   10 mm @ 83 and 90°
Turret Front   30 mm @ 10°
Gun Mantle   35 mm rounded
Superstructure Roof   11 mm @ 85 and 90°
Driver's Front Plate   30+30 mm @ 9°
Glacis   20 mm @ 72°
Hull Nose   50 mm @ 14°
Hull Belly   10 mm @ 90°

Turret Side   20 mm @ 24°
Superstructure Side   20+20 mm @ 0°
Engine Deck Side   20 mm @ 0°
Hull Side   20+20 mm @ 0°

Turret Rear   20 mm @ 14°, curved
Engine Deck Roof   10 mm @ 88°
Engine Deck Rear   20 mm @ 10°
Hull Rear   20 mm @ 10°

Automotive Capabilities:
Average Speed
    a) Road: 25 km/hr
    b) Cross Country: 20 km/hr
Maximum Speed: 42 km/hr
Range
    a) Road: 210 km
    b) Cross Country: 130 km
Fuel Capacity: 470 liter
Grade: 30°
Step: 60 cm
Trench Crossing: 230 cm
Fording Depth: 80 cm
Motor: 265 metric HP, water cooled, 12 cylinder
Maybach HL 120 TRM, 12 liter gasoline
HP/Weight Ratio: 12.0 metric HP/ton
Transmission: 6 speed Zahnradfabrik S.S.G.76
Steering: Differential steering
Suspension: 8 roadwheels, leaf springs

Measurements:
Length Overall: 5.92 m
Width Overall: 2.84 m
Height Overall: 2.68 m
Ground Clearance: 0.40 m
Combat Loaded: 22 metric tons
Ground Pressure: 0.91 kg/cm^2

Official Title: **Carro L.3-33 & L.3-35**

Weapons: Two Fiat 35 machineguns, or
                                        Two Breda 38 machineguns, or
                                        One Fiat 35 machinegun and Lanciafiamme
Elevation: -12 °, + 15°
Traverse: 12° left and right of center by hand
Ammunition Types: Ball and AP for machineguns
Ammunition Stowage: 2400 rounds for the machineguns
                                        500 kg liquid for the flamethrower

Crew: Commander/Gunner and Driver

Communications: No radio

Armor (Thickness at Angle from Vertical):

Superstructure Roof   6 mm @ 85°
Driver's Front Plate   13.5 mm @ 12°
Glacis   13.5 mm @ 63° + 8.5 mm @ 78°
Hull Nose   13.5 mm @ 0°
Lower Hull Nose   8 mm @ 68°
Hull Belly   6 mm @ 90°

Superstructure Side   8.5 mm @ 0-12°
Hull Side   8.5 mm @ 0°

Superstructure Rear   8.5 mm @ ??°
Engine Deck Roof   6 mm @ 90°
Hull Rear   8.5 mm @ 0°

Automotive Capabilities:
Average Speed
    a) Road: ?? km/hr
    b) Cross Country: 15 km/hr
Maximum Speed: 41.3 km/hr
Range
    a) Road: 120 km
    b) Cross Country: 4-5 hours
Fuel Capacity: 65 liter
Grade: 45°
Step: 0.65 cm
Trench Crossing: 1.45 cm
Fording Depth: 0.70 cm
Motor: 43 H.P., water cooled, 4 in-line cylinder

HP/Weight Ratio: 12.5 H.P./ton
Transmission:

	On-Road	Off-Road
1.Gear	8.3 km/hr	3.0 km/hr
2.Gear	16.7	6.1
3.Gear	26.0	9.9
4.Gear	41.3	15.2
R.Gear	6.5	2.3

Steering: Epicyclic clutch
Suspension: Two sets of leaf springs,
                                        one set for three roadwheels

Measurements:
Length Overall: 3.15 m
Width Overall: 1.40 m
Height Overall: 1.28 m
Ground Clearance: 0.23 m
Combat Loaded: 3.435 metric tons
Ground Pressure: 0.59 kg/cm^2

Official Title: **Carro armato M.13-40**

Weapons: One cannone da 47-32
                                             Four Breda 38 machineguns
Elevation Main Gun: - 10°, + 20°
Turret Traverse: 360° by hydraulic motor and by hand
Hull Machineguns   - 15°, + 23°, 28° traverse
Ammunition Types: Mod.39 APBC/HE-Shell and Mod.35 HE-Shells for 47-32
                                             Ball and AP for machineguns
Ammunition Stowage: 85 rounds for 47-32
                                             3000 rounds for the machineguns
                                             (24 x 125)
Gun Sight: Telescope (1.25 x 30°)
Range: Graduated to 1200 meters for APBC/HE-Shell with adjustable range scale

Crew: Commander/gunner, loader, hull machine-gunner, and driver

Communications: No radio

Armor (Thickness at Angle from Vertical):

Turret Roof   14 mm @ 85°
Turret Front   40 mm @ 16°
Gun Mantle   33 mm rounded
Superstructure Roof   14 mm @ 90°
Driver's Front Plate   30 mm @ 11°
Glacis   25 mm @ 81°
Hull Nose   30 mm rounded
Lower Hull Nose   15 mm @ 81°
Hull Belly   15 mm @ 90°

Turret Side   25 mm @ 22°
Superstructure Side   25 mm @ 9°
Engine Deck Side   9 mm @ 76°
Hull Side   25 mm @ 0°

Turret Rear   25 mm @ 22°
Engine Deck Roof   9 mm @ 88°
Superstructure Rear   25 mm @ 0°
Hull Rear   25 mm @ 0°
Stowage Compartment Lid   25 mm @ 62°
Rear Stowage Compartment   25 mm @ 20°

Automotive Capabilities:
Average Speed
    a) Road: ?? km/hr
    b) Cross Country: 15 km/hr
Maximum Speed: 31.8 km/hr
Range
    a) Road: 200 km
    b) Cross Country: 10 hours
Fuel Capacity: 210 liter
Grade: 40°
Step: 90 cm
Trench Crossing: 210 cm
Fording Depth: 100 cm
Motor: 125 H.P. @ 1800 rpm, water cooled diesel, V-8 cylinder
HP/Weight Ratio: 8.9 metric H.P./ton
Transmission:

	On-Road	Off-Road
1.Gear	6.46 km/hr	2.37 km/hr
2.Gear	11.2	4.12
3.Gear	19.1	7.04
4.Gear	31.8	11.63
R.Gear	4.84	1.81

Steering: Epicyclic clutch
Suspension: Two sets of leaf springs for four paired roadwheels

Measurements:
Length Overall:	4.915 m
Width Overall:	2.230 m
Height Overall:	2.370 m
Ground Clearance:	0.410 m
Combat Loaded:	14.00 metric tons
Ground Pressure:	0.94 kg/cm^2

APPENDIX B - GERMAN UNITS TRANSPORTED BY SHIP TO TRIPOLI

Convoy Number	Date and Time of Arrival	Name of the Units
1	11Feb41	Feldlazerett 4/572 kl.Kw.Kol.800 und 804 kl.Kw.Kol. fuer Filtergeraet Reifenstaffel 13
2	1830 on 14Feb41	Panzer-Jaeger-Abteilung 39 Aufklaerung-Abteilung 3
3	Morning of 20Feb41	Stab, 1., 2., und 3.Batterie/ I.Abteilung/Flak-Regiment 33
4	1900 on 25Feb41	4. und 5.Batterie/I./ Flak-Regiment 33 le.Kol./I./Flak-Regiment 33 Part of 2.(H)/14.Pz. 3./Nachrichten-Abteilung 39 Kw.Kol.797, 801, 803, und 822
5	Evening of 27Feb41	M.G.-Bataillon 8 5.Pionier-Kompanie/M.G.-Bataillon 2 One-half of Vers.-Kdo./Panzer-Regiment 5 Stabsqu./5.leichte Division
6	1800 on 3Mar41	Regiments-Stab z.b.V.200 Kw.Kol.5/619
7	1900 on 6Mar41	M.G.-Bataillon 2 Kw.Kol.6/619 und 662
8	8Mar41	Regiments-Stab/Panzer-Regiment 5 II.Abteilung/Panzer-Regiment 5
9	Midday on 10Mar41	I.Abteilung/Panzer-Regiment 5
10	Unrecorded	
11&12	18Mar41	Kurierstaffel Part of Panzer-Jaeger-Abteilung 605 I./Jagdgeschwader 27 (Luftwaffe)
13	21Mar41	I.Abteilung/Artillerie-Regiment 75 (minus the 1.Batterie) Stab und Funk-Kompanie/Korps-Nachrichten- Abteilung Rest of Panzer-Jaeger-Abteilung 605 Kw.Kol.1./533, 2./533, 1./686 und 3./686

14	23Mar41	1.Batterie/Artillerie-Regiment 75 Fernsprech-Kompanie/Nachrichten-Abteilung Libyen 3., 4., und 5./Kol.Abt.533
15	30Mar41	I.Abteilung/Flak-Regiment 18 Part of Fla-M.G.-Bataillon 606 6./Kol.Abt.533 2. und 4./Kol.Abt.686
	Sank:	30 men and the equipment for: 2.Kompanie/Fla-M.G.-Bataillon 606 Part of 6./M.G.-Bataillon 2 Part of Panzerspaehzug/Aufklaerungs-Abteilung 3 7./Kol.Abt.686
16	1Apr41	Panzer-Jaeger-Abteilung 33
17	5Apr41	Stab, 1., 2., und 3.Kompanie/ Kradschuetzen-Bataillon 15 1., 2., 3., und 7./Kol.Abt.529 5. und 6./Kol.Abt.686
18	10Apr41	4. und 5.Kompanie/Kradschuetzen -Bataillon 15 4., 5., 6. und 9./Kol.Abt.534 10. und 11./Kol.Abt.529
19	14Apr41	1.Staffel, Ia, Ic, und IIa Stab/ 15.Panzer-Division Stab I.Bataillon, 1., 3., 4., 5., und 6.Kompanie/Schuetzen-Regiment 115 II.Abteilung/Artillerie-Regiment 33 2., 5., 6., 7., 9., und 10./Kol.Abt.33
20	Sank on 16Apr41:	28 officers and 315 men missing Part of Stab/15.Panzer-Division Stab und 11.Geschuetz-Kompanie/ Schuetzen-Regiment 115 Stab und Stabs-Batterie/Artillerie-Regiment 33 Part of Panzer-Nachrichten-Abteilung 33 Part of Sanitaets-Kompanie 2/83 Part of kl.Kw.Kol. 9/33 und 10/33 with all weapons, vehicles, and equipment.
21	Morning of 20Apr41	Panzer-Aufklaerung-Abteilung 33 Stabs-Kompanie/Schuetzen-Regiment 115 Erkundungskommando Panzer-Pionier-Bataillon 33 2.Staffel Qu./Stab 15.Panzer-Divsion Rest of Panzer-Nachrichten-Abteilung 33 Schlaechtereizug Part of Baeckerie-Kompanie 33 Part of Sanitaets-Kompanie 2/83

22	24Apr41	Stab und Stabskompanie/I.Abteilung und 1.Kompanie/Panzer-Regiment 8 7., 9., und 10.Kompanie/Schuetzen-Regiment 115 Horch-Kompanie 3./Nachrichten-Abteilung 56 7./Kol.Abt.533 Part of Baeckerie-Kompanie 33
23	2May41	Stab, 2., 3., und 5.Kompanie, und le.Kol./Panzer-Regiment 8 Stab II.Abteilung, 2. und 8.Kompanie, und le.Kol./Schuetzen-Regiment 115 III.Abteilung/Artillerie-Regiment 33 Lichtstaffel/Beobachtungs-Batterie 326 12./Kol.Abt.33 Part of 1./Nachschub Kol.Abt.572
24	6May41	Stab II.Abteilung, 6. und 7.Kompanie, und Werkstatt-Kompanie/Panzer-Regiment 8 One M.G.Kompanie, one M.G.Zug, one Pak-Zug, and two s.Gr.W.Truppe as replacements for M.G.-Bataillon 8 Schallstaffel/Beobachtungs-Batterie 326 Vehicles for Stab 15.Schuetzen-Brigade, Stab und Stabskompanie, and 2., 3., 4., und 5.Kompanie/Schuetzen-Regiment 104, and Stab und 1.Kompanie/Panzer-Pionier-Bataillon 33 le.Pz.Kol.13/33
25	1100 on 13May41	Stab I., 1. und 2.Batterie/Artillerie-Regiment 33 Vehicles for 6., 7., und 9.Kompanie/Schuetzen-Regiment 104 1., 3., und 8./Kw.Kol.33 Stab, 2., 3., 7., und 8./gr.Kw.Kol.572
26	1100 on 21May41	3.Batterie/Artillerie-Regiment 33 Gr.Kw.Kol.4./572 Werkstatt-Kompanie 1/33 Panzer-Ersatzteile-Kol.33 Vehicles for 8.Kompanie/Schuetzen-Regiment 104
27	25May41	Panzer-Jaeger-Kompanie and Krad-M.G.Zug for M.G.Bataillon 8
28	28May41	1.Batterie/Kuesten-Artillerie-Abteilung 533 4. und 11./Kol.Abt.33
29		No new units
30	1930 on 22Jun41	Part of: 1.Kompanie/Pionier-Bataillon 33 Pionier-Bataillon 900 3.Batterie/Artillerie-Abteilung 408 9.Batterie/Flak-Regiment 25
31	0900 on 28Jun41	III.Bataillon/Infanterie-Regiment 258 III.Bataillon/Infanterie-Regiment 241 Bau-Bataillon 85

APPENDIX B - GERMAN UNITS TRANSPORTED BY AIR TO LIBYA

Location	Date of Arrival	Name of the Units
Benina	27Apr41	Stab 15.Schuetzen-Brigade Stab I.Bataillon, 3. und 4.Kompanie/ Schuetzen-Regiment 104
Benina	28Apr41	Stab, 1. und 2.Kompanie/Pionier-Bataillon 33
Benina	29Apr41	1., 2., 5., und 6.Kompanie, und Stab II.Bataillon/Schuetzen-Regiment 104
Benina	2May41	Stab Schuetzen-Regiment 104
Benina	3May41	7., 8., und 9.Kompanie/Schuetzen -Regiment 104
Tripoli	4May41	Stabs-Kompanie, 10. und 11.Geschuetz-Kompanie/Schuetzen-Regiment 104 6. und 10.Oasen-Kompanie
Tripoli	6May41	2.Oasen-Kompanie
Tripoli	21May41	Two Zuege Pionier-Bataillon 900
Tripoli	24May41	2.Kompanie/Pionier-Bataillon 900
Tripoli	25May41	Stab/Pionier-Bataillon 900
Benina	26May41	1.Kompanie/Pionier-Bataillon 900
Tripoli	31May41	13.Oasen-Kompanie
Tripoli	10Jun41	64 personnel for Panzer-Nachrichten-Abteilung 78
Tripoli	11Jun41	Personnel for Panzer-Nachrichten-Abteilung 78 and 3.Batterie/Artillerie-Regiment 408

APPENDIX C - RECOMMENDED BOOKS

The Desert Rats (History of the 7th Armoured Division 1938 - 1945) by Major General G.L. Verney, Published by Hutchinson & Co., Ltd., 1956.

Krieg Ohne Hass by Erwin Rommel, Published by Heidenheimer Verlagsanstalt, 1950.

The Mediterranean and Middle East, Vol.I (British Official History) by Major General I.S.O. Playfair, Published by H.M.Stationary Office, 1956.

The Seventh and Three Enemies (The Story of World War II and the 7th Queen's Own Hussars) by Brigadier G.M.O. Davy, Published by W.Heffer & Sons, Ltd., Cambridge.

The Tanks, Vol Two 1939-1945 (History of the Royal Tank Regiment) by Captain B.H. Liddell Hart, Published by Frederick A. Praeger Publishers, 1959.

Tobruk and El Alamein (Australian History) by Barton Maughan, Published by Australian War Memorial, Canberra, 1966.

APPENDIX D - GLOSSARY OF GERMAN MILITARY TERMS

Abteilung	Abt. - battalion with less than five companies
Abwehr	defense
Armee	army
Armee Oberkommando	A.O.K. - army command
Art	type
Artillerie	artillery
Aufklaerung	reconnaissance
Ausbildung	training
Ausfuehrung	Ausf. - model designation
Bataillon	battalion of five companies
Batterie	artillery battery
Befehlspanzer	command tank
Begleitwagen	B.W. - code name for the Pz.Kpfw.IV
Beobachtungs	observation
Breitkeil	reverse "V" formation
Chef des Stabes	chief of staff
Erkunder	scouting
Fahrgestell	Fgst. - chassis
Feldwebel	army rank equivalent to American army sergeant
Fla	anti-aircraft
Flak	anti-aircraft gun
Flammenwerfer	flamethrower
Fliegerabwehr	Fla - anti-aircraft
Fliegerkorps	Luftwaffe unit
Fuehrer	leader
Funk	Fu - radio
Funkgeraet	FuG - radio set
Gefechtstross	combat trains
Gefreiter	army rank equivalent to American army corporal
Generalstab des Heeres	GenStdH - army chief of staff
Gepanzerte	armored
Geschuetz	gun
Gliederung	organization
Gr.38 HL	shaped charge shell
gr.Pz.Bef.Wg.	large armored command vehicle
Gruppe	section or Kampfgruppe
Halbzug	section
Haubitze	howitzer
Hauptmann	army rank equivalent to American army captain
Heeres	German army
Heeresgruppe	command over several armies
Heereswaffenamt	army ordnance department
Hohlgranate	HL - shaped charge shells
Infanterie	infantry
Instandsetzung	repair
Kampfgruppe	battle group
Kampfstaffel	small mixed combat unit
kl.Pz.Bef.Wg.	small armored command vehicle
Kolonne	supply column
Kommando	Kdo. - command
Kompanie	Kp. - company

Kompanie-Trupp	Kp.Tr. - company headquarters
Korps	corps
Korps-Truppen	units assigned to a corps
Kradschuetzen	motorcycle-borne infantry
Kreuz	cross
Kurskreisel	course indicating gyro-compass
Kurz	kz - short
Kw.K.	tank gun
Ladung	Ldg. - charge
La.S.100	code name for the Pz.Kpfw.II
Landwirtschaftlicher Schlepper	La.S. - agricultural tractor - code name for the Pz.Kpfw.I
Lang	lg - long
Lastkraftwagen	trucks
leichte	light
Leichttraktor	light tank
Leutnant	army rank equivalent to American army second lieutenant
Luftflotte	Luftwaffe unit
Luftwaffe	air force
Minen	land mines
mittlere	medium
mot	abbreviation for motorized
Munition	ammunition
Nachrichten	signals
Nebelgranate	smoke shells
Nebelkerzen	smoke candles
Neu	new
Neubau Fahrzeug	Nb.Fz. - code name for a medium tank
Obergefreiter	army rank with no American equivalent, between a corporal and a sergeant
Oberfeldwebel	army rank equivalent to staff American army sergeant
Oberkommando des Heeres	OKH - army high command
Oberkommando des Wehrmacht	OKW - armed forces high command
Oberleutnant	army rank equivalent to American army first lieutenant
Oberst	army rank equivalent to American army colonel
Oberstleutnant	army rank equivalent to American army lieutenant colonel
Pak	anti-tank gun
Panzer-Abwehr	anti-tank
Panzer-Abteilung	armored battalion
Panzer-Armee	armored army
Panzerbefehlswagen	armored command vehicle
Panzerbeobachtungswagen	armored artillery observation vehicle
Panzer-Brigade	armored brigade
Panzerbuechse	PzB - anti-tank rifle
Panzer-Division	armored division
Panzergranate	Pzgr. - armor-piercing shell
Panzergranate 38	Pzgr.38 - capped armor-piercing shell
Panzergranate 39	Pzgr.39 - capped armor-piercing shell with a ballistic cap
Panzergranate 40	Pzgr.40 - solid high density core armor-piercing round
Panzer-Gruppe	Panzer-Kampfgruppe
Panzer-Jaeger	anti-tank unit
Panzerkampfwagen	Pz.Kpfw. - generic name for tank
Panzer-Kompanie	armored company
Panzer-Regiments	armored regiment
Panzerspaehtrupp	section of armored cars
Panzerspaehwagen	armored car
Panzertruppen	armored troops, after February 1943 used to designate a separate branch of the army
Panzer-Zug	armored platoon
Pionier	combat engineer

Reihe	formation of tanks in a row
Ritterkreuz	knight's cross
Rueckhalt	backstop
Sanitaets	medics
S.m.K.	steel core ammunition
S.m.K.H.	special hard core ammunition
Schuetzen	motorized infantry
Schwadron	squadron
schwere	heavy
Schwerpunkt	primary area selected for concentrating an attack or a concentrated point for defense
Sd.Kfz.	special vehicle
Selbsfahrlafette	Sfl. or Sf. - self-propelled
Sonder	special
Sondergeraet	special equipment
Spaehgruppe	reconnaissance Kampfgruppe
Sperrverband	blocking force
Spezial	Sp - special, designation used in North Africa for Panzers with the longer guns
Sprenggranaten	Sprgr. - high-explosive fragmentation shells
Stab	headquarters
Stabsfeldwebel	army rank equivalent to American army staff sergeant
Stabskompanie	headquarters company
Stanzpfropfen	plug
Stossgruppe	assault Kampfgruppe
Stuetzpunkt	defensive position prepared for all-round defense
Tiefladeanhaenger	low-bed trailers
Tropen	tropical
Turmzielfernrohr	T.Z.F. - telescopic gunsight
Verband	unit
verlastet	transported
Versorgung	supply
Versuchs	experimental
Vorausabteilung	advanced element
Waffe	weapon or branch of service
Waffenamt	ordnance department
Waffenzug	weapons platoon
Wa Pruef 6	automotive design office under the Heeres Waffenamt
Wehrmacht	armed forces encompassing the Heeres, Luftwaffe, and Kriegsmarine
Werkstatt-Kompanie	maintenance company
z.b.V.	for special employment
Zuege	platoons
Zug	platoon
Zugfuehrerwagen	Z.W. - code name for the Pz.Kpfw.III
Zugkraftwagen	three-quarter tracked towing vehicle
Zugmaschine	towing vehicle

Also from the Publisher

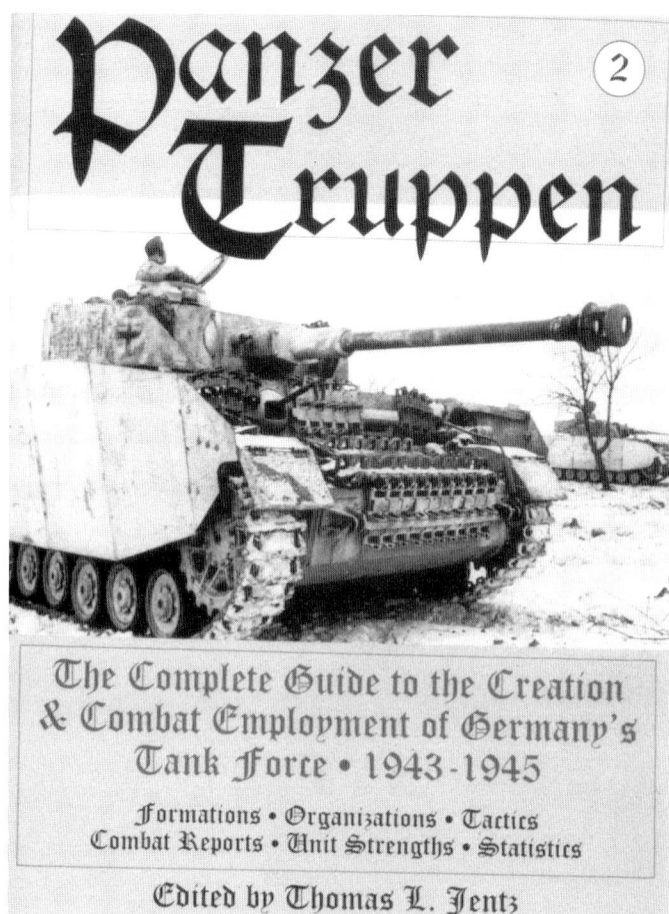

PANZERTRUPPEN
The Complete Guide to the Creation & Combat Employment of Germany's Tank Force 1933-1942

Edited by Thomas L. Jentz

In September of 1939, the world was astounded by Germany's ability to defeat Poland in less than a month. With the world still puzzled by the suddenness of this event, Denmark, Norway, Holland, Belgium, and France fell in rapid succession to the German onslaught, leaving Britain in shock. Greece and Yugoslavia were rapidly overrun during April of 1941, while German-Italian forces advanced rapidly in North Africa. Russia's turn was next, when German forces began pulverizing their forces in June of 1941. How had Germany achieved victory after victory, often against numerically superior enemy forces? The answer came in two words – Panzer and Blitzkrieg. When and how had Germany built its Panzer forces and trained them for the Blitzkrieg? When was each Panzer unit formed? What was their organization? Why were Panzer units disbursed among the Panzer-Divisions, leichte Divisions, and Armee-Korps? When were the various types of Panzers developed? What were their armament, armor protection, and capability? How many of each type were produced? What tactics did they use? How successful were they in combat? This is the only book that provides detailed answers to these and other questions related to how German tankers trained and fought from 1933-1942.

Size: 8 1/2" x 11" over 100 b/w photographs, maps, charts, appendices
288 pages, hard cover
ISBN: 0-88740-915-6 $49.95

PANZERTRUPPEN
The Complete Guide to the Creation & Combat Employment of Germany's Tank Force 1943-1945

Edited by Thomas L. Jentz

Having failed to win their strategic objectives, the Heeres (German Army) was overextended deep in enemy territory facing numerically superior forces in the Fall of 1942. Now it was the Allies turn to launch the offensives that would keep the Heeres off balance. With few exceptions the days of employing massed Panzer formations to gain strategically decisive objectives had come to an end. And, these few exceptions were almost invariably failures. Forced onto the defensive the Panzertruppen modified their tactics becoming expert at counterattacks that spoiled their opponents drives and inflicted heavy casualties. They became so proficient that the Allied armies took years to retake territory that the Heeres had overran in a few weeks or months. This companion volume to *Panzertruppen 1933-1942* presents how the Panzertruppen fought during their defensive struggle with details on the units, organizations, types of Panzers, and tactics. The first volume presents the offensive phase up to October 1942.

Size: 8 1/2" x 11" 47 b/w photographs, maps, charts, appendices
304 pages, hard cover
ISBN: 0-7643-0080-6 $49.95